LIVY

VII

LCL 367

LIVY

HISTORY OF ROME

BOOKS 26–27

EDITED AND TRANSLATED BY

J. C. YARDLEY

HARVARD UNIVERSITY PRESS

CAMBRIDGE, MASSACHUSETTS

LONDON, ENGLAND

2020

Copyright © 2020 by the President and Fellows
of Harvard College
All rights reserved

First published 2020

LOEB CLASSICAL LIBRARY® is a registered trademark
of the President and Fellows of Harvard College

Library of Congress Control Number 2016957655
CIP data available from the Library of Congress

ISBN 978-0-674-99735-6

*Composed in ZephGreek and ZephText by
Technologies 'N Typography, Merrimac, Massachusetts.
Printed on acid-free paper and bound by
Maple Press, York, Pennsylvania*

CONTENTS

.

PREFACE

I am again grateful to John Briscoe for his many sugges-
tions and corrections on earlier drafts, especially in the
textual notes.

As he has noted in his discussion of the Spirensian
tradition, in Books 26–30 (Vol. V, pp. lxxx–lxxxii), Σ indicates the reading of the Spirensian tradition if it is either
cited by Rhenanus or found in at least two of the other
witnesses, while Σ? indicates a reading found in only one
such witness. On some occasions, however, it has seemed
to him desirable to cite in a parenthesis individual witnesses other than those that have the reading attributed
to Σ.

J.C.Y.

HISTORY OF ROME

LIBER XXVI

1. Cn. Fulvius Centumalus P. Sulpicius Galba consules
cum idibus Martiis magistratum inissent, senatu in Capitolium vocato de re publica, de administratione belli, de
2 provinciis exercitibusque patres consuluerunt. Q. Fulvio
Ap. Claudio prioris anni consulibus prorogatum imperium
est atque exercitus quos habebant decreti; adiectumque
ne a Capua quam obsidebant abscederent priusquam ex-
3 pugnassent. ea tum cura maxime intentos habebat Romanos non ab ira tantum, quae in nullam unquam civitatem
4 iustior fuit, quam quod urbs tam nobilis ac potens, sicut
defectione sua traxerat aliquot populos, ita recepta incli-
natura rursus animos videbatur ad veteris imperii respec-
5 tum. et praetoribus prioris anni M. Iunio in Etruria, P.
Sempronio in Gallia cum binis legionibus quas habuerant
prorogatum est imperium.

---

1 The first meeting of the senate at this time took place on the
Ides of March (15th) in the temple of Capitoline Jupiter. This
changed in 153, when the Kalends of January (1st) became the
start of the consular and civil year.

2 Q. Fulvius Flaccus, also consul in 237, 224, and 212; Ap.
Claudius Pulcher had been praetor in Sicily in 215.

3 The power to command in peace and in war; its holders
could impose the death penalty within the army and had supreme
authority over the Roman civilian population.

BOOK XXVI

1. When the consuls Gnaeus Fulvius Centumalus and Publius Sulpicius Galba began their terms of office on the Ides of March, they convened the senate on the Capitol[1] and sought members' opinions on matters of state, the management of the war, and the question of provinces and armies. Quintus Fulvius and Appius Claudius, the previous year's consuls,[2] had their *imperium*[3] prorogued and were assigned the armies that they were already commanding, and they were further instructed not to raise their blockade of Capua until they had captured the city.[4] That was the matter on which the Romans were then most focused, not so much from the anger they felt—though this was more justified than with any state in the past—as because it seemed likely that, since a city so famous and powerful had drawn several different peoples into defection with it, so recovering it would reestablish respect for the former regime. The previous year's praetors, Marcus Junius and Publius Sempronius,[5] also had their *imperium* prorogued, Junius in Etruria and Sempronius in Gaul, each retaining the two legions that they had been commanding.

[4] It had been under siege since autumn 212 (25.22.7–16).
[5] M. Junius Silanus; P. Sempronius Tuditanus, praetor in Gaul in 213, with *imperium* prorogued to 212.

3

6   Prorogatum et M. Marcello ut pro consule in Sicilia
7 reliqua belli perficeret eo exercitu quem haberet: si supplemento opus esset, suppleret de legionibus quibus P.
8 Cornelius pro praetore in Sicilia praeesset, dum ne quem
militem legeret ex eo numero quibus senatus missionem
9 reditumque in patriam negasset ante belli finem. C. Sulpicio, cui Sicilia evenerat, duae legiones quas P. Cornelius
habuisset decretae et supplementum de exercitu Cn.
Fulvi, qui priore anno in Apulia foede caesus fugatusque
10 erat. huic generi militum senatus eundem quem Cannen-
sibus finem statuerat militiae. additum etiam utrorumque
ignominiae est ne in oppidis hibernarent, neve hiberna
propius ullam urbem decem milibus passuum aedifica-
11 rent. L. Cornelio in Sardinia duae legiones datae quibus
Q. Mucius praefuerat; supplementum si opus esset con-
12 sules scribere iussi. T. Otacilio et M. Valerio Siciliae
Graeciaeque orae cum legionibus classibusque quibus
praeerant decretae; quinquaginta Graecia cum legione
una, centum Sicilia cum duabus legionibus habebant[1]
13 naves. tribus et viginti legionibus Romanis eo anno bellum
terra marique est gestum.

---

[1] habebant *P*: habebat *Walters*

---

6 M. Claudius Marcellus (consul 222, 215, 214, 210, and 208)
had been proconsul in Sicily since 213.

7 P. Cornelius Lentulus, praetor in Sicily in 214, prorogued as
propraetor in 213 and 212.   8 Praetor in Sicily for 211.

9 Cn. Fulvius Flaccus, praetor in 212, had suffered a defeat at
Herdonea in Apulia (*Barr.* 45 C2) that was attributed to incom-
petence by Livy (25.20.6–21.10); cf. 2.7 below for his impeach-
ment. Some have considered this a doublet of the defeat suffered
at Herdonea in 210 by Cn. Fulvius Centimalus (27.3–15).

Marcus Marcellus' *imperium* was likewise prorogued to enable him to terminate as proconsul what remained of the war in Sicily with the army under his command;[6] if he needed it supplemented he was to supplement it from the legions that Publius Cornelius commanded as propraetor in Sicily,[7] but without taking any soldier from those whom the senate had denied discharge or repatriation before the war ended. Gaius Sulpicius,[8] who had been allotted Sicily, was assigned the two legions that Publius Cornelius had commanded and a supplementary force from the army of Gnaeus Fulvius that had been shamefully cut to pieces and routed in Apulia the previous year.[9] For this class of soldier the senate had stipulated the same term of service as for those from Cannae.[10] Another mark of censure for the two groups was that they were not to winter in towns or build winter quarters within ten miles of any city. In Sardinia, Lucius Cornelius was assigned the two legions that Quintus Mucius had commanded[11] and the consuls were ordered to raise reinforcements, if necessary. The coastlines of Sicily and Greece were assigned to Titus Otacilius and Marcus Valerius[12] together with the legions and fleets already under their command. (Greece had fifty ships with one legion, Sicily a hundred ships with two legions.) Land and sea operations were that year conducted with twenty-three Roman legions.

[10] That is, until the enemy was driven from Italy (24.18.9; 25.7.4).   [11] L. Cornelius Lentulus, praetor this year; Q. Mucius Scaevola, praetor in 215, with his *imperium* in Sardinia annually prorogued until this year.   [12] T. Otacilius, fleet commander in Sicily since his first praetorship in 217. M. Valerius Laevinus, praetor in 217, had, apart from his naval command, also been a legionary commander since 213 (24.44.5).

2. Principio eius anni cum de litteris L. Marci referretur, res gestae magnificae senatui visae; titulus honoris, quod imperio non populi iussu, non ex auctoritate patrum dato "propraetor senatui" scripserat, magnam partem
2 hominum offendebat. rem mali exempli esse imperatores legi ab exercitibus et sollemne auspicandorum comitiorum in castra et provincias procul ab legibus magistra-
3 tibusque ad militarem temeritatem transferri. et cum quidam referendum ad senatum censerent, melius visum differri eam consultationem donec proficiscerentur
4 equites qui ab Marcio litteras attulerant. rescribi de frumento et vestimentis exercitus placuit eam utramque rem curae fore senatui; adscribi autem "propraetori L. Marcio" non placuit, ne id ipsum quod consultationi reliquerant pro praeiudicato ferret.
5 Dimissis equitibus de nulla re prius consules rettulerunt, omniumque in unum sententiae congruebant agendum cum tribunis plebis esse, primo quoque tempore ad plebem ferrent quem cum imperio mitti placeret in Hispaniam ad eum exercitum cui Cn. Scipio imperator prae-
6 fuisset. ea res cum tribunis acta promulgataque est, sed

---

13 L. Marcius Septimius. For his success in Spain, cf. 25.37.2–25.39.17.

14 That is, he was not a propraetor with *imperium*. Livy calls him a Roman knight (25.37.2), Cicero a centurion *primipilus* (*Balb*. 34), and Valerius Maximus (who also records the senate's displeasure with his presumption) a military tribune (2.7.15a).

15 The auspices, taken by consuls and other high-ranking magistrates, involved various kinds of divination (especially from celestial phenomena or the behavior of birds or sacred chickens)

2. When a dispatch from Lucius Marcius[13] was brought up at the start of that year, the senate did find his achievements outstanding; but the title attached to his office irked many members because he had written "from the propraetor to the senate" although *imperium* had not been granted him by the people or authorized by the senate.[14] It was a bad precedent being set, they felt—generals being chosen by armies, and the solemn electoral process with its obligatory *auspices*[15] transferred to unruly soldiers in camps and provinces far from the law and the magistrates! Although some proposed raising the matter for debate in the house, it seemed preferable for discussion to be postponed until the riders who had delivered the dispatch from Marcius should leave. As for grain and clothing for Marcius' army, it was decided that the reply to be given was that the senate would attend to both items, but that it not be addressed to "Lucius Marcius propraetor" in case Marcius thereby attained—as though it were already decided—the very thing they had shelved for later consideration.

When the horsemen had been dismissed, the consuls moved (and everyone was of the same opinion) that they must discuss with the plebeian tribunes the matter of putting before the people as soon as possible the question of the man they wanted sent with *imperium* to Spain, to the army that Gnaeus Scipio had commanded. That matter was discussed with the tribunes and public notice was

to ascertain the will of the gods. They attended all public acts, such as elections and military operations: *OCD* s.v. *auspicium*; Levene *Religion*, 3–4, 129–31.

7 aliud certamen occupaverat animos. C. Sempronius Blaesus die dicta Cn. Fulvium ob exercitum in Apulia amissum
in contionibus vexabat, multos imperatores temeritate atque inscitia exercitum in locum praecipitem perduxisse
8 dictitans, neminem praeter Cn. Fulvium ante corrupisse
omnibus vitiis legiones suas quam proderet. itaque vere
dici posse prius eos perisse quam viderent hostem, nec ab
Hannibale sed ab imperatore suo victos esse.

9 Neminem cum suffragium ineat satis cernere cui imperium, cui exercitum permittat. quid interfuisse inter Ti.
10 Sempronium ⟨et Cn. Fulvium? Ti. Sempronium,⟩[2] cum ei
servorum exercitus datus esset, brevi effecisse disciplina
atque imperio ut nemo eorum generis ac sanguinis sui
memor in acie esset, ⟨sed⟩[3] praesidio sociis, hostibus ter-
rori essent; Cumas Beneventum aliasque urbes eos velut
e faucibus Hannibalis ereptas populo Romano restituisse.
11 Cn. Fulvium Quiritium Romanorum exercitum, honeste
genitos liberaliter educatos, servilibus vitiis imbuisse. ergo
effecisse ut feroces et inquieti inter socios, ignavi et im-
belles inter hostes essent, nec impetum modo Poenorum
12 sed ne clamorem quidem sustinere possent. nec hercle
mirum esse ⟨cessisse⟩[4] milites in acie cum primus om-

---

2 ⟨et . . . Sempronium⟩ *Madvig*
3 ⟨sed⟩ *Walters:* ⟨ut⟩ *Walsh*
4 esse ⟨cessisse⟩ *Alschefski:* esse *P:* cessisse *Gron.*

---

16 C. Sempronius Blaesus, one of the plebeian tribunes for
211.

17 At Herdonea: cf. 1.9 and note, above. The charge is *per-
duellio* ("activity hostile to the state" [*OCD*]).

18 Ti. Sempronius Gracchus. His success with slave volunteers

given; but another dispute had now seized their attention. Gaius Sempronius Blaesus[16] had arraigned Gnaeus Fulvius over the loss of his army in Apulia,[17] and he was now harassing him in public meetings. Many commanders had taken their army into dangerous terrain from recklessness and inexperience, he would say, but none apart from Gnaeus Fulvius had corrupted his legions with all sorts of vices and then betrayed them to the enemy. Thus it could be truly said that Fulvius' men were done for before setting eyes on their foe, and that it was not by Hannibal that they had been defeated but by their own general.

No one, when proceeding to the vote, had much idea of the person to whom he was confiding *imperium* and an army, he said. What had been the difference between Tiberius Sempronius and Gnaeus Fulvius? When he was given an army of slaves, Tiberius Sempronius had by his discipline and authority soon ensured that none of those slaves gave any thought in battle to his lineage and bloodline, that they provided defense for the allies and terror for the enemy.[18] Cumae, Beneventum, and other cities— these they had virtually snatched from Hannibal's jaws and restored to the people of Rome. But Gnaeus Fulvius— given an army of Roman citizens, men well born and honorably brought up, in these he had instilled the vices of slaves! Thus, what *he* ensured was that that they would be hotheaded ruffians with the allies but spineless cowards with the enemy, unable to withstand even the Carthaginians' war cry and much less their charge. Indeed, that his men gave way in battle is no surprise, not when their

(*volones*) at Beneventum came when he was proconsul in 214: cf. 24.14.3–24.16.19 and *OCD* s.v.

13   nium imperator fugeret; magis mirari se aliquos stantes
cecidisse, et non omnes comites Cn. Fulvi fuisse pavoris
ac fugae. C. Flaminium L. Paulum L. Postumium Cn. ac
P. Scipiones cadere in acie maluisse quam deserere cir-
cumventos exercitus; Cn. Fulvium prope unum nuntium
14   deleti exercitus Romam redisse. facinus indignum esse
Cannensem exercitum, quod ex acie fugerit, in[5] Siciliam
deportatum ne prius inde dimittatur quam hostis ex Italia
decesserit, et hoc idem in Cn. Fulvi legionibus nuper
15   decretum, Cn. Fulvio fugam ex proelio ipsius temeritate
commisso impunitam esse, et eum in ganea lustrisque ubi
16   iuventam egerit senectutem acturum, milites qui nihil
aliud peccaverint quam quod imperatoris similes fuerint
relegatos prope in exsilium ignominiosam pati militiam.
adeo imparem libertatem Romae diti ac pauperi, honorato
atque inhonorato esse.

    3. Reus ab se culpam in milites transferebat: eos fero-
citer pugnam poscentes, productos in aciem non eo quo
voluerint, quia serum diei fuerit, sed postero die et tempore et loco aequo instructos seu famam seu vim hostium
2   non sustinuisse. cum effuse omnes fugerent, se quoque
turba ablatum ut Varronem Cannensi pugna, ut multos
3   alios imperatores. qui autem solum se restantem prodesse

    [5] in P: ita in *Allen*

commander was the very first to flee—he was more surprised that some had actually died making a stand and that they had not all shared Gnaeus Fulvius' panic-stricken flight! Gaius Flaminius, Lucius Paullus, Lucius Postumius, and Gnaeus and Publius Scipio had preferred to fall in the battle line rather than desert their encircled armies; but Gnaeus Fulvius had returned to Rome virtually the only man left to report his army's annihilation! The army at Cannae had been shipped off to Sicily for having fled the battle, the men not to be released from there until the enemy had left Italy; and now the same conditions had been recently decreed for Gnaeus Fulvius' army; and it was a shocking crime that Gnaeus Fulvius' flight from a battle that he himself had irresponsibly begun should go unpunished and that he would pass his old age in a low dive and brothels in which he had passed his younger days, while soldiers whose only sin was to have been like their commander should be virtually exiled and made to endure ignominious service! So different at Rome was freedom for the rich and freedom for the poor, so different for a man who had held office and one who had not!

3. The defendant began shifting the blame from himself to his men. They had been aggressively demanding action, he said, but even when led them out into the line of battle—not on the day they wanted (because it was too late) but the next one—when both the timing and the site of their deployment favored them, they had not been able to face either the enemy's reputation or his attack. When all were in disordered flight, he too had been swept away in the crowd, like Varro in the battle at Cannae and like many other commanders. How could he have helped the republic by making a stand all alone—unless his own

rei publicae, nisi si mors sua remedio publicis cladibus
4 futura esset, potuisse? non se inopia commeatus in loca
iniqua incaute deductum, non agmine inexplorato euntem
insidiis circumventum; vi aperta armis acie victum. nec
suorum animos nec hostium in potestate habuisse; suum
cuique ingenium audaciam aut pavorem facere.

5 Bis est accusatus pecuniaque anquisitum. tertio testi-
bus datis cum, praeterquam quod omnibus probris onera-
batur, iurati permulti dicerent fugae pavorisque initium a
6 praetore ortum, ab eo desertos milites cum haud vanum
timorem ducis crederent terga dedisse, tanta ira accensa
7 est ut capite anquirendum contio succlamaret. de eo quoque novum certamen ortum. nam cum bis pecunia anqui-
8 sisset, tertio capitis se anquirere diceret, tribuni plebis
appellati collegae negarunt se in mora esse quominus,
quod ei more maiorum permissum esset, seu legibus seu
moribus mallet, anquireret quoad vel capitis vel pecuniae
9 iudicasset privato. tum Sempronius perduellionis se iudi-
care Cn. Fulvio dixit, diemque comitiis ab C. Calpurnio
praetore urbano petit.

10 Inde alia spes ab reo temptata est, si adesse in iudicio
Q. Fulvius frater posset, florens tum et fama rerum ges-
11 tarum et propinqua spe Capuae potiundae. id cum per
litteras miserabiliter pro fratris capite scriptas petisset
Fulvius, negassentque patres e re publica esse abscedi a

---

[19] The appeal (made of course by the accused, Gnaeus Fulvius) focused on the change of punishment now demanded. Capital punishment (*poena capitalis*) could mean death or (as here)
exile (cf. *OLD* s.v. caput, 5).

[20] That is, a meeting of the *comitia centuriata*.

death could be the remedy for national disasters! It was not as if he had been incautiously led onto unfavorable terrain through shortage of provisions or taken by ambush on a path he had failed to reconnoiter—it was with an open attack, with weapons, on the field of battle that he had been defeated. His men's courage had been no more under his control than his enemy's; it was a man's own nature that gave him bravery or cowardice.

Fulvius was twice accused, with a fine demanded. On the third, witnesses were produced and, apart from the defendant being subjected to all manner of insults, many declared on oath that the panic-stricken flight had started with the praetor and that the soldiers, abandoned by him, had turned to flee believing their leader's fear to be well-founded. Such anger then flared up that the assembly noisily demanded that Fulvius be arraigned on a capital charge. Over that a new squabble also arose. For when the plaintiff, after twice asking for fines, on the third occasion said that he was asking for capital punishment, an appeal was made to the tribunes of the plebs,[19] who declared they would not obstruct their colleague's efforts to press under the laws or customary practice. Sempronius then said he was seeking Gnaeus Fulvius' condemnation for treason, and he asked the praetor Gaius Calpurnius to set a date for the assembly.[20]

Another approach he thought promising was then tried by the defendant, that his brother Quintus Fulvius could attend the trial (he enjoyed celebrity at the time both for his famous exploits and for his prospects of soon taking Capua). When, in an emotional letter in defense of his brother's life, Quintus Fulvius requested permission for that, the senators replied that it was not in the state's in-

12 Capua, postquam dies comitiorum aderat Cn. Fulvius
exsulatum Tarquinios abiit. id ei iustum exsilium esse scivit plebs.

4. Inter haec vis omnis belli versa in Capuam erat.
obsidebatur tamen acrius quam oppugnabatur, nec aut
famem tolerare servitia ac plebs poterant aut mittere nun-
2 tios ad Hannibalem per custodias tam artas. inventus est
Numida qui acceptis litteris evasurum se professus prae-
staret promissum. per media Romana castra nocte egressus spem accendit Campanis, dum aliquid virium super-
3 esset, ab omni parte eruptionem temptandi. ceterum in
multis certaminibus equestria proelia ferme prospera faciebant, pedites[6] superabantur. sed nequaquam tam lae-
tum vincere quam triste vinci ulla parte erat ab obsesso et
4 prope expugnato hoste. inita tandem ratio est ut quod viribus deerat arte aequaretur.

Ex omnibus legionibus electi sunt iuvenes maxime vigore ac levitate corporum veloces; eis parmae breviores
quam equestres et septena iacula quaternos longa pedes
5 data, praefixa ferro quale hastis velitaribus inest. eos singulos in equos suos accipientes equites adsuefecerunt et
vehi post sese et desilire perniciter ubi datum signum es-
6 set. postquam id[7] adsuetudine cotidiana satis intrep⟨id⟩e

---

[6] pedites *P*: pedite *Gron.*
[7] ⟨id⟩ *hic Koch*: *ante* postquam *M. Müller*

---

[21] Modern Tarquinia. It was the most important of the Etru-
rian cities, lying some fifty-six miles northwest of Rome (*Barr.* 42
B4).   [22] There were in fact three Roman armies and camps
involved in the siege; cf. 25.22.8, and 8.6–9, below.

[23] Latin *Campani*, literally, "Campanians," but also applied to
residents of Capua, the chief city of Campania.

terests for him to leave Capua, and when the day of the assembly arrived Gnaeus Fulvius went into exile at Tarquinii.[21] The plebs declared that his exile was justified.

4. Meanwhile, the entire brunt of the war had been brought to bear on Capua. It was, however, being blockaded intensively rather than directly attacked, and slaves and the masses could neither endure the lack of food nor send messengers to Hannibal because the guard posts were so closely spaced. A Numidian was found who, taking a letter, declared he would get through with it, and kept his promise. Making his way through the Roman camp[22] at night, he fired the people of Capua[23] with hopes of mounting a counterattack at all points while they still had a modicum of strength. However, while in many encounters their cavalry battles were for the most part successful, their infantry would suffer defeat; but the joy of the Romans over their infantry victories was nothing like the dejection they felt at their defeat in any action by a foe under siege and almost vanquished. Finally, a new expedient was adopted so what they lacked in strength could be compensated for by skill.

From all the legions young men were picked out who had exceptional speed because of their strength and light build; and they were issued shields smaller than the cavalry's plus seven four-foot long javelins tipped with iron, like *velites*'[24] spears. Each taking one of these men on their horses, the cavalrymen would train them to ride mounted behind them and dismount briskly on being given the signal. When, after daily training, that seemed to be done

[24] The skirmishers posted before the three lines of the legion; 1,200 in number, they were armed with small shields, swords, and light javelins.

15

fieri visum est, in campum qui medius inter castra murumque erat adversus instructos Campanorum equites
7 processerunt, et ubi ad coniectum teli ventum est, signo dato velites desiliunt. pedestris inde acies ex equitatu repente in hostium equites incurrit, iaculaque cum impetu
8 alia super alia emittunt; quibus plurimis in equos virosque passim coniectis permultos volneraverunt. pavoris tamen plus ex re nova atque inopinata iniectum est, et in perculsum hostem equites invecti fugam stragemque eorum us-
9 que ad portas fecerunt. inde equitatu quoque superior
10 Romana res fuit. ⟨ita⟩[8] institutum ut velites in legionibus essent; auctorem peditum equiti immiscendorum centurionem Q. Navium ferunt, honorique id ei apud imperatorem fuisse.

5. Cum in hoc statu ad Capuam res essent, Hannibalem in diversum Tarentinae arcis potiundae Capuaeque reti-
2 nendae trahebant curae. vicit tamen respectus Capuae, in quam omnium sociorum hostiumque conversos videbat animos, documento futurae qualemcumque eventum de-
3 fectio ab Romanis habuisset. igitur magna parte impedimentorum relicta in Bruttiis et omni graviore armatu, cum delectis peditum equitumque, quam poterat aptissimis[9] ad maturandum iter, in Campaniam contendit; secuti tamen tam raptim euntem tres et triginta elephanti.

---

[8] ⟨ita⟩ *Walsh*: ⟨et⟩ *Ussing*
[9] aptissimis *M^{c}LA^p*: aptissimus *P*

---

25 For Navius, see below, 5.12–17; also Frontin. *Str.* 4.7.29; Val. Max. 2.3.3. Broughton (*MRR* 261 and note 8) suggests identification with a prefect of the allies, Q. Naevius Crista.

26 Since Hannibal has only one elephant in 217 (22.2.10), those mentioned here were probably the ones brought by Bomil-

quite confidently, they advanced into the plain that lay between the camp and the city wall to face Capuan cavalry that was drawn up for battle, and on coming within javelin range the *velites* would dismount when given the signal. An infantry line emerging from the cavalry then suddenly attacked the enemy horsemen and unleashed javelin after javelin as they charged. Hurling these weapons in large numbers at horses and riders indiscriminately, they inflicted heavy casualties; but even greater was the panic inspired in the Capuans by the new and unexpected tactic, and the cavalry then bore down on their frightened enemy and chased them in bloody flight right up to their gates. From then on the Romans also enjoyed cavalry superiority. Thus began the practice of *velites* being deployed among the legions; and the man responsible for incorporating infantry within the cavalry was, they say, the centurion Quintus Navius,[25] and for it he was given special recognition by the general.

5. When matters stood thus in Capua, Hannibal had two conflicting priorities: taking the citadel of Tarentum and holding Capua. It was his concern for Capua that prevailed, however; he could see that everyone's attention, his allies' and his enemy's, was focused on the town, and that how Capua's defection from Rome turned out would be a bellwether for the future. He therefore left most of his baggage and all his more heavily armed forces in Bruttium and hastened into Campania at the head of some elite infantry and cavalry troops that were as well equipped as possible for a speedy march; and despite the swift pace there were thirty-three elephants with him.[26]

car when he arrived in Locri in 215 (23.41.10). No elephants appear in Polybius' account (9.3).

4   In valle occulta post Tifata, montem imminentem Capuae, consedit. adveniens cum castellum Calatiam praesidio vi pulso cepisset, in circumsedentes Capuam se ver-

5   tit, praemissisque[10] nuntiis Capuam quo tempore castra Romana adgressurus esset ut eodem et illi ad eruptionem parati portis omnibus sese effunderent, ingentem prae-

6   buit terrorem. nam alia parte ipse adortus est, alia Campani omnes equites peditesque, et cum iis Punicum prae-

7   sidium, cui Bostar et Hanno praeerant, erupit. Romani ut in re trepida, ne ad unam concurrendo partem aliquid indefensi relinquerent, ita inter sese copias partiti sunt:

8   Ap. Claudius Campanis, ⟨Q.⟩[11] Fulvius Hannibali est oppositus; C. Nero propraetor cum equitibus sex legionum via quae Suessulam fert, C. Fulvius Flaccus legatus cum sociali equitatu constitit e regione Volturni amnis.

9   Proelium non solito modo clamore ac tumultu est coeptum, sed ad alium virorum, equorum armorumque sonum disposita in muris Campanorum imbellis multitudo tantum cum aeris crepitu, qualis in defectu lunae silenti nocte cieri solet, edidit clamorem ut averteret

10   etiam pugnantium animos. Campanos facile a vallo Appius arcebat; maior vis ab altera parte Fulvium Hannibal et

---

10 praemissisque *det.*: praemissis namque *P*: praemissisque iam *Walsh*   11 ⟨Q.⟩ *H.J.M.*

---

27 Mt. Tifata, north of Capua: *Barr.* 44 F3.

28 On the Via Appia, about six miles southeast of Capua (*Barr.* 44 F3).

29 This Bostar and this Hanno remain unidentified.

30 Bronze cymbals were regarded as being capable, in a witch's hands, of drawing down the moon and also counteracting

He encamped in a secluded valley behind Tifata, the hill overlooking Capua.[27] Since he had on his arrival taken the stronghold of Calatia[28] and driven out its garrison, he turned to the force that was blockading Capua; and by sending messengers ahead to Capua to report when he would assault the Roman camp (so the townspeople would synchronize a sortie with his attack, charging from all the gates) he struck great fear into the Romans. For he attacked on one side himself while, on the other, the Capuan cavalry and infantry came charging out in full force together with the Carthaginian garrison that Bostar and Hanno[29] commanded. Caught in a critical situation, the Romans so divided their forces between them as not to leave any point undefended by rushing off to one point all together: Appius Claudius faced the Capuans and Quintus Fulvius faced Hannibal; the propraetor Gaius Nero took up his position on the road leading to Suessa with the cavalry of six legions, and the legate Gaius Fulvius Flaccus did so close to the River Volturnus with the allied cavalry.

The engagement did not begin only with the customary battle cry and clamor; in addition to the noise from the men, horses, and weapons, there was also that from a crowd of noncombatant Capuans on the walls, and such was the clamor they produced, together with the clashing of bronze instruments (a noise like that normally raised at dead of night during a lunar eclipse),[30] that they even distracted the fighters. Appius easily kept the Capuans away from the rampart; but on the other side Fulvius faced greater pressure from Hannibal and the Carthaginians.

a lunar eclipse; cf. Plin. *HN* 2.54; Tac. *Ann.* 1.28.2; Plut. *Aem.* 17.8. As a battle tactic, cf. 43.10.5–6.

11 Poeni urgebant. legio ibi sexta loco cessit; qua pulsa cohors Hispanorum cum tribus elephantis usque ad vallum pervasit, ruperatque mediam aciem Romanorum et in ancipiti spe ac periculo erat utrum in castra perrumperet an intercluderetur a suis.

12 Quem pavorem legionis periculumque castrorum Fulvius ubi vidit, Q. Navium primoresque alios centurionum hortatur ut cohortem hostium sub vallo pugnantem inva-

13 dant: in summo discrimine rem verti; aut viam dandam iis esse—et minore conatu quam condensam aciem rupissent

14 in castra inrupturos—aut conficiendos sub vallo esse. nec magni certaminis rem fore; paucos esse et ab suis interclusos; et quae dum paveat Romanus interrupta acies videatur, eam si se utrimque in hostem vertat ancipiti pugna medios circumventuram.

15 Navius ubi haec imperatoris dicta accepit, secundi hastati signum ademptum signifero in hostes infert, iacturum in medios eos minitans ni se propere sequantur milites et

16 partem capessant pugnae. ingens corpus erat, et arma honestabant; et sublatum alte signum converterat ad spec-

17 taculum cives hostesque. ceterum postquam iam ad signa pervenerat Hispanorum, tum undique in eum tragulae coniectae et prope tota in unum acies versa, sed neque multitudo hostium neque telorum vis arcere impetum eius viri potuerunt.

6. Et M. Atilius legatus primi principis ex eadem le-

---

31 M. Atilius Regulus, praetor urbanus in 213 (24.44.2).

There the sixth legion gave ground, and when it was driven back a Spanish unit penetrated as far as the rampart with three elephants; and this had broken through the Roman center and was now weighing up hope against possible danger—hope of breaking into the camp and danger of being cut off from its own people.

When he saw the legion's fear and the danger facing the camp, Fulvius urged Quintus Navius and other first centurions to attack the enemy cohort that was fighting at the foot of their rampart. The situation was becoming critical, he said: they must either let the enemy through—and for them breaking into the camp would be less difficult than breaking through the Roman line's closed ranks—or finish them off at the foot of the rampart. That would not be a hard fight; they were few and cut off from their side; and when the Romans panicked their line had apparently been broken—so if both parts of that line now turned to face the enemy on both sides they would catch them in a pincer movement.

On hearing his commander's words, Navius seized the standard of the second maniple of the *hastati* from its bearer and carried it toward the enemy, threatening to hurl it into their midst if his men did not swiftly follow him and join the fight. He had a large physique, and his weapons enhanced it; and the standard that he held high in the air had also attracted the attention of citizen and enemy alike. When he reached the Spaniards' standards, however, he was the target of spears from all around, and almost the whole enemy line turned on the one man; but neither enemy numbers nor the quantity of their weapons could stop that man's charge.

6. The legate Marcus Atilius[31] also started to carry the

gione signum inferre in cohortem Hispanorum coepit,[12]
et qui castris praeerant L. Porcius Licinus et T. Popillius
legati pro vallo acriter propugnant elephantosque trans-
2 gredientes in ipso vallo conficiunt. quorum corporibus
cum oppleta fossa esset, velut aggere aut ponte iniecto
transitum hostibus dedit. ibi <su>per[13] stragem iacentium
elephantorum atrox edita caedes.

3   Altera in parte castrorum iam impulsi erant Campani
Punicumque praesidium, et sub ipsa porta Capuae quae
4 ad[14] Volturnum fert pugnabatur; neque tam armati in-
rumpentibus Romanis resistebant quam quod[15] porta bal-
listis scorpionibusque instructa missilibus procul hostes
5 arcebat. et suppressit impetum Romanorum volnus imperatoris Ap. Claudi, cui suos ante prima signa adhortanti
sub laevo umero summum pectus gaeso ictum est. magna
vis tamen hostium ante portam est caesa, ceteri trepidi in
6 urbem compulsi. et Hannibal postquam cohortis Hispanorum stragem vidit summaque vi castra hostium defendi,
omissa oppugnatione recipere signa et convertere agmen
peditum, obiecto ab tergo equitatu ne hostis instaret, coe-
7 pit. legionum ardor ingens ad hostem insequendum fuit;
Flaccus receptui cani iussit, satis ad utrumque profectum

---

12 inferre . . . coepit *Ruperti*: inferri . . . coegit *P*
13 <su>per *Ussing*: per *P*   14 <ad> *Wesenberg*
15 quod *A^p*: quo *P*: *del. Gron.*

---

32 The river Volturnus rather than the town of Volturnum lying at its mouth (*Barr.* 44 E3); cf. Jal *ad loc.*

33 "A quick-firing piece of artillery for discharging arrows or
sim. at close range" (*OLD* scorpio, 3).

34 Latin *gaesum*, a long, heavy javelin used mainly, but not

22

standard of the *principes* of the first maniple of that same legion toward the Spanish cohort, and the legates in charge of the camp, Lucius Porcius Licinus and Titus Popillius, fought vigorously before the rampart and dispatched a number of elephants on the rampart itself as they were crossing. Since the ditch was now filled with their carcasses, it provided the enemy with a passageway, as if a mole or bridge had been laid down for them. There, over the supine bodies of slaughtered elephants, a furious and bloody struggle broke out.

On the other side of the camp the Capuans and the Punic garrison had already been repelled, and fighting was continuing right up to the Capuan gate that leads to the Volturnus.[32] And resistance to the Romans as they attempted to break into the town was provided less by soldiers than by a gate equipped with *ballistas* and "scorpions"[33] that kept their enemies at bay with projectiles. The Roman thrust was further checked by a wound to the general Appius Claudius who, while urging on his men at the front, was struck by a javelin[34] in the upper chest below the left shoulder. Even so, large numbers of the enemy were killed before the gate and the rest were driven back panic-stricken into the city. And when Hannibal saw his Spanish unit being cut to pieces and the enemy camp defended with maximum force, he abandoned the assault and started withdrawing the standards and pulling back his infantry, setting cavalry to their rear to curtail his enemy's pressure. The legions' ardor for pursuing the foe was great, but Flaccus ordered the retreat sounded, thinking

exclusively, by Gallic and Iberian tribes (cf. Caes. *BGall.* 3.4.1; Verg. *Aen* 8.662).

ratus ut et Campani quam haud multum in Hannibale praesidii esset et ipse Hannibal sentiret.

8   Caesa eo die qui[16] huius pugnae auctores sunt octo milia hominum de Hannibalis exercitu, tria ex Campanis tradunt, signaque Carthaginiensibus quindecim adempta,

9 duodeviginti Campanis. apud alios nequaquam tantam molem pugnae inveni, plusque pavoris quam certaminis fuisse cum inopinato in castra Romana Numidae Hispa-

10 nique cum elephantis inrupissent, elephanti per media castra vadentes stragem tabernaculorum ingenti sonitu ac

11 fugam abrumpentium vincula iumentorum facerent. fraudem quoque super tumultum adiectam, immissis ab Hannibale qui habitu Italico gnari Latinae linguae iuberent consulum verbis, quoniam amissa castra essent, pro se

12 quemque militum in proximos montes fugere. sed eam celeriter cognitam fraudem oppressamque magna caede hostium; elephantos igni e castris èxactos.

13   Hoc ultimum, utcumque initum finitumque est, ante deditionem Capuae proelium fuit. medix tuticus, qui summus magistratus apud Campanos est, eo anno Seppius

14 Loesius erat, loco obscuro tenuique fortuna ortus. matrem eius quondam pro pupillo eo procurantem familiare os-

---

16 qui *P*: ‹quidam qui› *Luchs*

---

35 One of whom was probably Valerius Antias, whom Livy frequently accuses of gross exaggeration (e.g., 49.3, below).

36 They were proconsuls; Livy often refers to proconsuls as consuls: cf. Briscoe, *A Commentary on Livy Books 31–33*, 161 (on 31.49.4).

37 The senior officer among Campanian and other Oscan-speaking peoples (cf. *OCD* s.v. *meddix*).

that two ends had been sufficiently achieved: making the Capuans aware of how little support they had in Hannibal, and making Hannibal himself also aware of it.

Casualties that day, according to authors[35] who discuss this battle, were eight thousand from Hannibal's army and three thousand Capuans, with fifteen standards taken from the Carthaginians and eighteen from the Capuans. In others I have found the battle to be in no way so momentous, that there was more panic than fighting when the Numidians and Spaniards unexpectedly broke into the Roman camp with elephants, and that the elephants, trumpeting loudly, trampled down the tents as they passed through the center of the camp and stampeded the pack animals, making them break their tethers and run off. They also claim that, in addition to the affray, there was some trickery involved, that men dressed in Italian clothing and familiar with the Latin language were sent among the Romans by Hannibal to tell them, in the name of the consuls,[36] to look out for themselves and run for the nearest hills since the camp had been lost; the trickery, however, was quickly discovered and foiled, which resulted in heavy enemy losses; and the elephants were driven from the camp with fire.

Whatever the details of its beginning and end, this was the final battle before the capitulation of Capua. That year the *medix tuticus* (the supreme magistrate among the Capuans)[37] was Seppius Loesius, a man of low birth and slender means. The story goes that his mother was once performing an expiatory sacrifice on his behalf, since Loesius was still a minor,[38] in connection with an omen affect-

---

[38] Latin *pupillus* (under the care of a guardian), which suggests that he had lost his father.

tentum, cum respondisset haruspex summum quod esset
15 imperium Capuae perventurum ad eum puerum, nihil ad
eam spem adgnoscentem dixisse ferunt: "Ne tu perditas
res Campanorum narras, ubi summus honos ad filium
meum perveniet." ea ludificatio veri et ipsa in verum ver-
16 tit. nam cum fame ferroque urgerentur, nec spes ulla
superesset sisti ⟨posse, iis qui nati⟩[17] in spem honorum
17 erant honores detractantibus, Loesius, querendo desertam ac proditam a primoribus Capuam, summum magistratum ultimus omnium Campanorum cepit.

7. Ceterum Hannibal, ut nec hostes elici amplius ad
pugnam vidit neque per castra eorum perrumpi ad Ca-
2 puam posse, ne suos quoque commeatus intercluderent
novi consules, abscedere inrito incepto et movere a Capua
3 statuit castra. multa secum quonam inde ire pergeret
volventi subiit animum impetus caput ipsum belli Romam
petendi, cuius rei semper cupitae praetermissam occasionem post Cannensem pugnam et alii volgo fremebant
4 et ipse non dissimulabat. necopinato pavore ac tumultu
non esse desperandum aliquam partem urbis occupari
5 posse, et si Roma in discrimine esset Capuam extemplo
omissuros aut ambo imperatores Romanos aut alterum ex
iis; et si divisissent copias, utrumque infirmiorem factum
aut sibi aut Campanis bene gerendae rei fortunam daturos

---

[17] ⟨posse . . . nati⟩ *Alschefski*

---

[39] "A diviner of a class originating in Etruria; according to
Cicero they were interpreters of internal organs, prodigies and
lightning" (*OLD* s.v.).
[40] Cf. Maharbal's comment: "You know how to win a battle,
Hannibal; you do not know how to use the victory" (22.51.4).

ing the family, and that the *haruspex*[39] told her that the highest power in Capua would come to that boy. At this, the mother, who saw no reason to entertain such hopes, said "You must be saying that the state of Capua is lost when its top office will come to my son!" This derisory remark about the truth of the prophecy did prove to be true. When the Capuans were hard pressed by starvation and the sword, when no hope of resistance remained, and when all men born to expect public offices were refusing them, Loesius, by complaining that Capua had been abandoned and betrayed by its dignitaries, became the last of all Campanians to gain the city's highest magistracy.

7. However, when he saw that it was no longer possible for his enemy to be enticed into battle or for a passage to Capua to be forced through their lines, and also fearing that the new consuls might cut off his supplies, Hannibal decided to abandon his venture and move his camp away from Capua. As he thought long and hard about where to proceed from there, the urge took him to head for Rome, the very heart of the war. This he had always wanted to do, but he had let the opportunity slip after the battle of Cannae—a criticism that others often leveled at him and he did not himself deny.[40] With a sudden outbreak of panic and public disorder, seizing some section of the city was not, he felt, beyond hope, and if Rome were in danger either both Roman commanders, or one of the two, would immediately abandon Capua; and if they divided their troops, they would by weakening both halves give him or the Capuans some chance of success. One thing alone both-

6 esse. una ea cura angebat, ne ubi abscessisset extemplo
dederentur Campani.

Numidam promptum ad omnia ⟨agenda⟩[18] auden-
daque donis pellicit ut litteris acceptis specie transfugae
castra Romana ingressus altera parte clam Capuam per-
7 vadat. litterae autem erant adhortatione plenae: profectionem suam quae salutaris illis foret abstracturam ad
defendendam Romam ab oppugnanda Capua duces atque
8 exercitus Romanos. ne desponderent animos; tolerando
9 paucos dies totam soluturos obsidionem. inde naves in
flumine Volturno comprehensas subigi ad id quod iam
10 ante praesidii causa fecerat castellum iussit. quarum ubi
tantam copiam esse ut una nocte traici posset exercitus
allatum est, cibariis decem dierum praeparatis deductas
nocte ad fluvium legiones ante lucem traiecit.

8. Id priusquam fieret ita futurum compertum ex transfugis Fulvius Flaccus senatui Romam cum scripsisset,
varie animi hominum pro cuiusque ingenio adfecti sunt.
2 ut in re tam trepida senatu extemplo vocato, P. Cornelius
cui Asinae cognomen erat omnes duces exercitusque ex
tota Italia, neque Capuae neque ullius alterius rei memor,
3 ad urbis praesidium revocabat. Fabius Maximus abscedi a
Capua terrerique et circumagi ad nutus comminatio-
4 nesque Hannibalis flagitiosum ducebat: qui ad Cannas

---

18 ⟨agenda⟩ *Alschefski*: ⟨subeunda⟩ *Weiss.*: ⟨conanda⟩ *Oakley cl. 35.31.12*

---

41 Not according to Polybius (9.6.1), who claims that the news
caused "total confusion and panic" in Rome.

42 P. Cornelius Scipio Asina. He had been consul in 221 (*MRR*
233 and note 1) and interrex in 217 (22.34.1).

ered him: when he withdrew, the Capuans might immediately capitulate.

He bribed a Numidian, a man ready for any risky venture, to take a letter, enter the Roman camp posing as a deserter and then slip furtively away to Capua from the other side. The letter was full of encouragement: his leaving would prove their salvation (it said) as that would divert the Roman leaders and their armies from besieging Capua to defending Rome. They should not be dismayed; by holding out for a few days they would raise the entire siege. He then ordered ships to be commandeered on the Volturnus river and brought up to a fort that he had earlier built as a guard post. Informed that the number of these vessels was great enough for his army to be ferried over in one night, he had ten days' worth of rations prepared and, leading his legions down to the river at night, he ferried them over before dawn.

8. Before this happened, Fulvius Flaccus had received information from deserters that it was coming, and when he had reported it by letter to the senate in Rome reactions varied according to people's temperaments.[41] As could be expected in a serious crisis, the senate was immediately convened, and Publius Cornelius, whose *cognomen* was Asina,[42] with no thought for Capua or anything else, was for recalling all generals and armies to the defense of Rome from all over Italy. Fabius Maximus[43] felt that withdrawing from Capua, and being intimidated by Hannibal and led around at his beck and call, was humiliating: a man who after his victory at Cannae had not

---

[43] Probably Fabius Maximus Verrucosus, the famous "Cunctator."

victor ire tamen ad urbem ausus non esset, eum a Capua
5 repulsum spem potiundae urbis Romae cepisse. non ad
Romam obsidendam sed ad Capuae liberandam obsidionem ire. Romam cum eo exercitu qui ad urbem esset
Iovem foederum ruptorum ab Hannibale testem deosque
alios defensuros esse.
6 Has diversas sententias media sententia P. Valeri Flacci
vicit, qui utriusque rei memor imperatoribus qui ad Capuam essent scribendum censuit quid ad urbem praesidii
esset; quantas autem Hannibal copias duceret aut quanto
7 exercitu ad Capuam obsidendam opus esset, ipsos scire. si
ita Romam e ducibus alter et exercitus pars mitti posset ut
ab reliquo et duce et exercitu Capua recte obsideretur,
8 inter se compararent Claudius Fulviusque utri obsidenda
Capua, utri ad prohibendam obsidione patriam Romam
veniundum esset.
9 Hoc senatus consulto Capuam perlato Q. Fulvius
proconsul, cui collega ex volnere aegro redeundum Romam erat, e tribus exercitibus milite electo ad quindecim
10 milia peditum mille equites Volturnum traducit. inde cum
Hannibalem Latina via iturum satis comperisset, ipse per
Appiae municipia quaeque propter eam viam sunt Setiam
11 Coram Lanuvium[19] praemisit, ut commeatus paratos et in
urbibus haberent et ex agris deviis in viam proferrent,

---

19 Lanuvium *Cluverius*: Lavinium *P*

---

44 P. Valerius Flaccus, consul in 227, and in 219 an envoy to
Hannibal in Saguntum and Carthage (21.6.8).

45 From a point some twenty miles northwest of Capua, the
two roads run roughly parallel, about twenty miles apart, the gap
narrowing on the approach to Rome (*Barr.* 44 C–E 2–3).

dared march on the city now hoping to take the city of Rome after being driven from Capua! No, the aim of his march was not to blockade Rome but to raise the siege of Capua! As for Rome, Jupiter—witness to the treaties broken by Hannibal—and the other gods would defend her with the army that was in the city.

In this clash of opinions the compromise position of Publius Valerius Flaccus[44] prevailed. He, remaining focused on both situations, proposed that a letter be written to the generals at Capua informing them of what was available for defending the city, but adding that they themselves best knew the size of the force Hannibal was bringing and how great an army was needed for besieging Capua. If one of the generals and part of the army could be sent to Rome while the siege of Capua remained effectively conducted by the general and troops that remained, then Claudius and Fulvius should agree on which should continue the siege of Capua and which come to prevent a blockade of Rome, their homeland.

When this senatorial decree was brought to Capua, the proconsul Quintus Fulvius (whose colleague had to return to Rome as he was still incapacitated with his wound) selected men from the three armies and led about fifteen thousand infantry and a thousand cavalry across the Volturnus. Since he had discovered that Hannibal would be proceeding along the Latin Way, he sent instructions ahead for townships on the Appian Way[45] and those in its vicinity—Setia, Cora, and Lanuvium[46]—to have provisions stockpiled in the towns and also, in the case of more remote farms, brought down to the road; and they were to

[46] *Barr.* 44 C–D 2.

praesidiaque in urbes contraherent ut sua cuique res publica in manu esset.

9. Hannibal quo die Volturnum est transgressus haud
2 procul a flumine castra posuit; postero die praeter Cales in agrum Sidicinum pervenit. ibi diem unum populando moratus per Suessanum Allifanumque et Casinatem agrum via Latina ducit. sub Casinum[20] biduo stativa habita
3 et passim populationes factae. inde praeter Interamnam Aquinumque in Fregellanum agrum ad Lirim fluvium ventum, ubi intercisum pontem a Fregellanis morandi itineris causa invenit.

4 Et Fulvium Volturnus tenuerat amnis, navibus ab Hannibale incensis, rates ad traiciendum exercitum in magna
5 inopia materiae aegre comparantem. traiecto ratibus exercitu reliquum Fulvio expeditum iter, non per urbes modo sed circa viam expositis benigne commeatibus, erat; alacresque milites alius alium ut adderet gradum, memor ad defendendam iri patriam, hortabantur.

6 Romam Fregellanus nuntius diem noctemque itinere continuato ingentem attulit terrorem. tumultuosius quam
   〈quod〉[21] allatum erat 〈con〉cursu[22] hominum adfingen-
7 tium vana auditis, totam urbem concitat. ploratus mulie-

---

20 Casinum *P*: Casino *Ussing*

21 quam 〈quod〉 *Weiss*.: quam *P*

22 〈con〉cursu *Friedersdorff*

---

47 Cales and the Sidicini: *Barr.* 44 F3. All other towns mentioned here (and the River Liris) are located in 44 E–F 2–3.

48 Because the Oscan town of Cales and its neighbor Teanum Sidicinum, a Latin colony, had remained loyal to Rome.

muster troops for the towns so each community could look after itself.

9. Hannibal pitched camp not far from the Volturnus the day that he crossed the river, and the next day he came past Cales into the territory of the Sidicini.[47] There he spent one day plundering the countryside[48] and then took his army along the Latin Way through the country of Suessa, Allifae, and Casinum. He remained encamped for two days before the walls of Casinum and conducted widespread raids. He next came past Interamna and Aquinum to the River Liris in the territory of Fregellae,[49] where he found that the bridge had been broken down by the Fregellans in order to slow his progress.

Fulvius, too, had been held up by the River Volturnus, where the boats had been burned by Hannibal; and because of the dire shortage of timber he had difficulty putting together rafts for ferrying over his army. Once the army was taken across on the rafts, the rest of Fulvius' march was easy, since generous quantities of supplies had been left out for him not only in towns but also along the road; and the men enthusiastically urged each other to pick up the pace, remembering that they were marching to defend their fatherland.

A messenger from Fregellae, making a nonstop day and night journey, brought great panic to Rome. He threw the entire city into even worse turmoil than the news merited since people were running about adding pure fiction to what they heard. It was now not only women's lamenta-

---

[49] A Latin colony in the Liris valley loyal to Rome against both Hannibal and (earlier) Pyrrhus: Barr. 44 E2.

rum non ex privatis solum domibus exaudiebatur, sed
undique matronae in publicum effusae circa deum delu-
8 bra discurrunt crinibus passis aras verrentes, nixae geni-
bus, supinas manus ad caelum ac deos tendentes oran-
tesque ut urbem Romanam e manibus hostium eriperent
matresque Romanas et liberos parvos inviolatos servarent.
9 senatus magistratibus in foro praesto est si quid consulere
velint. alii accipiunt imperia disceduntque ad suas quisque
officiorum partes, alii offerunt se si quo usus operae sit.
praesidia in arce, in Capitolio, in muris, circa urbem, in
10 monte etiam Albano atque arce Aefulana ponuntur. inter
hunc tumultum Q. Fulvium proconsulem profectum cum
exercitu Capua adfertur. cui ne minueretur imperium si in
urbem venisset, decernit senatus ut Q. Fulvio par cum
consulibus imperium esset.
11   Hannibal, infestius perpopulato agro Fregellano propter intercisos pontes, per Frusinatem Ferentinatemque
12 et Anagninum agrum in Labicanum venit. inde Algido
Tusculum petiit, nec receptus moenibus infra Tusculum
dextrorsus Gabios descendit. inde in Pupiniam exercitu
13 demisso, octo milia passuum ab Roma posuit castra. quo

---

50 The Alban Mount is today Monte Cavo: *Barr.* 43 C2. Aefula
was an old Latin town close to Tibur (*Barr.* 43 D2), which did not
survive beyond the first century AD.

51 As proconsul, Fulvius would forfeit his *imperium* if he
crossed the *pomerium*, the city's sacred boundary. (On the problem of the *pomerium*, however, cf. Beard 204–5).

52 Frusino, Ferentinum, Anagnia: *Barr.* 44 D2; Labicum:
Barr. 43 C2.

53 Mt. Algidus: *Barr.* 43 D3.

tions being heard coming from private homes—everywhere married ladies, pouring into the streets, were running around the gods' shrines, sweeping altars with their disheveled hair, falling to their knees, and, with hands held palm-up to heaven and the gods, begging heaven to rescue the city of Rome from the enemy's hands and save Roman mothers and little children from abuse. The senate put itself at the disposal of the magistrates in the forum in case they wanted to raise any matter. Some took on military assignments and went off to their various duties; others volunteered for anything that might be of service. Defensive units were posted on the citadel, the Capitol, the walls, and around the city, and even on the Alban Mount and the citadel of Aefula.[50] Amid this upheaval news arrived that the proconsul Quintus Fulvius had left Capua with an army. So his *imperium* might not be invalidated by entering the city, the senate decreed that Quintus Fulvius' *imperium* should be on a par with that of the consuls.[51]

After devastating the Fregellan farmlands all the more ferociously because of the bridges' destruction, Hannibal passed through the territory of Frusino, Ferentinum, and Anagnia into that of Labicum.[52] He then made for Tusculum by way of Algidus;[53] but on being refused entry within its walls he veered to the right below Tusculum toward Gabii. From there he brought the army down into Pupinia[54] and encamped eight miles[55] from Rome. The

---

[54] The area, mentioned also by Valerius Maximus (4.4.4), remains unlocated.

[55] Roman miles, slightly shorter than the UK/U.S. mile. Polybius (9.5.9) has him "not more than 40 stades" away (approx. 5 miles).

propius hostis accedebat, eo maior caedes fiebat fugientium praecedentibus Numidis, pluresque omnium generum atque aetatium capiebantur.

10. In hoc tumultu Fulvius Flaccus porta Capena cum
exercitu Romam ingressus media urbe per Carinas Esquilias contendit; inde egressus inter Esquilinam Collinam-
que portam posuit castra. aediles plebis commeatum eo
2 comportarunt; consules senatusque in castra venerunt; ibi
de summa re publica consultatum. placuit consules circa
portas Collinam Esquilinamque ponere castra, C. Calpur-
nium praetorem urbanum Capitolio atque arci praeesse;
et senatum frequentem in foro contineri si quid in tam
subitis rebus consulto opus esset.

3 Inter haec Hannibal ad Anienem fluvium tria milia passuum ab urbe castra admovit. ibi stativis positis ipse cum
duobus milibus equitum ad portam Collinam usque ad
Herculis templum est progressus, atque unde proxime
poterat moenia situmque urbis obequitans contempla-
4 batur. id eum tam licenter atque otiose facere Flacco indignum visum est; itaque immisit equites summoverique
atque in castra redigi hostium equitatum iussit.

---

56 Gate in the Servian wall between the Caelian hill and the
Aventinus Minor, where the Via Appia ends (Richardson 301).

57 A quarter between the Caelian and Esquiline hills that became very fashionable. The name purportedly arose from some
buildings there resembling ships' keels: Richardson 71–72.

58 Gates in the eastern and the northern sectors of the city
wall: Richardson 263 (fig. 58); for the Porta Collina (58.5) and
Porta Esquilina (58.7). Cf. p. 302.

59 Richardson 185: Hercules, Templum (1). However, the
precise location is unknown, and Richardson's estimate is based
on what Livy says here.

closer the enemy came, the heavier became the casualties among fugitives (since the Numidians were riding ahead of the army) and the greater the number of all classes and ages that was being captured.

10. Amid this chaos Fulvius Flaccus marched into Rome with his army through the Porta Capena,[56] coming swiftly through the city center to the Esquiline by way of the Carinae;[57] then, leaving the city again, he encamped between the Porta Esquilina and the Porta Collina.[58] There the plebeian aediles brought him supplies; and the consuls and senate also came to his camp, and there the most important concerns of state were discussed. It was decided that the consuls should also pitch their camp near the Porta Collina and the Porta Esquilina, and that the urban praetor Gaius Calpurnius should have charge of the Capitol and citadel. The senate would meet in full in the forum in case consultation was needed in such a critical situation.

Hannibal meanwhile advanced his camp to the River Anio, three miles from the city. After establishing a base there, he proceeded with two thousand cavalry right to the temple of Hercules near the Porta Collina,[59] and riding up to the walls he began to examine them and the lie of the city as closely as he could.[60] For him to be doing this so brazenly and nonchalantly seemed outrageous to Flaccus; and so he sent some riders against him and ordered them to see that the enemy cavalry were repelled and driven back to their camp.

[60] More dramatically, Valerius Maximus (3.7.10b) and Silius Italicus (12.565–66) have Hannibal ride around the city and beat on a gate(s) with his spear (cf. also Cic. *Fin.* 4.22).

37

5   Cum commissum proelium esset, consules transfugas Numidarum, qui tum in Aventino ad mille et ducenti

6   erant, media urbe transire Esquilias iusserunt, nullos aptiores inter convalles tectaque hortorum et sepulcra et cavas undique vias ad pugnandum futuros rati. quos cum ex arce Capitolioque clivo Publicio in equis decurrentes

7   quidam vidissent, captum Aventinum conclamaverunt. ea res tantum tumultum ac fugam praebuit ut, nisi castra Punica extra urbem fuissent, effusura se omnis pavida multitudo fuerit; tunc in domos atque in tecta refugiebant, vagosque in viis suos pro hostibus lapidibus telisque in-

8   cessebant. nec comprimi tumultus aperirique error poterat, refertis itineribus agrestium turba pecorumque quae repentinus pavor in urbem compulerat.

9   Equestre proelium secundum fuit, summotique hostes sunt. et quia multis locis comprimendi tumultus erant qui temere oriebatur, placuit omnes qui dictatores consules censoresve fuissent cum imperio esse donec recessisset a

10   muris hostis. et diei quod reliquum fuit et nocte insequenti multi temere excitati tumultus sunt compressique.

11. Postero die transgressus Anienem Hannibal in aciem omnes copias eduxit; nec Flaccus consulesque cer-

2   tamen detractavere. instructis utrimque exercitibus in eius pugnae casum, in qua urbs Roma victori praemium

---

61 The main road on the Aventine, built between 241 and 238 and named after its builders, the aediles L. and M. Publicius Malleolus: Richardson 90 and fig. 14 (p. 47). It descended (*clivus* means "slope") to the Forum Boarium.

When the battle started, the consuls ordered some Numidian deserters, of whom there were then about twelve hundred on the Aventine, to go through the city center and cross the Esquiline; none, they thought, would be better suited for fighting on land among gullies, garden buildings, sepulchers and roads high-banked at every point. But when some people in the citadel and the Capitol spotted them swiftly descending the Clivus Publicius[61] on horseback, they yelled out that the Aventine had been captured. That precipitated such a headlong stampede that, had there been no Punic camp outside the city, the whole panic-stricken crowd would have poured out of town; but in fact they ran for their homes and other buildings and, assuming their own comrades wandering the streets to be the enemy, they started pelting them with stones and projectiles. Nor could the panic be suppressed and their mistake made clear, since the roads were choked with crowds of peasants and farm animals that the sudden panic had driven into the city.

The cavalry engagement was successful and the enemy was pushed back. And because any disturbances randomly erupting at various points needed to be quelled, it was decided that all who had been dictators, consuls, or censors should hold *imperium* until the enemy left the walls. In fact, throughout the rest of that day and the following night, many such disturbances did randomly break out and were suppressed.

11. The following day Hannibal crossed the Anio and brought all his troops into battle formation; nor did Flaccus and the consuls decline the fight. When both armies were deployed for that critical engagement, in which the victor's prize would be the city of Rome, there was a heavy

esset, imber ingens grandine mixtus ita utramque aciem
turbavit ut vix armis retentis in castra sese receperint, nul-
3 lius rei minore quam hostium metu. et postero die eodem
loco acies instructas eadem tempestas diremit; ubi re-
cepissent se in castra, mira serenitas cum tranquillitate
4 oriebatur. in religionem ea res apud Poenos versa est,
auditaque vox Hannibalis fertur potiundae sibi urbis Ro-
5 mae modo mentem non dari, modo fortunam. minuere
etiam spem eius duae[23] aliae parva magnaque res, magna
illa quod, cum ipse ad moenia urbis Romae armatus sede-
ret, milites sub vexillis in supplementum Hispaniae pro-
6 fectos audiit; parva autem quod per eos dies eum forte
agrum in quo ipse castra haberet venisse, nihil ob id demi-
7 nuto pretio, cognitum ex quodam captivo est. id vero adeo
superbum atque indignum visum, eius soli quod ipse bello
captum possideret haberetque inventum Romae emp-
torem, ut extemplo vocato praecone tabernas argentarias
quae circa forum Romanum essent iusserit venire.
8   His motus ad Tutiam fluvium castra rettulit sex milia
passuum ab urbe. inde ad lucum Feroniae pergit ire, tem-
9 plum ea tempestate inclutum divitiis. Capenates aliique
qui accolae eius erant primitias frugum eo donaque alia

---

23 duae *Madvig*: et P

---

62 None of this is found in Polybius (9.6.3–9, 9.7.2), who only
has Hannibal turn to looting and burning in the face of Roman
resistance, and then withdraw when the consuls encamp nearby.

63 Mentioned by Silius Italicus (13.5) as a "slender, insignificant stream," emptying into the Tiber, it remains unidentified.

64 Feronia: an old Italian goddess, perhaps of Sabine origin;
the grove at Capena (*Barr.* 42 D4) was her main place of worship.

rain shower intermixed with hail that caused such havoc in each of the battle lines that they retired to their camps scarcely able to hold their weapons, and fearing nothing less than their enemy. And when the lines were drawn up in the same spot the following day, the same storm parted them; but on their return to camp amazingly bright and tranquil weather would appear. For the Carthaginians the phenomenon had religious significance, and Hannibal was purportedly heard to remark that he had once been denied the will to take the city of Rome, and later the opportunity. His hopes were also diminished by two other incidents, one of lesser and one of greater significance. The greater was hearing that, although he was himself sitting with an army before the walls of Rome, Roman soldiers had set out under their standards as reinforcements for the Spanish campaign; the lesser was learning from a prisoner of war that the land on which he was encamped happened to have been sold around that time but with no corresponding drop in price. That for sure struck him as so outrageously presumptuous—a buyer found in Rome for land that he himself now possessed and owned after taking it in war!—that he immediately summoned an auctioneer and ordered the bankers' shops around the forum to be put up for sale.[62]

Shaken by this, Hannibal withdrew his camp to the River Tutia,[63] six miles from the city. From there he proceeded to the Grove of Feronia, whose temple was famous for its wealth at that time. The people of Capena[64] and others living close by kept it well endowed with

pro copia portantes multo auro argentoque id exornatum habebant. iis omnibus donis tum spoliatum templum. aeris acervi, cum rudera milites religione inducti iacerent, post profectionem Hannibalis magni inventi.

10 Huius populatio templi haud dubia inter scriptores est. Coelius Romam euntem ab Ereto devertisse eo Hannibalem tradit, iterque eius ab Reate Cutiliisque et ab Ami-

11 terno orditur; ex Campania in Samnium, inde in Paelignos pervenisse, praeterque oppidum Sulmonem in Marrucinos transisse; inde Albensi agro in Marsos, hinc Amiter-

12 num Forulosque vicum venisse. neque ibi error est quod tanti ducis tantique exercitus vestigia intra tam brevis aevi

13 memoriam potuerint confundi. isse enim ea constat; tantum id interest, veneritne eo itinere ad urbem an ab urbe in Campaniam redierit.

12. Ceterum non quantum Romanis pertinaciae ad premendam obsidione Capuam fuit tantum ad defen-

2 dendam Hannibali. namque per Samnium Apuliamque et Lucanos in Bruttium agrum ad fretum ac Regium eo cursu contendit ut prope repentino adventu incautos oppresse-

3 rit. Capua etsi nihilo segnius obsessa per eos dies fuerat,

---

65 On Coelius (Antipater), see Introduction to vol. V, xxliii; on the problems presented by Coelius' description of the route, see Hoyos *HW*, 667.   66 Eretum, Reate: *Barr.* 42 D4; Amiternum and (Aquae) Cutiliae: E4.

67 Sulmo (later Ovid's birthplace, today Sulmona): *Barr.* 44 E1; Marrucini: 42 F4; Alba (Fucens): 42 E4; Marsi: 42 F4; Foruli: 42 E4.   68 *Barr.* 46 C5 (mod. Reggio di Calabria), the most important town of southern Italy remaining loyal to the Romans. As it lies about 430 miles from Rome, the march must have taken about two weeks.

gold and silver, bringing there their first fruits and other gifts, according to their resources. Of all these offerings the temple was then stripped. Great heaps of bronze were found after Hannibal's departure since his soldiers would from contrition throw down chunks of the metal.

About the pillaging of this temple there is no discrepancy in our sources. Coelius[65] records that Hannibal made a diversion to it on his way to Rome from Eretum; and he has him coming by way of Reate, Cutiliae, and Amiternum.[66] He came into Samnium from Campania and from there into Paelignian territory, he says, then went past the town of Sulmo into the land of the Marrucini, and from there, by way of Alban territory, into that of the Marsi, then reaching Amiternum and the village of Foruli.[67] Nor can there be uncertainty about this, because the path of so great a leader and so great an army could not have become confused in anyone's mind in so short a space of time. There *is* agreement on it, in fact; the only disaccord is on whether this was the path he took when he came *to* the city or when he returned to Campania *from* the city.

12. Hannibal's determination to defend Capua, however, was not as great as was the Romans' to tighten their blockade. For he instead pressed on into Bruttian territory through Samnium, Apulia, and the land of the Lucanians, reaching the strait and the town of Rhegium[68] with such speed as to take its people by surprise and almost overwhelm them with his sudden appearance. Although the siege of Capua had lost none of its intensity at the time,

tamen adventum Flacci sensit, et admiratio orta est non
4 simul regressum Hannibalem. inde per conloquia intel-
lexerunt relictos se desertosque, et spem Capuae retinen-
5 dae deploratam apud Poenos esse. accessit edictum proconsulum ex senatus consulto propositum volgatumque
apud hostes ut qui civis Campanus ante certam diem
6 transisset sine fraude esset. nec ulla facta est transitio,
metu magis eos quam fide continente quia maiora in de-
7 fectione deliquerant quam quibus ignosci posset. ceterum
quemadmodum nemo privato consilio ad hostem trans-
ibat, ita nihil salutare in medium consulebatur. nobilitas
rem publicam deserverant,[24] neque in senatum cogi pot-
8 erant; in magistratu erat qui non sibi honorem adiecisset,
sed indignitate sua vim ac ius magistratui quem gerebat
9 dempsisset. iam ne in foro quidem aut publico loco principum quisquam apparebat; domibus inclusi patriae occa-
sum cum suo exitio in dies exspectabant.

10   Summa curae omnis in Bostarem Hannonemque praefectos praesidii Punici versa erat, suo non sociorum peri-
11 culo sollicitos. ii conscriptis ad Hannibalem litteris non
libere modo sed etiam aspere, quibus[25] non Capuam so-
lam traditam in manum hostibus sed se quoque et praesi-
12 dium in omnes cruciatus proditos incusabant; abisse eum
in Bruttios velut avertentem sese ne Capua in oculis eius

24 deserverant P: deserverat $M^c\Lambda$
25 quibus P: del. Doering

69 Cf. 6.13–17 above.
70 Cf. 5.6 above.

its people were nevertheless aware of Flaccus' arrival, and some surprise arose that Hannibal had not returned at the same time. They then discovered through discussions that they had been abandoned and deserted, and that the Carthaginians had lost hope of holding Capua. In addition, an edict of the proconsuls had been enacted following a decree of the senate, and had been made known to the enemy, that any Capuan citizen going over to the Romans before a certain date would come to no harm. There was, however, no defection, though it was fear more than loyalty that kept them on side because their atrocities in seceding from Rome were, they felt, too great for pardon. But while no one was defecting to the enemy by individual decision there was also no discussion of measures for collective safety. The aristocracy had abandoned the government and could not be brought together for a senate meeting; and in the top magistracy was a man who had brought no distinction upon himself but had robbed his office of its power and authority by his own unfitness for it.[69] By now none of their leading people was appearing even in the forum or any public place; shut up in their houses, they were every day awaiting their fatherland's downfall and their own destruction.

Overall responsibility for operations had devolved entirely upon the Carthaginian garrison commanders Bostar and Hanno,[70] who were concerned about their own, not their allies', predicament. They wrote Hannibal a letter that was not just frank but downright bitter, reproaching him not only for handing Capua over to the enemy but also for leaving them and their garrison to face all sorts of torture: he had gone off to Bruttium, virtually turning his back on them not to have Capua captured before his eyes!

45

caperetur. at hercle Romanos ne oppugnatione quidem
13 urbis Romanae abstrahi a Capua obsidenda potuisse; tanto
constantiorem inimicum Romanum quam amicum Poenum esse. si redeat Capuam bellumque omne eo vertat, et
14 se et Campanos paratos eruptioni fore. non cum Reginis
neque Tarentinis bellum gesturos transisse Alpes; ubi
Romanae legiones sint, ibi et Carthaginiensium exercitus
debere esse. sic ad Cannas, sic ad Trasumennum rem bene
gestam, coeundo conferundoque cum hoste castra, fortunam temptando.

15 In hanc sententiam litterae conscriptae Numidis, pro-
posita mercede eam professis operam, dantur. ii specie
transfugarum cum ad Flaccum in castra venissent ut inde
tempore capto abirent, famesque quae tam diu Capuae
erat nulli non probabilem causam transitionis faceret,
16 mulier repente Campana in castra venit scortum transfugarum unius, indicatque imperatori Romano Numidas
fraude composita transisse, litterasque ad Hannibalem
17 ferre; id unum ex iis qui sibi rem aperuisset arguere sese
paratam esse.

Productus primo satis constanter ignorare se mulierem
simulabat; paulatim dein convictus veris cum tormenta
posci et parari videret, fassus id ita esse, litteraeque pro-
18 latae; additum[26] etiam indicio quod celabatur, et alios
specie transfugarum Numidas vagari in castris Romanis.

---

[26] additum *Duker*: et additum *P*

---

[71] That is, Bostar, Hanno, and the garrison.

But the Romans, for heaven's sake—it had still proved impossible to divert *them* from the siege of Capua even by attacking the city of Rome; so much more constant was the Roman as an enemy than the Carthaginian as a friend! If he returned to Capua and made it the focus of the whole war, then both they[71] and the Capuans would be ready for a counterattack. It was not to fight the people of Rhegium or Tarentum that they had crossed the Alps; where the Roman legions were—that was where the Carthaginian armies should also be! Thus had they succeeded at Cannae and thus at Trasimene—by tackling the enemy, setting their camp down next to his, and putting fortune to the test.

The letter, written in such terms, was handed to some Numidians who, on the promise of a reward, undertook to deliver it. Posing as deserters, these men came to Flaccus in his camp, intending to slip away at the first opportunity (and the food shortages had lasted so long in Capua that no one lacked a credible pretext for deserting), when a Capuan woman, the mistress of one of the "deserters," suddenly came into the camp and informed the Roman commander that the Numidians' desertion had been a trick and they were carrying a letter to Hannibal. She was ready to offer proof about of one of them, she said, the one who had disclosed the affair to her.

When brought in, the man at first steadfastly claimed no knowledge of the woman. Then, his case gradually collapsing before the facts, and seeing instruments of torture called for and prepared for use, he admitted the truth and the letter was produced. A piece of information that was being kept hidden was also added: there were other Numidians at large in the Roman camp, posing as deserters.

47

19 ii supra septuaginta comprehensi, et cum transfugis novis
mulcati virgis manibusque praecisis Capuam rediguntur.

13. Conspectum tam triste supplicium fregit animos
Campanorum. concursus ad curiam populi factus coegit
Loesium senatum vocare; et primoribus qui iam diu publicis consiliis aberant propalam minabantur, nisi venirent in
senatum, circa domos eorum ituros se et in publicum om-
2 nes vi extracturos esse. is timor frequentem senatum magistratui praebuit. ibi cum ceteri de legatis mittendis ad
3 imperatores Romanos agerent, Vibius Virrius, qui defectionis auctor ab Romanis fuerat, interrogatus sententiam
negat eos qui de legatis et de pace ac deditione loquantur
meminisse nec quid facturi fuerint si Romanos in potestate habuissent, nec quid ipsis patiendum sit.

4 "Quid? vos" inquit "eam deditionem fore censetis qua
quondam, ut adversus Samnites auxilium impetraremus,
nos nostraque omnia Romanis dedidimus? iam e[27] memoria excessit quo tempore et in qua fortuna a populo Ro-
5 mano defecerimus? iam quemadmodum in defectione
praesidium quod poterat emitti per cruciatum et ad contu-
6 meliam necarimus? quotiens in obsidentes quam inimice

---

[27] iam e *P*: iamne *Fügner*

---

[72] For this virulently anti-Roman Capuan, who advocated a
treaty with Hannibal after Cannae, cf. 23.6–7; Sil. 13.65–72.

[73] In the mid-fourth century the Capuans were under attack
from the Samnites, who were Roman allies. Knowing the Romans
to be too honorable to break with allies, the Capuans, to gain their
assistance, surrendered "the people of Campania and the city of
Capua" (7.30–31).

These, more than seventy in number, were arrested and, along with the new "deserters," returned to Capua after a flogging and having their hands cut off.

13. The sight of such savage punishment broke the Capuans' will. A swift rush to the senate house by the people forced Loesius to convene the senate, and they also openly threatened the leading citizens who had long been absenting themselves from the public meetings: if they did not come to the senate, they would go round their houses and forcibly drag all of them out into the streets. Fear of that gave the magistrate a well-attended senate. There, while all others were talking about sending a deputation to the Roman commanders, Vibius Virrius, the man responsible for the defection from the Romans,[72] declared when asked his opinion that those talking about a deputation and about peace and surrender were bearing in mind neither what they themselves had intended doing if they had had the Romans at their mercy, nor what treatment they must face themselves.

"Well," he continued, "do you think this surrender is going to be same as before, when we surrendered ourselves and all our possessions to the Romans to gain their help against the Samnites?[73] Have you already forgotten just when it was that we rebelled from the Roman people, and in what circumstances? Have you forgotten how, when we defected, we put to death with torture and shameful abuse a garrison that could have been released?[74] Have you forgotten how often and how fiercely we conducted

[74] The Capuans had seized allied prefects and Roman citizens and locked them in the baths, where they were suffocated by the heat (23.7.3).

eruperimus, castra oppugnarimus, Hannibalem vocaveri-
mus ad opprimendos eos, hoc quod recentissimum est ad
oppugnandam Romam hinc eum miserimus?

7   "Age contra, quae illi infeste in nos fecerint repetite, ut
ex eo quid speretis habeatis. cum hostis alienigena in Italia esset et Hannibal hostis et cuncta bello arderent, omissis omnibus, omisso ipso Hannibale, ambo consules et duo
consulares exercitus ad Capuam oppugnandam miserunt.

8   alterum annum circumvallatos inclusosque nos fame ma-
cerant, et ipsi nobiscum ultima pericula et gravissimos
labores perpessi, circa vallum ac fossas saepe trucidati ac
prope ad extremum castris exuti.

9   "Sed omitto haec; vetus atque usitata res est in oppugnanda hostium urbe labores ac pericula pati. illud irae
atque odii ⟨inexpiabilis⟩[28] exsecrabilisque indicium est.

10   Hannibal ingentibus copiis peditum equitumque castra
oppugnavit et ex parte cepit; tanto periculo nihil moti sunt
ab obsidione. profectus trans Volturnum perussit Cale-

11   num agrum; nihil tanta sociorum clade avocati sunt. ad
ipsam urbem Romam infesta signa ferri iussit; eam quoque tempestatem imminentem spreverunt. transgressus
Anienem amnem tria milia passuum ab urbe castra posuit,
postremo ad moenia ipsa et ad portas accessit, Romam se

12   adempturum eis nisi omitterent Capuam ostendit; non
omiserunt. feras bestias caeco impetu ac rabie concitatas,

---

[28] ⟨inexpiabilis⟩ *Alschefski*

---

[75] Cf. 9.2 and note, above.

sorties against the blockading forces, attacked their camp, called on Hannibal to crush them and (the most recent thing) sent him from here to attack Rome?

"On the other hand, so you can gather from that what to expect, recall their hostile acts against us. When there was an enemy from abroad in Italy, when that enemy was Hannibal, and when the whole country was engulfed in the flames of war, they still forgot everything else, forgot even Hannibal himself, and sent two consuls and two consular armies to blockade Capua. It is now the second year that they are grinding us down with hunger, surrounded by siege works and under blockade, although, like us, they too have faced the severest dangers and most punishing hardships, often massacred around their rampart and ditches and ultimately almost driven from their camp.

"But I pass over this—facing hardships and dangers in blockading an enemy city has a long history and is commonplace. What is evidence of a rage and hatred that is implacable and deadly, however, is this: Hannibal attacked their camp with massive infantry and cavalry forces and took part of it; not even by danger on that scale could they be in any way dislodged from their blockade. Proceeding over the Volturnus, he put the land of Cales[75] to the torch; not even by such a catastrophe for their allies could they be deterred. He ordered an attack on the city of Rome itself; even to that gathering storm they paid no heed. Crossing the River Anio, he encamped three miles from the city and finally came right up to the walls and gates and made it clear to them that he would take Rome unless they abandoned Capua. They did not abandon it. When wild beasts are in the grip of blind and furious rage you

si ad cubilia et catulos earum ire pergas, ad opem suis
13 ferendam avertas; Romanos Roma circumsessa coniuges,
liberi, quorum ploratus hinc prope exaudiebantur, arae,
foci, deum delubra, sepulcra maiorum temerata ac violata
a Capua non averterunt. tanta aviditas supplicii expetendi,
tanta sanguinis nostri hauriendi est sitis. nec iniuria; forsitan nos quoque idem fecissemus, si data fortuna esset.

14 "Itaque quoniam aliter dis immortalibus est visum,
cum mortem ne recusare quidem debeam, cruciatus con-
tumeliasque quas parat hostis dum liber, dum mei potens
sum, effugere morte praeterquam honesta, etiam leni pos-
15 sum. non videbo Ap. Claudium et Q. Fulvium victoria
insolenti subnixos, neque vinctus per urbem Romanam
triumphi spectaculum trahar, ut coniectus in carcerem[29]
aut ad palum deligatus, lacerato virgis tergo, cervicem
securi Romanae subiciam; nec dirui incendique patriam
videbo, nec rapi ad stuprum matres Campanas virgines-
16 que et ingenuos pueros. Albam unde ipsi oriundi erant a
fundamentis proruerunt ne stirpis, ne memoria originum
suarum exstaret, nedum eos Capuae parsuros credam cui
infestiores quam Carthagini sunt.

17 "Itaque quibus vestrum ante fato cedere quam haec tot
tam acerba videant in animo est, iis apud me hodie epulae
18 instructae parataeque sunt. satiatis vino ciboque poculum
idem quod mihi datum fuerit circumferetur; ea potio cor-

---

[29] coniectus in carcerem *Oakley*: deinde in carcerem *P*: deinde in carcere *Madvig*: demissus in carcerem *Jal*

---

[76] Alba Longa in Latium, reputedly founded by Aeneas' son
Ascanius, was destroyed by the third king of Rome, Tullus Hostilius (reign traditionally dated to 672–641).

can make them turn aside to help their own kind if you approach their lairs and their young. In the Romans' case, Rome under siege could not turn them aside from Capua, nor could their wives and children, whose weeping and wailing could be heard almost from here—nor could the desecration and violation of their altars, their hearths, the shrines of their gods, and their ancestors' tombs. So great is their hunger for punishment, so great their thirst for our blood! And not without reason; perhaps we would have done the same if given the chance.

"And so, since the gods have decided otherwise, and as I must not even shrink back from the prospect of death, I can, while still free and my own master, escape the tortures and indignities that the enemy is preparing, with a death honorable and even merciful. I shall not see Appius Claudius and Quintus Fulvius high and mighty in insolent victory, nor will I be dragged in chains through the city of Rome as an exhibit in their triumph to then be thrown in prison or tied to a post and set my neck beneath a Roman ax, after my back has been lacerated by the whip; nor will I see my native city being destroyed and burned or Capuan mothers, girls, and freeborn boys being taken off to face sexual abuse. Alba, from which they themselves are descended, the Romans razed to its foundations to leave no memory of their lineage and origins.[76] Much less will I believe they will spare Capua, which they hate more than they hate Carthage.

"And so, for those among you who have it in mind to yield to fate before witnessing so many painful sights, a dinner has been today arranged and prepared at my house. When you have had your fill of wine and food, a cup that will have been given to me first will also be passed around

pus a cruciatu, animum a contumeliis, oculos aures a vi-
dendis audiendisque omnibus acerbis indignisque quae
manent victos vindicabit. parati erunt qui magno rogo in
19 propatulo aedium accenso corpora exanima iniciant. haec
una via et honesta et libera ad mortem. et ipsi virtutem
mirabuntur hostes, et Hannibal fortes socios sciet ab se
desertos ac proditos esse."

14. Hanc orationem Virri plures cum adsensu audie-
runt quam forti animo id quod probabant exsequi potue-
2 runt. maior pars senatus, multis saepe bellis expertam
populi Romani clementiam haud diffidentes sibi quoque
placabilem fore, legatos ad dedendam Romanis Capuam
3 decreverunt miseruntque. Vibium Virrum septem et viginti ferme senatores domum secuti sunt; epulatique cum
eo et quantum facere potuerant alienatis mentibus vino ab
4 imminentis sensu mali, venenum omnes sumpserunt. inde
misso convivio, dextris inter se datis ultimoque complexu
conlacrimantes suum patriaeque casum, alii ut eodem
rogo cremarentur manserunt, alii domos digressi sunt.
5 impletae cibis vinoque venae minus efficacem in matu-
randa morte vim veneni fecerunt. itaque noctem totam
plerique eorum et diei insequentis partem [is] cum ani-
mam egissent, omnes tamen prius quam aperirentur
hostibus portae exspirarunt.
6 Postero die porta Iovis quae adversus castra Romana
erat iussu proconsulum aperta est. ea intromissa legio una
7 et duae alae cum C. Fulvio legato. is cum omnium primum

---

the company. That is a drink that will rescue your body from torment, your spirit from humiliation, your eyes and ears from all the painful and degrading sights and sounds that await the conquered. Men will be at hand to hurl the lifeless bodies onto a pyre set alight in the courtyard of the house. This is the only path to death honorable and befitting a free man. Our enemies themselves will marvel at our courage, and Hannibal, too, will know of the valiant allies he deserted and betrayed."

14. More heard with agreement what Virrius said than were able to carry out with firm resolve a plan that they approved. Most of the senate had little doubt that the clemency of the Roman people that they had often witnessed in many wars would also serve them well; and they decided to send a delegation to surrender Capua to the Romans, and then sent it. Some twenty-seven senators went home with Vibius Virrus and, after dining with him and doing all they could to deaden their minds with wine to the prospect of the torment ahead, they all took the poison. The banquet then broke up and they clasped each other's right hands and embraced for the last time, shedding tears for their own and their country's lot. Some then stayed on so they could be burned together on the same pyre; others went off to their homes. That their veins were replete with food and wine diminished the poison's potency to hasten death. As a result most were gasping for breath throughout the night and part of the following day, but all met their end before the gates were opened to their enemy.

The following day the Jupiter Gate that faced the Roman camp was thrown open by order of the proconsuls. A single legion and two cavalry squadrons were sent in under the command of the legate Gaius Fulvius.[77] His first

arma telaque quae Capuae erant ad se conferenda curasset, custodiis ad omnes portas dispositis ne quis exire aut emitti posset, praesidium Punicum comprehendit, senatum Campanum ire in castra ad imperatores Romanos

8 iussit. quo cum venissent, extemplo iis omnibus catenae iniectae, iussique ad quaestores deferre quod auri atque argenti haberent. auri pondo duo milia septuaginta fuit,

9 argenti triginta milia pondo et mille ducenta. senatores quinque et viginti Cales in custodiam, duodetriginta Teanum missi, quorum de sententia maxime descitum ab Romanis constabat.

15. De supplicio Campani senatus haudquaquam inter Fulvium Claudiumque conveniebat. facilis impetrandae

2 veniae Claudius, Fulvio[30] durior sententia erat. itaque Appius Romam ad senatum arbitrium eius rei totum rei-

3 ciebat; percontandi etiam aequum esse potestatem fieri patribus num communicassent consilia cum aliquis sociorum Latini nominis,[31] et num ope eorum in bello forent

4 adiuti. id vero minime committendum esse Fulvius dicere, ut sollicitarentur criminibus dubiis sociorum fidelium animi, et subicerentur indicibus quis neque ⟨quid dicerent neque⟩[32] quid facerent quicquam unquam pensi fuisset; itaque se eam quaestionem oppressurum exstincturumque.

5 Ab hoc sermone cum digressi essent, et Appius quam-

---

[30] Fulvio *P*: Fulvii Λ   [31] nominis *Madvig*: nominis municipiorum *P*   [32] ⟨quid dicerent neque⟩ *Alschefski*

---

[78] Because Cales and Teanum had remained loyal to Rome.

[79] Appius' sympathy for the Capuans may have arisen from his daughter being married to Pacuvius Calavius, a former chief mag-

act was to have all arms and projectiles in Capua brought to him and then, stationing sentries at all the gates so none could leave or be let out, he arrested the Punic garrison and ordered the Capuan senate to proceed to the Roman commanders in their camp. When they reached there all the senators were immediately clapped in irons and ordered to bring out to the quaestors whatever gold and silver they owned. This amounted to 2,070 pounds of gold and 31,200 pounds of silver. Twenty-five senators whose views were generally known to have been responsible for the defection from Rome were sent to Cales for imprisonment, and twenty-eight to Teanum.[78]

15. On punishment for the Capuan senate there was no agreement whatsoever between Fulvius and Claudius. Claudius was amenable to granting pardon,[79] but Fulvius was more obdurate. Appius therefore kept suggesting that they refer the entire matter to the senate; it was also fair, he said, that the senators be given the opportunity to question the prisoners on whether they had shared their plans with any Latin allies, and whether they had received assistance from them during the hostilities. Fulvius, however, maintained that they must at all costs avoid the loyalty of faithful allies being exposed to vague insinuations, and left at the mercy of informers who had no concern whatsoever about what they said or did, and he said he would therefore overrule and quash that line of inquiry.

When they parted after this conversation, Appius was

istrate (*medix tuticus*) at Capua (cf. 23.2.6). His failure to intervene later may have been because he had already died from his wound (cf. 6.5 and 16.1, above).

vis ferociter loquentem collegam non dubitaret tamen
6 litteras super tanta re ab Roma exspectaturum, Fulvius,
ne id ipsum impedimentum incepto foret, dimittens praetorium tribunis militum ac praefectis socium imperavit uti
duobus milibus equitum delectis denuntiarent ut ad tertiam bucinam praesto essent.

7   Cum hoc equitatu nocte Teanum profectus prima luce
portam intravit atque in forum perrexit; concursuque ad
primum equitum ingressum facto, magistratum Sidicinum
citari iussit, imperavitque ut produceret Campanos quos
8 in custodia haberet. producti omnes virgisque caesi ac
securi percussi. inde citato equo Cales percurrit. ubi cum
in tribunali consedisset productique Campani deligaren-
tur ad palum, eques citus ab Roma venit, litterasque a C.
Calpurnio praetore Fulvio et senatus consultum tradit.
9 murmur ab tribunali totam contionem pervasit differri
rem integram ad patres de Campanis; et Fulvius id ita esse
ratus acceptas litteras neque resolutas cum in gremio re-
posuisset, praeconi imperavit ut lictorem lege agere iuberet. ita de iis quoque qui Calibus erant sumptum suppli-
10 cium. tum litterae lectae senatusque consultum serum ad
impediendam rem actam quae summa ope approperata
erat ne impediri posset.

11   Consurgentem iam Fulvium Taurea Vibellius Campanus per mediam vadens turbam nomine inclamavit, et

---

80 Literally, "Sidicine magistrate," Teanum being the chief
city of the Sidicini.

81 Livy earlier calls him a distinguished soldier (23.8.5) and
"one of the bravest cavalrymen of Capua" (23.46.12), but then
reports his contest with a Roman cavalryman from which he
emerges the loser (23.46.13–23.47.8).

convinced that, for all his defiant words, his colleague would still await written orders from Rome on a matter of such importance. Fulvius, however, feared that this very thing would interfere with what he intended doing, and while he was dismissing his council he ordered his military tribunes and allied officers to have two thousand select cavalrymen at the ready when the bugle sounded the third watch.

Leaving for Teanum at night with this cavalry force, Fulvius passed through the gate at dawn and headed straight for the forum. People gathered around when the cavalry first entered; and he then ordered the chief magistrate[80] summoned and commanded him to bring out the Capuan citizens that he had in custody. All were brought out, flogged, and beheaded. From there he rode at a gallop to Cales. After he had taken his seat on the podium and the Capuans had been brought out and were actually being tied to the stake, a horseman arrived posthaste from Rome who delivered to Fulvius a dispatch from the praetor Gaius Calpurnius and a decree of the senate. A rumor then spread from the podium throughout the gathering that the Capuans' case was being postponed pending senatorial adjudication; and Fulvius, accepting that as being the case, took the letter, placed it unopened in his lap, and told the herald to give the lector the order to carry out the lawful sentence. So the execution of the prisoners at Cales was also carried out. Only then were the letter and senatorial decree actually read, too late to obstruct something that had been speeded up by all possible means to make obstructing it impossible.

Fulvius was already rising to his feet when Taurea Vibellius,[81] a Capuan citizen, came striding through the

cum mirabundus quidnam sese vellet resedisset Flaccus,
12 "Me quoque" inquit "iube occidi ut gloriari possis multo
13 fortiorem quam ipse es virum abs te occisum esse." cum
Flaccus negaret profecto satis compotem mentis esse,
modo prohiberi etiam se si id vellet senatus consulto dice-
14 ret, tum Vibellius "quando quidem" inquit "capta patria,
propinquis amicisque amissis, cum ipse manu mea con-
iugem liberosque interfecerim ne quid indigni paterentur,
mihi ne mortis quidem copia eadem est quae his civibus
15 meis, petatur a virtute invisae huius vitae vindicta." atque
ita gladio quem veste texerat per adversum pectus trans-
fixus ante pedes imperatoris moribundus procubuit.

16. Quia et quod ad supplicium attinet Campanorum
et pleraque alia de Flacci unius sententia acta erant, mortuum Ap. Claudium sub deditionem Capuae quidam tra-
2 dunt. hunc quoque ipsum Tauream neque sua sponte venisse Cales neque sua manu interfectum, sed dum inter
ceteros ad palum deligatur,[33] quia parum inter strepitus
exaudiri possent quae vociferaretur, silentium fieri Flac-
3 cum iussisse. tum Tauream illa quae ante memorata sunt
dixisse, virum se fortissimum ab nequaquam pari ad virtutem occidi; sub haec dicta iussu proconsulis praeconem
ita pronuntiasse: "Lictor, viro forti adde virgas et in eum
4 primum lege age." lectum quoque senatus consultum
priusquam securi feriret quidam auctores sunt, sed quia

---

[33] dum . . . deligatur *Fr. 2*: cum . . . deligatus *P*: cum . . . deligatur *Drak.*: cum inter ceteros ‹esset› . . . deligatus *Walsh*

---

[82] Presumably from his wound; cf. 6.5 and 16.1, above.

midst of the crowd and called on him by name; and when, Flaccus, wondering what the man wanted of him, sat down again, Vibellius said: "Have me executed, too, so you can boast that a man much braver than you yourself was executed by you." Flaccus declared the man was clearly deranged and that, in any case, he was prevented by the senate's decree from doing what he asked even if he wanted to. "My native city has been captured," replied Vibellius, "and my relatives and friends are gone—with my own hand I killed my wife and children so they would not be subjected to any outrage. But I do not even have the same opportunity to die as these fellow citizens of mine, so let my release from this life that I hate come from my courage." With that he took a sword that he had hidden under his clothes, plunged it straight through his breast, and fell dead at the general's feet.

16. Because both the matter of the Capuans' execution and several other things arose from a unilateral decision of Flaccus, some record that Appius Claudius was dead before the surrender of Capua.[82] They add that this man Taurea had himself not come to Cales of his own volition or died by his own hand; while he was being tied to a stake along with the others, they claim, Flaccus called for silence because what the man was shouting could barely be heard amid the clamor, and Taurea then made the declaration recorded above, that he was a very brave man being put to death by one nowhere near his equal in courage; and at this the herald, on the proconsul's order, called out: "Lictor, apply the lash to the brave man and on him carry out the lawful sentence first!" Some authors also record that the senatorial decree was read by Fulvius before he carried out the execution but that, because there was a

adscriptum in senatus consulto fuerit si ei videretur integram rem ad senatum reiceret, interpretatum esse quid magis e re publica duceret aestimationem sibi permissam.

5   Capuam a Calibus reditum est, Atellaque et Calatia in deditionem acceptae; ibi quoque in eos qui capita rerum
6   erant animadversum. ita ad septuaginta principes senatus interfecti. trecenti ferme nobiles Campani in carcerem conditi, alii per sociorum Latini nominis urbes in custodias dati variis casibus interierunt; multitudo alia civium Campanorum venum data.

7   De urbe agroque reliqua consultatio fuit, quibusdam delendam censentibus urbem praevalidam propinquam inimicam. ceterum praesens utilitas vicit; nam propter agrum, quem omni fertilitate terrae satis constabat primum in Italia esse, urbs servata est ut esset aliqua ara-
8   torum sedes. urbi frequentandae multitudo incolarum libertinorumque et institorum opificumque retenta; ager
9   omnis et tecta publica populi Romani facta. ceterum habitari tantum tamquam urbem Capuam frequentarique placuit, corpus nullum civitatis nec senatum nec plebis con-
10   cilium nec magistratus esse. sine consilio publico, sine imperio multitudinem nullius rei inter se sociam ad consensum inhabilem fore; praefectum ad iura reddenda ab Roma quotannis missuros.

11   Ita ad Capuam res compositae consilio ab omni parte laudabili severe et celeriter in maxime noxios animadver-

---

83 This was the conventional formula employed by the senate when issuing instructions to magistrates and promagistrates (cf. 22.33.9, 25.41.9, etc.), but Fulvius perversely takes the formula at face value.   84 Adjacent Campanian towns among those that defected from Rome (cf. 22.61.11): Calatia, *Barr.* 44 F3; Atella, F4.   85 Cf. Cic. *Leg. agr.* 1.19–20.

rider in the decree stating that "he should refer the whole matter back to the senate for adjudication if he saw fit,"[83] he interpreted it as meaning that the decision on what was in the state's best interests had been left to him.

From Cales he returned to Capua and accepted the surrender of Atella and Calatia;[84] there, too, punishment was meted out to those who were the ringleaders. About seventy prominent members of the senate were put to death. Around three hundred Campanian nobles were imprisoned, and others that had been kept in custody throughout the cities of the Latin allies perished in various ways; the remaining horde of Capuan citizens was sold into slavery.

There remained discussion of the city and its lands, some advocating destruction of a city that was very strong, close by, and hostile. Immediate practical considerations prevailed, however; for, since its land was widely seen as the best in Italy for overall fertility, the city was preserved to be a sort of agricultural base. To keep the city inhabited, its population of resident foreigners, freedmen, traders, and craftsmen was retained, and all farmlands and buildings became the public property of the Roman people. It was decided, however, that Capua should only be inhabited and populated like a city but would have no political structure—no senate, no plebeian council, no magistrates.[85] Without a public council, without authority, and with no shared interest in anything, the population would be incapable of any uniform policy. The Romans would each year send a prefect from Rome to conduct judicial proceedings.

The Capuan question was thus settled by implementing a program praiseworthy in every respect: punishment of the most culpable was harsh and swift; the bulk of the

sum; multitudo civium dissipata in nullam spem reditus;
12 non saevitum incendiis ruinisque in tecta innoxia murosque, et cum emolumento quaesita etiam apud socios lenitatis species incolumitate urbis nobilissimae opulentissimaeque, cuius ruinis omnis Campania, omnes qui
13 Campaniam circa accolunt populi ingemuissent; confessio expressa hosti quanta vis in Romanis ad expetendas poenas ab infidelibus sociis, et quam nihil in Hannibale auxilii ad receptos in fidem tuendos esset.

17. Romani patres perfuncti quod ad Capuam attinebat cura, C. Neroni ex iis duabus legionibus quas ad Capuam habuerat sex milia peditum et trecentos equites quos ipse legisset, et socium Latini nominis peditum numerum pa-
2 rem et octingentos equites decernunt. eum exercitum Puteolis in naves impositum Nero in Hispaniam transportavit. cum Tarraconem navibus venisset, expositisque ibi copiis et navibus subductis socios quoque navales multi-
3 tudinis augendae causa armasset, profectus ad Hiberum flumen exercitum ab Ti. Fonteio et L. Marcio accepit. inde
4 pergit ad hostes ire. Hasdrubal Hamilcaris ad Lapides Atros castra habebat; in Oretanis[34] is locus est inter oppida Iliturgim et Mentisam. huius saltus fauces Nero occupavit.

---

34 Oretanis *Glar.*: Ausetanis *P*

---

86 C. Claudius Nero, already mentioned at 5.8, above. Praetor for 212, he had participated in the siege of Capua (25.22.7–13). He became consul in 207.

87 Ti. Fonteius had been Scipio's legate in Spain (25.37.4). For L. Marcius, cf. 2.1 and note, above.

88 Hannibal's youngest brother, who later died in the battle at the River Metaurus in 207 (27.49.3–4).

citizen body was dispersed with no prospect of return; there was no wreaking havoc with fire and destruction on inoffensive buildings and walls, and in addition to their economic gain the Romans could appear lenient with their allies by leaving unharmed a very famous and wealthy city, the destruction of which would have brought anguish to Campania and all in the environs of Campania; and the enemy was forced to acknowledge Rome's ability to punish disloyal allies and Hannibal's total inability to safeguard those he had taken under his protection.

17. After settling problems related to Capua, the Roman senators decreed to Gaius Nero[86] six thousand infantry and three hundred cavalry that he could select from the two legions he had commanded at Capua, and the same number of infantry and eight hundred cavalry from allies and men of Latin status. Nero boarded this army on ships at Puteoli and transported it to Spain. On reaching Tarraco with the fleet, he disembarked the troops, hauled the ships ashore and, in order to increase his strength, also armed his crews; then he left for the River Ebro, where he received command of their army from Tiberius Fonteius and Lucius Marcius.[87] From there he proceeded against the enemy. Hasdrubal son of Hamilcar[88] was encamped at the Black Rocks; this is an area between the towns of Iliturgi and Mentisa.[89] As it lay in a pass, Nero seized the entrance.

[89] The precise location of the Black Rocks is unknown. For Iliturgi, cf. *Barr.* 27 B4; TIR *J-30*, 202–3. For Mentisa, cf. *Barr.* 27 C3 (Mentesa); TIR *J-30*, 234–35. Instead of Oretani the manuscripts all read Ausetani, but as they lived close to the Pyrenees (*Barr.* 25 H4), Oretani, Glareanus' emendation (*Barr.* 27 B3, Oretania), accepted by Jal, is preferable.

5   Hasdrubal, ne in arto res esset, caduceatorem misit qui promitteret si inde emissus foret se omnem exercitum ex
6   Hispania deportaturum. quam rem cum laeto animo Romanus accepisset, diem posterum Hasdrubal conloquio petivit, ut coram leges conscriberentur de tradendis arcibus urbium dieque statuenda ad quam praesidia deducerentur, suaque omnia sine fraude Poeni deportarent.
7   quod ubi impetravit, extemplo primis tenebris atque inde tota nocte quod gravissimum exercitus erat Hasdrubal
8   quacunque posset evadere e saltu iussit. data sedulo opera est ne multi ea nocte exirent, ut ipsa paucitas cum ad hostem silentio fallendum aptior tum ad evadendum per artas semitas ac difficiles esset.

9   Ventum insequenti die ad conloquium est, sed loquendo plura scribendoque dedita opera quae in rem non
10   essent die consumpto, in posterum dilatum est. addita insequens nox spatium dedit et alios emittendi; nec
11   postero die res finem invenit. ita aliquot dies disceptando palam de legibus, noctesque emittendis clam e castris Carthaginiensibus absumptae. et postquam pars maior emissa exercitus erat, iam ne iis quidem quae ultro dicta erant stabatur, minusque ac minus, cum timore simul fide decrescente, conveniebat. iam ferme pedestres omnes
12   copiae evaserant e saltu, cum prima luce densa nebula saltum omnem camposque circa intexit. quod ubi sensit Hasdrubal, mittit ad Neronem qui in posterum diem conloquium differret: illum diem religiosum Carthaginien-

Not to be penned in, Hasdrubal sent a herald to Nero with a promise to remove his entire army from Spain if he were allowed out of there. When the Roman gladly accepted the offer, Hasdrubal requested a meeting on the following day so terms for surrendering the citadels in the cities could be drawn up in face-to-face discussions, and for a date to be set for withdrawing the garrisons and removing all their property with impunity. When granted this, Hasdrubal immediately ordered his heaviest troops to slip out of the pass by any means possible as soon as darkness fell and then throughout the night. Care was taken for not many to leave that coming night; a smaller number would be better for eluding the enemy by their silence, and also for slipping away along narrow and difficult pathways.

They came to the meeting the following day, but as the day was consumed with inordinately long discussions and documentation of irrelevancies it was adjourned to the next. The oncoming night gave Hasdrubal further time for sending out even more men, and the business did not reach a conclusion the next day, either. Thus several days were spent on openly discussing terms and several nights on secretly slipping Carthaginians out of the camp. Then, when most of the army had been slipped out, there was no longer any support even for terms that they had actually proposed themselves, and agreement was less and less forthcoming as their integrity decreased along with their fear. Nearly all their infantry troops had already left the pass when, at break of day, a dense mist covered the whole pass and the surrounding plains. Noting that, Hasdrubal sent someone to Nero to postpone the meeting to the following day; on that present day, he said, religion forbade

13 sibus ad agendum quicquam rei seriae esse. ne tum quidem suspecta fraus cum esset, data venia eius diei,
exemploque Hasdrubal cum equitatu elephantisque
14 castris egressus sine ullo tumultu in tutum evasit. hora
ferme quarta dispulsa sole nebula aperuit diem, vacuaque
15 hostium castra conspexerunt Romani. tum demum Claudius Punicam fraudem adgnoscens ut se dolo captum sensit, proficiscentem institit sequi, paratus confligere acie.
16 sed hostis detractabat pugnam; levia tamen proelia inter
extremum Punicum agmen praecursoresque Romanorum
fiebant.

18. Inter haec Hispaniae populi nec qui post cladem
acceptam defecerant redibant ad Romanos, nec ulli novi
2 deficiebant; et Romae senatui populoque post receptam
Capuam non Italiae iam maior quam Hispaniae cura erat;
3 et exercitum augeri et imperatorem mitti placebat. nec
tam quem mitterent satis constabat quam illud, ubi duo
summi imperatores intra dies triginta cecidissent, qui in
locum duorum succederet extraordinaria cura deligen-
4 dum esse. cum alii alium nominarent, postremum eo
decursum est ut populus proconsuli creando in Hispaniam
comitia haberet,[35] diemque comitiis consules edixerunt.
5 primo exspectaverant ut qui se tanto imperio dignos cre-

---

[35] ut populus . . . proconsuli . . . haberet *P*: ut proconsuli . . .
haberentur *Madvig*

---

[90] Latin *Punica fraus* (Punic deceit), frequently attributed to
the Carthaginians by the Romans. It is an expression that occurs
five times in this decade and elsewhere only in Florus (influenced
by Livy) and much later in Orosius. This episode figures among

Carthaginians from conducting any serious business. As there was no suspicion of duplicity even then, Hasdrubal was excused for that day; and immediately on leaving camp with his cavalry and elephants he slipped quietly away to safety. At about the fourth hour the mist, dispersed by the sun, revealed the light of day, and the Romans set eyes on a deserted enemy camp. Only then did Claudius recognize the Carthaginian perfidy,[90] and when he realized that he had been hoodwinked he followed hard on the heels of the departing Hasdrubal, ready to face him in regular battle. The enemy, however, refused to engage, though there were some skirmishes between the Punic rearguard and the advance troops of the Romans.

18. Meanwhile, those peoples of Spain that had defected after the defeat[91] were not returning to the Roman alliance, although there were no new defections either; and at Rome, after the recovery of Capua, the senate and people's concern was now as much for Spain as for Italy. It was decided that the army there should be augmented and also that a commander be sent out; but about the man to send there was less agreement than there was about the notion that, when two of their best commanders had perished in thirty days, the man succeeding them must be chosen with extra-special care. When various people suggested various candidates, the expedient eventually accepted was that the people should hold an election to appoint a proconsul for Spain; and the consuls announced a date for the election. At first people had expected those

Frontinus' *Stratagems* (1.5.19), most probably deriving from Livy.

[91] That is, the defeat of the two Scipio brothers (25.32–36).

derent nomina profiterentur; quae ut destituta exspectatio est, redintegratus luctus acceptae cladis desideriumque imperatorum amissorum.

6   Maesta itaque civitas prope inops consilii comitiorum die tamen in campum descendit; atque in magistratus versi circumspectant ora principum aliorum alios intuentium, fremuntque adeo perditas res desperatumque de re publica esse ut nemo audeat in Hispaniam imperium acci-
7 pere, cum subito P. Cornelius, P. Corneli qui in Hispania ceciderat filius quattuor et viginti ferme annos natus, professus se petere in superiore unde conspici posset loco
8 constitit. in quem postquam omnium ora conversa sunt, clamore ac favore ominati extemplo sunt felix faustumque
9 imperium. iussi deinde inire suffragium ad unum omnes non centuriae modo sed etiam homines P. Scipioni impe-
10 rium esse in Hispania iusserunt. ceterum post rem actam ut iam resederat impetus animorum ardorque, silentium
11 subito ortum et tacita cogitatio quidnam egissent. nonne favor plus valuisset quam ratio? aetatis maxime paenitebat; quidam fortunam etiam domus horrebant nomenque ex funestis duabus familiis in eas provincias ubi inter sepulcra patris patruique res gerendae essent proficiscentis.

---

92 P. Cornelius Scipio, later Africanus. He had been military tribune in 216, when he rallied the dispirited survivors of Cannae at Canusium (22.53.3–13), and curule aedile in 213. Livy's sketch of Scipio is based on Polybius (10.2–5) with some details added (e.g., Scipio's purported divine birth).

93 According to Polybius (10.6.10), Scipio was twenty-seven in 210 (and so twenty-six in 211), but Livy later has him personally declare his age as twenty-four when given the Spanish command (28.4311). This would be the turning point in the war.

believing themselves worthy of such an important command to put their names forward; but when that expectation came to nothing melancholy over the defeat and grief for the lost commanders resurfaced.

Thus it was with sadness and practically at a loss for a plan that the community went down into the Campus on election day. Turning toward the magistrates, they scrutinized their leading citizens' faces in turn—and these also kept looking at each other—and started murmuring that things were so bad, and hope for the state so low, that no one dared accept authority for Spain, when suddenly Publius Cornelius,[92] son of the Publius Cornelius who had fallen in Spain, now about twenty-four years of age, declared his candidacy and stood on higher ground from which he could be easily seen. Everyone's gaze turned on him, and with shouts and cheers they all immediately envisioned an auspicious and successful command. Then, instructed to cast their ballots, not only the centuries but individuals, too, voted unanimously that command in Spain should go to Publius Scipio. When this was over, however, and the excitement and fervor had subsided, silence suddenly fell, and there was quiet reflection on what they had done. Had not partiality prevailed over reason? His age was what was causing most concern;[93] but some also had morbid fears about the family's fortunes and the man's name—he would be setting off from two ill-fated households[94] into provinces where his campaigns must be conducted amid the tombs of his father and uncle.

[94] Livy omits to mention that the deaths of his father and uncle occurred about a year earlier.

19. Quam ubi ab re tanto impetu acta sollicitudinem curamque hominum animadvertit, advocata contione ita de aetate sua imperioque mandato et bello quod gerundum esset magno elatoque animo disseruit ut ardorem

2 eum qui resederat excitaret rursus novaretque, et impleret homines certioris spei quam quantam fides promissi humani aut ratio ex fiducia rerum subicere solet.

3 Fuit enim Scipio non veris tantum virtutibus mirabilis sed arte quoque quadam ab iuventa in ostentationem ea-

4 rum compositus, pleraque apud multitudinem aut per nocturnas visa species aut velut divinitus mente monita agens, sive et ipse capti quadam superstitione animi, sive ut imperia consiliaque velut sorte oraculi missa sine

5 cunctatione exsequerentur. ad hoc iam inde ab initio praeparans animos, ex quo togam virilem sumpsit nullo die prius ullam publicam privatamque rem egit quam in Capitolium iret, ingressusque aedem consideret et plerumque

6 solus in secreto ibi tempus tereret. hic mos, ⟨quem⟩ per omnem vitam servabat,[36] seu consulto seu temere volgatae opinioni fidem apud quosdam fecit stirpis eum divinae

7 virum esse, rettulitque famam in Alexandro Magno prius volgatam, et vanitate et fabula parem, anguis immanis concubitu conceptum, et in cubiculo matris eius visam persaepe prodigii eius speciem, interventuque hominum

---

[36] ⟨quem⟩ . . . servabat *Weiss.*: per omnem vitam servabat *P*: *sic, sed* servabatur *MΓ*: ⟨qui⟩ . . . servabatur *Drak.*

---

[95] Cf. Polyb. 10.5.5–8.

[96] The plain white toga of manhood that boys of high birth assumed in their mid-teens, leaving behind the toga praetexta.

[97] For the story, cf. Plut. *Alex.* 2.4; Just. 11.11.3, 12.16.2. It

19. Noting people's anxiety and concern over a step they had so impetuously taken, Scipio called an assembly and discussed his age, the command entrusted to him, and the war to be fought, and he did so with such a magnanimous and noble spirit as to revive their waning enthusiasm and fill men with expectations higher than trust in a human's promise or assessment based on confidence in the circumstances would usually generate.

For Scipio won admiration not simply for his undeniable merits; he had from his early years also developed some talent for showcasing them.[95] In addressing a crowd he would represent most of his actions as prompted by dreams at night or divine inspiration, perhaps because he had a superstitious bent himself, or perhaps because he sought unhesitating acceptance of his orders and plans by vesting them with oracular authority. He had been preparing people for this from the beginning, ever since he assumed the *toga virilis*;[96] for since then he had passed no day on any public or private business without first going to the Capitol, entering the temple, taking a seat and spending time there, usually alone and in seclusion. This practice, which he maintained throughout his life, instilled in some people belief in the story (whether deliberately or just fortuitously circulated) that he was a man of divine descent, and it also revived the rumor earlier circulated about Alexander the Great (an equally fatuous piece of fiction) that his conception came from sexual union with a huge snake,[97] that this miraculous creature was often seen in his mother's bedroom, and that it immediately

---

was also recycled for the birth of Augustus (Suet. *Aug.* 94.4). Cf. also Levene *HW*, 119–21.

8 evolutam repente atque ex oculis elapsam. his miraculis
nunquam ab ipso elusa fides est; quin potius aucta arte
quadam nec abnuendi tale quicquam nec palam adfir-
9 mandi. multa alia eiusdem generis, alia vera alia adsimu-
lata, admirationis humanae in eo iuvene excesserant
modum; quibus freta tunc civitas aetati haudquaquam
maturae tantam molem rerum tantumque imperium per-
misit.

10 Ad eas copias quas ex vetere exercitu Hispania habebat
quaeque a Puteolis cum C. Nerone traiectae erant decem
milia militum et mille equites adduntur, et M. Junius Sila-
11 nus propraetor adiutor ad res gerendas datus est. ita cum
triginta navium classe—omnes autem quinqueremes
erant—ostiis Tiberinis profectus praeter oram Tusci maris
Alpesque et Gallicum sinum et deinde Pyrenaei circumvectus promunturium, Emporiis urbe Graeca—oriundi et
12 ipsi a Phocaea sunt—copias exposuit. inde sequi navibus
iussis Tarraconem pedibus profectus conventum omnium
sociorum—etenim legationes ad famam adventus eius ex
13 omni se provincia effuderant—habuit. naves ibi subduci
iussit, remissis quattuor triremibus Massiliensium quae

---

98 Cf. 1.5, above. Silanus was praetor in 212, and Livy has
Scipio say later that he was sent to Spain with authority equal to
his own (28.28.14; cf. also Polyb. 10.6.7).

99 From Greek *emporion* (trading place), it is now Ampurias/
Empuries, a much visited tourist site (*Barr.* 25 I3). For a fuller
account of the town, inhabited by Spaniards, Greeks and, later,
Romans, cf. 34.9.1–12.

100 A city in Asia Minor (*Barr.* 56 D4); "also hail from" must
refer to the inhabitants of Massilia (Marseille), the most famous
Phocaean colonists in the western Mediterranean. Scipio's Mas-

slithered away and vanished from sight when people arrived on the scene. Belief in these supernatural tales was never ridiculed by the man himself; indeed, it was actually promoted by a sort of knack he had for neither rejecting nor openly affirming anything of the kind. There were many other instances of that sort of thing, some genuine, some fabricated, that had won this young man superhuman admiration; and it was relying on this that the state then bestowed such great responsibility and so great a command on a person by no means mature in years.

To the forces that he had from the old army in Spain and those that had crossed from Puteoli with Gaius Nero were added ten thousand infantry and a thousand cavalry, and the propraetor Marcus Junius Silanus was assigned as his assistant in the campaign.[98] And so, with a fleet of thirty ships (all of them quinqueremes) Scipio set off from the mouth of the Tiber, skirted the coast of the Etruscan Sea, the Alps, and the Gulf of Gaul, and then, after rounding the promontory of the Pyrenees, he put his troops ashore at Emporiae,[99] a Greek city (its people also hail from Phocaea).[100] From there, ordering his ships to follow, he set out for Tarraco[101] on foot and held a meeting of all the allies; for delegations had flooded to him from every part of the province as soon as they got word of his coming. There, after sending back four triremes from Massilia that

siliot escort (mentioned below) and Massilia's appearance in Silius' account of Scipio's journey to Spain (Sil. 15.168–69) have led some to think that a visit there by Scipio has dropped out of the text somewhere in this section.

101 Modern Tarragona on the northeast coast of Spain (*Barr.* 25 G4).

14 officii causa ab domo prosecutae fuerant. responsa inde
legationibus suspensis varietate tot casuum dare coepit, ita
elato ab ingenti virtutum suarum fiducia animo ut nullum
ferox verbum excideret, ingensque omnibus quae diceret
cum maiestas inesset tum fides.

20. Profectus ab Tarracone et civitates sociorum et
hiberna exercitus adiit; collaudavitque milites quod duabus tantis deinceps cladibus icti provinciam obtinuissent,
2 nec fructum secundarum rerum sentire hostes passi, omni
cis Hiberum agro eos arcuissent sociosque cum fide tutati
essent.

3 Marcium secum habebat cum tanto honore ut facile
appareret nihil minus vereri quam ne quis obstaret gloriae
4 suae. successit inde Neroni Silanus, et in hiberna milites
novi deducti. Scipio omnibus quae adeunda agendaque
erant mature aditis peractisque Tarraconem concessit.
5 nihilo minor fama apud hostes Scipionis erat quam apud
cives sociosque, et divinatio quaedam futuri, quo minus
ratio timoris reddi poterat oborti temere, maiorem infe-
6 rens metum. in hiberna diversi concesserant Hasdrubal
Gisgonis usque ad Oceanum et Gades, Mago in mediter-
ranea maxime super Castulonensem saltum; Hasdrubal
Hamilcaris filius proximus Hibero circa Saguntum hiber-
navit.

---

102 Father of the beautiful but ill-starred wife of Syphax, Sophonisba, whose tragic story Livy recounts in Book 30 (12.11–
15.8). He commanded a Carthaginian army in Spain from his
arrival in 214 until 206.   103 In the eastern sector of the Sierra
Morena (*Barr.* 27 B3; TIR *J-30*, 141–42), it was by Cicero's time
notorious for banditry. Livy's account of the location of the Carthaginian armies cannot be reconciled with Polyb. 10.7.4–6.

had, as a courtesy, escorted him from their home, he ordered the ships to be hauled ashore. He then started issuing replies to delegations that were perturbed by the many changes of fortune, and he did so in such a stately a manner, which came from great confidence in his abilities, that no arrogant word fell from his lips, and in everything he said there was both great dignity and great sincerity.

20. Setting off from Tarraco, he put in at allied states and also at the army's winter quarters. He praised the soldiers for having held the province even after suffering two such disastrous defeats one after the other, for having kept the enemy out of all territory north of the Ebro, not allowing him to feel any benefit from his successes, and for having steadfastly defended the allies.

He kept Marcius with him, showing him such respect as to make it clear that he feared nothing less than anyone being an obstacle to his own renown. Silanus then succeeded Nero, and the new recruits were led into winter quarters. After making all the obligatory visits and doing all that needed to be done, Scipio retired to Tarraco. Scipio's reputation was no less great among the enemy than among his citizens and allies; and some sort of premonition brought them anxiety all the more intense from their inability to rationalize a fear welling up within them. The Carthaginians had left for their winter quarters in different directions, Hasdrubal son of Gisgo[102] going as far as Gades on the Ocean and Mago into the interior (mostly above the Forest of Castulo).[103] Hasdrubal son of Hamilcar wintered the closest to the Ebro, in the neighborhood of Saguntum.

7   Aestatis eius extremo qua capta est Capua et Scipio in
Hispaniam venit, Punica classis ex Sicilia Tarentum accita,
8   arcendo[37] commeatus praesidii Romani quod in arce Tarentina erat clauserat quidem omnes ad arcem a mari aditus, sed adsidendo diutius artiorem annonam sociis quam
9 hosti faciebat. non enim tantum subvehi oppidanis per
pacata litora apertosque portus praesidio navium Punica-
rum poterat quantum frumenti classis ipsa turba navali
10 mixta ex omni genere hominum absumebat, ut arcis praesidium etiam sine invecto quia pauci erant ex ante prae-
parato sustentari posset, Tarentinis classique ne invectum
11 quidem sufficeret. tandem maiore gratia quam venerat
classis dimissa est; annona[38] haud multum laxaverat, quia
remoto maritimo praesidio subvehi frumentum non poterat.

    21. Eiusdem aestatis exitu M. Marcellus ex Sicilia pro-
vincia cum ad urbem venisset, a C. Calpurnio praetore
2 senatus ei ad aedem Bellonae datus est. ibi cum de rebus
ab se gestis disseruisset, questus leniter non suam magis
quam militum vicem quod provincia confecta exercitum
deportare non licuisset, postulavit ut triumphanti urbem
3 inire liceret. id non impetravit. cum multis verbis actum

---

[37] arcendo *LA^P*: arcendos *P*: ad arcendos *C^c*
[38] annona *P*: annonam *C^c*

---

[104] Outside the *pomerium*, a favorite location for the senate
to meet a successful general requesting a triumph (cf. Beard
201–5). It has now been identified as lying just east of the temple
of Apollo Medicus (Richardson 57–58).
[105] Marcellus evidently had little support in the senate: the
previous year he had also been denied a request to recruit survivors of Cannae for his force (25.5.10–25.7.4). However, the tri-

At the end of that summer in which Capua was taken and Scipio reached Spain, a Punic fleet had been summoned from Sicily to Tarentum, and by cutting off supplies to the Roman garrison in the citadel of Tarentum it had succeeded in blocking every seaward approach to the citadel, but by remaining too long in place it was making grain provisioning more difficult for their allies than for their enemy. For any grain that could be brought in to the townspeople along peaceful shores and through ports kept open under Carthaginian naval protection was less than was being consumed by the fleet with its motley crowd of sailors from every race. Thus, thanks to its small numbers, the garrison in the citadel could survive on what had been stockpiled earlier without actually importing anything, while for the Tarentines and the fleet even what was imported was insufficient. Eventually, the fleet moved off, leaving the townspeople more grateful than they had been for its arrival, though this had not much lowered the price of food because, with naval protection gone, grain could not be brought in.

21. At that same summer's end, Marcus Marcellus arrived in the city from his province of Sicily and was granted an audience with the senate in the temple of Bellona[104] by the praetor Gaius Calpurnius. After giving an account of his achievements, Marcellus lodged a mild complaint—no more on his own behalf than his men's—that he had not been allowed to bring his army home on completing his mission, and he asked to be allowed to enter the city in triumph. He was not granted this request.[105] There had

umph may have been refused because the army had not been brought back to Rome (see below and Beard 206).

esset utrum minus conveniret, cuius nomine absentis ob
res prospere ductu eius gestas supplicatio decreta foret

4 et dis immortalibus habitus honos, ei praesenti negare
triumphum, an quem tradere exercitum successori ius-
sissent—quod nisi manente in provincia bello non decer-
neretur—eum quasi debellato triumphare cum exercitus
testis meriti atque immeriti triumphi abesset, medium
visum ut ovans urbem iniret.

5   Tribuni plebis ex auctoritate senatus ad populum tule-
runt ut M. Marcello, quo die urbem ovans iniret, imperium esset. pridie quam urbem iniret in monte Albano

6 triumphavit; inde ovans multam prae se praedam in ur-

7 bem intulit. cum simulacro captarum Syracusarum catapultae ballistaeque et alia omnia instrumenta belli lata et
pacis diuturnae regiaeque opulentiae ornamenta, argenti

8 aerisque fabrefacti vis, alia supellex pretiosaque vestis et
multa nobilia signa, quibus inter primas Graeciae urbes

9 Syracusae ornatae fuerant. Punicae quoque victoriae signum octo ducti elephanti; et non minimum fuere spectacu-

---

106 The supplication (*supplicatio*) was a period of collective
prayer decreed by the senate in times of crisis or calamity, or for
thanksgiving, especially for military success, as here (on victory
supplications, cf. Oakley 2.735).

107 Often referred to as a lesser triumph. Precise details are
not forthcoming, but it is known that the general went on foot or
horseback to the Capitoline, not in the triumphal chariot, and was
crowned with myrtle rather than laurel.

108 A "more drastic response to a refusal (of a full triumph)"
(Beard). A general refused a triumph might celebrate one unof-
ficially on the Alban Mount, today Monte Cavo, about seventeen
miles from the city: *OCD* s.v.; Beard 62–63, 314–15.

been a wordy debate in the house over which of two courses of action was less appropriate; should they refuse a triumph to a man now present when a supplication[106] had been decreed in his name during his absence, with honor formally paid to the immortal gods, for successes achieved under his command? Or should he celebrate a triumph as if the war were over, when the senators had instructed him to pass his army on to his successor—a decree that would not have been passed unless there was still war in the province—and celebrate it, too, when the army was not there to bear witness to whether or not the triumph was merited? A compromise was reached: Marcellus would enter the city in ovation.[107]

With senatorial authorization, the tribunes of the plebs brought before the people a proposal that Marcus Marcellus should have *imperium* on the day he entered the city with an ovation. On the day before he was to enter the city, he celebrated his triumph on the Alban Mount;[108] then, in his ovation, he had large quantities of plunder precede him into the city. Together with a model of the captured Syracuse,[109] catapults, ballistae, and a whole panoply of other war engines were carried along, as well as objets d'art amassed from the long period of peace and prosperity under the kings. There were heaps of silver and bronze artifacts as well as furniture, precious clothing, and many famous statues, with which Syracuse had been one of the most richly endowed among Greek cities. Also to represent victory over Carthage, eight elephants were led along,

---

109 Such pictorial displays were a regular feature of the triumph: cf. Tac. *Ann.* 2.41.2; Joseph *BJ* 7.132; Ov. *Am.* 1.220, *Tr.* 4.2.37–46; Beard 46–49, 124–27.

lum cum coronis aureis praecedentes Sosis Syracusanus et
10 Moericus Hispanus, quorum altero duce nocturno Syracusas introitum erat, alter Nassum quodque ibi praesidii
11 erat prodiderat. his ambobus civitas data et quingena iugera agri, Sosidi in agro Syracusano qui aut regius aut
hostium populi Romani fuisset, et aedes Syracusis cuius
12 vellet eorum in quos belli iure animadversum esset; Moe-
rico Hispanisque qui cum eo transierant urbs agerque in
Sicilia ex iis qui a populo Romano defecissent iussa dari.
13 id M. Cornelio mandatum ut ubi ei videretur urbem
agrumque eis adsignaret. in eodem agro Belligeni, per
quem inlectus ad transitionem Moericus erat, quadringenta iugera agri decreta.
14   Post profectionem ex Sicilia Marcelli Punica classis
octo milia peditum, tria Numidarum equitum exposuit. ad
eos Murgentia et Ergetium urbes defecere. secutae defectionem earum Hybla et Macella et ignobiliores quaedam
15 aliae; et Numidae praefecto Muttine vagi per totam Sici-
16 liam sociorum populi Romani agros urebant. super haec

---

[110] The identity of Sosis is uncertain, but he probably assisted
with the Romans' entry into the Hexapylon by night (25.23.15–
25.24.7) (so Jal, 129 n. 5); on Moericus, who admitted the Romans
to Achradina, cf. 25.30.2–12.   [111] Nassus is a form of the
Greek *nesos* (island) and refers to the island Ortygia (which also
figured prominently in the Athenians' Sicilian expedition).

[112] A *iugerum* is about two-thirds of an acre.

[113] M. Cornelius Cethegus, one of the praetors for 211, who
succeeded Marcellus in Sicily. He later became consul in 204
(*MRR* 305).   [114] Cf. 25.30.2.

[115] The location of Sicilian towns mentioned in this chapter is
uncertain. Murgentia is possibly Morgantina (*Barr.* 47 E4), and

and not the least impressive spectacle was the Syracusan Sosis and the Spaniard Moericus[110] walking ahead of Marcellus with crowns of gold (one of them had acted as guide the night when entry was gained into Syracuse, and the other had handed over the Nassus[111] and its garrison). These were both granted Roman citizenship and five hundred *iugera* of land,[112] that of Sosis being in Syracusan territory that had belonged either to the king or to former enemies of Rome, and any house he liked in Syracuse belonging to those punished under the rules of war; Moericus and the Spaniards who had seceded with him were to be given a city and its lands in Sicily, to be taken from those who had defected from the Roman people. Marcus Cornelius[113] was charged with assigning to them a town and land where he thought suitable. Belligenes,[114] the man responsible for Moericus' change of allegiance, was also decreed four hundred *iugera* in the same area.

After Marcellus' departure from Sicily, a Punic fleet put ashore eight thousand infantry and three thousand Numidian cavalry. The cities of Murgentia and Ergetium defected to them.[115] Hybla, Macella, and some lesser-known towns followed them in defecting; and the Numidians, led by Muttines,[116] roaming the length of Sicily, began torching farmland belonging to allies of the Roman

Hybla perhaps Hybla Gereatis, southwest of Aetna (47 F3), or Hybla Heraea, further south (47 F5).

116 An enterprising Libyphoenician, he had gained a thorough mastery of the arts of war under Hannibal, by whom he had been sent to Sicily to join Epicydes and Hanno (25.40.5). Switching sides, he provided the turning point in the war in Sicily (40.3–18, below) and was well rewarded by the senate (27.5.6–7).

exercitus Romanus iratus partim quod cum imperatore
non devectus ex provincia esset, partim quod in oppidis
hibernare vetiti erant, segni fungebantur militia, magis-
17 que eis auctor ad seditionem quam animus deerat. inter
has difficultates M. Cornelius praetor et militum animos
nunc consolando nunc castigando sedavit, et civitates omnes quae defecerant in dicionem redegit; atque ex iis Mur-
gentiam Hispanis quibus urbs agerque debebatur ex senatus consulto attribuit.

22. Consules cum ambo Apuliam provinciam haberent,
minusque iam terroris a Poenis et Hannibale esset, sortiri
iussi Apuliam Macedoniamque provincias. Sulpicio Macedonia evenit, isque Laevino successit.

2 Fulvius Romam comitiorum causa arcessitus cum comitia consulibus rogandis haberet, praerogativa Voturia
iuniorum T. Manlium Torquatum et T. Otacilium ‹con-
3 sules dixit. cum ad Manlium›,[39] qui praesens erat, gratu-
landi causa turba coiret, nec dubius esset consensus populi, magna circumfusus turba ad tribunal consulis venit,
4 petitque ut pauca sua verba audiret centuriamque quae
5 tulisset suffragium revocari iuberet. erectis omnibus exspectatione quidnam postulaturus esset, oculorum valetu-

[39] ‹consules . . . Manlium› *Walters*

[117] M. Valerius Laevinus, praetor 215, with *imperium* prorogued every year until now.

[118] This is the Centuriate Assembly, which met for the election of senior magistrates and comprised 193 "centuries," or voting blocks. The century to vote first (*centuria praerogativa*) was
selected by lot, thus making it the choice of the gods.

people. In addition, the Roman army was performing its duties lethargically, resentful partly because it had not been shipped home from the province with its commander and partly because the soldiers had been forbidden to winter in the towns; and it was lack of a leader rather than lack of will that staved off mutiny. Amid such difficulties, the praetor Marcus Cornelius calmed the men with a combination of reassurance and punishment, and he also suppressed all the communities that had defected; and of these it was Murgentia that Cornelius awarded to the Spaniards to whom a city and its lands were owed by decree of the senate.

22. As both consuls had Apulia as their province and there was by now less to be feared from the Carthaginians and Hannibal, they were instructed to proceed to sortition for Apulia and Macedonia as their provinces. Macedonia fell to Sulpicius, and he succeeded Laevinus.[117]

Fulvius was summoned to Rome for the elections, and when he held the meeting for the election of consuls the juniors of the Voturia, who had the first ballot,[118] declared their vote for Titus Manlius Torquatus and Titus Otacilius as consuls.[119] The crowd then converged on Manlius, who was present, to congratulate him, and that he had the unanimous support of the people was not in doubt. Manlius, however, with a great crowd swarming around him, proceeded to the consul's dais and appealed to the consul to hear a few words from him and order the century that had voted to be recalled. With all on tenterhooks, wondering what he was going to ask for, he then declined on

---

[119] T. Manlius Torquatus, consul twice (235 and 224), and censor in 231. On T. Otacilius Crassus, cf. 1.12 and note, above.

6 dinem excusavit: impudentem et gubernatorem et imperatorem esse qui, cum alienis oculis ei omnia agenda sint,
postulet sibi potius aliorum capita ac fortunas committi.
7 proinde si videretur ei, redire in suffragium Voturiam iuniorum iuberet et meminisse in consulibus creandis belli
8 quod in Italia sit temporumque rei publicae; vixdum re-
quiesse aures a strepitu et tumultu hostili quo paucos ante
menses ⟨qu⟩assa sint[40] prope moenia Romana.

Post haec cum centuria frequens succlamasset nihil se
9 mutare sententiae eosdemque consules dicturos esse, tum
Torquatus "neque ego vestros" inquit "mores consul ferre
potero, neque vos imperium meum. redite in suffragium,
et cogitate bellum Punicum in Italia et hostium ducem
10 Hannibalem esse." tum centuria et auctoritate mota viri
et admirantium circa fremitu, petiit a consule ut Voturiam
11 seniorum citaret: velle sese cum maioribus natu conloqui
et ex auctoritate eorum consules dicere. citatis Voturiae
senioribus, datum secreto in Ovili cum iis conloquendi
12 tempus. seniores de tribus consulendum dixerunt esse,
duobus plenis iam honorum Q. Fabio et M. Marcello, et,
si utique novum aliquem adversus Poenos consulem creari
vellent, M. Valerio Laevino; egregie adversus Philippum
regem terra marique rem gessisse.

[40] ⟨qu⟩assa sint *Ussing*: asserint *P*: cesserint *M^c*: arserint
Alschefski

---

[120] Latin *ovile* (sheepfold), also called the *saepta*. It was an
enclosure (perhaps near the Villa Publica) where the *comitia centuriata* met to vote during assemblies, so-named either because it
looked like a sheep's pen or because that was its original function:
Richardson 278.   [121] In 214 he sailed from his post at Brundisium and recaptured Oricum from Philip's garrison (24.40.1–6).

grounds of an eye ailment: only a shameless ship's pilot or general would ask for other people's lives and fortunes to be entrusted to him when everything had to be done with somebody else's eyes, he said. So, if he agreed, Fulvius should order the juniors of the Voturia century to retake the vote, and tell them, in electing the consuls, to keep in mind the war that was in progress in Italy and the crisis facing the republic; their ears had barely recovered from the enemy's tumultuous upheaval with which the walls of Rome had almost been shaken a few months earlier, he said.

At this, most of the century's members cried out that their minds were unchanged and they would appoint the same consuls as before, and Torquatus then retorted: "As consul, I shall be unable to bear your conduct, and you will be unable bear my authority. Go back to the vote, and reflect that there is a war with Carthage in Italy and that the enemy commander is Hannibal." Then, moved both by the man's authority and by the murmurs of astonishment all around, the century asked the consul to call in the seniors of Voturia: they wanted to discuss it with their elders and have their approval in appointing the consuls. The seniors of Voturia were summoned, and time was granted for a private discussion with them in the voting enclosure.[120] The seniors declared that three men ought to be considered: two of them, Quintus Fabius and Marcus Marcellus, had already been showered with honors, and if they really wanted some "new man" elected consul to face the Carthaginians there was Marcus Valerius Laevinus—he had to his credit outstanding land and sea operations against King Philip.[121]

13   Ita de tribus consultatione data, senioribus dimissis
iuniores suffragium ineunt. M. Claudium fulgentem tum
Sicilia domita et M. Valerium absentes consules dixerunt.
auctoritatem praerogativae omnes centuriae secutae sunt.

14   Eludant nunc antiqua mirantes; non equidem, si qua
sit sapientium civitas quam docti fingunt magis quam
norunt, aut principes graviores temperantioresque a cupi-
dine imperii aut multitudinem melius moratam censeam

15   fieri posse. centuriam vero iuniorum seniores consulere
voluisse quibus imperium suffragio mandaret, vix ut veri
simile sit parentium quoque hoc saeculo vilis levisque
apud liberos auctoritas fecit.

23. Praetoria inde comitia habita. P. Manlius Vulso[41] et
L. Manlius Acidinus et C. Laetorius et L. Cincius Alimen-

2   tus creati sunt. forte ita incidit ut comitiis perfectis nun-
tiaretur T. Otacilium, quem T. Manlio nisi interpellatus
ordo comitiorum esset collegam absentem daturus fuisse

3   videbatur populus, mortuum in Sicilia esse. ludi Apollinares et priore anno fuerant et eo anno ut fierent referente
Calpurnio praetore senatus decrevit ut in perpetuum voverentur.

4   Eodem anno prodigia aliquot visa nuntiataque sunt. in
aede Concordiae Victoria quae in culmine erat fulmine

---

[41] Vulso *Sig.*: valens *P*

---

[122] P. Manlius Vulso: he received Sardinia as his province,
where he had two legions (28.12, below) and repulsed a Carthaginian raid at Olbia (27.6.13–14); L. Manlius Acidinus became
praetor urbanus; C. Laetorius (curule aedile in 216) was perhaps
praetor peregrinus; L. Cincius Alimentus (who later wrote a history of Rome in Greek) received Sicily.

Thus discussion of the three followed, the senior members were discharged, and the younger men proceeded to the vote. They declared as consuls Marcus Claudius, then in the limelight through his conquest of Sicily, and Marcus Valerius, both of them *in absentia*. All the centuries followed the lead of the one voting first.

Let people laugh now at admirers of antiquity! If a state of philosophers does exist anywhere—something that scholars hypothesize about rather than know—I certainly would not believe its leaders could be more serious-minded or moderate than this, or its ordinary people more principled. A century of younger men wanting to consult their elders about whom they should grant power to with their vote—that is rendered scarcely believable in this age when parental authority over children is slight and ineffectual.

23. The praetorian elections were held next. Those appointed were Publius Manlius Vulso, Lucius Manlius Acidinus, Gaius Laetorius, and Lucius Cincius Alimentus.[122] It so happened that when the elections were over news arrived of the death in Sicily of Titus Otacilius,[123] the man whom, though absent, the people would probably have given to Titus Manlius as colleague had the electoral proceedings not been interrupted. The Games of Apollo had been presented the previous year, and when the praetor Calpurnius moved that they be put on again this year the senate decreed that a vow be taken to make them permanent.

That same year a number of prodigies were observed and reported. The statue of Victory on the roof of the

123 Cf. 1.12 and note, above.

icta decussaque ad Victorias quae in antefixis erant haesit
5 neque inde procidit. et Anagniae et Fregellis nuntiatum
est murum portasque de caelo tacta, et in foro Subertano
sanguinis rivos per diem totum fluxisse, et Ereti lapidibus
6 pluvisse, et Reate mulam peperisse. ea prodigia hostiis
maioribus sunt procurata, et obsecratio in unum diem
populo indicta et novendiale sacrum.
7   Sacerdotes publici aliquot eo anno demortui sunt, no-
vique suffecti; in locum M.' Aemilii Numidae decemviri
sacrorum M. Aemilius Lepidus, in locum M. Pomponi
Mathonis pontificis C. Livius, in locum Sp. Carvili Maximi
8 auguris M. Servilius. T. Otacilius Crassus pontifex quia
exacto anno mortuus erat, ideo nominatio in locum eius
non est facta. C. Claudius flamen Dialis quod exta perpe-
ram dederat flamonio abiit.
24. Per idem tempus M. Valerius Laevinus temptatis
prius per secreta conloquia principum animis ad indictum
ante ad id ipsum concilium Aetolorum classe expedita ve-

---

124 There were two temples of Concord at this time (cf. Richardson 98–99), and it is uncertain which is referred to here.

125 Anagnia: *Barr.* 43 E3. Subertum: location unknown, but
presumably a town of the Subertani, a mid-Etrurian people mentioned by the elder Pliny (3.52); Eretum: *Barr.* 44 C1; Reate: 42
D4.

126 Sacrificial victims were either unweaned (*lactantes*) or
full-grown (*maiores*) animals, the latter being used for major
thanksgivings/crises. The nine-day rite is particularly associated
with "stone showers": cf. 21.62.6, 23.31.15, 25.7.9, 27.37.1.

temple of Concord was struck by lightning, and although knocked down it became lodged among the statues of Victory amid the antefixes and fell no further.[124] It was also reported that the wall and gates at both Anagnia and Fregellae had been struck by lightning; that in the forum of Subertum streams of blood had flowed for an entire day; that at Eretum there had been a stone shower; and that at Reate a mule had given birth.[125] To expiate the prodigies full-grown animals were sacrificed, with a one-day session of prayer plus the nine-day rite prescribed for the people.[126]

Some state priests died that year and were replaced by new ones: Marcus Aemilius Lepidus replaced Manius Aemilius Numida as decemvir for religious rites;[127] Gaius Livius replaced Marcus Pomponius Matho the pontiff; and Marcus Servilius replaced the augur Spurius Carvilius Maximus. Because the pontiff Titus Otacilius Crassus died after the end of his year there was no nomination made for replacing him. The flamen of Jupiter, Gaius Claudius, resigned his office over his incorrect placing of the entrails.[128]

24. About this same time Marcus Valerius Laevinus came with a swift fleet to a council of the Aetolians that had been previously scheduled expressly for this purpose. (He had earlier held clandestine meetings with its leaders

---

[127] The decemvirs for sacrifices were a priestly college that gave advice on religious matters. Their prime function was to guard and interpret the Sibylline Books, which were consulted in times of disaster or dire prodigies.

[128] The rite involving animal entrails was elaborate, and any mistake indicated the flamen no longer enjoyed Jupiter's favor.

2   nit. ubi cum Syracusas Capuamque captas[42] in fidem in
3   Sicilia[43] Italiaque rerum secundarum ostentasset, adiecissetque[44] iam inde a maioribus traditum morem Romanis
colendi socios, ex quibus alios in civitatem atque aequum
secum ius accepissent, alios in ea fortuna haberent ut socii
4   esse quam cives mallent. Aetolos eo in maiore futuros
honore quod gentium transmarinarum in amicitiam primi
5   venissent; Philippum eis et Macedonas graves accolas
esse, quorum se vim ac spiritus et iam fregisse et eo redac-
turum esse ut non iis modo urbibus quas per vim ademissent Aetolis excedant, sed ipsam Macedoniam infes-
6   tam habeant; et Acarnanas quos aegre ferrent Aetoli a
corpore suo diremptos restituturum se in antiquam for-
mulam, iurisque ac dicionis[45] eorum.
7   Haec dicta promissaque a Romano imperatore Scopas,
qui tum praetor gentis erat, et Dorimachus princeps Aetolorum adfirmaverunt auctoritate sua, minore cum verecundia et maiore cum fide vim maiestatemque populi
8   Romani extollentes; maxime tamen spes potiundae move-
bat Acarnaniae. igitur conscriptae condiciones quibus in

---

[42] captas Σ: captam P

[43] Sicilia Italiaque A[p]: Italiaque P: Italia <Sicilia>que Alschefski

[44] adiecissetque M[c]C[c]Γ: adiecisseque P

[45] dicionis P: dicionis <facturum> Walsh

---

[129] An alliance with the Aetolians was desirable to counter
Hannibal's alliance with Philip V (with whom the Aetolians were
continually at odds). Laevinus probably came there in 212, but
possibly 211 (cf. Jal *ad loc.*).

to gauge their sympathies.)[129] After pointing to the capture of Syracuse and Capua to illustrate Roman success in Sicily and Italy, he added that he followed traditional Roman practice in dealing with allies, one inherited from their ancestors: some they accepted as citizens in equal partnership with themselves, and others they kept in such a prosperous state that they preferred remaining allies to being citizens. The Aetolians, he said, would be all the more honored for being the first overseas people to enter into friendship with Rome;[130] Philip and the Macedonians were difficult neighbors for the Aetolians, but he had already broken their violent and haughty temper, and he was going to bring them to the point of not only quitting cities they had forcibly taken from the Aetolians, but of finding Macedonia itself under threat. As for the Acarnanians, whose forceful separation from their league the Aetolians resented, he would also bring them back to their old status, subject to their authority and control.

These statements and promises from the Roman commander were confirmed by Scopas, who was praetor[131] of their people at the time, and by Dorimachus, the leading Aetolian citizen, with their authority, both men extolling the Roman people's power and majesty with less reserve and even greater conviction; but it was the prospect of gaining Acarnania that most impressed the Aetolians. Conditions were therefore drafted on which they would

---

130 However, *Per.* 14 refers to some form of alliance (*societas*) earlier made with Ptolemy Philadelphus.

131 As usual, Livy uses what he considers a Roman equivalent for a Greek office (here *strategos*). For Scopas, Dorimachus, and the chronology here, see Walbank 2.12–14.

9 amicitiam societatemque populi Romani venirent; additumque ut, si placeret vellentque, eodem iure amicitiae
Elei Lacedaemoniique et Attalus et Pleuratus et Scerdilaedus essent, Asiae Attalus, hi Thracum et Illyriorum
10 reges; bellum ut extemplo Aetoli cum Philippo terra ge-
rerent; navibus ne minus viginti quinque quinqueremibus
11 adiuveret Romanus; urbium Corcyra tenus ab Aetolia inci-
pienti solum tectaque et muri cum agris Aetolorum, alia
omnis praeda populi Romani esset, darentque operam
12 Romani ut Acarnaniam Aetoli haberent. si Aetoli pacem
cum Philippo facerent, foederi adscriberent ita ratam
fore[46] pacem si Philippus arma ab Romanis sociisque qui-
13 que eorum dicionis essent abstinuisset; item si populus
Romanus foedere iungeretur regi, ut caveret ne ius ei belli
inferendi Aetolis sociisque eorum esset.
14 Haec convenerunt, conscriptaque biennio post Olympiae ab Aetolis, in Capitolio ab Romanis ut testata sacratis
15 monumentis essent sunt posita. morae causa fuerant re-
tenti Romae diutius legati Aetolorum, nec tamen impedi-
mento id rebus gerendis fuit. et Aetoli extemplo moverunt
adversus Philippum bellum, et Laevinus Zacynthum—
parva insula est propinqua Aetoliae, urbem unam eodem
quo ipsa est nomine habet; eam praeter arcem vi cepit—et
Oeniadas Nassumque Acarnanum captas Aetolis contri-

---

[46] fore *Muret*: eorum *P*: ⟨fore⟩ eorum *Walsh*

---

[132] *Barr.* 54 A5, inset.

enter into friendship and alliance with the Roman people; and a rider was added that, if such was their pleasure and wish, the Eleans and the Lacedaemonians, and Attalus, Pleuratus, and Scerdilaedus, would have the same treaty rights (Attalus was king of Asia, Pleuratus and Scerdilaedus the kings of the Thracians and Illyrians, respectively). The Aetolians were to proceed immediately to war against Philip on land; the Roman was to help with no fewer than twenty-five quinqueremes; in the cities from Aetolia as far as Corcyra, the soil, buildings, and farmlands would be the Aetolians', and everything else would be booty of the Roman people, and the Romans would do their best to see that the Aetolians should have Acarnania. If the Aetolians made peace with Philip, they were to subjoin to the treaty that the peace remained valid only if Philip avoided armed conflict with the Romans, their allies, and those subject to them. Likewise, should the Roman people make a treaty with the king, they were to ensure that he had no right to make war on the Aetolians and their allies.

The terms were agreed upon, and two years later they were transcribed and put on display (at Olympia by the Aetolians, and on the Capitol by the Romans) so they should have sacred monuments witnessing them. The cause of this delay had been the Aetolian envoys being detained in Rome for some time, though this did not impede implementation of the provisions. The Aetolians did immediately open hostilities against Philip, and Laevinus captured Zacynthus—a small island close to Aetolia that has a single city with the same name as the island; that city Laevinus took by storm, apart from its citadel,[132] and he also captured Oeniadae and Nassus, two Acarnanian

16 buit. Philippumque[47] satis implicatum bello finitimo ratus ne Italiam Poenosque et pacta cum Hannibale posset respicere, Corcyram ipse se recepit.

25. Philippo Aetolorum defectio Pellae hibernanti allata est. itaque quia primo vere moturus exercitum in
2 Graeciam erat, Illyrios finitimasque eis urbes ab tergo metu quietas ut Macedonia haberet, expeditionem subitam in Oricinorum atque Apolloniatium fines fecit, egressosque Apolloniatas cum magno terrore ac pavore com-
3 pulit intra muros. vastatis proximis Illyrici in Pelagoniam eadem celeritate vertit iter; inde Dardanorum urbem Sintiam, in Macedoniam transitum Dardanis facturam,
4 cepit. his raptim actis, memor Aetolici iunctique cum eo Romani belli, per Pelagoniam et Lyncum et Bottiaeam in
5 Thessaliam descendit—ad bellum secum adversus Aetolos capessendum incitari posse homines credebat—et relicto ad fauces Thessaliae Perseo cum quattuor milibus
6 armatorum ad arcendos aditu Aetolos, ipse priusquam maioribus occuparetur rebus in Macedoniam atque inde
7 in Thraciam exercitum ac Maedos duxit. incurrere ea gens in Macedoniam solita erat ubi regem occupatum externo

---

[47] Philippumque *Weiss.*: Philippum quoque *P*

---

[133] Both lay on the Paracheloitis peninsula (*Barr.* 54 D5).

[134] That is, from Philip; by their alliance with Rome, they renounced the peace of Naupactus signed with him at the end of the Social War in 217.

[135] Two important ports of Illyricum (mod. Albania): *Barr.* 49 B3.

[136] *Barr.* 50 D2.

[137] Pelagonia: *Barr.* 49 D2; Lyncus: D3; Bottiaea: E3.

towns,[133] and annexed them to Aetolia. Thinking Philip to be also sufficiently embroiled in a local war as to be unable to turn his attention to Italy, the Carthaginians, and his pact with Hannibal, Laevinus withdrew to Corcyra.

25. Philip was brought news of the Aetolians' defection[134] while he was wintering at Pella. His plan was to lead his troops into Greece in early spring; and so that Macedonia could have the Illyrians and the adjacent towns to her rear inactive from fear, he made a lightning raid on the lands of Oricum and Apollonia,[135] and when the people of Apollonia came out he drove them back within their walls in terror-stricken panic. After laying waste the closer parts of Illyria he veered just as speedily into Pelagonia; and after that he took Sintia,[136] a city of the Dardanians that might allow the Dardanians passage into Macedonia. Then, with these operations speedily completed, and keeping in mind the Aetolian war and the Roman war linked with it, he went down into Thessaly by way of Pelagonia, Lyncus, and Bottiaea.[137] (He believed its people could be induced to join him in hostilities against the Aetolians.) He left Perseus[138] at the pass into Thessaly with four thousand troops to prevent the Aetolians from entering, and before he should become preoccupied with more serious matters he himself led his force back to Macedonia and from there against the Maedi in Thrace.[139] That people would often swoop down on Macedonia whenever they

---

[138] Evidently, one of Philip's generals, not his son Perseus, then only eleven years old.

[139] A people hostile to Macedon inhabiting the Strymon valley (Strabo 7.36.331): *Barr.* 51 A1 (Maidoi); Walbank 2.256.

8 bello ac sine praesidio esse regnum sensisset; ad frangendas igitur ⟨vires⟩[48] vastare agros et urbem Iamphorynnam, caput arcemque Maedicae, oppugnare coepit.

9 Scopas ubi profectum in Thraciam regem occupatumque ibi bello audivit, armata omni iuventute Aetolorum

10 bellum inferre Acarnaniae parat. adversus quos Acarnanum gens, et viribus impar et iam Oeniadas Nassumque amissa cernens Romanaque insuper arma ingruere, ira

11 magis instruit quam consilio bellum. coniugibus liberisque et senioribus supra sexaginta annos in propinquam Epirum missis, ab quindecim ad sexaginta annos con-

12 iurant nisi victores se non redituros. qui victus acie excessisset, eum ne quis urbe tecto mensa lare reciperet diram exsecrationem in populares, obtestationem quam sanctis-

13 simam potuerunt adversus hospites composuerunt, precatique simul Epirotas sunt ut qui suorum in acie cecidissent eos uno tumulo contegerent, adicerentque[49] humatis titu-

14 lum: "Hic siti sunt Acarnanes qui adversus vim atque iniuriam Aetolorum pro patria pugnantes mortem occubuerunt."

15 Per haec incitatis animis castra in extremis finibus suis obvia hosti posuerunt. nuntiis ad Philippum missis quanto res in discrimine esset, omittere[50] id quod in manibus erat coegerunt bellum, Iamphorynna per deditionem recepta

---

[48] ⟨vires⟩ *Madvig*: ⟨vires gentis simul⟩ *Conway*

[49] adicerentque *Weiss.*: adliberentque *P*: adhiberentque *MᶜCΓ*: adfigerentque *Madvig*

[50] omittere *Walsh*: omittere Philippum *P*

---

[140] Not in *Barr*. Walbank (2.188) suggests that it is the Phorounna mentioned as "a city in Thrace" by Polybius (9.45.3).

became aware that the king was engrossed in some foreign war and his kingdom was unprotected. To break their power he therefore proceeded to destroy their fields and assault Iamphorynna,[140] the capital and stronghold of Medic territory.

When Scopas heard that the king had left for Thrace and was preoccupied with a war there, he put all Aetolians of fighting age under arms and prepared to invade Acarnania. Although the Acarnanian people were no match for them in strength, and could see that Oeniadae and Nassus were lost and that war with Rome was also coming, they nonetheless put up a fight, but with anger rather than strategy. Wives, children, and older men more than sixty years of age were sent to the closest parts of Epirus, and those between fifteen and sixty took an oath not to return home unless they were victorious. Against their own people they framed a terrible curse should anyone receive in his city, in his house, at his table, or by his hearth, anyone leaving the field in defeat, and they also made a most solemn appeal to their Epirot hosts to observe the injunction. They at the same time begged the Epirots to bury under a single mound those of their men who fell in battle, and to set over those buried the following epitaph: "Here lie the Acarnanians who met their end fighting for their country against Aetolian aggression and injustice."

Their courage fired by this, the Acarnanians encamped right on their own borders, facing the enemy. By sending messengers to Philip to inform him of their precarious situation, they forced him to abandon the war in which he was engaged, although Iamphorynna had been recovered

16 et prospero alio successu rerum. Aetolorum impetum tardaverat primo coniurationis fama Acarnanicae; deinde auditus Philippi adventus regredi etiam in intimos coegit
17 fines. nec Philippus, quamquam ne opprimerentur Acarnanes itineribus magnis ierat, ultra Dium est progressus. inde cum audisset reditum Aetolorum ex Acarnania et ipse Pellam rediit.

26. Laevinus veris principio a Corcyra profectus navibus superato Leucata promunturio cum venisset Naupactum, Anticyram inde se petiturum edixit: ut praesto ibi
2 Scopas Aetolique essent. sita Anticyra est in Locride laeva parte sinum Corinthiacum intranti; breve terra iter eo,
3 brevis navigatio ab Naupacto est. tertio ferme post die utrimque oppugnari coepta est. gravior a mari oppugnatio erat, quia et tormenta machinaeque omnis generis in navibus erant, et Romani inde oppugnabant. itaque intra paucos dies recepta urbs per deditionem Aetolis traditur;
4 praeda ex pacto Romanis cessit. litterae Laevino redditae consulem eum absentem declaratum et successorem venire P. Sulpicium; ceterum diuturno ibi morbo implicitus serius spe omnium Romam venit.

5 M. Marcellus cum idibus Martiis consulatum inisset, senatum eo die moris modo causa habuit, professus nihil se absente collega neque de re publica neque de provinciis
6 acturum. scire se frequentes Siculos prope urbem in villis obtrectatorum suorum esse; quibus tantum abesse ut per

---

141 *Barr.* 50 B4.   142 About fifty miles east of Naupactus (*Barr.* 55 D4), it actually lies in Phocis.
143 P. Sulpicius Galba Maximus, consul the previous year (cf.1.1, above).

100

and his other operations had been successful. The Aetolian attack had first been delayed by word of the Acarnanians' oath; and then news of Philip's coming even made them fall back into the interior of their country. And despite forced marches to prevent the Acarnanians from being overwhelmed, Philip did not advance beyond Dium;[141] then, on hearing of the Aetolians' withdrawal from Acarnania he, too, retired to Pella.

26. Sailing from Corcyra at the start of spring and reaching Naupactus after rounding the promontory of Leucas, Laevinus announced that he would head for Anticyra; Scopas and the Aetolians were to meet him right there. Anticyra lies in Locris, to the left as one enters the Corinthian Gulf; from Naupactus it is only a short journey by land or a short sail by sea.[142] An assault on the town from both sides started about two days later. The attack from the sea was more intense because there was all manner of artillery and assault apparatus aboard the ships, and on that side it was the Romans who were attacking. Thus the city capitulated in few days and was handed over to the Aetolians; the booty, as had been agreed, fell to the Romans. Laevinus was brought a letter informing him that he had been declared consul during his absence and that Publius Sulpicius[143] was coming to succeed him; but, caught there with a lingering illness, he reached Rome later than anyone expected.

Entering his consulship on the Ides of March, Marcus Marcellus on that day convened the senate, as was usual, but he also declared that he would not conduct any state or provincial business. He knew that large numbers of Sicilians housed on estates belonging to his political opponents, he said, and far from not permitting them to

se non liceat palam Romae crimina edita[51] ab inimicis
7 volgare, ut ni simularent aliquem sibi timorem absente
collega dicendi de consule esse, ipse eis extemplo daturus
senatum fuerit. ubi quidem collega venisset, non passu-
rum quicquam prius agi quam ut Siculi in senatum intro-
8 ducantur. dilectum prope a M. Cornelio per totam Siciliam habitum ut quam plurimi questum de se Romam
venirent; eundem litteris falsis urbem implesse bellum
9 in Sicilia esse ut suam laudem minuat. moderati animi
gloriam eo die adeptus consul senatum dimisit, ac prope
iustitium omnium rerum futurum videbatur donec alter
consul ad urbem venisset.

10 Otium ut solet excitavit plebis rumores. belli diuturni-
tatem, et vastatos agros circa urbem qua infesto agmine
isset Hannibal, ⟨et⟩[52] exhaustam dilectibus Italiam et
11 prope quotannis caesos exercitus querebantur, et consules
bellicosos ambo viros acresque nimis et feroces creatos qui
vel in pace tranquilla bellum excitare possent, nedum in
bello respirare civitatem forent passuri.

27. Interrupit hos sermones nocte quae pridie Quinquatrus fuit pluribus simul locis circa forum incendium
2 ortum. eodem tempore septem tabernae quae postea
quinque, et argentariae quae nunc novae appellantur, ar-

---

[51] edita *Madvig*: edita ficta *P*: ficta *Ussing*
[52] ⟨et⟩ *ald.*

---

[144] A festival of Minerva, so named because it began on March
19, which was by inclusive counting the fifth day (*quinque* =
"five") after the Ides of March. It lasted until March 23. It was
the festival that the emperor Nero later used to draw his mother
to Baiae for her murder.

disseminate in Rome charges concocted against him by his enemies, he would personally have granted them an immediate hearing before the senate if they were not pretending to have some fear of talking about the consul in his colleague's absence. In fact, when his colleague arrived, he would allow no business to be discussed before the Sicilians were brought into the senate. There had almost been a levy of people conducted throughout Sicily by Marcus Cornelius to ensure that as many as possible came to Rome to lodge complaints about him, he said; and that same man, to blacken his reputation, had also filled the city with letters falsely claiming there was war in Sicily. Having that day earned a reputation for restraint, the consul adjourned the senate, and it looked as if there would be a suspension of all business until the other consul returned to the city.

Inactivity, as usual, gave rise to talk among the masses. They complained about the war's length, about farmlands devastated around the city wherever Hannibal had attacked with his troops, about Italy depleted by troop levies, and about armies cut to shreds almost every year; and they also complained that both men elected consuls were warmongers, all too impetuous and aggressive, the sort able to foment war in the midst of peace and tranquility, much less allow the state a breathing space in time of war!

27. Such talk was interrupted on the night preceding the Quinquatrus[144] by a fire breaking out around the forum in a number of places simultaneously. At the very same time seven shops (which later became five) and the bankers' establishments now called the "New Banks" all

3 sere; comprehensa postea privata aedificia—neque enim
  tum basilicae erant—, comprehensae lautumiae forumque
4 piscatorium et atrium regium. aedes Vestae vix defensa est
  tredecim maxime servorum opera, qui in publicum re-
5 dempti ac manu missi sunt. nocte ac die continuatum incendium fuit, nec ulli dubium erat humana id fraude factum esse, quod pluribus simul locis et iis diversis ignes
6 coorti essent. itaque consul ex auctoritate senatus pro contione edixit qui quorum opera id conflatum ‹esset›[53] incendium profiteretur, praemium fore libero pecuniam,
  servo libertatem.
7   Eo praemio inductus Campanorum Calaviorum ser-
  vus—Manus ei nomen erat—indicavit dominos et quinque praeterea iuvenes nobiles Campanos, quorum parentes a Q. Fulvio securi percussi erant, id incendium
  fecisse; volgoque facturos alia ni comprehendantur. com-
8 prehensi ipsi familiaeque eorum. et primo elevabatur in-
  dex indiciumque: pridie eum verberibus castigatum ab
  dominis discessisse; per iram ac levitatem ex re fortuita

53 ‹esset› *hic C-J, post* incendium *Madvig*

[145] The nature of the buildings is unclear, but the "seven shops," located on a street leading to the Forum, were replaced the following year by five new ones, above which cantilevered galleries gave spectators a view of events in the forum. The "bankers' establishments" (*argentariae*) were also later replaced: Richardson 375–76 (Tabernae Circum Forum).

[146] The Lautumiae (on the northeast slope of the Capitoline: Richardson 234) were stone quarries that also served as prisons (named after the Syracusan quarries also so used). The Fish Market (*forum piscatorium*) is another name for the *Macellum*, the

went up in flames.[145] After that, private houses caught fire—there were no basilicas there then—as did the Lautumiae, the Fish Market and the Royal Atrium.[146] The Temple of Vesta was barely saved, thanks mainly to the efforts of thirteen slaves, who were bought with state funds and manumitted. The fire continued for a night and a day, and no one doubted that it was a case of arson since it had broken out in several spots simultaneously and also in different areas. So, on the authority of the senate, the consul publicly announced at an assembly that there would be a reward for anyone identifying those responsible for the fire, monetary in the case of a free man and freedom in the case of a slave.

A slave of the Calavii family of Capua[147]—his name was Manus—was induced by the reward to denounce his masters and five noblemen of Capua (men whose fathers had been beheaded by Quintus Fulvius)[148] for having set that fire; and if they were not arrested they would set others far and wide, he said. Arrested they were, they and their slaves. At first there was some attempt to discredit the informer and his information: he had purportedly been punished with a whipping the day before, had run away from his masters; and, angry and irresponsible, he had

great food market lying northeast of the Forum Romanum (Richardson 169). The nature of the Royal Atrium (*atrium regium*) is unknown. For rebuilding contracts for these buildings, cf. 27.11.16.   [147] An old and distinguished Campanian family: cf. 9.26.7, where Ofilius Calavius supports Rome after the Caudine Forks disaster, and 23.2.2–3, in which Pacuvius Calavius has become chief magistrate (*medix tuticus*), but by dishonorable means.   [148] Cf. chapter 15, above.

9 crimen commentum. ceterum ut coram coarguebantur et
quaestio ex ministris facinoris foro medio haberi coepta
est, fassi omnes, atque in dominos servosque conscios animadversum est. indici libertas data et viginti milia aeris.

10 Consuli Laevino Capuam praetereunti circumfusa
multitudo Campanorum est obsecrantium cum lacrimis ut
sibi Romam ad senatum ire liceret oratum, si qua miseri-
cordia tandem flecti possent, ne se ad ultimum perditum
irent nomenque Campanorum a Q. Flacco deleri sinerent.

11 Flaccus sibi privatam simultatem cum Campanis negare
ullam esse. publicas inimicitias hostiles et esse et futuras

12 quoad eo animo esse erga populum Romanum sciret; nullam enim in terris gentem esse, nullum infestiorem populum nomini Romano. ideo se moenibus inclusos tenere
eos; quippe si qui evasissent aliqua, velut feras bestias per
agros vagari, et laniare et trucidare quodcunque obvium

13 detur; alios ad Hannibalem transfugisse, alios ad Romam
incendendam profectos. inventurum in semusto foro con-

14 sulem vestigia sceleris Campanorum, Vestae aedem peti-
tam et aeternos ignes et conditum in penetrali fatale
pignus imperii Romani. se minime censere tutum esse
Campanis potestatem intrandi Romana moenia fieri.

15 Laevinus Campanos iure iurando a Flacco adactos
quinto die quam ab senatu responsum accepissent Ca-

---

149 The Palladium, an ancient statue of Athena (Minerva),
purportedly brought to Italy by Aeneas and so well known to
Romans that the allusive reference would be easily understood.

fabricated the charge out of what was just an accident. But when the accusation was brought against them before their accuser, and the process of interrogating their henchmen began in the forum, everyone confessed, and both the masters and their slave accomplices were executed. The informant was granted freedom and twenty thousand *asses*.

While the consul Laevinus was passing by Capua, he was surrounded by a crowd of Capuans tearfully begging for permission to approach the senate in Rome to plead with the senators (if they could finally be moved to pity) not to allow them to be utterly destroyed and the Capuan name wiped out by Quintus Flaccus. Flaccus denied having any personal animosity against the Capuans. His antipathy and anger was and would be a public matter for as long as he knew that they maintained their present attitude toward the Roman people—for there was no race and no people on the face of the earth hating the Roman name more than they. That was why he kept them confined within their walls: for any who had somehow found a way out were roaming the countryside like wild animals, mutilating and butchering whatever got in their way. Some had gone over to Hannibal, others had left to set fire to Rome. The consul would find traces of the Capuans' mischief in the half-burned forum; Vesta's temple and her ever-burning fires had been targeted and so too, hidden away in the inner sanctum, had destiny's pledge of Roman imperial power.[149] He personally thought it very unsafe for Capuans to be given leave to enter the walls of Rome, he said.

After making the Capuans swear on oath to Flaccus that they would return to Capua four days after receiving

16 puam redituros, sequi se Romam iussit. hac circumfusus
multitudine, simul Siculis obviam egressis secutisque
Romam, praebuit ⟨dolentis speciem duarum⟩[54] clarissi-
marum urbium excidio, ac celeberrimis viris victos bello
17 accusatores in urbem adducentis. de re publica tamen
primum ac de provinciis ambo consules ad senatum ret-
tulere.

28. Ibi Laevinus quo statu Macedonia et Graecia, Aetoli, Acarnanes Locrique essent, quasque ibi res ipse egis-
2 set terra marique exposuit. Philippum inferentem bellum
Aetolis in Macedoniam retro ab se compulsum ad intima
penitus regni abisse, legionemque inde deduci posse; classem satis esse ad arcendum Italia regem.

3 Haec de se deque provincia cui praefuerat consul; tum
de provinciis communis relatio fuit. decrevere patres ut
alteri consulum Italia bellumque cum Hannibale provincia esset, alter classem cui T. Otacilius praefuisset Sici-
liamque provinciam cum L. Cincio praetore obtineret.
4 exercitus eis duo decreti qui in Etruria Galliaque essent;
eae quattuor erant legiones. urbanae duae superioris anni
in Etruriam, duae quibus Sulpicius consul praefuisset in
5 Galliam mitterentur. Galliae et legionibus praeesset quem
6 consul cuius Italia provincia esset praefecisset; in Etruriam C. Calpurnius post praeturam prorogato in annum
imperio missus. et Q. Fulvio Capua provincia decreta pro-

---

[54] ⟨dolentis speciem duarum⟩ *Johnson*: ⟨speciem dolentis
duarum⟩ *M. Müller*

the senate's answer, Laevinus ordered them to follow him to Rome. Surrounded by this crowd, and with Sicilians also pouring out to meet him and following him on the road to Rome, he presented a picture of a man grieving for the overthrow of two very famous cities, but also of one bringing the defeated peoples into his city to prosecute its celebrated heroes. But it was matters of state and the provinces that the two consuls first brought before the senate.

28. There Laevinus laid out the situation in Macedonia and Greece vis-à-vis the Aetolians, Acarnanians, and Locrians, and his own land and naval operations there: Philip, on starting to invade Aetolia, had been driven back into Macedonia by him and had retreated deep into the heart of his kingdom, and the legion could now be withdrawn from there—the fleet sufficed for keeping the king away from Italy.

Such was the consul's report on himself and the province he had held; then the matter of both consuls' provinces was raised. The senators decreed that one should have Italy and the war with Hannibal as his province, the other command of the fleet formerly under Titus Otacilius and (jointly with the praetor Lucius Cincius) Sicily. They were assigned the two armies that were in Etruria and Gaul; these comprised four legions. The two urban legions of the previous year were to be sent into Etruria and the two formerly commanded by the consul Sulpicius into Gaul. Command of Gaul and its legions would go to whomsoever the consul whose province was Italy put in place; after his praetorship Gaius Calpurnius was dispatched into Etruria with his *imperium* prorogued for a year. Quintus Fulvius was decreed Capua as his province,

109

7 rogatumque in annum imperium; exercitus civium sociorumque minui iussus ut ex duabus legionibus una legio,
8 quinque milia peditum et trecenti equites, essent, dimissis
qui plurima stipendia haberent, et sociorum septem milia
peditum et trecenti equites relinquerentur, eadem ratione
stipendiorum habita in veteribus militibus dimittendis.
9 Cn. Fulvio consuli superioris anni nec de provincia
Apulia nec de exercitu quem habuerat quicquam mutatum; tantum in annum prorogatum imperium est. P. Sulpicius collega eius omnem exercitum praeter socios na-
10 vales iussus dimittere est. item ex Sicilia exercitus cui M.
Cornelius praeesset ubi consul in provinciam venisset di-
11 mitti iussus. L. Cincio praetori ad obtinendam Siciliam
12 Cannenses milites dati duarum instar legionum. totidem
legiones in Sardiniam P. Manlio Vulsoni praetori decretae,
quibus L. Cornelius in eadem provincia priore anno prae-
13 fuerat. urbanas legiones ita scribere consules iussi ne
quem militem facerent qui in exercitu M. Claudi M. Valeri
Q. Fulvi fuisset, neve eo anno plures quam una et viginti
Romanae legiones essent.
29. His senatus consultis perfectis sortiti provincias
consules. Sicilia et classis Marcello, Italia cum bello adver-
2 sus Hannibalem Laevino evenit. quae sors velut iterum
captis Syracusis ita exanimavit Siculos, exspectatione sor-

---

[150] The number here has been thought too high; cf. P. A.
Brunt, *Italian Manpower 225 BC–AD 14* (Oxford, 1971), 679.

[151] There had been twenty-three the previous year (1.13,
above).

and his *imperium* was also prorogued for a year; his army made up of citizens and allies was ordered to be reduced in size, with a single legion of five thousand infantry and three hundred cavalry formed from the two then in operation, and the men with the longest service records discharged; and of the allies only seven thousand infantry and three hundred cavalry were to remain operative, the same principle of length of service also being applied in discharging veterans.[150]

In the case of Gnaeus Fulvius, consul the previous year, no change was made either in the allocation of Apulia as his province or in the army that he had been commanding; he merely had his *imperium* prorogued for a year. Fulvius' colleague, Publius Sulpicius, was ordered to demobilize his entire army apart from ships' crews. There were likewise orders for the army under the command of Marcus Cornelius in Sicily to be demobilized when the consuls reached the province. The praetor Lucius Cincius was given the Cannae veterans (representing about two legions) for holding Sicily. For Sardinia the praetor Publius Manlius Vulso was also assigned the same number of legions; these troops Lucius Cornelius had commanded in that same province the previous year. The consuls were ordered to raise city legions without enlisting anyone who had served in the army of Marcus Claudius, Marcus Valerius, or Quintus Fulvius, and without the total number of Roman legions that year exceeding twenty-one.[151]

29. Once these senatorial resolutions were put into effect, the consuls proceeded to sortition of provinces. Sicily and the fleet fell to Marcellus, Italy and the war against Hannibal to Laevinus. For the Sicilians, who were awaiting it standing in full view of the consuls, that sortition

tis in consulum conspectu stantes, ut comploratio eorum
flebilesque voces et extemplo oculos hominum converte-
3 rint et postmodo sermones praebuerint. circumibant enim
senatorum ⟨domos⟩[55] cum veste sordida, adfirmantes se
non modo suam quosque patriam sed totam Siciliam relic-
4 turos si eo Marcellus iterum cum imperio redisset. nullo
suo merito eum ante implacabilem in se fuisse; quid ira-
tum quod Romam de se questum venisse Siculos sciat
facturum? obrui Aetnae ignibus aut mergi freto satius illi
insulae esse quam velut dedi noxae inimico.

5   Hae Siculorum querellae domos primum nobilium cir-
cumlatae celebrataeque sermonibus, quos partim miseri-
cordia Siculorum partim invidia Marcelli excitabat, in se-
6 natum etiam pervenerunt. postulatum a consulibus est ut
de permutandis provinciis senatum consulerent. Marcellus si iam auditi ab senatu Siculi essent aliam forsitan
7 futuram fuisse sententiam suam dicere; nunc ne quis timore frenari eos dicere posset quo minus de eo libere
querantur in cuius potestate mox futuri sint, si collegae
8 nihil intersit, mutare se provinciam paratum esse. depre-
cari senatus praeiudicium; nam cum extra sortem collegae
optionem dari provinciae iniquum fuerit, quanto maiorem
iniuriam, immo contumeliam esse sortem suam ad eum
transferri?

9   Ita senatus, cum quid placeret magis ostendisset quam
decrevisset, dimittitur. inter ipsos consules permutatio

[55] ⟨domos⟩ hic Weiss., ante senatorum Riemann

112

came as such a blow—like a second capture of Syracuse—
that their lamentation and tearful remarks immediately
drew people's attention and then raised discussion. For
they would go around senators' homes in mourning garb,
declaring that they would leave not only their home towns
but the whole of Sicily if Marcellus returned there with
imperium. They had done nothing to deserve his implacable rancor toward them, they said; what would he now
do in his anger at knowing Sicilians had come to Rome to
complain about him? Better for that island to be engulfed
in the flames of Aetna or swallowed by the sea than be
virtually surrendered to their enemy for punishment!

These grievances of the Sicilians, first circulating
among homes of the nobility and becoming common top-
ics of conversation—raised partly by pity for the Sicilians
and partly by jealousy felt for Marcellus—also reached the
senate. The consuls were asked to discuss with the senate
the possibility exchanging provinces. Marcellus stated that
if the Sicilians had already been heard by the senate his
opinion might perhaps have been different; but, so no one
could say they were being held back by fear from freely
complaining about someone in whose power they were
soon to be, he was prepared to exchange his province if
it made no difference to his colleague; but he petitioned
the senate not to prejudge the matter; for, unfair as it
would have been for his colleague to be granted the choice
of his province without sortition, how much greater an
injustice—no, insult!—was it for his own allotment in the
sortition to be transferred to him?

Thus, after making its wishes known rather than passing a decree, the senate was adjourned. An exchange of

provinciarum, rapiente fato Marcellum ad Hannibalem,
10 facta est, ut ex quo primus post ‹adversa omnia haud›[56]
adversae pugnae gloriam ceperat, in eius laudem post-
remus Romanorum imperatorum prosperis tum maxime
bellicis rebus caderet.

30. Permutatis provinciis Siculi in senatum introducti
multa de Hieronis regis fide perpetua erga populum Romanum verba fecerunt, in gratiam publicam ea verten-
2 tes:[57] Hieronymum ac postea Hippocraten atque Epi-
cyden tyrannos cum ob alia tum propter defectionem
ab Romanis ad Hannibalem invisos fuisse sibi. ob eam
causam et Hieronymum a principibus iuventutis prope
3 publico consilio interfectum, et in Epicydis Hippocratis-
que caedem septuaginta nobilissimorum iuvenum coniu-
rationem factam, quos Marcelli mora destitutos quia ad
praedictum tempus exercitum ad Syracusas non admovis-
4 set indicio facto omnes ab tyrannis interfectos. eam quoque Hippocratis et Epicydis tyrannidem Marcellum ex-
5 citasse Leontinis crudeliter direptis. nunquam deinde
principes Syracusanorum desisse ad Marcellum transire

---

[56] ‹adversa omnia haud› *Riemann*: ‹adversissimas haud›
Madvig   [57] ‹e›a vertentes *Harant*: avertentes *P*

---

[152] Destiny (*fatum*) because the exchange of provinces will
lead to Marcellus' death (in an ambush in Bruttium in 208:
27.27.7–11).

[153] The "not-a-defeat" battle was at Nola in 216 (cf. Livy's
comment at 23.16.16), after Flaminius had earlier fallen at Trasimene (22.6.3–4) and Aemilius Paullus at Cannae (22.49.12).

[154] Hieronymus, tyrant only from 215 until his assassination
in 214, was replaced by Hippocrates and Epicydes, who were

provinces was arranged by the consuls as destiny swept Marcellus on to confront Hannibal,[152] making him the first to win the glory of a battle that after all the failures was not a defeat, and the last of the Roman generals to enhance Hannibal's reputation by falling in combat,[153] and just when the war was going well.

30. The provinces being exchanged, the Sicilians, brought into the senate, talked at length about King Hieron's undying loyalty toward the Roman people, trying to turn that to the credit of their state. Hieronymus, and the tyrants Hippocrates and Epicydes after him, they claimed to have hated for various reasons, but mostly because of their defection from the Romans to Hannibal.[154] That, they said, was the reason for Hieronymus being killed by the leaders of Syracuse's youth after what was virtually a public resolution, and for a group of seventy of their most prominent young noblemen hatching a conspiracy to assassinate Epicydes and Hippocrates (but they had been let down by Marcellus' tardiness—he had not brought his army to Syracuse at the appointed time, and when informed upon, they had all been killed by the tyrants). Furthermore, that tyranny of Hippocrates and Epicydes had been precipitated by Marcellus with his ruthless sacking of Leontini.[155] The leaders of Syracuse had never stopped going over to Marcellus after that, promising to

born in Carthage, where their Syracusan grandfather was in exile. Sent to Syracuse by Hannibal in 215 (24.6.2), they gradually gained influence with the tyrant, persuaded him to abandon the alliance with Rome, and eventually, after his murder, became masters of the city (Book 24.21–32).

155 Cf. 24.30.1–5.

6 pollicerique se urbem cum vellet ei tradituros; sed eum
primo vi capere maluisse, dein cum id neque terra neque
mari omnia expertus potuisset, auctores traditarum Syracusarum fabrum aerarium Sosim et Moericum Hispanum
quam principes Syracusanorum habere totiens id nequiquam ultro offerentes praeoptasse, quo scilicet iustiore de
causa vetustissimos socios populi Romani trucidaret ac
7 diriperet. si non Hieronymus ad Hannibalem defecisset
sed populus Syracusanus et senatus, si portas Marcello
Syracusani publice et non oppressis Syracusanis tyranni
eorum Hippocrates et Epicydes clausissent, si Carthaginiensium animis bellum cum populo Romano gessissent,
8 quid ultra quam quod fecerit, nisi ut deleret Syracusas,
9 facere hostiliter Marcellum potuisse? certe praeter moenia et tecta exhausta urbis et refracta ac spoliata deum
delubra, dis ipsis ornamentisque eorum ablatis, nihil relic-
10 tum Syracusis esse. bona quoque multis adempta ita ut ne
nudo quidem solo reliquiis direptae fortunae alere sese ac
suos possent. orare se patres conscriptos ut si nequeant
omnia, saltem quae compareant cognoscique possint re-
stitui dominis iubeant.
11 Talia conquestos cum excedere ex templo ut de postu-
latis eorum patres consuli possent Laevinus iussisset,
12 "maneant immo" inquit Marcellus "ut coram iis respon-
deam, quando ea condicione pro vobis, patres conscripti,

---

[156] On Sosis and Moericus, cf. 21.9 note, above.

deliver the city to him whenever he wished; but from the beginning he had preferred to take it by force. Then, when he could not, for all his efforts, achieve that either by land or sea, he chose the coppersmith Sosis and the Spaniard Moericus[156] as his agents for delivering Syracuse rather than leading Syracusan citizens, whose numerous offers were in vain—evidently to have more justification for massacring and pillaging the Roman people's oldest allies! Suppose that not Hieronymus but the whole Syracusan people and their senate had defected to Hannibal, that it had been the Syracusans who had closed the gates on Marcellus by official decision, that their tyrants Hippocrates and Epicydes had not kept the Syracusans in subjection and closed their gates, and that the Syracusans had fought the Roman people with the resolve of the Carthaginians! Even then what damage, short of actually destroying Syracuse, could Marcellus have inflicted on them greater than he did? Apart from their city's walls and some looted buildings, and the plundered and despoiled temples of their gods' temples, with the gods themselves and their ornaments hauled away, the Syracusans had certainly been left with nothing. Many had also had their property confiscated to the point where fortunes were so wrecked that they did not even have bare land for supporting themselves and their families. They were pleading with the conscript fathers: if all could not be returned, at least they should order what could be found and identified to be returned to its owners.

When, after such complaints from them, Laevinus ordered the Syracusans to leave the temple so the senators could discuss their petition, Marcellus said: "No, let them stay so I can answer them face to face, since these are the

bella gerimus, ut victos armis accusatores habeamus, duae<que>[58] captae hoc anno urbes Capua Fulvium reum, Marcellum Syracusae habeant."

31. Reductis in curiam legatis tum consul "Non adeo maiestatis" inquit "populi Romani imperiique huius oblitus sum, patres conscripti, ut,[59] si de meo crimine ambigeretur, consul dicturus causam accusantibus Graecis

2 fuerim. sed non quid ego fecerim in disquisitionem venit, quem[60] quidquid in hostibus feci ius belli defendit, sed quid isti pati debuerint. qui si non fuerunt hostes, nihil

3 interest nunc an vivo Hierone Syracusas violaverim; sin autem desciverunt a populo Romano, si legatos nostros ferro atque armis petierunt, urbem ac moenia clauserunt exercituque Carthaginiensium adversus nos tutati sunt, quis passos esse hostilia cum fecerint indignatur?

4 "Tradentes urbem principes Syracusanorum aversatus sum; Sosim et Moericum Hispanum quibus rem tantam crederem potiores habui. non estis extremi Syracusano-

5 rum, quippe qui aliis humilitatem obiciatis. quis est vestrum qui se mihi portas aperturum, qui armatos milites meos in urbem accepturum promiserit? odistis et exsecramini eos qui fecerunt, et ne hic quidem contumeliis in eos

---

[58] duae<que> C-J: <et> duae Ussing
[59] ut P: velut Walsh
[60] quem quidquid . . . quid Σ: nam quidquid P

---

[157] Spoken disdainfully; anti-Greek prejudice is commonplace in Roman literature.

[158] In fact, the ambassadors escaped in their quinquereme but a quadrireme escorting them was captured (24.33.2).

conditions on which we fight wars for you, conscript fathers—having men defeated in war accuse us and seeing this year's two captured cities put us on trial, Capua Fulvius and Syracuse Marcellus."

31. When the Sicilian ambassadors were brought back into the senate house, the consul then said: "Not so oblivious am I to the Roman People's eminence and this *imperium* of mine, Senators, that I, a consul, would defend myself before Greek accusers,[157] if it were a charge brought against me personally. However, it is not what *I* did that is at issue—in the case of an enemy whatever I did is sanctioned by the rules of war—but what those people deserved to suffer. If they were not our enemies, then it makes no difference whether my 'violation' of Syracuse occurred now or when Hieron was alive; but if they defected from the Roman people, if they drew their swords for an armed attack on our ambassadors,[158] closed up their city and fortifications, and defended themselves against us with a Carthaginian army,[159] who can protest against their suffering acts of aggression when they committed them themselves?

"I turned away some leading Sicilians who were offering to surrender the city. I thought Sosis and the Spaniard Moericus to be better men to whom to entrust such an important matter; you people are not the lowest of Syracusans, for you criticize the humble condition of others. And who among you promised to open the gates to me and who to let my armed forces into the city? You hate and curse those who did, and not even here do you refrain

[159] Cf. 24.35.7, but it was Hannibal's men Epicydes and Hippocrates who joined Himilco (24.6.3).

dicendis parcitis; tantum abest ut et ipsi tale quicquam
6 facturi fueritis. ipsa humilitas eorum, patres conscripti,
quam isti obiciunt maximo argumento est me neminem
qui navatam operam rei publicae nostrae velit[61] aversatum
esse.

7   "Et antequam obsiderem Syracusas nunc legatis mittendis nunc ad conloquium eundo temptavi pacem, et
posteaquam neque legatos violandi verecundia erat nec
mihi ipsi congresso ad portas cum principibus responsum
dabatur, multis terra marique exhaustis laboribus tandem
8 vi atque armis Syracusas cepi. quae captis acciderint, apud
Hannibalem et Carthaginienses victos iustius quam apud
9 victoris populi senatum quererentur. ego, patres conscripti, Syracusas spoliatas si negaturus essem, nunquam
spoliis earum urbem Romam exornarem. quae autem singulis victor aut ademi aut dedi, cum belli iure tum ex
10 cuiusque merito satis scio me fecisse. ea vos rata habeatis,
patres conscripti, necne magis rei publicae interest quam
mea. quippe mea fides exsoluta est; ad rem publicam per-
tinet ne acta mea rescindendo alios in posterum segniores
11 duces faciatis. et quoniam coram et Siculorum et mea
verba audistis, patres conscripti, simul templo excedemus
ut me absente liberius consuli senatus possit." ita dimissi
Siculi et ipse in Capitolium ad dilectum discessit.

    32. Consul alter de postulatis Siculorum ad patres ret-
tulit. ibi cum diu[62] sententiis certatum esset et magna pars

---

[61] velit Λ: velitet *P*: vellet *Gron.*
[62] diu *Gron.*: diu de *P*

---

[160] This attempted parley is not mentioned in Books 24 or 25
but is found in Plutarch (*Marc.* 2).

from insulting them—so far were you yourselves from taking any such action! Senators, those people's low status, with which these men reproach me, is the most solid argument that no one ready to serve our country has been turned away by me.

"Even before I blockaded Syracuse I tried to establish peace, sending spokesmen to them at one time, going to parley with them at another,[160] and when they showed no restraint in maltreating my legates and I was being given no answer when I myself went to meet their leaders at their gates, I finally, after enduring many hardships on land and sea, took Syracuse by armed force. What befell them after their capture, that they could more justifiably complain about to Hannibal and his defeated Carthaginians than to the senate of the victorious people. As for me, conscript fathers, had I been going to deny that Syracuse was sacked, never would I be beautifying the city of Rome with its spoils. As for what I as victor took from individuals, or gave to them, I know for sure it was justified by the rules of war as well as the merits of each case. Whether or not you ratify these things, conscript fathers, is more the state's concern than mine. For my responsibility has been loyally discharged; as regards the state, it is important that you not, by revoking my acts, make other leaders more hesitant in future. And since you have, in our presence, heard both what the Sicilians and I have to say, we shall leave the temple together so the senate can discuss things more freely in my absence." With that, the Sicilians were sent off and Marcellus himself left for the Capitol to levy troops.

32. The other consul raised the Sicilians' demands with the senators. Opinions were there long divided, and most

2 senatus, principe eius sententiae T. Manlio Torquato, cum
tyrannis bellum gerendum fuisse censerent hostibus et
Syracusanorum et populi Romani; et urbem recipi, non
capi, et receptam legibus antiquis et libertate stabiliri, non
3 fessam miseranda servitute bello adfligi; inter tyrannorum
et ducis Romani certamina praemium victoris in medio
positam urbem pulcherrimam ac nobilissimam perisse,
horreum atque aerarium quondam populi Romani, cuius
munificentia ac donis multis tempestatibus, hoc denique
4 ipso Punico bello, adiuta ornataque res publica esset; si ab
inferis exsistat rex Hiero fidissimus imperii Romani cultor,
quo ore aut Syracusas aut Romam ei ostendi posse cum,
ubi semirutam ac spoliatam patriam respexerit, ingrediens
Romam in vestibulo urbis, prope in porta, spolia patriae
suae visurus sit?

5   Haec taliaque cum ad invidiam consulis miserationem-
que Siculorum dicerentur, mitius tamen decreverunt
6 patres. acta M. Marcelli quae is gerens bellum victorque
egisset rata habenda esse; in reliquum curae senatui fore
rem Syracusanam, mandaturosque consuli Laevino ut
quod sine iactura rei publicae fieri posset fortunis eius
civitatis consuleret.

---

161 For Hieron's generosity to Rome, cf. 22.37.1–13 and
23.21.5; on the morality of the Roman treatment of Sicily, cf.
Polyb. 9.10.2–13.   162 This has been thought to refer to a
temple of Honos et Virtus (Honor and Courage), vowed by Marcellus after the battle Clastidium in 222 and later adorned with
spoils from Syracuse. However, the temple (outside the Porta
Capena) seems to have been built much earlier and dedicated
only to Honos. Marcellus tried to have it refurbished and re-
dedicated in 208 but was blocked by the pontiffs (27.25.7–10). Cf.
Richardson 190 (Honos et Virtus, Aedes [1]).

of the senate was of the view, with Titus Manlius Torquatus its leading advocate, that they should have opened hostilities against the tyrants, enemies both of the Syracusans and the Roman people; that the city should have been recovered, not taken by force; and that, after being recovered, it should have been stabilized with its earlier constitution and independence, not crushed militarily when it was exhausted from a wretched despotism; set up as the victor's prize in struggles between the tyrants and the Roman commander, a beautiful and famous city had perished, a city once the breadbasket and treasury of the Roman people, through whose generous gifts the Roman republic had many times been aided and beautified—and actually been so in this very war with Carthage.[161] Suppose King Hieron, a most loyal supporter of the Roman empire, rose from the dead and were shown either Syracuse or Rome; and then suppose that, walking into Rome, he saw the spoils taken from his country[162] in the approach to the city and practically at its gate—what expression would he have on his face looking upon his half-ruined and pillaged country?

These and similar remarks were made to arouse animosity against the consul and pity for the Sicilians, but the senators nevertheless showed moderation in their decision. The measures taken by Marcellus during his conduct of the war and after his victory were to be ratified, but in future the state of Syracuse would be the concern of the senate, and the senators would order the consul Laevinus to promote, as far as was possible without detriment to the republic, the fortunes of that state.

7   Missis duobus senatoribus in Capitolium ad consulem
uti rediret in curiam et introductis Siculis, senatus con-
8   sultum recitatum est; legatique benigne appellati ac dimissi ad genua se Marcelli consulis proiecerunt, obse-
crantes ut quae deplorandae ac levandae calamitatis causa
dixissent veniam eis daret, et in fidem et clientelam se
urbemque Syracusas acciperet. potens senatus consulto[63]
consul clementer appellatos eos dimisit.

33. Campanis deinde senatus datus est, quorum oratio
2   miserabilior, causa durior erat; neque enim meritas poenas negare poterant nec tyranni erant in quos culpam conferrent. sed satis pensum poenarum tot veneno absumptis,
3   tot securi percussis senatoribus credebant: paucos nobilium superstites esse, quos nec sua conscientia ut quicquam de se gravius consulerent impulerit nec victoris ira
capitis damnaverit; eo se[64] libertatem sibi suisque et bono-
rum aliquam partem orare cives Romanos, adfinitatibus
plerosque et propinquis iam cognationibus ex conubio
vetusto iunctos.

4   Summotis deinde e templo paulisper dubitatum an
arcessendus a Capua Q. Fulvius esset—mortuus enim
post captam Claudius consul erat—ut coram imperatore

[63] potens senatus consulto *Walters*: potens oc *P*: pollicens hoc
Boettcher   [64] eo se *Harant*: eos *P*

[163] Cf. 23.4.7 (on 216, the year Capua defected), where all
that kept the Capuans from defection was that "the time-honored
right of intermarriage had connected many of their distinguished
and powerful families with Roman families." An example is the
Capuan marriage of Appius Claudius' daughter (cf. 23.2.6, and
note on 15.1, above).

After two senators were sent to the consul on the Capitol to request his return to the senate house, and the Sicilians had been admitted, the senatorial decree was read out; then the envoys, when called upon and dismissed with some congenial remarks, flung themselves at Marcellus' feet, begging his pardon for what they had said in bemoaning and trying to lighten their calamity, and asking him to take them and the city of Syracuse under his protection and patronage. Armed with the senate's decree, the consul sent them off with a few kind words.

33. The Capuans were granted a senate hearing next, and their presentation was more pitiful and their case harder to make; for they could not deny that they deserved punishment and there were no tyrants for them to blame. But they believed they had paid a great enough penalty with so many of their senators killed by poison and so many beheaded: few of the nobility had survived, those whom a guilty conscience had not driven to drastic measures or the victor's anger not condemned to death, they said; and so they were begging for freedom for themselves and their families and for some part of their property—they were Roman citizens, several of them connected to Rome by marriage and by now even by blood relationships from their long-established right of intermarriage.[163]

When the Capuans were then taken from the temple, the senators briefly considered whether Quintus Fulvius should be summoned from Capua—for the consul Claudius had died after the city's capture—so the matter

qui res gessisset sicut inter Marcellum Siculosque discep-
5 tatum fuerat disceptaretur. dein cum M. Atilium C. Fulvium fratrem Flacci legatos eius, et Q. Minucium et L.
Veturium Philonem item Claudi legatos qui omnibus gerendis rebus adfuerant in senatu viderent, nec Fulvium
avocari a Capua nec differri Campanos vellent, interroga-
6 tus sententiam M. Atilius Regulus, cuius ex iis qui ad
Capuam fuerant maxima auctoritas erat,

7   "In consilio" inquit "arbitror me fuisse consulibus Capua capta cum quaereretur ecqui Campanorum bene
8 meritus de re publica nostra esset. duas mulieres fuisse
compertum est, Vestiam Oppiam Atellanam Capuae habi-
tantem et Fauculam[65] Cluviam quae quondam quaestum
corpore fecisset; illam cottidie sacrificasse pro salute et
victoria populi Romani, hanc captivis egentibus alimenta
9 clam suppeditasse. ceterorum omnium Campanorum
eundem erga nos animum quem Carthaginiensium fuisse,
securique percussos a Q. Fulvio fuisse magis quorum di-
gnitas inter alios quam quorum culpa eminebat.

10   "Per senatum agi de Campanis qui cives Romani sunt
iniussu populi non video posse, idque et apud maiores
nostros in Satricanis factum esse cum defecissent, ut M.
Antistius tribunus plebis prius rogationem ferret scisce-
retque plebs uti senatui de Satricanis sententiae dicendae

---

65 Fauculam *P*: Paculam *Mommsen*

---

164 Q. Minucius Rufus, later praetor (200) and consul (197);
L. Veturius Philo, praetor in 209 and consul in 206.
165 Valerius Maximus (5.2.1b) has the same story, and gives
her name as Cluvia Facula.

could be discussed in the presence of the commander who had conducted operations, as in the case of Marcellus and the Sicilians. They then saw his legates, Marcus Atilius and Flaccus' brother Gaius Flavius, present in the senate, and also Quintus Minucius and Lucius Veturius Philo,[164] who were legates of Claudius, and, as these had been present throughout the campaign and the senators did not want Fulvius recalled from Capua or the Capuans' case deferred, Marcus Atilius Regulus (who had the greatest authority of those who had been at Capua) was asked his opinion.

"I was, I believe, on the consuls' advisory board," said Regulus, "when, after Capua's capture, the question arose whether there was among the Capuans anyone deserving our republic's gratitude. Two women were found: Vestia Oppia, a lady from Atella resident in Capua, and Faucula Cluvia,[165] who had once earned her living by prostitution. The former had offered daily sacrifice for the safety and victory of the Roman people; the latter had secretly provided starving prisoners with food. The rest of the people of Capua, it was felt, all had the same feelings toward us as did the Carthaginians, and what distinguished the men beheaded by Quintus Fulvius from the others was more their rank than their guilt.

"In the case of Capuans who are Roman citizens, I do not see how steps can be taken by the senate without the people's authorization, and I also note that the action taken in our ancestors' time over the people of Satricum's defection was that the plebeian tribune Marcus Antistius presented a proposal on the issue and the plebs voted that the senate should have the right to prescribe the Satricans'

11 ius esset. itaque censeo cum tribunis plebis agendum esse
ut eorum unus pluresue rogationem ferant ad plebem qua
nobis statuendi de Campanis ius fiat."

12 L. Atilius tribunus plebis ex auctoritate senatus plebem
in haec verba rogavit: "Omnes Campani Atellani Calatini
Sabatini qui se dediderunt in arbitrium dicionemque po-

13 puli Romani Q. Fulvio proconsuli, quosque una secum
dedidere, quaeque una secum dedidere agrum urbemque
divina humanaque utensiliaque sive quid aliud dediderunt, de iis rebus quid fieri velitis vos rogo, Quirites."

14 plebes sic iussit: "Quod senatus iuratus maxima pars cen-
seat qui adsient, id volumus iubemusque."

34. Ex hoc plebei scito senatus consultus Oppiae
Cluviaeque primum bona ac libertatem restituit; si qua
alia praemia petere ab senatu vellent, venire eas Romam.

2 Campanis in familias singulas decreta facta quae non

3 operae pretium est omnia enumerare. aliorum bona publicanda, ipsos liberosque eorum et coniuges vendendas
extra filias quae enupsissent priusquam in populi Romani

4 potestatem venirent; alios in vincula condendos, ac de iis
posterius consulendum. aliorum Campanorum summam
etiam census distinxerunt, publicanda necne bona essent;

---

166 Satricum, northeast of Antium (*Barr.* 43 D3), was taken by
Papirius Cursor in 319 and severely punished for revolting after
the Caudine Forks episode: Livy 9.16.10; but there he records no
such procedure.   167 For Atella and Calatia, cf. 16.5, above.
Sabate, however, if it lay on the Lacus Sabatinus (mod. Lago di
Bracciano), was in Etruria, northwest of Rome (Frontin. *Aq.* 71;
Columella, *Rust.* 6.18.2; *Barr.* 44 B1), and either Livy is mistaken
or Sabate and the Sabatini were in different areas.

168 This clearly refers only to aristocratic families.

sentence.[166] I therefore recommend that we discuss with the plebeian tribunes whether one or more of them might bring a proposal to the plebs by which we are authorized to decide the Capuans' case."

The plebeian tribune Lucius Atilius, on senatorial authority, then brought before the plebs a bill worded as follows: "With regard to all the people of Capua, Atella, Calatia, and Sabate[167] who have put themselves under the Roman People's authority and power, in the hands of the proconsul Quintus Fulvius, and with regard to the persons they surrendered together with themselves and to the property they surrendered together with themselves— land and city, objects divine and secular, implements and whatever else they surrendered—I ask you, citizens, what you wish to be done with them." The plebs decreed as follows: "Whatever decision the senate reaches under oath with a majority of those present, that is our wish and command."

34. When consulted after this plebiscite, the senate first restored their property and freedom to Oppia and Cluvia; if they wished to claim further recompense from the senate, they were to come to Rome. Decrees were passed against individual Capuan households,[168] but it is not worthwhile listing them all. Some were to have their property expropriated, with them and their children and wives sold into slavery, apart from girls who had married outside the community before falling under authority of the Roman people; others faced imprisonment, with discussion of their fate postponed. For other Campanians they used census evaluations to determine whether or not property should be confiscated; and they also decided that

129

LIVY

5 pecua captiva praeter equos, et mancipia praeter puberes
virile secus,[66] et omnia quae solo non continerentur resti-
6 tuenda censuerunt dominis. Campanos omnes Atellanos
Calatinos Sabatinos, extra quam qui eorum aut ipsi aut
7 parentes eorum apud hostes essent, liberos esse iusserunt,
ita ut nemo eorum civis Romanus aut Latini nominis esset,
neve quis eorum qui Capuae fuisset dum portae clausae
essent in urbe agrove Campano intra certam diem mane-
8 ret; locus ubi habitarent trans Tiberim qui non contingeret
Tiberim daretur. qui nec Capuae nec in urbe Campana
quae a populo Romano defecisset per bellum fuissent, eos
9 cis Lirim amnem Romam versus, qui ad Romanos trans-
issent priusquam Capuam Hannibal veniret cis Volturnum
emovendos censuerunt, ne quis eorum propius mare
quindecim milibus passuum agrum aedificiumve haberet.
10 qui eorum trans Tiberim emoti essent, ne ipsi posterive
eorum uspiam pararent haberentve nisi in Veiente aut
Sutrino Nepesinove agro, dum ne cui maior quam quinquaginta iugerum agri modus esset.
11 Senatorum omnium quique magistratus Capuae Atellae Calatiae gessissent bona venire Capuae iusserunt; libera corpora quae venum dari placuerat Romam mitti ac
12 Romae venire. signa, statuas aeneas, quae capta de hosti-

---

[66] virile secus *J. Gron.*: viriles sexus *P*: virilis sexus *C*

[169] In fact, by 188 Capua was again on the Roman census
(38.28.4): Briscoe, *A Commentary on Livy Books 38–40*, 104.

[170] That is, beyond the limits of Campania. R. Liris: *Barr.* 44
E2–3.   [171] This was presumably to bar them from maritime
trading (R. Volturnus: *Barr.* 44 E–F3).

[172] Veii: *Barr.* 44 B1; Sutrium and Nepet(e): 42 C4.

captured farm animals apart from horses should be returned to their owners, as well as slaves (apart from adults of male sex) and all property not fixed to the ground. They ordained that all citizens of Capua, Atella, Calatia, and Sabate should have free status, apart from those who had either themselves served with the enemy or whose fathers had done, with the proviso that none was to become a Roman citizen or have Latin status, and no one present in Capua during the time when the gates were shut was to remain in the city or on the farmland of Capua beyond a certain date;[169] these would be given a place to live beyond the Tiber but not on its banks. As for those neither in Capua during the hostilities nor in any Campanian city that had defected from the Roman people, the senators voted that they be removed to a point beyond the River Liris, in the direction of Rome.[170] Those who had switched to the Romans before Hannibal's arrival in Capua they voted to have transferred to an area north of the River Volturnus, with the proviso that none possess land or a building within fifteen miles of the sea.[171] Those relocated across the Tiber were forbidden, both themselves and their descendants, to acquire or possess land anywhere other than in the territory of Veii, Sutrium, or Nepete,[172] their holdings there being restricted to no more than fifty *iugera* per person.

The senate also ordered property belonging to all senators and officeholders in Capua, Atella, or Calatia to be put up for sale in Capua; and the free persons that they had decided should be sold into slavery were to be sent to Rome and sold in the city. Art work and bronze statues

bus dicerentur, quae eorum sacra ac profana essent ad
13 pontificum collegium reiecerunt. ob haec decreta maes-
tiores aliquanto quam Romam venerant Campanos dimi-
serunt, nec iam Q. Fulvi saevitiam in sese sed iniquitatem
deum atque exsecrabilem fortunam suam incusabant.

35. Dimissis Siculis Campanisque dilectus habitus.
scripto deinde exercitu de remigum supplemento agi
2 coeptum. in quam rem cum neque hominum satis nec ex
qua pararentur stipendiumque acciperent pecuniae quic-
3 quam ea tempestate in publico esset, edixerunt consules
ut privati[67] ex censu ordinibusque sicut antea remiges
4 darent cum stipendio cibariisque dierum triginta. ad id
edictum tantus fremitus hominum, tanta indignatio fuit ut
magis dux quam materia seditioni deesset: secundum Siculos Campanosque plebem Romanam perdendam lace-
5 randamque sibi consules sumpsisse. per tot annos tributo
exhaustos nihil reliqui praeter terram nudam ac vastam
habere. tecta hostes incendisse, servos agri cultores rem
publicam abduxisse, nunc ad militiam parvo aere emendo
6 nunc remiges imperando; si quid cui argenti aerisve fuerit,
stipendio remigum et tributis annuis ablatum. se ut dent
quod non habeant nulla vi, nullo imperio cogi posse. bona

---

[67] privati *Fr. 1*: privatim P

[173] In 214: 24.11.7–9.

[174] Possibly because booty from both Syracuse and Capua
(see below) might have been expected to keep the treasury in
good order.

that were said to have been taken from the enemy the senators referred to the college of pontiffs for a decision on which of them were sacred and which profane. Because of these decrees, they sent the Capuans off considerably more downcast than when they had arrived in Rome, and they were railing now not against Quintus Fulvius' cruel treatment of them but against the gods' unfairness and their own execrable fortune.

35. The Sicilian and Capuan delegations dismissed, troop mobilization got under way. Then, once the army had been enrolled, discussion began of supplementing the number of oarsmen. As there was insufficient manpower available for that, and at the time no money in the public purse for buying rowers and providing their pay, the consuls proclaimed that private individuals should supply the oarsmen, together with their pay and thirty days' worth of food rations, on the basis of their property rating and their class, as before.[173] That proclamation met with such a howl of protest from the people, and such indignation,[174] that what was lacking for a riot was not the conditions but a leader; after the people of Sicily and Capua the consuls had now picked on the common folk of Rome as their next victim for ruin and persecution, they said. Drained year after year by tribute, they were left with nothing but their land, which was bare and desolate. The enemy had burned their houses and the state had taken away the slaves that worked their land, buying them up cheaply for the army or commandeering them as oarsmen; any silver or bronze in anyone's possession had been taken to pay oarsmen and the annual taxes. There now was no coercion and no authority by which they could be forced to give what they did not have. The state could sell their property and

133

sua venderent, in corpora quae reliqua essent saevirent;
ne unde redimantur quidem quicquam superesse.

7 Haec non in occulto sed propalam in foro atque oculis
ipsorum consulum ingens turba circumfusi fremebant;
nec eos sedare consules nunc castigando nunc consolando
8 poterant. spatium deinde iis tridui se dare ad cogitandum
dixerunt, quo ipsi ad rem inspiciendam expediendam[68] usi
9 sunt. senatum postero die habuerunt de remigum supplemento, ubi cum multa disseruissent cur aequa plebis recu-
satio esset, verterunt orationem eo ut dicerent privatis id
10 seu aequum seu iniquum onus iniungendum esse; nam
unde, cum pecunia in aerario non esset, paraturos navales
socios? quomodo autem sine classibus aut Siciliam obti-
neri aut Italia Philippum arceri posse aut tuta Italiae litora
esse?

36. Cum in hac difficultate rerum consilium haereret
ac prope torpor quidam occupasset hominum mentes,
2 tum Laevinus consul: magistratus senatui et senatum populo, sicut honore praestet,[69] ita ad omnia quae dura atque
aspera essent subeunda ducem[70] debere esse.

3 "Si, quod[71] iniungere inferiori velis, id prius in te ac
tuos ipse iuris statueris, facilius omnes oboedientes ha-
beas. nec impensa gravis est, cum eam[72] plus quam pro
4 virili parte sibi quemque capere principum vident. itaque
⟨si⟩ classes[73] habere atque ornare volumus populum

[68] expediendam *P*: expediendamque *C^c*: ⟨et⟩ expediendam
Alschefski   [69] praestet Σ: praestent *P*

[70] ducem *P*: duces *Crév.*

[71] quod *Madvig*: quid *P*

[72] eam Σ: ea *P*

[73] ⟨si⟩ classes *Madvig*

maltreat their bodies, which was all they had left; there remained nothing with which they could even be ransomed!

These complaints they made not in secret but quite openly in the forum before the eyes of the consuls as they milled about them in a huge crowd; and the consuls, in turn censuring and comforting them, could not calm them down. They then declared that they were giving the people a three-day period to mull things over, time that they themselves devoted to examining the problem and seeking a solution. The next day they convened the senate to consider supplementing the oarsmen, and after much talk of why the people's refusal was quite justified they then changed direction, going on to say that, fair or unfair, the burden had to be placed on private citizens; for with no money in the treasury, how would they acquire naval crews? And if they had no crews, how could Sicily be secured or Philip kept away from Italy or Italy's coasts safeguarded?

36. At this difficult moment, when debate was bogged down and a sort of paralysis had seized men's minds, the consul Laevinus then spoke: as the magistrates ranked above the senate and the senate above the people, he said, that precedence in rank obliged them to take the lead in accepting all that was hard and difficult.

"If you want to impose something on an inferior," he said, "you will the more easily have everyone listening to you if you first accept it as an obligation on yourself and your family; nor is the expense burdensome when they see each of their leading men take on more than his fair share. So if we want the Roman people to have fleets and to man them, and to have private individuals providing

135

Romanum, privatos sine recusatione remiges dare, nobis-
5 met ipsis primum imperemus. aurum argentum ⟨aes⟩[74]
signatum omne senatores crastino die in publicum confe-
ramus, ita ut anulos sibi quisque et coniugi et liberis, et
filio bullam, et quibus uxor filiaeve sunt singulas uncias
6 pondo auri relinquant. argenti qui curuli sella sederunt
equi ornamenta et ⟨duas⟩[75] libras pondo, ut salinum patel-
lamque deorum causa habere possint; ceteri senatores li-
7 bram argenti tantum. aeris signati quina milia in singulos
8 patres familiae relinquamus. ceterum omne aurum argentum aes signatum ad triumviros mensarios extemplo de-
feramus nullo ante senatus consulto facto, ut voluntaria
conlatio et certamen adiuvendae rei publicae excitet ad
aemulandum animos primum equestris ordinis, dein reli-
9 quae plebis. hanc unam viam multa inter nos conlocuti
consules invenimus; ingredimini dis bene iuventibus. res
publica incolumis et privatas res facile salvas praestat;
publica prodendo tua nequiquam serves."
10   In haec tanto animo consensum est ut gratiae ultro
11 consulibus agerentur. senatu inde misso pro se quisque
aurum argentum aes[76] in publicum conferunt, tanto certamine iniecto ut prima aut inter primos nomina sua
vellent in publicis tabulis esse ut nec triumviri accipiendo
12 nec scribae referendo sufficerent. hunc consensum senatus equester ordo est secutus, equestris ordinis plebs. ita

---

[74] ⟨aes⟩ *Mog.: om.* P   [75] ⟨duas⟩ *C-J*
[76] aes *ald.*: et aes P

---

[175] A golden locket containing an amulet worn around the
neck by boys of patrician class.

[176] Latin *triumviri mensarii*, a board of officials (formed per-

oarsmen without objecting, let us first impose that on ourselves. Let us, the senators, bring to the treasury tomorrow all our gold, silver, and bronze, with the following
exceptions: a ring for each man, his wife and each child, a
bulla[175] for a son and, for those with a wife and daughters,
an ounce of gold for each. In the case of silver, those who
have occupied curule offices may retain the decorative
emblems of their horse and two pounds of that metal, so
they can have a saltcellar and plate for offerings to the
gods; all other senators should keep just one pound per
person. And bronze coins—let us leave five thousand asses
to each family head. All other gold, silver, and bronze coin
let us immediately deposit with the treasury officials[176]
before issuing any senatorial decree, so that our volun-
tarily contribution and rivalry in assisting the state may
also inspire the equestrian order to emulate us, and then
the plebeians too. After long discussions, we the consuls
have found this to be the only road to follow; embark on
it, with the gods' help! Kept healthy, the state can also
easily safeguard private property; by abandoning the public cause you will have no chance of saving what is yours."

On this agreement was so strong that the consuls were
actually thanked by the senators. The senate being then
adjourned, every member brought his own gold, silver,
and bronze to the treasury; and so heated was rivalry to
have names listed first in the public records, or among the
first, that the treasury officials were incapable of taking the
deposits or the secretaries of recording them. This unanimity of the senate was followed by the equestrian order,

haps in 216, the year of their first appearance in Livy: 23.21.6)
charged with supervising the war finances of the state.

sine edicto, sine coercitione magistratus nec remige in supplementum nec stipendio res publica eguit, paratisque omnibus ad bellum consules in provincias profecti sunt.

37. Neque aliud tempus belli fuit quo Carthaginienses Romanique pariter variis casibus immixti magis in ancipiti
2 spe ac metu fuerint. nam Romanis et in provinciis hinc in Hispania adversae res, hinc prosperae in Sicilia luctum et
3 laetitiam miscuerant; et in Italia cum Tarentum amissum damno et dolori tum arx cum praesidio retenta praeter
4 spem gaudio fuit, et terrorem subitum pavoremque urbis Romae obsessae et oppugnatae Capua post dies paucos
5 capta in laetitiam vertit. transmarinae quoque res quadam vice pensatae; Philippus hostis tempore haud satis opportuno factus, Aetoli novi adsciti socii Attalusque Asiae rex, iam velut despondente fortuna Romanis imperium orientis.

6 Carthaginienses quoque Capuae amissae Tarentum captum aequabant; et ut ad moenia urbis Romanae nullo
7 prohibente se pervenisse in gloria ponebant, ita pigebat inriti incepti pudebatque adeo se spretos ut sedentibus ipsis ad Romana moenia alia porta exercitus Romanus in
8 Hispaniam duceretur. ipsae quoque Hispaniae quo propius spem venerant tantis duobus ducibus exercitibusque caesis debellatum ibi ac pulsos inde Romanos esse, eo plus ab L. Marcio tumultuario duce ad vanum et inritum vic-

---

177 Cf. 24.9–10, above.

and that of the equestrian order by the plebs. Thus, with no senatorial edict and no coercion from a magistrate, the republic lacked neither oarsmen to make up the numbers nor money for their pay; and with everything prepared for war, the consuls set off for their provinces.

37. There was no other point in the war at which Carthaginians and Romans, both having experienced mixed fortunes, fluctuated more between hope and fear. For in the case of the Romans and their provinces failure in Spain and success in Sicily had brought a mixture of grief and joy; and in Italy, while the loss of Tarentum was painful, retaining the citadel with its garrison brought unexpected elation; and the sudden panic and fear when Hannibal blockaded and attacked the city of Rome turned to jubilation a few days later with the capture of Capua. Overseas, too, there was some balance in oscillating fortunes, Philip becoming an enemy at what was hardly a favorable time, but the Aetolians and King Attalus being enlisted as new allies,[177] as if destiny were already promising the Romans mastery of the East.

The Carthaginians also balanced the capture of Tarentum with the loss of Capua; and though they prided themselves on reaching the walls of the city of Rome without resistance they were also galled by the failure of the enterprise and embarrassed at being held in such contempt that, while they sat right before the walls of Rome, a Roman army was being led off to Spain through another gate. Then there were the Spanish provinces themselves where, the closer they had come to hope of finishing off the war and driving out the Romans after killing two great commanders and their armies, the greater was their exasperation over their victory being rendered null and void

9 toriam redactam esse indignationis praebebant. ita aequante fortuna suspensa omnia utrimque[77] erant, integra spe, integro metu, velut illo tempore primum bellum inciperent.

38. Hannibalem ante omnia angebat quod Capua pertinacius oppugnata ab Romanis quam defensa ab se mul-

2 torum Italiae populorum animos averterat. quos neque omnes tenere praesidiis nisi vellet in multas parvasque partes carpere exercitum, quod minime tum expediebat, poterat, nec deductis praesidiis spei liberam vel obnoxiam

3 timori sociorum relinquere fidem. praeceps in avaritiam et crudelitatem animus ad spolianda quae tueri nequibat,

4 ut vastata hosti relinquerentur, inclinavit. id foedum consilium cum incepto tum etiam exitu fuit. neque enim indigna patientium modo abalienabantur animi sed ceterorum etiam, quippe ad plures exemplum quam ‹pericu-

5 lum›[78] pertinebat; nec consul Romanus temptandis urbibus sicunde spes aliqua se ostendisset deerat.

6 Salapiae principes erant Dasius et Blattius. Dasius Hannibali amicus, Blattius quantum ex tuto poterat rem Romanam fovebat; et per occultos nuntios spem proditionis fecerat Marcello, sed sine adiutore Dasio res transigi

7 non poterat. multum ac diu cunctatus, et tum quoque magis inopia consilii potioris quam spe effectus, Dasium

---

[77] utrimque Σ: utriusque P: utrisque M[c]
[78] ‹periculum› *Walsh*: ‹calamitas› *ald.*: ‹pernicies› *Weiss.*

---

[178] Modern Salpi, a town in northern Apulia southeast of Arpi (*Barr.* 45 C2). The story of Dasius and Blattius is also found in Valerius Maximus (3.8.ext.1).

[179] The Dasii, a prominent Apulian family, had long been opposed to Rome; cf. 21.48.9, where a Dasius of Brundisium turned

by Lucius Marcius, a makeshift commander. So, with fortune evening things up, everything hung in the balance on both sides, with hope still alive and fear still alive, as if at that time they were just beginning the war.

38. What vexed Hannibal more than anything was that the Romans' blockade of Capua, mounted with greater resolve than his defense of it, had lost him the support of many of the peoples of Italy. All these he could not hold down with garrisons unless he were willing to split his army into many small sections, something not at all to his advantage; but neither could he leave his allies' loyalty open to their own aspirations or subject to intimidation by withdrawing his garrisons. A temperament prone to greed and cruelty now leaned toward pillaging what he could not protect so his enemy would be left with devastated lands. A terrible plan in its inception, so was it also in its outcome. For he was cut off not only by those suffering an undeserved fate but by everybody else, too, since the example touched more people than did the danger; and the Roman consul was losing no opportunity to win over cities wherever any hope appeared.

The most prominent men in Salapia[178] were Dasius and Blattius. Dasius favored Hannibal;[179] Blattius, as far as he safely could, espoused the cause of Rome, and in clandestine messages he had led Marcellus to hope that the town could be betrayed to him; but without Dasius' complicity that object could not be achieved. After much hesitation and long delay, and then only from lack of a better plan rather than hope of success, Blattius started

Clastidium over to Hannibal, and 24.45.1, where Dasius Altinius offered to betray Arpi. The two (but with Blassius for Blattius) also appear in Valerius Maximus (3.8.ext.1).

appellabat; at ille, cum ab re aversus tum aemulo poten-
8 tatus inimicus, rem Hannibali aperit. arcessito utroque
Hannibal cum pro tribunali quaedam ageret mox de Blat-
tio cogniturus, starentque summoto populo accusator et
9 reus, Blattius de proditione Dasium appellabat.[79] enimvero ille velut in manifesta re exclamat sub oculis Hannibalis secum de proditione agi. Hannibali atque eis qui
aderant, quo audacior res erat, minus similis veri visa est:
10 aemulationem profecto atque odium esse, et id crimen
adferri quod, quia testem habere non posset, liberius fin-
11 genti sit ita inde dimissi sunt. nec Blattius ante abstitit
tam audaci incepto quam idem obtundendo docendoque
quam ea res ipsis patriaeque salutaris esset, pervicit
ut praesidium Punicum—<quingenti>[80] autem Numidae
erant—Salapiaque traderetur Marcello.
12 Nec sine caede multa tradi potuit; longe fortissimi
equitum toto Punico exercitu erant. itaque quamquam
improvisa res fuit nec usus equorum in urbe erat, tamen
13 armis inter tumultum captis et eruptionem temptaverunt
et cum evadere nequirent pugnantes ad ultimum occubuerunt, nec plus quinquaginta ex iis in potestatem ho-
14 stium vivi venerunt. plusque aliquanto damni haec ala
equitum amissa Hannibali quam Salapia fuit; nec deinde
unquam Poenus, quo longe plurimum valuerat, equitatu
superior fuit.

[79] appellabat *P*: appellat *Madvig*
[80] <quingenti> *Sig. cl. Val. Max. 3.8.ext.1*

[180] But he would attempt to recapture it in 208 (27.28.5–6).

making overtures to Dasius; but he, being opposed to the idea and also his rival for power, divulged the matter to Hannibal. When both men were summoned, Hannibal was conducting some business at his tribunal, intending to hear the matter of Blattius a little later; and as the two stood there, accuser and accused, with others kept at some remove, Blattius was making overtures to Dasius about the betrayal. And Dasius, of course, thinking the truth self-evident, cried out that the town's betrayal was being discussed with him then and there before Hannibal's eyes. For Hannibal and those present the more brazen the act the less plausible it seemed to be; it was surely just rivalry and personal animosity, and the accusation was made because, since there could be no witness, there was greater scope for fabrication, and with that the men were dismissed. Blattius, however, did not abandon such a bold project until, by drumming the same thing into the man's ears and explaining how good it was for them and their homeland, he convinced him that the Punic garrison (it comprised five hundred Numidians) should be delivered to Marcellus along with Salapia.

It could not be delivered without much bloodshed; the Numidians were by far the bravest horsemen in the whole Punic army. Thus, although the coup was a surprise and horses were of no use in the city, they still took up weapons in the melee and tried to break out; but, unable to escape, they went down fighting to the bitter end, with no more than fifty of them falling into their enemies' hands alive. The loss of this unit of horsemen was considerably more damaging to Hannibal than the loss of Salapia;[180] never after that did the Carthaginian enjoy superiority in cavalry, in which he had earlier been by far the stronger.

39. Per idem tempus cum in arce Tarentina vix inopia tolerabilis esset, spem omnem praesidium quod ibi erat Romanum praefectusque praesidii atque arcis M. Livius
2 in commeatibus ab Sicilia missis habebant; qui ut tuto praeterveherentur oram Italiae, classis viginti ferme na-
3 vium Regii stabat. praeerat classi commeatibusque D. Quinctius, obscuro genere ortus, ceterum multis fortibus
4 factis militari gloria inlustris. primo quinque naves, qua-rum maximae duae triremes a Marcello ei traditae erant, habuit;[81] postea rem impigre saepe gerenti tres additae
5 quinqueremes. postremo ipse a sociis Reginisque et a Velia et a Paesto debitas ex foedere exigendo classem vi-ginti navium, sicut ante dictum est, effecit.[82]

6 Huic ab Regio profectae classi Democrates cum pari navium Tarentinarum numero quindecim milia ferme
7 ab urbe ad Sapriportem obvius fuit. velis tum forte im-providus futuri certaminis Romanus veniebat, sed circa Crotonem Sybarimque suppleverat remigio naves, in-structamque et amatam egregie pro magnitudine navium
8 classem habebat; et tum forte sub idem tempus et venti vis omnis cecidit et hostes in conspectu fuere, ut ad com-ponenda armamenta expediendumque remigem ac mili-tem ad imminens certamen satis temporis esset.

---

[81] habuit *P*: *del. Duker*   [82] effecit Δ: efficit *P*

---

[181] Perhaps M. Livius Macatus; cf. Walbank 2.102.

[182] Rhegium: *Barr.* 46 C5; Velia and Paestum: 45 B4.

[183] He is given no introduction but may be the naval officer Democrates killed with Nico when Tarentum was later retaken in 209 by the Romans (27.16.1–3).

[184] *Barr.* 46 F3 (Croton); D2 (Sybaris). Sybaris was destroyed

39. At this same time, since food shortages in the citadel of Tarentum were hardly tolerable, the Roman garrison there and Marcus Livius, commander[181] of the garrison and citadel, had all their hope focused on provisions sent from Sicily; and, to safeguard the transportation along the Italian coastline, a fleet of some twenty ships was riding at anchor at Rhegium. In charge of the fleet and the provisions was Decimus Quinctius who despite his undistinguished background had an outstanding military record from many brave exploits. He had five ships at first, the largest being two triremes put under him by Marcellus; later, because of his energetic conduct on many occasions, three quinqueremes were added. Finally, by requisitioning himself ships due under treaty from the allies Rhegium, Velia, and Paestum,[182] he built up a fleet of twenty ships (as noted above).

This fleet, setting off from Rhegium, was confronted with a similar number of Tarentine vessels by Democrates[183] at Sapriportis, some fifteen miles from the city of Tarentum. The Roman commander happened then to be advancing under sail, not expecting a fight ahead, but near Croton and Sybaris[184] he had taken on board a full complement of oarsmen and was in possession of a fleet extremely well equipped and well armed, given the size of its vessels. Then it so happened that the wind completely dropped and the enemy came into view at the same moment, giving Quinctius no time to stow the rigging and get his oarsmen and fighters ready for the impending engagement.

in 510, and the town of Thurii (cf. 25.7.11 and note) was later founded nearby. It is to this that Livy refers but uses the old name, though Thurii occurs later in the chapter (18, below).

9   Raro alias tantis animis iustae concurrerunt classes,
quippe cum in maioris discrimen rei quam ipsae erant
10 pugnarent, Tarentini ut reciperata urbe ab Romanis post
centesimum prope annum, arcem etiam liberarent, spe
commeatus quoque hostibus si navali proelio posses-
11 sionem maris ademissent interclusuros, Romani ut retenta
possessione arcis ostenderent non vi ac virtute sed proditione ac furto Tarentum amissum.

12   Itaque ex utraque parte signo dato cum rostris concurrissent, neque retro navem inhiberent nec dirimi ab se
host<il>em[83] paterentur quam quis indeptus navem erat
ferrea iniecta manu, ita conserebant ex propinquo pugnam ut non missilibus tantum sed gladiis etiam prope con-
13 lato pede gereretur res. prorae inter se iunctae haerebant;
puppes alieno remigio circumagebantur. ita in arto stipa-
tae erant naves ut vix ullum telum in mare[84] vanum inter-
cideret; frontibus velut pedestres acies urgebant, perviae-
que naves pugnantibus erant.

14   Insignis tamen inter ceteras pugna fuit duarum quae
15 primae agminum concurrerant inter se. in Romana nave
ipse Quinctius erat, in Tarentina Nico cui Perconi fuit
cognomen, non publico modo sed privato etiam odio invisus atque infestus Romanis quod eius factionis erat quae
16 Tarentum Hannibali prodiderat. hic Quinctium simul

[83] host<il>em *Luchs*
[84] mare *dett.*: mari *P*

---

[185] Actually, fifty-nine to sixty years; it was captured by the
Romans in 272.
[186] Possibly *perkos*, a kind of hawk mentioned by Aristotle
(*Hist. an.* 9.36.1).

Rarely have conventional fleets clashed with such fe-
rocity, for they were fighting to decide something greater
than their own fate. The Tarentines, with their city now
recovered from the Romans after nearly a century,[185] were
fighting to liberate its citadel, too, and also hoping to cut
their enemy's supply line by depriving him of dominance
at sea with a naval battle; and the Romans, having retained
possession of the citadel, were fighting to show that their
loss of Tarentum had been brought about not by force and
courage but by treachery and deceit.

Thus, with the signal given on both sides, the vessels
charged each other with their prows and did not back
water or allow the enemy ship to disengage; rather, throwing grappling irons onto any ship they encountered, they
engaged at such close quarters that it became almost
hand-to-hand fighting at the same moment, a battle fought
not so much with projectiles as with swords. Prows remained stationary, locked together, and sterns were being
swung round by the enemy vessel's oars. So closely grouped
were the ships that hardly any weapon landed harmlessly
in the sea between them; and they pushed against each
other front to front like lines of infantry, with the fighters
able to move from ship to ship.

An engagement standing out from all the others, however, was one between two ships that had clashed at the
head of their lines. In the Roman vessel was Quinctius himself, and in the Tarentine was Nico (surnamed
Perco),[186] who loathed the Romans and was in turn de-
tested by them, the animosity being as much a personal as
it was a public matter, for he belonged to the faction that
had betrayed Tarentum to Hannibal. As Quinctius was
fighting and simultaneously urging on his men, this man

pugnantem hortantemque suos incautum hasta transfigit.
17 ille ut praeceps cum armis procidit ante proram, victor
Tarentinus in turbatam duce amisso navem impigre transgressus cum summovisset hostes et prora iam Tarentinorum esset, puppim male conglobati tuerentur Romani,
18 repente et alia a puppe triremis hostium apparuit. ita in
medio circumventa Romana navis capitur. hinc ceteris terror iniectus ubi praetoriam navem captam videre, fugien-
tesque passim aliae in alto mersae, aliae in terram remis
19 abreptae mox praedae fuere Thurinis Metapontinisque. ex
onerariis quae cum commeatu sequebantur perpaucae in
potestatem hostium venere; aliae ad incertos ventos hinc
atque illinc obliqua transferentes vela in altum evectae
sunt.
20   Nequaquam pari fortuna per eos dies Tarenti res gesta.
nam ad quattuor milia hominum frumentatum egressa
21 cum in agris passim vagarentur, Livius qui arci prae-
sidioque Romano praeerat intentus in omnes occasiones
gerendae rei, C. Persium impigrum virum cum duobus
22 milibus et ⟨quingentis⟩[85] armatorum ex arce emisit. qui
vage effusos per agros palatosque adortus cum diu passim
cecidisset, paucos ex multis trepida fuga incidentes semi-
apertis portarum foribus in urbem compulit, ⟨neque
23 multum afuit quin⟩[86] urbs eodem impetu caperetur. ita

[85] ⟨quingentis⟩ *Alschefski*
[86] ⟨nec (neque *C-J*) multum afuit quin⟩ *Alschefski*

[187] Both cities had abandoned Rome for Hannibal in 212
(25.15.4–17). Thurii: *Barr.* 46 D2; Metapontum: 45 F4.
[188] That is, for the Tarentines.

caught him off guard and ran him through. When the man, together with his weapons, fell headlong in front of the prow, the victorious Tarentine leaped nimbly over to the Roman ship, now in confusion after the loss of its commander. He pushed his enemy back and, when the prow was now in Tarentine hands and the Romans, all crowded together, were having little success defending the stern, a second enemy trireme also suddenly appeared astern. Thus, caught between the two, the Roman vessel was captured. With that, on seeing the flagship taken, the other ships were panic-stricken, and fleeing in all directions some were sunk on the open sea and others, hurriedly rowing to shore, soon became plunder for the people of Thurii and Metapontum.[187] Of the freighters that were following with supplies very few fell into the enemy's hands; others, orienting their sails one way or another to catch the shifting winds, sailed out to the open sea.

The fighting at Tarentum during that period went nothing like as well for them.[188] About four thousand men who had left on a foraging expedition were wandering at large through the fields when Livius, who was in command of the citadel and the Roman garrison and on the lookout for any opportunity, dispatched an energetic officer, Gaius Persius, against them from the citadel with an armed force of twenty-five hundred. Attacking the foragers as they drifted widely dispersed through the fields, and for a long time cutting them down everywhere, he drove the large force's few survivors into the city through its half-open gates in panic-stricken flight; and the city was not far from being taken in that same attack. Thus things remained on

aequatae res ad Tarentum, Romanis ‹terra, Tarentinis›[87]
victoribus mari. frumenti spes quae in oculis fuerat utros-
que frustrata pariter.

40. Per idem tempus Laevinus consul iam magna parte
anni circumacta in Siciliam veteribus novisque sociis ex-
spectatus cum venisset, primum ac potissimum omnium
ratus Syracusis nova pace inconditas componere res,
2 Agrigentum inde, quod belli reliquum erat tenebaturque
a Carthaginiensium valido praesidio, duxit legiones. et
adfuit fortuna incepto.

3 Hanno erat imperator Carthaginiensium, sed omnem
4 in Muttine Numidisque spem repositam habebant. per
totam Siciliam vagus praedas agebat ex sociis Romanorum, neque intercludi ab Agrigento vi aut arte ulla nec
5 quin erumperet ubi vellet prohiberi poterat. haec eius
gloria quia iam imperatoris quoque famae officiebat postremo in invidiam vertit, ut ne bene gestae quidem res iam
6 Hannoni propter auctorem satis laetae essent. postremo
praefecturam eius filio suo dedit, ratus cum imperio
auctoritatem quoque ei inter Numidas erepturum.

7 Quod longe aliter evenit. nam veterem favorem eius
sua insuper invidia auxit; neque ille indignitatem iniuriae
tulit confestimque ad Laevinum occultos nuntios misit de
8 tradendo Agrigento. per quos ut est facta fides compositus-
que rei gerendae modus, portam ad mare ferentem Nu-

---

[87] ‹terra, Tarentinis› *ed. Mediol 1505*: ‹terra, Carthaginiensibus› *C-J*

---

[189] On Muttines, cf. 21.15 and note, above.

a par at Tarentum, the Romans victorious on land and the Tarentines at sea. The hope of the grain that they had been eying eluded both.

40. At this same time, with most of the year already gone, the consul Laevinus arrived in Sicily, his coming awaited by allies old and new; and thinking his first and most urgent priority to be settling the disorder still reigning in Syracuse in the early days of peace, he led his legions to Agrigentum, which represented the last phase of the war and was being held by a strong Carthaginian force. And fortune attended his enterprise.

Hanno was the commander of the Carthaginians, but they really had all their hopes pinned on Muttines and the Numidians.[189] Roving throughout Sicily, Muttines kept carrying off plunder from Roman allies, and neither by force nor by any other means could he be cut off from Agrigentum or prevented from making forays from that town whenever he chose. The man's celebrity, because it had already also been eclipsing the commander's reputation, eventually aroused such resentment in Hanno that even success brought him little pleasure because of the person responsible for it. Finally, he transferred command to his own son, believing that he would thus take from him his standing among the Numidians, along with the command.

It turned out very differently. The support he had long enjoyed was only increased by Hanno's own unpopularity; Muttines did not accept the undeserved slight, either, and he immediately sent undercover agents to Laevinus about handing over Agrigentum. After mutual confidence was established through these men and a plan of action drawn up, the Numidians seized the gate facing the sea, expelling

151

midae cum occupassent pulsis inde custodibus aut caesis,
9 Romanos ad id ipsum missos in urbem acceperunt. et cum
agmine iam in media urbis ac forum magno tumultu iretur,
ratus Hanno non aliud quam tumultum ac secessionem, id
quod et ante acciderat, Numidarum esse, ad compri-
10 mendam seditionem processit. atque ille cum ei multitudo
maior quam Numidarum procul visa ‹esset›[88] et clamor
Romanus haudquaquam ignotus ad aures accidisset,
11 priusquam ad ictum teli veniret capessit fugam. per aver-
sam portam emissus adsumpto comite Epicyde cum paucis ad mare pervenit; nactique opportune parvum navi-
gium, relicta hostibus Sicilia de qua per tot annos certatum
12 erat, in Africam traiecerunt. alia multitudo Poenorum
Siculorumque ne temptato quidem certamine, cum caeci
in fugam ruerent clausique exitus essent, circa portas
13 caesa. oppido recepto Laevinus qui capita rerum Agrigenti
erant virgis caesos securi percussit, ceteros praedamque
vendidit; omnem pecuniam Romam misit.
14   Fama Agrigentinorum cladis Siciliam cum pervasisset,
omnia repente ad Romanos inclinaverunt. prodita brevi
sunt viginti oppida, sex vi capta; voluntaria deditione in
15 fidem venerunt ad quadraginta. quarum civitatium principibus cum pro cuiusque merito consul pretia poenasque
exsolvisset, coegissetque Siculos positis tandem armis
16 ad agrum colendum animos convertere, ut esset non incolarum modo alimentis frugifera insula sed urbis Romae

[88] ‹esset› *anon.*

or killing the guards, and accepted into the city some Romans sent specifically for that purpose. When these went in a column into the town center and forum with a great commotion, Hanno thought it no more than a noisy protest by the Numidian troops, something that had also occurred earlier, and he went forth to calm the disturbance. But there, after a crowd too large to be the Numidians was sighted in the distance, and Roman shouting that was by no means unfamiliar to him came to his ears, he ran off before coming within weapon range. Slipping away through a back gate and taking Epicydes along with him, he reached the sea with a few men. There, fortuitously coming upon a small sailing vessel, and leaving to their enemy Sicily, for which they had fought for so many years, they crossed to Africa. The remaining horde of Carthaginians and Sicilians rushed off in blind flight without even attempting resistance, and finding the exits blocked they were killed near the gates. Taking possession of the town, Laevinus flogged and beheaded those in charge at Agrigentum, and the rest he sold off with the booty. All money there he sent to Rome.

When news of the Agrigentines' defeat spread throughout Sicily, there was suddenly a complete shift to the Romans. Twenty cities were soon betrayed, six more taken by force, and some forty came under Roman protection through voluntary surrender. To the leading men of these communities the consul meted out such rewards and punishments as each deserved, and he forced the Sicilians to finally lay down their arms and turn their attention to farming the land (not only to make their island fertile enough to support its inhabitants, but also so it could alleviate grain supply difficulties for the city of Rome and

atque Italiae—id quod multis saepe tempestatibus fecerat—annonam levaret, ab Agathyrna inconditam multitu-
17 dinem secum in Italiam transvexit. quattuor milia hominum erant, mixti ex omni conluvione exsules obaerati,
capitalia ausi plerique et[89] cum in civitatibus suis ac sub
legibus vixerant, et postquam eos ex variis causis fortuna
similis conglobaverat Agathyrnam per latrocinia ac rapi-
18 nam tolerantes vitam. hos neque relinquere Laevinus in
insula tum primum nova pace coalescente velut materiam
novandis rebus satis tutum ratus est, et Reginis usui futuri
erant ad populandum Bruttium agrum adsuetam latroci-
niis quaerentibus manum. et quod ad Siciliam attinet eo
anno debellatum est.

41. In Hispania principio veris P. Scipio, navibus deductis evocatisque edicto Tarraconem sociorum auxiliis,
classem onerariasque ostium inde Hiberi fluminis petere
2 iubet. eodem legiones ex hibernis convenire cum iussisset,
ipse cum quinque milibus sociorum ab Tarracone profectus ad exercitum est. quo cum venisset adloquendos maxime veteres milites qui tantis superfuerunt cladibus ratus,
contione advocata ita disseruit.

---

[89] et cum *P*: cum *Madvig*

---

[190] Cf. 27.5.5, where Laevinus, informing the senate of the
Carthaginians' expulsion from Sicily, boasts that its land was once
more Rome's most dependable source of grain.   [191] Port on
the northeast coast of Sicily: *Barr.* 47 F2 (Agathyrnum).

[192] Cf. Polyb. 9.27.11–12, who says that Laevinus promises
the Agathyrnians personal security on condition that they plunder
Bruttium, for which they would be paid by the people of Rhegium
and also allowed to keep the booty.

Italy, something it had often done in the past),[190] and he then crossed to Italy, taking with him a disorderly crowd from Agathyrna.[191] This comprised four thousand men, a ragtag bunch of all sorts of unsavory individuals—exiles, debtors, and many who had committed capital offenses (even when living in their own communities and under their own laws) and who, after similar fortunes had for various reasons concentrated them at Agathyrna, had been supporting themselves by robbery and pillage. Laevinus did not feel it very safe to leave them behind on an island just then achieving unity under the new peace, since they would provide fuel for revolution; and they would also be of service to the people of Rhegium, who were searching for a band of men experienced in robbery for raids on the territory of Bruttium.[192] And as far as Sicily is concerned the war ended that year.

41. In Spain Publius Scipio launched his ships at the start of spring,[193] summoned the allied auxiliaries to Tarraco by edict, and ordered the fleet and transport vessels to head from there to the mouth of the River Ebro. Ordering the legions to muster in this same location on leaving winter quarters, he himself set off from Tarraco with five thousand allied troops to join the army. On arriving there, and thinking he should make an address—especially to the veteran soldiers who had survived such terrible defeats— he called an assembly and spoke as follows:[194]

---

[193] Livy is here at fault in placing the following chapters relating to the capture of New Carthage in 210 instead of in 209.

[194] Livy has, as often, greatly expanded the speech found in Polybius 10.6.2–6.

3   "Nemo ante me novus imperator militibus suis priusquam opera eorum usus esset gratias agere iure ac merito
4 potuit; me vobis priusquam provinciam aut castra viderem
obligavit fortuna, primum quod ea pietate erga patrem
5 patruumque meum vivos mortuosque fuistis, deinde quod
amissam tanta clade provinciae possessionem integram et
populo Romano et successori mihi virtute vestra obtinuis-
6 tis. sed cum iam benignitate deum id paremus atque aga-
mus non ut ipsi maneamus in Hispania sed ne Poeni maneant, nec ut pro ripa Hiberi stantes arceamus transitu
hostes sed ut ultro transeamus transferamusque bellum,
7 vereor ne cui vestrum maius id audaciusque consilium
quam aut pro memoria cladium nuper acceptarum aut pro
8 aetate mea videatur. adversae pugnae in Hispania nullius
in animo quam meo minus oblitterari possunt, quippe cui
pater et patruus intra triginta dierum spatium, ut aliud
super aliud cumularetur familiae nostrae funus, interfecti
9 sunt; sed ut familiaris paene orbitas ac solitudo frangit
animum, ita publica cum fortuna tum virtus desperare de
summa rerum prohibet. ea fato quodam data nobis sors
est, ut magnis omnibus bellis victi vicerimus.
10   "Vetera omitto, Porsennam Gallos Samnites; a Punicis
bellis incipiam. quot classes, quot duces, quot exercitus
priore bello amissi sunt! iam quid hoc bello memorem?
11 omnibus aut ipse adfui cladibus aut, quibus afui, maxime
unus omnium eas sensi. Trebia Trasumennus Cannae quid

---

195 Lars Porsenna, king of Clusium (*Barr.* 42 B2), besieged
Rome in the early days of the republic in an effort to reestablish
the exiled last king, Tarquinius Superbus; wars with the Gauls
were frequent from the early fourth century; and the Samnite
wars occurred in the second half of the fourth century.

"No new commander prior to me has been able to give his soldiers due and well-earned thanks before using their services. In my case, fortune put me in your debt even before I set eyes on my province or my camp, first because you showed such devotion to my father and uncle both when they were alive and dead, and then because of your valor in keeping secure, both for the Roman people and for me, their successor, a province that had been lost by so momentous a defeat. But since, through heaven's blessing, our preparations and actions are focused not on ourselves remaining in Spain but on seeing that the Carthaginians do *not* remain, and focused not on standing before the banks of the Ebro to prevent the enemy crossing but actually on our crossing and transferring the war to the other side, I fear that this plan might seem to any of you too great and too foolhardy in light of the recent defeats and my age. The battles lost in Spain can be erased from no one's mind less easily than mine, what with my father and uncle both killed within thirty days of each other, so that for our family there was one funeral after another; but though being left with almost no family daunts the spirit, the good fortune and valor of our commonwealth both forbid me to despair of the final outcome. Granted us by some divine providence, our destiny in all our major wars is to emerge victorious even after defeat.

"Old examples I pass over—Porsenna, the Gauls, the Samnites;[195] I shall start with the Punic Wars. How many fleets, how many generals, how many armies were lost in the earlier war! And now what am I to say of this war? In all its defeats I was either present myself or, if not present, I felt them more deeply than anyone. Trebia, Trasimene,

aliud sunt quam monumenta occisorum exercituum con-
12 sulumque Romanorum? adde defectionem Italiae maioris
partis,[90] Siciliae, Sardiniae; adde ultimum terrorem ac
pavorem, castra Punica inter Anienem ac moenia Romana
posita et visum prope in portis victorem Hannibalem. in
hac ruina rerum stetit una integra atque immobilis virtus
populi Romani; haec omnia strata humi erexit ac sustulit.
13 "Vos omnium primi, milites, post Cannensem cladem
vadenti Hasdrubali ad Alpes Italiamque, qui si se cum
fratre coniunxisset nullum iam nomen esset populi Romani, ductu auspicioque patris mei obstitistis; et hae se-
14 cundae res illas adversas sustinuerunt. nunc benignitate
deum omnia secunda prospera in dies laetiora ac meliora
15 in Italia Siciliaque geruntur. in Sicilia Syracusae Agrigentum captum, pulsi tota insula hostes, receptaque provincia
in dicionem populi Romani est. in Italia Arpi recepti,
16 Capua capta; iter omne ab urbe Roma trepida fuga emen-
sus Hannibal, in extremum angulum agri Bruttii compul-
sus nihil iam maius precatur deos quam ut incolumi ce-
17 dere atque abire ex hostium terra liceat. Quid igitur minus
conveniat, milites, quam cum aliae super alias clades cu-
mularentur ac di prope ipsi cum Hannibale starent, vos
hic cum parentibus meis—aequentur enim etiam honore
nominis—sustinuisse labantem fortunam populi Romani,
nunc eosdem cum iam illic omnia secunda laetaque sunt

---

[90] Italiae maioris partis, Siciliae *Forchhammer*: Italiae, Siciliae maioris partis *P*

---

[196] *Barr.* 45 C1.
[197] A reference to the joint command of Scipio's father and
uncle in Spain (cf. 25.3.6).

Cannae—what else are they but a history of massacred Roman armies and consuls? Add the defection of most of Italy, Sicily, Sardinia; add the sheer terror and panic of a Punic camp pitched between the Anio and the walls of Rome, and the sight of a victorious Hannibal almost at its gates. In this collapse all that stood unimpaired and unshakeable was the courage of the Roman people; this was what restored and revived everything that had collapsed.

"When Hasdrubal was making for the Alps and Italy after the Cannae disaster—and had he linked up with his brother, the name of Rome would no longer exist—you, men, were the very first to oppose him, under my father's leadership and *auspices*; and this success compensated for that earlier failure. Now, through heaven's blessing, all goes well and smoothly in Italy and Sicily, the situation better and brighter every day. In Sicily, Syracuse and Agrigentum have been taken, the enemy entirely driven from the island, and the province again brought under the sway of the Roman people. In Italy, Arpi[196] has been recovered and Capua taken; after making the whole journey from the city of Rome in panic-stricken flight, Hannibal has been pushed back into the farthest corner of Bruttian territory and is begging the gods for nothing more than to be allowed a safe retreat and withdrawal from his enemies' land. So, men, when defeats were being piled on defeats and the gods themselves were almost standing alongside Hannibal, and you joined my parents here (let them be honored equally with that title)[197] in shoring up the tottering fortunes of the Roman people, what could be more irrational than that you, those very same men, should now lack confidence when all goes well and successfully over

18 animis deficere? nuper quoque quae acciderunt—utinam
tam sine meo luctu quam ⟨. . .⟩

"Nunc di[91] immortales imperii Romani praesides qui
centuriis omnibus ut mihi imperium iuberent dari fuere
auctores, idem auguriis auspiciisque et per nocturnos
19 etiam visus omnia laeta ac prospera portendunt. animus
quoque meus, maximus mihi ad hoc tempus vates, prae-
sagit nostram Hispaniam esse, brevi extorre hinc omne
Punicum nomen maria terrasque foeda fuga impleturum.
20 quod mens sua sponte divinat, idem subicit ratio haud
fallax. vexati ab iis socii nostram fidem per legatos implo-
rant. tres duces discordantes prope ut defecerint alii ab
aliis trifariam exercitus[92] in diversissimas regiones di-
21 straxere. eadem in illos ingruit fortuna quae nuper nos
adflixit. nam et deseruntur ab sociis ut prius ab Celtiberis
nos, et diduxere exercitus, quae patri patruoque meo
22 causa exitii fuit; nec discordia intestina coire eos in unum
sinet, neque singuli nobis resistere poterunt. vos modo,
milites, favete nomini Scipionum, suboli imperatorum
23 vestrorum velut accisis recrescenti stirpibus. agite, veteres
milites, novum exercitum novumque ducem traducite
Hiberum, traducite in terras cum multis fortibus factis
24 saepe a vobis peragratas. brevi faciam ut quemadmodum

---

[91] nunc di . . . 43.8 Africa Σ: *om. P; v. Reeve, RFIC 114 (1986), 146–48*

[92] exercitus A^c: exercitum *Sp*

---

[198] There is a long lacuna in P at this point, extending to 43.8, but most of the missing text is preserved by manuscripts transmitting the Spirensian tradition (see Introduction to vol. V).

[199] Livy has already referred to Scipio's use of visions for cle-

there in Italy? I wish, too, that what happened recently were, for me, as free from grief . . .[198]

"The immortal gods, protectors of the Roman empire, who prompted all the centuries to authorize command to be vested in me, now also foretell by augury, *auspices,* and even nightly visions,[199] that all will go well and successfully. My intuition (until now my best forecaster) also portends that Spain is ours, and that the whole Punic race will soon be driven from here to cover sea and land in disgraceful flight. What my mind instinctively predicts is further supported by clear reasoning. Ill-treated by them, their allies beg for our protection through legates.[200] Their three commanders, squabbling almost to the point of mutiny, have drawn their armies away from each other in three directions into widely separated areas of the country. The same bad luck that recently afflicted us is now descending on them. For they, too, are being abandoned by their allies, as were we earlier by the Celtiberians,[201] and they have also divided their armies, which was what caused the deaths of my father and uncle. Internal conflicts will not allow them to coalesce, and individually they will not be able to resist us. Just give your support to the Scipio name, men, to the offspring of your commanders, like one growing again from stumps that were pruned. Come on, you seasoned soldiers, take your new army and new leader over the Ebro; take them over into lands often traversed by you with many heroic deeds. Just as you now recognize

verly presenting himself as divinely inspired and not denying the widespread belief in his divine birth (19.3–8, above).

[200] A claim also made by Scipio in Polybius (10.6.3–4, 34.8).

[201] They were bribed by Hasdrubal (25.33.1–9).

nunc noscitatis in me patris patruique similitudinem oris
25 voltusque et lineamenta corporis, ita ingenii fidei virtutis-
que exemplum effigiem[93] vobis reddam ut revixisse aut
renatum sibi quisque Scipionem imperatorem dicat."

42. Hac oratione accensis militum animis, relicto ad
praesidium regionis eius M. Silano cum tribus milibus peditum et trecentis equitibus, ceteras omnes copias—erant
autem viginti quinque milia peditum, duo milia quingenti
2 equites—Hiberum traiecit. ibi quibusdam suadentibus ut,
quoniam in tres tam diversas regiones discessissent Punici
exercitus, proximum adgrederetur, periculum esse ratus
ne eo facto in unum omnes contraheret nec par unus esset
3 tot exercitibus, Carthaginem Novam interim oppugnare
statuit, urbem cum ipsam opulentam suis opibus tum hostium omni bellico apparatu plenam—ibi arma, ibi pecu-
4 nia, ibi totius Hispaniae obsides erant—sitam praeterea
cum opportune ad traiciendum in Africam tum super portum satis amplum quantaevis classi, et nescio an unum in
Hispaniae ora qua nostro adiacet mari.
5   Nemo omnium quo iretur sciebat praeter C. Laelium.
is classe circummissus ita moderari cursum navium iussus

---

93 exemplum effigiem Σ: exemplum ‹ac› effigiem *Sig.*: exemplum ‹et› effigiem *Walsh*

---

202 M. Junius Silanus: cf. 19.10 and note, above.
203 Modern Cartagena. Scipio learned of the town's importance and the nature of its lagoon in the winter of 210–9 and spent
the rest of it preparing to attack it (Polyb. 10.8.1–10). Its lagoon,
which would prove of paramount importance for the attack, "will
have occupied the site of the modern marshy plain of Almajar"
(Walbank 2.208).

in me a similarity to my father and my uncle in face, expression, and physical features—just so shall I shortly see to it that I also exemplify and reflect their character, loyalty, and valor, making every one of you declare his general Scipio has been revived or reborn."

42. After rallying his men with this address, Scipio, leaving Marcus Silanus[202] to safeguard the region with three thousand infantry and three hundred cavalry, crossed the Ebro with the rest of his troops (they were twenty-five thousand infantry and twenty-five hundred cavalry). There, since the Punic armies had withdrawn into three widely separated regions, some pressed him to attack the closest one, but Scipio thought that in that lay danger of making them all come together and that his single force would be no match for so many armies. He therefore decided for the present to attack New Carthage,[203] a city rich from its own resources and also full of all kinds of enemy military equipment—there lay their arsenal, there their treasury and there their hostages from all over Spain—and it was also well situated for crossing to Africa, had the further advantage of overlooking a harbor large enough for a fleet of any size, and was possibly the only one on the coastline of Spain facing our sea.[204]

Absolutely no one knew the army's destination apart from Gaius Laelius.[205] He, sent around the coast with the

---

[204] The Mediterranean. The expression "overlooking a harbor" might suggest a hill city, but Polybius (10.10.7–11) correctly observes that the city is in fact surrounded by hills.

[205] He would become a close friend of Scipio, whose support ensured him a successful career: quaestor (202); plebeian aedile (197); praetor (196); consul (190). cf. *OCD* s.v. Laelius (1).

erat ut eodem tempore Scipio ab terra exercitum
6 ostenderet et classis portum intraret. septimo die ab Hibero Carthaginem ventum est simul terra marique. castra
ab regione urbis qua in septentrionem versa est posita; his
ab tergo—nam frons natura tuta erat—vallum obiectum.
7 Etenim sita Carthago sic est. sinus est maris media
ferme Hispaniae ora maxime Africo vento oppositus, ad
duo milia et quingentos passus introrsus retractus, paululo
plus passuum mille et ducentos in latitudinem patens.
8 huius in ostio sinus parva insula obiecta ab alto portum ab
omnibus ventis praeterquam Africo tutum facit. ab intimo
sinu paeneinsula excurrit; tumulus is ipse, in quo condita
urbs est, ab ortu solis et a meridie cincta mari. ab occasu
stagnum claudit paulum etiam ad septentrionem fusum,
incertae altitudinis utcumque exaestuat aut deficit mare.
9 continenti urbem iugum ducentos ferme et quinquaginta
passus patens coniungit. unde cum tam parvi operis muni-
tio esset, non obiecit vallum imperator Romanus, seu fiduciam hosti superbe ostentans sive ut subeunti saepe ad
moenia urbis recursus pateret.
43. Cetera quae munienda erant cum perfecisset,
naves etiam in portu velut maritimam quoque ostentans

---

[206] Six by Roman inclusive counting, though Jal and De Selin-
court take *septimo* (seventh) as seven (so also Walbank 2.204–5),
but even that is unrealistic for an army covering the distance
between the Ebro and New Carthage, which was 2,600 stades
(325 miles) according to Polybius (3.39.6).

[207] Literally, "facing the African wind," that is, the Scirocco,
which blows from the south or the southeast. Livy's description
of the town seems less accurate than that of Polybius (10.10), who
claims autopsy (10.11.4). Cf. Walbank 2.205–13 (with map).

fleet, had been ordered to so regulate his ships' speed that Scipio would appear with his army on land at the same time as Laelius' fleet would be entering the harbor. The land and sea journeys from the Ebro to New Carthage were both completed in six days.[206] A camp was set up on the north-facing side of the city, and an earth-work created to secure its rear, for the front was protected by its natural features.

Now the site of New Carthage is as follows. About half way down the coast of Spain is a bay facing mainly southwest,[207] receding inland about two and a half miles, and slightly more than twelve hundred paces wide. At the entrance to this bay a small island forms a barrier on the seaward side, keeping the harbor sheltered from all winds except the southwesterly. From the deepest recesses of the bay a peninsula runs out; and it is right on this higher ground that the city is built, its eastern and southern sections surrounded by the sea. To the west, access is blocked by a lagoon that also runs in a slightly northerly direction, its depth varying according to the rise and fall of the tide. A causeway roughly two hundred and fifty paces wide connects the city to the mainland. Although constructing one would have taken such little work, the Roman commander did not throw up a protective barrier on it, either brashly displaying his confidence to his enemy or so as to have a way back from frequent forays to the city walls.[208]

43. After completing the other necessary fortifications, Scipio also deployed his ships in the harbor as though

[208] Polybius (10.11.2–3) gives Scipio the same motivation for dispensing with any fortification.

obsidionem instruxit; circumvectusque classem cum monuisset praefectos navium ut vigilias nocturnas intenti servarent—omnia ubique primo obsessum hostem conari—, regressus in castra ut consilii sui rationem, quod ab urbe potissimum oppugnanda bellum orsus esset, militibus ostenderet et spem potiundae cohortando faceret, contione advocata ita disseruit.

3 "Ad urbem unam oppugnandam si quis vos adductos credit, is magis operis vestri quam emolumenti rationem exactam, milites, habet; oppugnabitis enim vere moenia unius urbis, sed in una urbe universam ceperitis Hispaniam. hic sunt obsides omnium nobilium regum populorumque, qui simul in potestate vestra erunt, extemplo omnia quae nunc sub Carthaginiensibus sunt in dicionem tradent. hic pecunia omnis hostium, sine qua neque illi gerere bellum possunt quippe qui mercenarios exercitus alant, et quae nobis maximo usui ad conciliandos animos barbarorum erit. hic tormenta armamenta arma, omnis apparatus belli est qui simul et vos instruet et hostes nudabit. potiemur praeterea cum pulcherrima opulentissimaque urbe tum opportunissima portu egregio, unde terra marique quae belli usus poscunt suppeditentur; quae cum magna ipsi habebimus tum dempserimus hostibus multo maiora. haec illis arx, hoc horreum aerarium armamentarium, hoc omnium rerum receptaculum est.

signaling that there was also a naval blockade in force; and sailing around the fleet he warned the ships' captains to maintain strict night watch—when first under siege, an enemy tried all sorts of tactics everywhere, he said—and then he returned to camp to explain to the soldiers his rationale for starting the campaign with an attack especially on the city, and also, with words of encouragement, to give them hope of taking it. Then, calling an assembly, he delivered an address as follows:

"Any of you thinking you have been brought here for an attack on only one city is more correct about the effort you face than the benefit forthcoming; you will, it is true, be attacking the walls of one city, but with that one city you will have captured all of Spain. Here are the hostages from all their important kings and peoples; and once they are in your power they will immediately put in your hands everything now under the Carthaginians. Here lies all of the enemy's money, without which they cannot conduct a war since they maintain mercenary armies, and you will find that money *very* useful for gaining support from the barbarians. Here are their artillery, their arsenal, their weapons, and all their war apparatus, which will see you well-stocked and the enemy deprived. We shall in addition be taking possession of a city of great beauty and great wealth, one also having the great advantage of an excellent harbor through which everything that is needed for the war can be supplied by land and sea; and while we ourselves shall have these great assets we shall also have deprived the enemy of far greater ones. This is their stronghold, this their granary, their treasury, their armory—this is their warehouse for everything. Here is the terminus for

huc rectus ex Africa cursus est, haec una inter Pyrenaeum et Gades statio, hinc omni Hispaniae imminet Africa ‹. . .›"

44. ‹. . .› armaverat, cum terra marique instrui oppugnationem videret, et ipse copias ita disponit. oppidanorum duo milia ab ea parte qua castra Romana erant opponit; quingentis militibus arcem insidit, quingentos tumulo urbis in orientem verso imponit. multitudinem aliam quo clamor, quo subita vocasset res intentam ad omnia occurrere iubet. patefacta deinde porta eos quos in via ferente ad castra hostium instruxerat emittit. Romani duce ipso praecipiente parumper cessere ut propiores subsidiis in certamine ipso summittendis essent. et primo haud impares stetere acies; subsidia deinde identidem summissa e castris non averterunt solum in fugam hostes sed adeo effusis institerunt ut, nisi receptui cecinisset, permixti fugientibus inrupturi fuisse in urbem viderentur. Trepidatio vero non in proelio maior quam tota urbe fuit. multae stationes pavore atque fuga desertae sunt relictique muri, cum qua cuique erat proximum desilvissent. quod ubi egressus Scipio in tumulum quem Mercuri vocant animadvertit multis partibus nudata defensoribus moenia esse, omnes e castris excitos ire ad oppugnandam

---

209 The lines that follow here in some manuscripts are spurious. I follow Walsh, Conway, and Jal in assuming a lacuna containing the end of Scipio's speech and the start of the assault on the town. The lost section probably contained rewards promised to the men and Scipio's claim that Neptune had appeared to him in a dream (cf. Polyb. 10.11.6–7).

210 The subject of this sentence is lost in the lacuna. That it was Mago is inferred from 46.8, below.

211 Today the Castillo de los Moros (Walbank 2.208).

the direct crossing from Africa; this is their one anchorage between the Pyrenees and Gades; and it is from here that Africa threatens the whole of Spain . . ."[209]

44. . . . ‹Mago›[210] had given them arms, and when he saw preparations being made for a land and sea assault he also proceeded with his own troop deployment. He ranged two thousand of the town's inhabitants as a buffer on the side facing the Roman camp; and he garrisoned the citadel with five hundred men and set five hundred more on a hill in the eastern sector of the city. The large numbers remaining he ordered to be ready for any contingency, and to rush wherever any shouting or sudden emergency might call them. Then, throwing open the gate, he sent forth men that he had deployed on the roadway leading toward the enemy camp. The Romans, on instructions from the commander himself, gave way a little so as to be closer to reinforcements that were to be sent in during the actual combat. And at first both lines stood their ground not unevenly matched; then waves of reinforcements sent in time and again from the Roman camp not only turned the enemy to flight but also put such pressure on them as they scattered that, if Scipio had not sounded the recall, it looked as if the Romans would have broken into the city intermingled with the fugitives.

The consternation on the battlefield was actually no greater than that throughout the city. Many guard posts were abandoned in panic-stricken flight, and walls were deserted after soldiers leaped down by the shortest route any could find. When, on mounting a hillock they call the Hill of Mercury,[211] Scipio observed that the fortifications had been stripped of their defenders at many points, he ordered everyone to be called from the camp for an assault

7 urbem et ferre scalas iubet. ipse trium prae se iuvenum
validorum scutis oppositis—ingens enim iam vis omnis
generis telorum e muris volabat—ad urbem succedit. hor-
8 tatur, imperat quae in rem sunt; quod plurimum ad ac-
cendendos militum animos intererat, testis spectatorque
9 virtutis atque ignaviae cuiusque adest. itaque in volnera ac
tela ruunt, neque illos muri neque superstantes armati
10 arcere queunt quin certatim adscendant. et ab navibus
eodem tempore ea quae mari adluitur pars urbis oppugnari coepta est. ceterum tumultus inde maior quam vis
11 adhiberi poterat. dum adplicant, dum raptim exponunt
scalas, militesque dum qua cuique proximum est in terram
evadere properant, ipsa festinatione et certamine alii alios
impediunt.

45. Inter haec repleverat iam Poenus armatis muros, et
vis magna ex ingenti copia congesta telorum suppeditabat.
2 sed neque viri nec tela nec quicquam aliud aeque quam
moenia ipsa sese defendebant. rarae enim scalae altitudini
aequari poterant, et quo quaeque altiores, eo infirmiores
3 erant. itaque cum summus quisque evadere non posset,
subirent tamen alii, onere ipso frangebantur. quidam stantibus scalis cum altitudo caliginem oculis offudisset, ad
4 terram delati sunt. et cum passim homines scalaeque
ruerent, et ipso successu audacia atque alacritas hostium
5 cresceret, signum receptui datum est. quod spem non

---

212 This section ("He himself . . . everyone") closely follows
Polyb. 10.13.1–5.
213 The end of this chapter (from "At that same time") is absent from Polybius (who mentions no sailors), although Livy
closely follows the earlier parts.

on the town, and to bring ladders. He himself moved up to the city with three sturdy young men holding shields before him (for large numbers of weapons of all kinds were already flying from the walls). He gave such encouragement and orders as the situation required; and, what best served to fire the men's spirit, he was present as witness and observer of everyone's courage or lack of spirit.[212] And so they charged forward into wounds and missiles, and neither walls nor the soldiers standing on them could stop them racing to clamber up. At that same time, too, the part of the city bordered by the sea came under attack from the ships. There, however, it could only be a chaotic scramble, not application of real pressure. As they landed, as they hurriedly brought out ladders, and as soldiers scurried to clamber onto land by the quickest path, they were actually obstructing one another with their very haste and competitiveness.[213]

45. The Carthaginian commander had meanwhile replenished his walls with troops, and these were having large quantities of javelins from their immense arsenal put at their disposal. But neither men nor javelins nor anything else could provide such effective a defense as did the walls themselves. For ladders long enough to reach such a height were few, and the longer they were the weaker they were. Thus, when a man at the top could not surmount the wall and others were nevertheless climbing up behind, they would break simply from the weight put on them. In some cases ladders held firm, but men still fell to ground when the height produced dizzy spells. And when both men and ladders were dropping everywhere, and their enemy's confidence and enthusiasm were increasing with their success, the retreat was sounded. That gave the

171

praesentis modo ab tanto certamine ac labore quietis ob-
sessis, sed etiam in posterum dedit scalis et corona capi
urbem non posse; opera et difficilia esse et tempus datura
ad ferendam opem imperatoribus suis.

6   Vix prior tumultus conticuerat cum Scipio ab defessis
iam volneratisque recentes integrosque alios accipere sca-
7 las iubet et vi maiore adgredi urbem. ipse ut ei nuntiatum
est aestum decedere, quod per piscatores Tarraconenses
nunc levibus cumbis nunc, ubi eae siderent, vadis perva-
gatos stagnum compertum habebat facilem pedibus ad
murum transitum dari, eo secum armatos ‹quingentos›[94]
8 duxit. medium ferme diei erat, et ad id quod sua sponte
cedente in mare aestu trahebatur aqua, acer etiam septen-
trio ortus inclinatum stagnum eodem quo aestus ferebat,
et adeo nudaverat vada ut alibi umbilico tenus aqua esset,
9 alibi genua vix superaret. hoc cura ac ratione compertum
in prodigium ac deos vertens Scipio, qui ad transitum
Romanis mare verterent et stagna auferrent viasque ante
nunquam initas humano vestigio aperirent, Neptunum
iubebat ducem itineris sequi ac medio stagno evadere ad
moenia.

[94] ‹quingentos› *hic Weiss., post* eo *Crév.*

214 During the previous winter: cf. Polyb. 10.8.6–7.
215 The Mediterranean is not completely tideless. The same
phenomenon appears in the accounts of both Appian (*Hisp.* 21)
and Polybius (10.14.8).
216 On this exploitation of the divine by Scipio, cf. 19.6–8,
41.1, above; also Walbank 2.192–93, Levene *Religion*, 18–19,
61–62.

beleaguered citizens not only hope of a temporary break from the arduous struggle but also, for the future, hope that the city could not be taken by scaling ladders and encirclement, and that siege works would both be difficult and also give their commanders time to bring aid.

The commotion of the first attempt had barely died down when Scipio ordered men who were fresh and un-injured to take the ladders from those now exhausted and wounded and assault the city with greater vigor. He himself had been informed by fishermen of Tarraco[214] (who had explored the whole lagoon both with light boats and, when they ran aground, by wading through the shallows) that crossing to the city wall on foot was easy; and when he was told the tide was ebbing[215] he took a band of five hundred armed men there himself. It was about the middle of the day, and in addition to the fact that with the tide naturally ebbing seaward the water level was dropping anyway, a brisk north wind had arisen and was helping to sweep the receding waters of the lagoon in the same direction as the tide; and this had exposed shallow areas, so much so that at some points the water came up to the navel and at others barely to the knee. This Scipio had established by careful observation and reason, but he made it out to be a miracle and the work of the gods: to grant the Romans a passage, they were turning back the sea, he said—draining the lagoon and exposing paths never trodden by a human foot! And he bade them follow Neptune as their guide for the journey and reach the walls through the middle of the lagoon.[216]

46. Ab terra ingens labor succedentibus erat; nec altitudine tantum moenium impediebantur, sed quod coeuntes[95] ad ancipites utrimque ictus subiectos habebant Romanos, ut latera infestiora subeuntibus quam adversa

2 corpora essent. at parte alia[96] quingentis et per stagnum facilis transitus et in murum adscensus inde fuit; nam neque opere emunitus erat ut ubi ipsius loci ac stagni praesidio satis creditum foret, nec ulla armatorum statio aut custodia opposita, intentis omnibus ad opem eo ferendam unde periculum ostendebatur.

3 Ubi urbem sine certamine intravere, pergunt inde quanto maximo cursu poterant ad eam portam circa quam

4 omne contractum certamen erat. in quod adeo intenti omnium non animi solum fuere sed etiam oculi auresque pugnantium spectantiumque et adhortantium pugnantes,

5 ut nemo ante ab tergo senserit captam urbem quam tela in aversos inciderunt et utrimque ancipitem hostem habe-

6 bant. tunc turbatis defensoribus metu et moenia capta et porta intus forisque pariter refringi coepta, et mox caedendo confractis[97] ac distractis ne iter impediretur foribus

7 armati impetum fecerunt. magna multitudo et muros transcendebat, sed ii passim ad caedem oppidanorum versi; illa quae portam ingressa erat iusta acies cum ducibus, cum ordinibus media urbe in[98] forum processit.

8 Inde cum duobus itineribus fugientes videret hostes, alios ad tumulum in orientem versum qui tenebatur quin-

95 <co>euntes *Jal*: <ad>euntes *Gron.*
96 alia *Weiss.*: in alia *P*
97 confractis Σ: confectis *P*
98 in *P*: usque in Σ?

46. Those on the landward approach to the town faced enormous difficulty: it was not just by the height of the walls that their progress was impeded, but the enemy, rallying, now also had the Romans open to attack from both sides, so that as they moved forward they faced greater danger from the flanks than from the front. On the other side, however, crossing the lagoon and then climbing from there to the top of the wall was easier; for it was not fortified, since its very location on the lagoon was thought to offer protection, and there were neither armed sentries nor guard posts facing them—everyone was concentrating on bringing assistance to where there was clearly danger.

After entering the city without a fight, they headed as fast they could for the gate where all the fighting was concentrated. To that not only was everyone's attention attracted, but the eyes and ears of combatants, their spectators and their supporters were all so focused on it that no one realized the city had been taken to their rear until javelins rained down on their backs and they had the enemy on both sides of them. Then, the defenders being thrown into a panic, the walls were taken and a start also made on breaking down the gate, inside and out; and soon, when the doors had been cut down and hacked to pieces so passage could not be obstructed, the soldiers mounted their charge. Large numbers were also scaling the walls, but these then turned to killing townspeople everywhere; and those who had entered by the gate advanced, keeping ranks, through the city center into the forum in an ordered column, and accompanied by their officers.

When Scipio observed the enemy fleeing in two directions, some eastward toward the hill occupied by a garri-

gentorum militum praesidio, alios in arcem in quam et
ipse Mago cum omnibus ferme armatis qui muris pulsi
fuerant refugerat, partem[99] copiarum ad tumulum ex-
9 pugnandum mittit, partem[100] ipse ad arcem ducit. et tumulus primo impetu est captus et Mago arcem conatus
defendere, cum omnia hostium plena videret neque spem
10 ullam esse, se arcemque et praesidium dedidit. quoad
dedita arx est, caedes tota urbe passim factae, nec ulli
puberum qui obvius fuit parcebatur; tum signo dato cae-
dibus finis factus. ad praedam victores versi quae ingens
omnis generis fuit.

47. Liberorum capitum virile secus ad decem milia
capta; inde qui cives Novae Carthaginis erant dimisit, urbemque et sua omnia quae reliqua eis bellum fecerat re-
2 stituit. opifices ad duo milia hominum erant; eos publicos
fore populi Romani edixit cum spe propinqua libertatis si
3 ad ministeria belli enixe operam navassent. ceteram multitudinem incolarum iuvenum ac validorum servorum in
classem ad supplementum remigum dedit; et auxerat na-
4 vibus duodeviginti[101] captivis classem. extra hanc multitudinem Hispanorum obsides erant, quorum perinde ac si
sociorum liberi essent cura habita.

[99] partem $M^cC^c\Sigma$: partim P
[100] partem C^cA^p: partim P: *om.* Σ
[101] duedeviginti *Sig. cl. Pol. 10.17.13*: octo P

[217] Polybius' account at this point is (unusually) more dra-
matic than Livy's and includes the killing of animals: "They do
this, I think, to inspire terror, so that when towns are taken by the
Romans one may often see not only the corpses of human beings,

son of five hundred soldiers, and others to the citadel to which Mago had fled himself with almost all his men after being driven from the walls, he sent part of his force to storm the hill while he himself led part to the citadel. The hill was taken with the first charge and Mago, attempting to hold the citadel, also surrendered himself, the citadel, and the garrison when he saw the enemy everywhere and the situation hopeless. Until the citadel was surrendered, the killing continued throughout the city, and no adult male they met was granted quarter; then, at a given signal, the killing ended.[217] The victors turned to the plunder, which was an enormous assortment of all kinds of things.

47. Some ten thousand free persons of male sex were taken; of these Scipio released those who were citizens of New Carthage and restored to them their city and all such property as the war had left them. There were also about two thousand skilled tradesmen; these he declared the property of the Roman people, but with expectation of early release if they were diligent in their work for the war effort. All the rest, large numbers of young resident aliens and able-bodied slaves, he turned over to the fleet to supplement the numbers of oarsmen (and he had also increased the size of the fleet with eighteen captured vessels). In addition to this crowd there were also the Spanish hostages, who were treated as if they were the children of allies.

but dogs cut in half, and the dismembered limbs of other animals, and on this occasion such scenes were very many" (Polyb. 10.15.5–6).

5   Captus et apparatus ingens belli; catapultae maximae formae centum viginti, minores ducentae octoginta una, 6 ballistae maiores viginti tres, minores quinquaginta duae, scorpionum maiorum minorumque et armorum telorumque ingens numerus, signa militaria septuaginta quattuor. 7 et auri argenti[102] relata ad imperatorem magna vis. paterae aureae fuerunt ducentae septuaginta sex, librales ferme omnes pondo; argenti infecti signatique decem et octo milia et trecenta pondo, vasorum argenteorum magnus 8 numerus. haec omnia C. Flaminio quaestori adpensa adnumerataque sunt. tritici quadringenta milia modium, 9 hordei ducenta septuaginta. naves onerariae sexaginta tres in portu expugnatae captaeque, quaedam cum suis oneribus frumento, armis, aere praeterea ferroque et linteis et 10 sparto et navali alia materia ad classem aedificandam, ut minimum omnium inter tantas opes belli captas Carthago ipsa fuerit.

48. Eo die Scipio, C. Laelio cum sociis navalibus urbem 2 custodire iusso, ipse in castra legiones reduxit, fessosque milites omnibus uno die belli operibus, quippe qui et acie dimicassent et capienda urbe tantum laboris periculique adissent et capta cum iis qui in arcem confugerant iniquo etiam loco pugnassent, curare corpora iussit.

---

[102] argenti *P*: et argenti *C^c*: argentique *M^cΛ*

---

[218] On scorpions, cf. 6.4 note, above.   [219] According to Polybius (10.19.1) more than six hundred talents (34,206 pounds on the Attic-Euboic standard).   [220] The Roman pound was about three-quarters of a pound (avoirdupois).

[221] C. Flaminius, later praetor (193) and consul (187), with Hither Spain as his province. He is the son of the consul of 217, who was killed at Trasimene.

A huge amount of military equipment was also taken: 120 catapults of the largest dimensions and 281 smaller ones; 23 larger and 52 smaller ballistas; a huge number of the larger and smaller scorpions,[218] and other weapons and projectiles; and 74 military standards. A large quantity of gold and silver was also brought to the commander.[219] There were 276 golden dishes, nearly all a pound in weight;[220] there were 18,300 pounds of silver in bullion and coin, and a large number of silver vessels. This was all weighed and counted for the quaestor Gaius Flaminius.[221] There were 400,000 measures of wheat and 270,000 of barley.[222] Sixty-three transport vessels were overpowered and captured in the harbor, some with their cargoes of grain and weapons, as well as bronze and iron, sail linen, rope, and other nautical materials for equipping a fleet. The result was that amid such riches taken as spoils of war New Carthage itself represented the least significant of all the prizes.

48. That day, after ordering Gaius Laelius to stand guard over the city with the marines, Scipio himself led the legions back to the camp. The men were exhausted from all the military operations packed into a single day: they had fought a pitched battle, faced extremes of hardship and danger in taking the city and after taking it had contended—on unfavorable ground, too—with those who had sought refuge in the citadel. Scipio told them to take food and rest.

[222] That is, 66,666 pecks of wheat and 45,000 of barley. The Roman *modius* (measure) was a dry measure that was one-sixth of a *medimnus* (peck).

3   Postero die militibus navalibusque sociis convocatis primum dis immortalibus laudes gratesque egit, qui se non urbis solum opulentissimae omnium in Hispania uno die compotem fecissent, sed ante eo congessissent omnes paene[103] Africae atque Hispaniae opes, ut neque hostibus quicquam relinqueretur et sibi ac suis omnia superessent.

4   militum deinde virtutem conlaudavit quod eos non eruptio hostium, non altitudo moenium, non inexplorata stagni vada, non castellum in alto tumulo situm, non munitissima arx deterruisset quo minus transcenderent omnia perrumperentque.

5   itaque quamquam omnibus omnia deberet, praecipuum muralis coronae decus eius esse qui primus murum adscendisset; profiteretur qui se dignum eo ducere dono.

6   Duo professi sunt, Q. Trebellius centurio legionis quartae et Sex. Digitius socius navalis. nec ipsi tam inter se acriter contendebant quam studia excitaverant uterque

7   sui corporis hominum. sociis C. Laelius praefectus classis,

8   legionariis M. Sempronius Tuditanus aderat. ea contentio cum prope seditionem veniret, Scipio tres recuperatores cum se daturum pronuntiasset, qui cognita causa testibusque auditis iudicarent uter prior in oppidum transcendis-

9   set, C. Laelio et M. Sempronio advocatis partis utriusque

---

103 omnes (-is) paene Σ: omnis P: omnes *Madvig*

---

223 The prize is mentioned earlier by Polybius: at 10.11.6 he has Scipio promising "gold crowns to those who should be the first to mount the wall." The event is a rare demonstration of esprit de corps in different units of the Roman army.

224 Livy uses a technical term, *recuperatores*, normally used of judges "dealing originally with disputes between *peregrini*

Calling a meeting of the soldiers and marines the next day, he first offered praise and thanks to the immortal gods, not only for making him master of the richest of all the cities in Spain in a single day but also for having earlier accumulated in that city nearly all the wealth of Africa and Spain, the enemy being left with nothing while he and his men had everything in abundance. He then praised his soldiers' courage: nothing, not the enemy counterattack, not the height of the walls, not the unexplored shallows of the lagoon, not the fort perched on a hill, not the citadel with its formidable defenses—nothing had deterred them from surmounting and bursting through every obstacle! And while he owed all his success to everyone, he said, the special honor attaching to the "mural crown" belonged to the man who had been first to climb the wall;[223] and whoever thought he deserved that prize should claim it.

There were two claimants: Quintus Trebellius, a centurion of the fourth legion, and Sextus Digitius, a marine. But the competition between the two was less heated than the fanatical support each had generated in the other men of the corps to which he belonged. The marines had Gaius Laelius as their champion, the legionaries Marcus Sempronius Tuditanus. When the dispute was verging on mutiny, Scipio announced that he would appoint three judges[224] who, examining the case after hearing witnesses, would render judgment on which had been the first over the wall into the town. Gaius Laelius and Marcus Sempronius represented their respective parties and to them

(foreigners) and Roman citizens, but later competent to deal also with cases between Romans" (*OLD* s.v. *reciperator*, 2).

P. Cornelium Caudinum de medio adiecit, eosque tres
10 recuperatores considere et causam cognoscere iussit. cum
res eo maiore agteretur certamine quod amoti tantae dig-
nitatis non tam advocati quam moderatores studiorum
fuerant, C. Laelius relicto consilio ad tribunal ad Sci-
11 pionem accedit, eumque docet rem sine modo ac modestia agi, ac prope esse ut manus inter se conferant: ceterum
etiamsi vis absit, nihilo minus detestabili exemplo rem agi,
12 quippe ubi fraude ac periurio decus petatur virtutis. stare
hinc legionarios milites, hinc classicos per omnes deos
paratos iurare magis quae velint quam quae sciant vera
esse, et obstringere periurio non se solum suumque caput
sed signa militaria et aquilas sacramentique religionem.
13 haec se ad eum de sententia P. Corneli et M. Semproni
deferre.

Scipio conlaudato Laelio ad contionem advocavit pro-
nuntiavitque se satis compertum habere Q. Trebellium et
Sex. Digitium pariter in murum escendisse, seque eos
14 ambos virtutis causa coronis muralibus donare. tum reli-
quos prout cuique[104] meritum virtusque erat donavit; ante
omnes C. Laelium praefectum classis et omni genere lau-
dis sibimet ipse aequavit, et corona aurea ac triginta bubus
donavit.

49. Tum obsides civitatium Hispaniae vocari iussit,
quorum quantus numerus fuerit piget scribere, quippe

---

[104] cuique *P*: cuiusque Σ.?

---

[225] That is, Laelius and Sempronius had been moderating in-
fluences before the impartial judges were appointed.

[226] Anachronistic: the eagle as legionary standard (only here
in Livy) belongs to the time of Marius nearly a century later.

Scipio added Publius Cornelius Caudinus as a disinterested third; and these three he ordered to sit as judges and hear the case. As the matter was becoming more heated (because both sides were now deprived of influential men to restrain rather than promote partisan fervor),[225] Gaius Laelius left the board and, coming to Scipio at his tribunal, told him that the matter was losing all semblance of moderation and decency and that men were almost fighting each other. Even in the absence of a violent outcome, he said, a deplorable precedent was nevertheless being set by the affair in that a prize for gallantry was being contested with cheating and lies The legionaries stood on one side, the marines on the other, ready to swear by all the gods to what they *wanted* to be true rather than what they *knew* to be true, and to taint with perjury not just their own persons but their military standards, their eagles,[226] and the sanctity of their oath of allegiance. He added that he was bringing this matter before Scipio on the advice of Publius Cornelius and Marcus Sempronius.

Commending Laelius, Scipio called the men to an assembly and announced that he was reliably informed that Quintus Trebellius and Sextus Digitius had scaled the wall at the same time, and he was awarding "mural crowns" to both. He then made awards to the rest in line with their service and bravery. Gaius Laelius, admiral of the fleet, he honored above all others with all manner of praise, putting him on a level with himself and awarding him a golden crown and thirty oxen.

49. He then had the hostages from the Spanish communities summoned. Their number I am reluctant to put

ubi[105] alibi trecentos ferme, alibi tria milia septingentos viginti quattuor fuisse inveniam; aeque et alia inter auc-
2 tores discrepant. praesidium Punicum alius decem, alius septem, alius haud plus quam duum milium fuisse scribit. capta alibi decem milia capitum, alibi supra quinque et
3 viginti invenio. scorpiones maiores minoresque ad sexaginta captos scripserim si auctorem Graecum sequar Silenum; si Valerium Antiatem, maiorum scorpionum sex milia, minorum tredecim milia—adeo nullus mentiendi
4 modus est. ne de ducibus quidem convenit. plerique Laelium praefuisse classi, sunt qui M. Iunium Silanum dicant;
5 Arinen praefuisse Punico praesidio deditumque Romanis
6 Antias Valerius, Magonem alii scriptores tradunt. non de numero navium captarum, non de pondere auri atque argenti et redacta pecunia[106] convenit; si aliquis adsentiri necesse est, media simillima veri sunt.

7 Ceterum vocatis obsidibus primum universos bonum
8 animum habere iussit: venisse enim eos in populi Romani potestatem, qui beneficio quam metu obligare homines malit, exterasque gentes fide ac societate iunctas habere
9 quam tristi subiectas servitio. deinde acceptis nominibus civitatium recensuit captivos quot cuiusque populi essent,

105 ubi *P*: cum Σ
106 redacta pecunia Σ: redactae pecuniae *P*

---

227 A Greek historian, probably Sicilian, who accompanied Hannibal on his expedition and wrote a history of it (cf. *OCD* s.v.). He is mentioned only here by Livy.

228 On Antias, see Introduction to vol. V, xxvii–xxviii.

229 Or perhaps "so unbridled is his (i.e., Antias') fabrication." This interpretation is quite likely, Antias being elsewhere criti-

on record as I find it about 300 in one source and 3,724 in another; and there is as much discrepancy between historians on other items, too. One records that the Punic garrison was 10,000 strong, another 7,000, and yet another that it was no more than 2,000. In one source I find the number of prisoners taken as 10,000, in another as more than 25,000. I should put at about 60 the larger and smaller scorpions captured if I follow the Greek author Silenus;[227] if I follow Valerius Antias,[228] then there were 6,000 larger scorpions and 13,000 smaller ones—so wild is the fabrication of historians![229] Even about commanders there is no agreement. Most claim that Laelius commanded the fleet, but some that was Marcus Junius Silanus. Valerius Antias informs us that Arines commanded the Punic garrison and surrendered to the Romans; other writers say it was Mago.[230] No agreement is found on the number of ships captured, and none on the weight of gold and silver taken or the amount of money realized for it. If one must follow a source, figures halfway between seem closest to the truth.

When the hostages were summoned, Scipio first told them all to be of good cheer: they had come into the power of the Roman people, who preferred to secure men's support by kindness rather than fear and have foreign nations joined to them in loyal alliance rather than downtrodden in wretched servitude. Then, taking note of their communities, he made an inventory of the prisoners, itemizing

cized by Livy for his inflation of numbers (33.10.8, "Valerius, who is guilty of gross exaggeration of numbers of all kinds").

[230] He is Aris in Silius Italicus (15.232), but Mago in Polybius (10.12.2).

et nuntios domum misit ut ad suos quisque recipiendos
10 veniret. si quarum forte civitatium legati aderant, eis prae-
sentibus suos restituit; ceterorum curam benigne tuendo-
rum C. Flaminio quaestori attribuit.

11 Inter haec e media turba obsidum mulier magno natu
Mandonii uxor, qui frater Indibilis Ilergetum reguli erat,
flens ad pedes imperatoris procubuit, obtestarique coepit
ut curam cultumque feminarum impensius custodibus
12 commendaret. cum Scipio nihil defuturum iis profecto
diceret, tum rursus mulier "Haud magni ista facimus" inquit; "quid enim huic fortunae non satis est? alia me angit[107] cura aetatem harum intuentem; nam ipsa iam extra
13 periculum iniuriae muliebris sum." simul aetate[108] et
forma florentes circa eam Indibilis filiae erant aliaeque
nobilitate pari, quae omnes eam pro parente colebant.

14 Tum Scipio "Meae populique Romani disciplinae causa
facerem" inquit "ne quid quod sanctum usquam esset
15 apud nos violaretur; nunc ut id curem impensius vestra
quoque virtus dignitasque facit, quae ne in malis quidem
16 oblitae decoris matronalis estis." spectatae deinde integri-
tatis viro tradidit eas, tuerique haud secus verecunde ac
modeste quam hospitum coniuges ac matres iussit.

50. Captiva deinde a militibus adducitur ad eum adulta
virgo adeo eximia forma ut quacumque incedebat conver-

---

107 alia me angit cura Σ: aliam cura (alia me N^c) P
108 simul aetate Σ: stimulat et aetate P

---

231 A powerful tribe north of the Ebro, allied to Carthage.
Ilerda (mod. Lleida) was a major city: *Barr.* 25 F4; TIR *K-30*, 131;
OCD s.v.

the numbers that belonged to each people, and he sent messengers to their homes with instructions for each community to come to recover its own citizens. Wherever ambassadors of the communities were present, he restored their hostages to them on the spot. The others he put under the care of the quaestor Gaius Flaminius, to be treated gently.

Meanwhile, from the midst of the crowd of hostages an elderly woman emerged, the wife of Mandonius, who was the brother of the Ilergetan chieftain Indibilis.[231] She, in tears, threw herself at the commander's feet and began begging him to give stricter injunctions to the guards about care and attention for the female hostages. When Scipio said they would certainly not be lacking anything, the woman replied: "That matters little to us; for in such a plight what is not having enough? It is another worry that torments me when I consider these ladies' ages, for I am myself beyond danger of such assault as a woman suffers." Surrounding her were Indibilis' daughters, at the peak of their youth and beauty, and other women of similar high birth, who all respected her like a mother.

"In line with my own and the Roman people's moral training," Scipio replied, "I would ensure that nothing in our keeping that is considered sacred would be violated. But the courage and dignity of you ladies now make me even more scrupulous in this regard; even in misfortune you have not forgotten the respect due to a lady." He then put the women in the care of a man of proven integrity, ordering him to guard them with as much consideration and respect as if they were wives and mothers of guests.

50. A female captive was then brought to Scipio by the soldiers, a grown girl of such strikingly good looks that

2   teret omnium oculos. Scipio percontatus patriam parentesque inter cetera accepit desponsam eam principi Cel-
3   tiberorum; adulescenti Allucio nomen erat. extemplo
igitur parentibus sponsoque ab domo accitis, cum interim
audiret deperire eum sponsae amore, ubi primum venit
accuratiore eum sermone quam parentes adloquitur.
4   "Iuvenis" inquit "iuvenem appello, quo minor sit huius
inter nos sermonis verecundia. ego cum sponsa tua capta
5   a militibus nostris ad me ducta esset, audiremque tibi eam
cordi esse et forma faceret fidem, quia ipse, si frui liceret
ludo aetatis praesertim in recto et legitimo amore et non
res publica animum nostrum occupasset, veniam mihi
dari, sponsam impensius amanti vellem, tuo cuius possum
6   amori faveo. fuit sponsa tua apud me eadem qua apud
soceros tuos parentesque suos verecundia; servata tibi est
ut inviolatum et dignum me teque dari tibi donum posset.
7   hanc mercedem unam pro eo munere paciscor: amicus
populo Romano sis, et si me virum bonum credis esse
quales patrem patruumque meum iam ante hae gentes
norant, scias multos nostri similes in civitate Romana esse,
8   nec ullum in terris hodie populum dici posse quem minus
tibi hostem tuisque esse velis aut amicum malis."[109]

---

[109] malis *P*: magis *Weir, fort. recte*

---

[232] The story of Scipio and the beautiful young captive appears in a number of authors, some versions being positive vis-à-
vis Scipio and others less so (cf. Jal *ad loc.*). Positive and negative
are found together in Aulus Gellius (7.8.3–6).

[233] On the much-debated question of romantic love and marriage in the Roman world, see S. Treggiari, *Roman Marriage: Iusti
Coniuges from the Time of Cicero to the Time of Ulpian* (Oxford,
1991), 229–61 (ch. 8, "Coniugalis Amor").

wherever she went she caught the eyes of all. Scipio inquired after her country and parents, and amid the information he received was that she was engaged to a chieftain of the Celtiberians; the young man's name was Allucius.[232] The parents and fiancé were therefore immediately summoned from her homeland, but meanwhile Scipio was informed that the young man was desperately in love with his intended bride,[233] and so, immediately on the fiancé's arrival, he addressed him in terms more carefully chosen than he did the parents:

"I speak to you as one young man to another," he said, "so there may be less unease in this conversation between us. Your fiancée was brought to me as a prisoner by our soldiers, and I was told that you are in love with her, something which her looks made quite understandable. Now, I would myself like to be pardoned for loving a fiancée too deeply, if I were granted the opportunity to enjoy the pleasures appropriate to my age, especially a correct and lawful love, and if affairs of state had not preoccupied me. Instead—something I *can* do—I give support to *your* love. Your fiancée has received in my care such respect as she would from her own parents, your future parents-in-law. She has been kept for you so she could be given to you as a gift, intact, as befits my dignity and yours. In return for that gift I ask this one recompense: that you be a friend of the Roman people, and if you think I am a good man, one such as the tribes here had earlier come to know in my father and uncle, then be assured that in the Roman state there are many like us, and that no people in the world today can be said to be one you would like less to have as your enemy or more to have as your friend."

9   Cum adulescens simul pudore et gaudio perfusus dex-
tram Scipionis tenens deos omnes invocaret ad gratiam illi
pro se referendam, quoniam sibi nequaquam satis faculta-
tis pro suo animo atque illius erga se merito esset, parentes
10   inde cognatique virginis appellati; qui, quoniam gratis sibi
redderetur virgo ad quam redimendam satis magnum at-
11   tulissent auri pondus, orare Scipionem ut id ab se donum
acciperet coeperunt, haud minorem eius rei apud se gratiam futuram esse adfirmantes quam redditae inviolatae
foret virginis.
12   Scipio, quando tanto opere peterent accepturum se
pollicitus, poni ante pedes iussit, vocatoque ad se Allucio
"Super dotem" inquit "quam accepturus a socero es, haec
tibi a me dotalia dona accedent"; aurumque tollere ac sibi
13   habere iussit. his laetus donis honoribusque dimissus domum, implevit populares laudibus meritis Scipionis: venisse dis simillimum iuvenem, vincentem omnia cum ar-
14   mis tum benignitate ac beneficiis. itaque dilectu clientium
habito cum delectis mille et quadringentis equitibus intra
paucos dies ad Scipionem revertit.
51. Scipio retentum secum Laelium dum captivos obsi-
2   desque et praedam ex consilio eius disponeret, satis rebus
omnibus compositis, data quinquereme captivisque Magone[110] et quindecim ferme senatoribus qui simul cum eo

---

[110] captivisque Magone *P*: captivis cum Magone Σ: e captivis
Magoneque *Walters*

---

[234] Livy possibly had in mind Virgil's famous first eclogue (*Ecl.*
1.6–7), where the herdsman Tityrus, on regaining his land, says
(referring to the emperor Augustus), *O Meliboee, deus nobis haec
otia fecit. namque erit ille mihi semper deus* (Meliboeus, a god
granted me this peace . . . for to me he will always be a god).

Overcome with both embarrassment and delight, the young man, holding Scipio's hand, called on all the gods to show him gratitude on his behalf, since he himself had nothing like the means to express his thanks as he might wish or as Scipio's kindness to him deserved. The girl's parents and relatives were then called and, since the girl was being returned to them free of charge and they had brought a considerable amount of gold to ransom her, they began to beg Scipio to accept it from them as a gift, declaring they would feel no less grateful for that than for his returning of the girl undefiled.

As they were so insistent, Scipio agreed to accept the gift, ordered it set at his feet, and then, calling Allucius to him, said: "In addition to the dowry that you shall receive from your father-in-law, this will also come to you as a wedding gift from me," and he told him to pick up the gold and keep it. The young man was then sent home, overjoyed with these gifts and the honors, and he filled the ears of his countrymen with well-deserved eulogies of Scipio. A young man had come who was very much like the gods,[234] he said, a man victorious everywhere thanks to his generosity and kindness as well as his military prowess. Then, holding a troop levy among his dependents, he returned to Scipio within a few days with fourteen hundred elite horsemen.

51. Scipio kept Laelius with him for as long as he was organizing captives, hostages, and booty with his advice, and when all was arranged he gave him a quinquereme,[235] put aboard his prisoners of war (Mago and some fifteen senators who had been captured with him) and sent him

[235] Cf. Polyb. 10.19.8.

capti erant in navem impositis, nuntium victoriae Romam
3 mittit. ipse paucos dies quibus morari Carthagine statuerat exercendis navalibus pedestribusque copiis absumpsit.
4 primo die legiones in armis quattuor milium spatio decur-
rerunt; secundo die arma curare et tergere ante tentoria
iussi; tertio die rudibus inter se in modum iustae pugnae
concurrerunt, praepilatisque missilibus iaculati sunt;
quarto die quies data; quinto iterum in armis decursum
5 est. hunc ordinem laboris quietisque quoad Carthagine
6 morati sunt servarunt. remigium classicique milites tran-
quillo in altum evecti agilitatem navium simulacris navalis
pugnae experiebantur.
7   Haec extra urbem terra marique corpora simul animosque ad bellum acuebant. urbs ipsa strepebat apparatu
belli, fabris omnium generum in publicam officinam in-
8 clusis. dux cuncta pari cura obibat. nunc in classe ac navali
erat, nunc cum legionibus decurrebat, nunc operibus ad-
spiciendis tempus dabat, quaeque in officinis quaeque in
armamentario ac navalibus fabrorum multitudo plurima
9 in singulos dies certamine ingenti faciebat. His ita incoha-
tis refectisque quae quassata erant muri dispositisque
10 praesidiis ad custodiam urbis Tarraconem est profectus, a
multis legationibus protinus in via aditus quas partim dato
responso ex itinere dimisit, partim distulit Tarraconem,
quo omnibus novis veteribusque sociis edixerat conven-

to Rome to announce the victory. The few days that he had decided to remain in New Carthage he himself spent drilling his naval and land forces. On the first day the legions underwent armed maneuvers over a four mile course; on the second they were ordered to burnish and clean their arms before their tents; on the third they fought a simulated battle with wooden swords and threw javelins tipped with a ball; on the fourth they were allowed to rest; and on the fifth they had armed maneuvers again. This cycle of work and rest they kept up the whole time they remained in New Carthage. The rowers and marines would put out to sea in calm weather and test the maneuverability of their vessels in mock naval battles.

Conducted on land and sea outside the city, these exercises were honing the men for war both physically and mentally. The city itself rang with the noise of war preparations, artisans of all kinds being shut up there in a public plant. The commander would supervise all the activities with equal care. At one moment he was with the fleet and in the dockyard; at another he was on maneuvers with the legions; on yet another he was spending his time inspecting works on which hordes of tradesmen were every day laboring in the workshops, arsenal, and dockyards in intense competition. After these initial steps, and after repairing battered sections of the wall and posting troops to provide for the city's defense, he set off for Tarraco; and as soon as he was en route he was approached by numerous delegations, to some of which he gave responses on the march and then sent on their way, while others he deferred until Tarraco, where he had scheduled a meeting for all the allies, old and new. And, in fact, nearly all the

11 tum. et cuncti ferme qui cis Hiberum incolunt populi,
multi etiam ulterioris provinciae convenerunt.

Carthaginiensium duces primo ex industria famam
captae Carthaginis compresserunt. deinde, ut clarior res
erat quam ut tegi ac dissimulari posset, elevabant verbis:
12 necopinato adventu ac prope furto unius diei urbem unam
Hispaniae interceptam, cuius[111] rei tam parvae praemio
elatum insolentem iuvenem immodico gaudio speciem
13 magnae victoriae imposuisse. at ubi appropinquare tres
duces, tres victores hostium exercitus audisset, occursu-
14 ram ei extemplo domesticorum funerum memoriam. haec
in volgus iactabant, haudquaquam ipsi ignari quantum sibi
ad omnia virium Carthagine amissa decessisset.

111 cuius *P*: eius Σ

tribes north of the Ebro assembled for the meeting, as also did many from the farther province.

The Carthaginian leaders at first deliberately suppressed news of New Carthage's capture. Then, when the facts became too well known to be hidden or ignored, they started downplaying it in their pronouncements: by the unexpected arrival of the Romans, almost by a piece of trickery, they said, a single town had one day been taken in Spain. Puffed up by such a paltry prize, a young show-off had in excessive euphoria made this out to be a great victory; but when he came to hear that three generals and three conquering armies of his enemy were coming, he would quickly be reminded of the deaths in his family. Such were the public comments of the Carthaginians, although they knew full well how much of their strength had gone in every way with the loss of New Carthage.

LIBRI XXVI PERIOCHA

Hannibal ad tertium lapidem ab urbe Roma super Anienem castra posuit. ipse cum duobus milibus equitum usque ad ipsam Capenam portam, ut situm urbis exploraret,
obequitavit. et cum per triduum in aciem utrimque exercitus omnis descendisset, certamen tempestas diremit;
nam cum in castra redisset, statim serenitas erat. Capua
capta est a Q. Fulvio et Ap. Claudio coss. principes Campanorum veneno sibi mortem consciverunt. cum senatus
Campanorum deligatus esset ad palos ut securi feriretur,
litteras a senatu missas Q. Fulvius consul, quibus iubeba-
tur parcere, antequam legeret, in sinu posuit et lege agi
iussit et supplicium peregit. cum comitiis apud populum
quaereretur cui mandaretur Hispaniarum imperium,
nullo id volente suscipere, P. Scipio, P. filius eius qui in
Hispania ceciderat, professus est se iturum, et suffragio
populi consensuque omnium missus Novam Carthaginem
expugnavit, cum haberet annos XXIIII videreturque divina stirpe, quia et ipse, postquam togam acceperat, coti-

---

236 As in Valerius Maximus (3.7.10); in Livy, Collina (as also
Plin. 15.76).

SUMMARY OF BOOK XXVI

Hannibal pitched camp on the bank of the River Anio at the third milestone from the city of Rome. He rode in person right up to the Porta Capena[236] with two thousand of his cavalry to examine the lie of the city. And although the entire army on each side had gone out into battle formation on three consecutive days, a storm broke off the engagement; for when each side returned to camp, there was immediately fine weather. Capua was taken by the consuls Quintus Fulvius and Appius Claudius. The leading men of the Capuans committed suicide with poison. When the Capuan senators had been tied to stakes for beheading, the consul Quintus Fulvius placed in the fold of his toga, before reading it, a letter sent to him by the senate, in which he was instructed to spare them; he then ordered the law to be applied and carried out the execution. At the elections the question arose before the people of who should be given command of the two Spanish provinces, and when no one was willing to take it Publius Scipio, son of the Publius who had fallen in Spain, declared that he would go; and, sent there by vote of the people and by general agreement, he stormed New Carthage. He was twenty-four years of age and appeared to be of divine descent, both because he himself, after as-

die in Capitolio erat et in cubiculo matris eius anguis saepe videbatur. res praeterea gestas in Sicilia continet et amicitiam cum Aetolis iunctam bellumque gestum adversus Acarnanas et Philippum, Macedoniae regem.

suming the toga, was on the Capitol every day and also because a snake was often spotted in his mother's bedroom. The book also contains the events in Sicily, the treaty of friendship established with the Aetolians, and the war against the Acarnanians and Philip, King of Macedonia.

LIBER XXVII

1. Hic status rerum in Hispania erat. in Italia consul Marcellus Salapia per proditionem recepta Marmoreas et
2 Meles de Samnitibus vi cepit. ad tria milia militum ibi Hannibalis, quae praesidii causa relicta erant, oppressa; praeda—et aliquantum eius fuit—militi concessa. tritici quoque ducenta quadraginta milia modium et centum decem milia hordei inventa.

3 Ceterum nequaquam inde tantum gaudium fuit quanta clades intra paucos dies accepta est haud procul Herdonea
4 urbe. castra ibi Cn. Fulvius proconsul habebat spe recipiendae Herdoneae, quae post Cannensem cladem ab Romanis defecerat, nec loco satis tuto posita nec praesidiis
5 firmata. neglegentiam insitam ingenio ducis augebat spes ea quod labare iis adversus Poenum fidem senserat postquam Salapia amissa excessisse iis locis in Bruttios Hanni-
6 balem auditum est. ea omnia ab Herdonea per occultos

---

1 Salapia is the Apulian town mentioned in the previous book (26.38.6 and note; *Barr.* 45 C2), but the other two are not mentioned elsewhere (though John Briscoe advises me that *Maronea* (Σ) is "clearly a corruption of the name of the Thracian town mentioned frequently in Books 31–45").

2 On the "measure" (*modius*), cf. 26.47.8 note.

BOOK XXVII

1. Such was the situation in Spain. In Italy the consul Marcellus gained Salapia through its betrayal, and Marmoreae and Meles[1] he took by force from the Samnites. Some three thousand of Hannibal's men who had been left to garrison the towns were overpowered, and the plunder taken—and its amount was considerable—was left to the soldiers. Two hundred and forty thousand measures of wheat and one hundred and ten thousand measures of barley[2] were also found.

Joy over this success, however, in no way balanced the disaster sustained not far from the city of Herdonea[3] a few days later. The proconsul Gnaeus Fulvius[4] had his camp in the area, hoping to recover Herdonea, which had defected from the Romans after the defeat at Cannae, but the camp was not in a very safe or well secured place. The carelessness ingrained in the general's nature was being increased by hope after he had become aware that the inhabitants' loyalty to the Carthaginian had been wavering ever since news arrived that, after losing Salapia, Hannibal had left the area for Bruttium. All this had been duly re-

---

[3] Called "obscure Herdonea" by Silius Italicus (8.567): *Barr.* 45 C2 (Herdoneae).   [4] Cn. Fulvius Centumalus Maximus, the previous year's consul.

nuntios delata Hannibali simul curam sociae retinendae urbis et spem fecere incautum hostem adgrediendi.

Exercitu expedito ita ut famam prope praeveniret magnis itineribus ad Herdoneam contendit, et quo plus
7 terroris hosti obiceret acie instructa accessit. par audacia Romanus, consilio et viribus impar, copiis raptim eductis conflixit. quinta legio et sinistra ala acriter pugnam inie-
8 runt. ceterum Hannibal signo equitibus dato ut, cum pedestres acies occupassent praesenti certamine oculos animosque, circumvecti pars castra hostium pars terga
9 pugnantium[1] invaderent, ipse Cn. Fulvi similitudinem nominis—quia Cn. Fulvium praetorem biennio ante in iisdem devicerat locis—increpans, similem eventum pugnae fore adfirmabat.
10 Neque ea spes vana fuit. nam cum comminus acie et
11 peditum certamine multi cecidissent Romanorum, starent tamen ordines signaque, equestris tumultus a tergo, simul a castris clamor hostilis auditus sextam ante legionem quae in secunda acie posita prior ab Numidis turbata est, quintam deinde atque eos qui ad prima signa erant avertit.
12 pars in fugam effusi, pars in medio caesi, ubi et ipse Cn.
13 Fulvius cum undecim tribunis militum cecidit. Romanorum sociorumque quot caesa in eo proelio milia sint quis pro certo adfirmet, cum tredecim milia alibi, alibi haud plus quam septem inveniam?

---

[1] pugnantium Φ: oppugnantium Λ: oppidantium *P*: trepidantium *Gron.*

---

[5] Cf. Book 25 chapter 21. The location of the two battles and the similarity of the Roman commanders' names has led some to believe that this battle is simply a doublet: contra, Jal, 97 n. 4.

ported to Hannibal by messengers sent covertly from Herdonea, making him anxious to hold on to an allied city and also giving him hope of catching his enemy off guard.

With a light-armed force he headed toward Herdonea by forced marches, so swiftly that he almost outran word of his coming; and in order to strike greater terror in his enemy he approached the town with a line deployed for battle. Hannibal's equal in daring but unequal in strategy and strength, the Roman swiftly led out his troops and engaged, and the fifth legion and allied left wing vigorously entered battle. Hannibal, however, had given a signal for his cavalry to ride around the field when the infantry lines had their eyes and attention focused on the immediate struggle, and for some to attack the enemy camp and others their rear; and because he had two years earlier defeated the praetor Gnaeus Fulvius in that same area[5] he would caustically repeat that Gnaeus Fulvius had the same name and the outcome of the battle would also be the same.

Nor was that a vain hope. For when many Romans had fallen in hand-to-hand fighting and in the clash of the infantry, but the ranks still held their ground with their standards, an uproar raised from the cavalry could be heard to their rear, and at the same time shouts of the enemy from their camp; and that first made the sixth legion retreat (stationed in the second line, it was the first thrown into disarray by the Numidians) and after it the fifth and those at the very front. Some were scattered in flight, and others were killed in the thick of the action, where Gnaeus Fulvius himself fell, together with eleven military tribunes. How many thousand Romans and allies were killed in that battle who could say for certain, when I find thirteen thousand in one author and no more than seven thousand in another?

14   Castris praedaque victor potitur. Herdoneam quia et
defecturam fuisse ad Romanos comperit nec mansuram in
fide si inde abscessisset, multitudine omni Metapontum
ac Thurios traducta incendit; occidit principes qui cum
15   Fulvio conloquia occulta habuisse comperti sunt. Romani
qui ex tanta clade evaserant diversis itineribus semermes
ad Marcellum consulem in Samnium perfugerunt.

    2. Marcellus nihil admodum tanta clade territus litteras
Romam ad senatum de duce atque exercitu ad Herdo-
2   neam amisso scribit: ceterum eundem se, qui post
Cannensem pugnam ferocem victoria Hannibalem contu-
disset, ire adversus eum, brevem illi laetitiam qua exultet
facturum.

3   Et Romae quidem cum luctus ingens ex praeterito tum
4   timor in futurum erat. consul ex Samnio in Lucanos transgressus ad Numistronem in conspectu Hannibalis loco
plano, cum Poenus collem teneret, posuit castra. addidit
5   et aliam fidentis speciem quod prior in aciem eduxit; nec
detractavit Hannibal ut signa portis efferri vidit. ita tamen
aciem instruxerunt ut Poenus dextrum cornu in collem
6   erigeret, Romani sinistrum ad oppidum adplicarent. ab
Romanis prima legio et dextra ala, ab Hannibale Hispani
milites et funditores Baliares, elephanti quoque commisso
iam certamine in proelium acti.

7   Diu pugna neutro inclinata stetit. ab hora tertia cum ad

---

    [6] Appian, who mentions only one Battle of Herdonea, gives a
different ending, with some survivors fighting bravely and saving
the camp (*Hann.* 48).

    [7] Cf. Book 23 chapters 16–17.

    [8] *Barr.* 45 C3 (tentatively).

The victor took the camp and its spoils.[6] Because he discovered that Herdonea would have defected to the Romans and not remained loyal if he had withdrawn from there, Hannibal removed the whole population to Metapontum and Thurii and burned the town; and he put to death leading citizens who were found to have been in clandestine discussions with Fulvius. Any Romans escaping such a slaughter fled by various routes and poorly armed to the consul Marcellus in Samnium.

2. Not at all dismayed by such a great defeat, Marcellus wrote to the senate in Rome reporting the loss of the general and army at Herdonea; but he was the very same man, he added, who after the battle of Cannae had stunned Hannibal while he gloated over his victory;[7] he would now face him and see that the joy of his exhilaration was short-lived.

In Rome, there was certainly deep melancholy over what had happened as well as fear for the future. The consul marched from Samnium into Lucania and encamped on level ground at Numistro,[8] in full view of Hannibal, while the Carthaginian was holding a hill. He then gave a further display of his confidence by being the first to deploy troops; and Hannibal did not back off when he saw the standards being brought out of the gates. But they so marshaled their battle lines that the Carthaginian had his right wing extended up the hill, while the Romans kept their left close to the town. By the Romans the troops sent in were the first legion and the allied right flank, and by Hannibal his Spanish troops and Balearic slingers, with the elephants also sent in once battle was joined.

For a long while the engagement favored neither. They

noctem pugnam extendissent, fessaeque pugnando primae acies essent, primae legioni tertia, dextrae alae sinistra subiit, et apud hostes integri a fessis pugnam accepere.

8 novum atque atrox proelium ex iam segni repente exarsit recentibus animis corporibusque; sed nox incerta victoria diremit pugnantes.

9 Postero die Romani ab sole orto in multum diei stetere in acie; ubi nemo hostium adversus prodiit, spolia per otium legere et congestos in unum locum cremavere suos.

10 nocte insequenti Hannibal silentio movit castra et in Apuliam abiit. Marcellus, ubi lux fugam hostium aperuit, sauciis cum praesidio modico Numistrone relictis praepositoque iis L. Furio Purpurione tribuno militum, vestigiis

11 institit sequi. ad Venusiam adeptus eum est. ibi per dies aliquot cum ab stationibus procursaretur, mixta equitum peditumque tumultuosa magis proelia quam magna,[2] et

12 ferme omnia Romanis secunda fuere. inde per Apuliam ducti exercitus sine ullo memorando certamine, cum Hannibal nocte signa moveret locum insidiis quaerens, Marcellus nisi certa luce et explorato ante non sequeretur.

3. Capuae interim Flaccus dum bonis principum vendendis, agro qui publicatus erat locando—locavit autem

---

[2] 2.11 quam magna . . . 3.7 Atellam Σ: *om.* P

---

[9] Livy says *incerta*, but Frontinus grants Hannibal "victory over a most renowned commander" (*Str.* 2.2.6).

[10] Venusia (mod. Venosa) in Apulia (*Barr.* 45 C3) saw the foundation of a large Latin colony in 291 and was later famous as Horace's birthplace. It was also where the Cannae survivors first congregated (22.49.14, 22.54.2–3).

drew out the action from the third hour until nightfall and, when the front lines were exhausted from fighting, the first legion was relieved by the third and the allies on the right by those on the left, while on the enemy side, too, fresh troops took over the fighting from those who were spent. After this injection of fresh spirit and strength, a renewed and savage struggle suddenly flared up from one that had been flagging, but night parted the combatants with victory left unclear.[9]

The following day the Romans stood in battle line from sunrise until well into the day; and when none of the enemy came forward to face them they took their time gathering up the spoils and then, heaping their dead together in one spot, they burned them. That coming night Hannibal quietly struck camp and went off into Apulia. When daylight revealed that his enemy had fled, Marcellus left his wounded lightly guarded at Numistro with the military tribune Lucius Furius Purpurio in charge and proceeded to dog Hannibal's footsteps. He caught up with him at Venusia.[10] There, for a number of days, there were forays from both sides' forward posts, scrappy infantry and cavalry encounters rather than serious battles, and they nearly all favored the Romans. After that the armies were marched through Apulia with no memorable encounter, since Hannibal would advance at night looking for a site for an ambush, and Marcellus would follow only in broad daylight and after reconnoitering.

3. In Capua, meanwhile, Flaccus had been spending his time selling off property of its leading citizens and renting out farmland appropriated by the Roman state

omnem frumento—tempus terit, ne deesset materia in Campanos saeviendi, novum in occulto gliscens per indicium protractum est facinus.

2   Milites aedificiis emotos simul ut cum agro tecta urbis fruenda locarentur, simul metuens ne suum quoque exercitum sicut Hannibalis nimia urbis amoenitas emolliret, in portis murisque sibimet ipsos tecta militariter coegerat

3   aedificare; erant autem pleraque ex cratibus ac tabulis facta, alia harundine texta stramento intecta, omne[3] velut

4   de industria alimentum[4] ignis. haec noctis una hora omnia ut[5] incenderent centum septuaginta Campani principibus

5   Blossiis fratribus coniuraverunt. indicio eius rei ex familia Blossiorum facto, portis repente iussu proconsulis clausis cum ad arma signo dato milites concurrissent, comprehensi omnes qui in noxa erant et quaestione acriter habita damnati necatique; indicibus libertas et aeris dena milia data.

6   Nucerinos et Acerranos querentes ubi habitarent non esse, Acerris ex parte incensis Nuceria deleta, Romam

7   Fulvius ad senatum misit. Acerranis permissum ut aedifi-

---

[3] omne Σ: omnia *Rhenanus*
[4] alimentum *A^p*: alimentis Σ
[5] ut *hic Madvig, ante* noctis *Vat. Pal. Lat. 879: om.* Σ

---

[11] C. Fulvius Flaccus, consul for the third time in 212 and now proconsul (cf. 26.1.2). His activities here were normally the charge of the censors (who did take them over the following year: cf. 11.8, below).
[12] Cf. 23.18.10–15.

(and he always rented it for grain),[11] when, so he should not lack any opportunity for savaging the Capuans, a new, furtively developing crime was revealed by informers.

He had removed his soldiers from the town buildings, partly so city houses as well as farmland could be leased for profit, and partly from fear that the city's all too seductive charms might soften his troops as they had Hannibal's, and he had forced them to build for themselves huts appropriate for soldiers at the gates and walls;[12] but several of the huts were made of wickerwork and planking, and some of interlaced reeds covered with straw—everything almost designed to feed a fire. A plot to set all of these on fire at the same time of night was hatched by a hundred and seventy Campanians, led by the Blossii brothers.[13] The affair was then divulged by slaves of the Blossii household, the city gates were promptly closed by order of the proconsul, and when the soldiers then rushed to arms at a given signal all the guilty parties were arrested; and after an intensive investigation these were condemned and executed, and the informants were granted freedom and ten thousand *asses* each.

When the peoples of Nuceria and Acerrae complained that they had nowhere to live, since Acerrae had been partly burned and Nuceria destroyed,[14] Fulvius sent them to the senate in Rome. The people of Acerrae were granted

---

[13] A noted Campanian family. A Marius Blossius was the chief magistrate (*meddix tuticus*) when Capua revolted in 216 (23.7.8). The philosopher Gaius Blossius of Cumae was a descendant.

[14] *Barr.* 42 D2 (Nuceria); 39 F3 (Acerrae). For their destruction, cf. 23.15.6 (Nuceria) and 17.7 (Acerrae).

carent quae incensa erant; Nucerini Atellam, quia id ma-
luerant, Atellanis Calatiam migrare iussis, traducti.

8   Inter multas magnasque res quae nunc secundae nunc
adversae occupabant cogitationes hominum, ne Tarenti-
9 nae quidem arcis excidit memoria. M. Ogulnius et P. Aquilius in Etruriam legati ad frumentum coemendum quod
Tarentum portaretur profecti; et mille milites de exercitu
urbano, par numerus Romanorum sociorumque, eodem
in praesidium cum frumento missi.

    4. Iam aestas in exitu erat comitiorumque consularium
instabat tempus; sed litterae Marcelli negantis e re publica
2 esse vestigium abscedi ab Hannibale, cui cedenti certa-
menque abnuenti gravis ipse instaret, patribus[6] curam
iniecerant ne aut consulem tum maxime res agentem a
3 bello avocarent aut in annum consules deessent. optimum
visum est quamquam extra Italiam esset Valerium potius
4 consulem ex Sicilia revocari. ad eum litterae iussu senatus
ab L. Manlio praetore urbano missae cum litteris consulis
M. Marcelli, ut ex iis nosceret quae causa patribus eum
potius quam collegam revocandi ex provincia esset.

5   Eo ferme tempore legati ab rege Syphace Romam venerunt, quae is prospera proelia cum Carthaginiensibus

---

[6] patribus Σ: *om.* P

---

[15] Atella: *Barr.* 44 F4: Calatia: F3.

[16] The Roman garrison was still installed in the city after
Tarentum's capture by Hannibal (Book 25.10–11).

[17] King of the Masaesylii in Numidia in North Africa, he has
already appeared at 24.48.2–24.49.6. He tried to maintain relations with both Rome and Carthage but veered toward the latter
under the influence of the beautiful Sophonisba. Their tragic
story appears in Book 30. Cf. *OCD* s.v. Syphax.

permission to rebuild what had been burned, the Nicerians were resettled at Atella, because that had been their preference, and the Atellans were ordered to move to Calatia.[15]

Amid many important matters on people's minds, some favorable, some unfavorable, the citadel of Tarentum was not forgotten either.[16] Marcus Ogulnius and Publius Aquilius set off as a delegation into Etruria to purchase grain that was to be transported to Tarentum; and a thousand soldiers from the city army, Romans and allies in equal numbers, were also sent with grain to the garrison there.

4. Summer was already at an end and time for the consular elections was close at hand; but a dispatch had come from Marcellus declaring that it was not in the state's interests for him to move one step away from Hannibal, on whom, he said, he was putting serious pressure as he retreated and refused battle; and this had caused the senators some concern: either they would be calling the consul away from the war just as he was making great gains, or they would be without consuls for the coming year. The best option seemed to be for the consul Valerius, although he was outside Italy, to be recalled from Sicily. By senatorial decree, a letter was sent to him, together with the consul Marcus Marcellus' letter, by the urban praetor Lucius Manlius, so Valerius could learn from them why it was he rather than his colleague that the senators were recalling from his province.

At about that time legates from King Syphax[17] came to Rome bearing news of successful battles that he had fought with the Carthaginians; there was no people to

6 fecisset memorantes: regem nec inimiciorem ulli populo
quam Carthaginiensi, nec amiciorem quam Romanis[7] esse
adfirmabant. misisse eum antea legatos in Hispaniam ad
Cn. et P. Cornelios imperatores Romanos; nunc ab ipso
7 velut fonte petere Romanam amicitiam voluisse. senatus
non legatis modo benigne respondit, sed et ipse legatos
cum donis ad regem misit L. Genucium P. Poetelium P.
8 Popillium. dona tulere togam et tunicam purpuream,
sellam eburneam, pateram auream ex quinque pondo
9 factam.[8] protinus et alios Africae regulos iussi adire; iis
quoque quae darentur portata, togae praetextae et terna
10 pondo paterae aureae. et Alexandream ad Ptolomaeum et
Cleopatram reges M. Atilius et M.' Acilius legati ad com-
memorandam renovandamque amicitiam missi dona tulere, regi togam et tunicam purpuream cum sella eburnea,
reginae pallam pictam cum amiculo purpureo.

11 Multa ea aestate qua haec facta sunt ex propinquis
urbibus agrisque nuntiata sunt prodigia: Tusculi agnum
cum ubere lactenti natum, Iovis aedis culmen fulmine
12 ictum ac prope omni tecto nudatum; iisdem ferme diebus
Anagniae terram ante portam ictam diem ac noctem sine
ullo ignis alimento arsisse, et aves ad compitum Anagni-

---

[7] Romanis Σ: Romamno P: Romano P[c]

[8] pateram auream . . . factam Σ: pateram ex quinque pondo
auri factam P

---

[18] Appropriate gifts for royalty: cf. chapter 10, below; 31.11.12;
42.14.10.   [19] These are Ptolemy IV Philopator, and his wife-
sister, Arsinoe. The "friendship" with Ptolemy II Philadelphus
was established in 273 by Q. Fabius Maximus Gurges, N. Fabius
Pictor, and Q. Ogulnius Gallus (*MRR* 197).

whom Syphax was a more implacable enemy than the Carthaginian, they declared, and none to whom he was a closer friend than the Romans. He had earlier sent legates to Gnaeus and Publius Cornelius in Spain, they said; now he had decided to seek Roman friendship directly from the source, as it were. The senate not only responded favorably to the legates but also sent its own legates, Lucius Genucius and Publius Poetelius, to the king with gifts. The gifts they brought were a purple toga and a purple tunic, a chair of ivory, and a golden bowl five pounds in weight.[18] They were also ordered to proceed immediately to other kings in Africa; and gifts to be presented to them were also brought (*togae praetextae* and golden bowls each weighing three pounds). In addition, Marcus Atilius and Manius Acilius were sent as legates to the royal couple Ptolemy and Cleopatra in Alexandria to remind them about their ties of friendship with Rome and renewing those ties;[19] and as gifts they brought for the king a toga and a purple tunic together with a chair of ivory, and for the queen an embroidered wrap and a purple cloak.

During the summer of these events numerous prodigies were reported from nearby towns and country areas. At Tusculum a lamb was said to have been born with its udder full of milk, and the top of the temple of Jupiter to have been struck by lightning and its roof almost completely torn off; at Anagnia,[20] at roughly the same time, the ground before the city gate was said to have been struck by lightning and to have burned for a day and a night although there was nothing to fuel the fire; and birds had

[20] Anagnia (mod. Anagni): *Barr.* 43 E3.

13 num in luco Dianae nidos in arboribus reliquisse. Tarraci-
nae in mari haud procul portu angues magnitudinis mirae
lascivientium piscium modo exultasse; Tarquiniis porcum
14 cum ore humano genitum; et in agro Capenate ad lucum
Feroniae quattuor signa sanguine multo diem ac noctem
15 sudasse. haec prodigia hostiis maioribus procurata decreto
pontificum, et supplicatio diem unum Romae ad omnia
pulvinaria, alterum in Capenate agro ad Feroniae lucum
indicta.

5. M. Valerius consul litteris excitus, provincia exercituque mandato L. Cincio praetori, M. Valerio Messalla
praefecto classis cum parte navium in Africam praedatum
simul speculatumque quae populus Carthaginiensis age-
2 ret pararetque misso, ipse decem navibus Romam profectus cum prospere pervenisset, senatum extemplo habuit.
3 ibi[9] de suis rebus gestis commemoravit: cum annos prope
sexaginta in Sicilia terra marique magnis saepe cladibus
4 bellatum esset, se eam provinciam confecisse. neminem
Carthaginiensem in Sicilia esse, neminem Siculum non
esse; qui fugati metu inde afuerint, omnes in urbes, in
5 agros suos reductos arare, serere. desertam recoli terram,
tandem frugiferam ipsis cultoribus, populoque Romano
6 pace ac bello fidissimum annonae subsidium. exim Mut-

[9] ibi Σ: ubi P

---

[21] Tusculum: *Barr.* 44 C2; Tarracina: D3; Tarquinii: 42 B4;
Capena/Grove of Feronia: D4 (cf. 26.11.7 note).

[22] L. Cincius Alimentus (the historian; cf. 21.38.3) assigned to
Sicily as praetor: 26.23.1 (and note), 28.11.

[23] M. Valerius Messalla Maximus (251), consul in 226.

[24] Cf. 26.40.15 for Laevinus' plans for Sicilian agriculture.

reportedly abandoned their nests in trees in the grove of Diana at the crossroads of Anagnia. At Tarracina, in the sea not far from the harbor, snakes of miraculous size were supposed to have jumped from the water like fish at play; at Tarquinii a pig to have been born with a human face; and, at the Grove of Feronia in the territory of Capena, four statues to have sweated out copious quantities of blood. Expiation ceremonies for these prodigies were, by decree of the pontiffs, conducted with full-grown sacrificial animals, and one day of supplication was prescribed at all the couches in Rome, and a second day at the Grove of Feronia in the territory of Capena.[21]

5. On receiving his letter of recall, the consul Marcus Valerius delegated his province and army to the praetor Lucius Cincius[22] and sent the fleet commander Marcus Valerius Messalla[23] to Africa with a number of his ships to conduct raids and at the same time gather intelligence on the activities and plans of the Carthaginian people; and Valerius himself set off for Rome with ten ships, and immediately on arrival after a successful voyage convened the senate. There he reported on his achievements, noting that after almost sixty years of war in Sicily on land and sea, often with dreadful defeats, he had now subdued that province. Not one Carthaginian was left in Sicily, he said, and no Sicilian was missing from there—those who had left out of fear had all been restored to their cities and farms, and were plowing and sowing. Abandoned land was being worked again, finally bearing crops for its cultivators—the Roman people's most reliable support for its grain supply in peace and war.[24] Muttines[25] and any oth-

[25] For Muttines, cf. 26.21.15–16 and note, and 26.40.3–12 for his part in the capture of Agrigentum.

tine et si quorum aliorum merita erga populum Romanum
erant in senatum introductis, honores omnibus ad ex-
7 solvendam fidem consulis habiti; Muttines etiam civis
Romanus factus, rogatione ab tribunis plebis ex auctoritate patrum ad plebem lata.

8   Dum haec Romae geruntur, M. Valerius quinquaginta
navibus cum ante lucem ad Africam accessisset, improviso
9 in agrum Vticensem escensionem fecit, eumque late de-
populatus multis mortalibus cum alia omnis generis
praeda captis ad naves rediit et ad Siciliam tramisit, tertio
decimo die quam profectus inde erat Lilybaeum revectus.
10 ex captivis quaestione habita haec comperta consulique
Laevino omnia ordine perscripta ut sciret quo in statu res
11 Africae essent: quinque milia Numidarum cum Masinissa
Galae filio, acerrimo iuvene, Carthagine esse, et alios per
totam Africam milites mercede conduci qui in Hispaniam
12 ad Hasdrubalem traicerentur, ut is quam maximo exercitu
primo quoque tempore in Italiam transgressus iungeret se
13 Hannibali; in eo positam victoriam credere Carthaginienses; classem praeterea ingentem apparari ad Siciliam
repetendam, eamque se credere brevi traiecturam.

14   Haec recitata a consule ita movere senatum ut non
exspectanda comitia consuli censeret,[10] sed dictatore
comitiorum habendorum causa dicto extemplo in pro-

---

[10] censeret Σ: censerent P

---

[26] Modern Marsala on Sicily's west coast (*Barr.* 47 A3).

[27] King of Numidia (238–148), Masinissa and his father, Gala,
were initially allied with Carthage. In 211, as a cavalry commander in Spain, he successfully fought P. Cornelius Scipio, who

ers who had well served the Roman people were then ushered into the senate, and in fulfillment of the consul's promise honors were conferred on all of them. Muttines was also made a Roman citizen after a bill authorized by the senate was brought before the people by the plebeian tribunes.

While this was taking place in Rome, Marcus Valerius, reaching Africa with fifty ships before dawn, made a surprise landing in the territory of Utica and plundered the area widely, taking many prisoners together with all other sorts of booty before he came back to his ships and crossed to Sicily, returning to Lilybaeum[26] twelve days after his departure. From interrogation of the captives the following facts were ascertained, and a full, detailed transcription made for the consul Laevinus for him to see how matters stood in Africa: five thousand Numidians were in Carthage with Masinissa son of Gala,[27] an extremely dynamic young man, and other soldiers were being hired throughout Africa to be shipped over to Hasdrubal in Spain for him to cross to Italy with the largest possible army and link up with Hannibal as soon as possible; it was in this strategy that the Carthaginians believed victory lay; moreover, a huge armada was being prepared for recovering Sicily, and they believed it would soon make the crossing.

Read out by the consul, this so concerned the senate that it voted that the consul not wait for the elections but appoint a dictator for the holding of elec-

died in the battle (25.34.2–14), but he later transferred his allegiance to Scipio Africanus, whom he loyally assisted when Scipio landed in Africa.

15 vinciam redeundum. illa disceptatio tenebat quod consul
in Sicilia se M. Valerium Messallam qui tum classi praeesset dictatorem dicturum esse aiebat, patres extra Romanum agrum—eum autem Italia terminari—negabant dic-
16 tatorem dici posse. M. Lucretius tribunus plebis cum de
ea re consuleret, ita decrevit senatus ut consul priusquam
ab urbe discederet populum rogaret quem dictatorem dici
placeret, eumque quem populus iussisset diceret dictatorem; si consul noluisset, praetor populum rogaret; si ne
17 is quidem vellet, tum tribuni ad plebem ferrent. cum consul se populum rogaturum negasset quod suae potestatis
esset praetoremque vetuisset rogare, tribuni plebem roga-
runt plebesque scivit ut Q. Fulvius qui tum ad Capuam
18 erat dictator diceretur. sed quo die id plebis concilium
futurum erat, consul clam nocte in Siciliam abiit; destitu-
tique patres litteras ad M. Claudium mittendas censuerunt ut desertae ab collega rei publicae subveniret, dice-
19 retque quem populus iussisset dictatorem. ita a M. Claudio
consule Q. Fulvius dictator dictus, et ex eodem plebis scito
ab Q. Fulvio dictatore P. Licinius Crassus pontifex maximus magister equitum dictus.

6. Dictator postquam Romam venit, C. Sempronium
Blaesum legatum quem ad Capuam habuerat in Etruriam

---

28 A position granted to an individual in an emergency (cf.
OCD s.v.).

29 P. Licinius Crassus Dives; Pontifex Maximus (212), praetor
(208), and consul with Scipio (205); cf. *MRR* 301.

tions[28] and immediately return to his province. But a disagreement kept holding the matter up because the consul kept saying that he would, when in Sicily, appoint as dictator Marcus Valerius Messalla (who was then in command of the fleet); but the senators told him that outside Roman territory, which was limited to the confines of Italy, a dictator could not be appointed. When the plebeian tribune Marcus Lucretius consulted the senate on the matter, the senate decreed that the consul should, before he left the city, put to the people the question of whom they wanted named dictator, and then he should appoint as dictator the man the people named. If the consul refused, then the praetor should put the question to the people; if even he refused, the tribunes should then bring the matter to the plebs. When the consul said he would not put before the people a matter he claimed was his to decide, and also ordered the praetor not to do so, the tribunes put the question to the plebs and the plebs decided that Quintus Fulvius, who was then at Capua, should be appointed dictator. But during the night before the assembly of the plebs was to be held the consul slipped furtively away to Sicily. Left at an impasse, the senators then voted to send a dispatch to Marcus Claudius for him to come to the assistance of a republic abandoned by his colleague, and to declare as dictator the man who was the people's choice. And so Quintus Fulvius was named dictator by the consul Marcus Claudius and, with the same resolution of the plebs, the Pontifex Maximus Publius Licinius Crassus[29] was appointed master of horse by the dictator Quintus Fulvius.

6. After arriving in Rome, the dictator dispatched his legate Gaius Sempronius Blaesus, whom he had had with

provinciam ad exercitum misit in locum C. Calpurni praetoris, quem ut Capuae exercituique suo praeesset litteris
2 excivit. ipse comitia in quem diem primum potuit edixit,
quae certamine inter tribunos dictatoremque iniecto per
3 fici non potuerunt. Galeria iuniorum quae sorte praerogativa erat Q. Fulvium et Q. Fabium consules dixerat, eodemque iure vocatae inclinassent ni se tribuni plebis C. et
4 L. Arrenii interposuissent, qui neque magistratum continuari satis civile esse aiebant et multo foedioris exempli
5 eum ipsum creari qui comitia haberet. itaque si suum
nomen dictator acciperet, se comitiis intercessuros; si aliorum praeterquam ipsius ratio haberetur, comitiis se mo
6 ram non facere. dictator causam comitiorum auctoritate
7 senatus, plebis scito, exemplis tutabatur: namque Cn. Servilio consule cum C. Flaminius alter consul ad Trasumennum cecidisset, ex auctoritate patrum ad plebem latum
plebemque scivisse ut, quoad bellum in Italia esset, ex iis
qui consules fuissent quos et quotiens vellet reficiendi
8 consules populo ius esset; exemplaque in eam rem se habere, vetus L. Postumi Megelli qui interrex iis comitiis
quae ipse habuisset consul cum C. Iunio Bubulco creatus

---

[30] He had been plebeian tribune the previous year and had
brought a charge against Cn. Fulvius Flaccus, the dictator's
brother, for the defeat at Herdonea (26.2.7, 26.3.9).

[31] C. Calpurnius Piso. He had been praetor urbanus for 211.

[32] The *centuria praerogativa*; cf. 26.22.2 and note.

[33] L. Postumius Megellus, consul in 305, 294, and (the year
when he was *interrex*) 291; *MRR* 182–83.

[34] Q. Fabius Maximus Verrucosus, the "delayer" (*cunctator*):
consul suffect in 215, consul in 214: *MRR* 254, 258.

him in Capua,[30] to the army in his province of Etruria to replace the praetor Gaius Calpurnius,[31] whom he summoned by letter to take charge of Capua and his army there. He himself then announced elections for the earliest possible day, something that, because of a dispute between the tribunes and the dictator, could not be arranged. The century of junior members of the tribe Galeria, which by lot had the right to vote first,[32] had declared Quintus Fulvius and Quintus Fabius their choice for consuls, and, when called on in their routine order, the other tribe would have been similarly inclined but for an intervention by the plebeian tribunes Gaius and Lucius Arrenius, who insisted that extending a period of office was unconstitutional and that electing the very man who was presiding over the voting set an even worse precedent. So if the dictator accepted his own nomination, they said, they would veto the election, but if other nominations and not his own were considered they would not obstruct the proceedings. The dictator kept trying to justify the election by appealing to the authority of the senate, the decision of the plebs, and precedents; when Gnaeus Servilius was consul, he said, and the other consul, Gaius Flaminius, had fallen at Trasimene, a proposal had been brought to the plebs with senatorial authorization—and one that the plebs ratified—that for as long as the war lasted in Italy the people should have the right to re-elect whatever former consuls they pleased and as often as they wished. He also had precedents supporting the procedure, he said, an old one being that of Lucius Postumius Megellus,[33] who had been elected consul with Gaius Junius Bubulcus in elections over which he himself had presided as *interrex,* and a recent one that of Quintus Fabius,[34] who would certainly

221

esset, recens Q. Fabi qui sibi continuari consulatum nisi
id bono publico fieret profecto nunquam sisset.

9   His orationibus cum diu certatum esset, postremo ita
inter dictatorem ac tribunos convenit ut eo quod censuis-
10 set senatus staretur. patribus id tempus rei publicae visum
est ut per veteres et expertos bellique peritos imperatores
res publica gereretur; itaque moram fieri comitiis non pla-
11 cere. concedentibus tribunis comitia habita; declarati consules Q. Fabius Maximus quintum Q. Fulvius Flaccus
12 quartum. praetores inde creati L. Veturius Philo, T.
Quinctius Crispinus, C. Hostilius Tubulus, C. Aurunculeius. magistratibus in annum creatis Q. Fulvius dictatura
se abdicavit.

13   Extremo aestatis huius classis Punica navium quadraginta cum praefecto Hamilcare in Sardiniam traiecta Ol-
14 biensem primo, dein postquam ibi P. Manlius Vulso praetor cum exercitu apparuit circumacta inde ad alterum
insulae latus Caralitanum agrum vastavit, et cum praeda
omnis generis in Africam rediit.[11]

15   Sacerdotes Romani eo anno mortui aliquot suffec-
tique. C. Servilius pontifex factus in locum T. Otacili
Crassi [Ti. Sempronius Ti. filius Longus augur factus in
16 locum T. Otacili Crassi].[12] decemvir item sacris faciundis

---

[11] rediit $C^c\Sigma$: redit P [12] [Ti. Sempronius . . . Crassi] P:
om. Σ; vide Briscoe comm. ad 41.21.7

---

[35] Greek for "happy, blessed, prosperous," a name given to
several Greek colonies; for this one in northern Sardinia, cf. Barr.
48 B2. The Romans took Sardinia from the Carthaginians in 238
and organized it as a province with Corsica in 227. The identity
of this Hamilcar remains uncertain.

never have allowed himself an extended consulship if it had not been in the public interest.

After lengthy wrangling over such arguments, an agreement was finally reached between the dictator and the tribunes to abide by whatever the senate decided. To the senators this critical moment for the republic seemed to call for affairs of state to be conducted by veteran commanders with experience and skill in warfare; and so they did not favor any delay in the elections. The tribunes acquiescing, elections were held; and Quintus Fabius Maximus was elected for the fifth time and Quintus Fulvius Flaccus for the fourth. The praetors were elected next: Lucius Veturius Philo, Titus Quinctius Crispinus, Gaius Hostilius Tubulus and Gaius Aurunculeius. The magistrates for the year thus elected, Quintus Fulvius resigned from the dictatorship.

At the end of this summer a Punic fleet of forty ships crossed to Sardinia under the command of Hamilcar. It first conducted raids on the farmlands of Olbia;[35] then, after Publius Manlius Volso appeared there with his army, it sailed around to other side of the island, plundered the lands of Carales,[36] and returned to Africa with all sorts of spoils.

A number Roman priests died that year and were replaced. Gaius Servilius was made pontiff in place of Titus Ocilius Crassus; Tiberius Sempronius Longus, son of Tiberius, was made augur in place of Gaius Atilius Serranus. Likewise Tiberius Sempronius Longus, son of Tiberius,

---

36 Modern Cagliari: *Barr.* 48 B3.

in locum Ti. Semproni C. filii Longi Ti. Sempronius Ti.
filius Longus suffectus. M. Marcius rex sacrorum mortuus
est et M. Aemilius Papus maximus curio, neque in eorum
17 locum sacerdotes eo anno suffecti. et censores hic annus
habuit L. Veturium Philonem et P. Licinium Crassum
maximum pontificem. Crassus Licinius nec consul nec
praetor ante fuerat quam censor est factus; ex aedilitate
18 gradum ad censuram fecit. sed hi censores neque senatum
legerunt neque quicquam publicae rei egerunt. mors dire-
19 mit L. Veturi; inde et Licinius censura se abdicavit. aediles
curules L. Veturius et P. Licinius Varus ludos Romanos
diem unum instaurarunt. aediles plebeii Q. Catius et L.
Porcius Licinus ex multaticio argento signa aenea ad Cereris dedere, et ludos pro temporis eius copia magnifice
apparatos fecerunt.

7. Exitu anni huius C. Laelius legatus Scipionis die
quarto et tricensimo quam a Tarracone profectus erat
Romam venit, isque cum agmine captivorum ingressus

---

[37] Also referred to as *rex sacrificiorum* or *rex sacrificulus* (king
of sacrifices). During the republic he fulfilled many of the religious functions earlier exercised by the king (cf. *OCD* s.v. *rex
sacrorum*). Marcius was perhaps the first plebeian to hold the
office (cf. *MRR* 284 n. 8).

[38] The chief *curio* was overall head of the *curiae*, the oldest of
the various divisions of the Roman people, thirty in number, ten
from each of the tribes: *OCD* s.v. *curia* (1).

[39] L. Veturius Philo, praetor in 209, consul in 206.

[40] P. Licinius Varus, urban praetor in 208.

[41] The Roman Games took place from September 4 to 19. As
games and festivals were religious ceremonies, correct protocol
and procedure were necessary, and any flaw or incorrect proce-

replaced Tiberius Sempronius Longus, son of Gaius, as *decemvir* for sacrifices. The *rex sacrorum* Marcus Marcius[37] and the head *curio*[38] Marcus Aemilius Papus also died, but no suffect priests replaced them that year. The year also saw Lucius Veturius Philo and Publius Licinius Crassus, the Pontifex Maximus, appointed censors. Licinius Crassus had previously been neither consul nor praetor before becoming censor; he made the step to the censorship directly from the aedileship. However, these censors did not revise the roll of senators or conduct any official business whatsoever. The death of Lucius Veturius preempted it; and Licinius also then resigned his censorship. The curule aediles Lucius Veturius[39] and Publius Licinius[40] repeated the Roman Games for a single day.[41] The Plebeian aediles Quintus Catius and Lucius Porcius Licinus established bronze statues at the temple of Ceres[42] with money raised from fines, and they put on games with considerable grandeur for the resources available at that time.

7. At the end of this year,[43] Scipio's legate Gaius Laelius came to Rome thirty-three days after leaving Tarraco, and he attracted large crowds when entering the city with a

dure led to partial or complete repetition (*instauratio*): *OCD* s.v. *ludi* and *instauratio*.

42 Northwest of the Circus Maximus, on the lower slope of the Aventine, the temple was a plebeian center, serving as headquarters for the plebeian aediles and possessing the right of asylum. It was dedicated in 493. Cf. Richardson 80–81.

43 Livy's chronology is faulty: it is now the end of 209 (the year of the capture of Cartagena) not 210.

2   urbem magnum concursum hominum fecit. postero die in senatum introductus captam Carthaginem caput Hispaniae uno die, receptasque aliquot urbes quae defecissent

3   novasque in societatem adscitas exposuit. ex captivis comperta iis ferme congruentia quae in litteris fuerant M. Valeri Messallae; maxime movit patres Hasdrubalis transitus in Italiam vix Hannibali atque eius armis obsistentem.

4   productus et in contionem Laelius eadem edisseruit. senatus ob res feliciter a P. Scipione gestas supplicationem in unum diem decrevit. C. Laelium primo quoque tempore cum quibus venerat navibus redire in Hispaniam iussit.

5   Carthaginis expugnationem in hunc annum contuli multis auctoribus, haud nescius quosdam esse qui anno inse-

6   quenti captam tradiderint, quod mihi minus simile veri visum est annum integrum Scipionem nihil gerendo in Hispania consumpsisse.

7   Q. Fabio Maximo quintum Q. Fulvio Flacco quartum consulibus idibus Martiis quo die magistratum inierunt Italia ambobus provincia decreta, regionibus tamen partitum imperium; Fabius ad Tarentum, Fulvius in Lucanis

8   ac Bruttiis rem gereret. M. Claudio prorogatum in annum imperium. praetores sortiti provincias, C. Hostilius Tubu-

---

[44] Cf. 26.51.2 for the embarkation of the captives along with "Mago and some fifteen senators who had been captured with him," but their departure was from Cartagena, not Tarragona. For Gaius Laelius, Scipio's close friend, cf. 26.42.5 and note.

[45] On supplication, cf. 26.21.3 note.

[46] Cf. 26.51.2, where only one quinquereme is mentioned; Moore suggests that smaller vessels (not thought worthy of mention) provided an escort, and others have suggested emendation.

[47] Livy is puzzled because he has misdated the disasters of the

train of captives.[44] Brought into the senate the next day, he recounted how New Carthage, the capital of Spain, had been captured in one day and how a number of cities that had defected had been recovered and some new ones brought into alliance. Information from the prisoners pretty well squared with what had been in the dispatch from Marcus Valerius Messalla; what most perturbed the senators was the threat of Hasdrubal's passage into an Italy that could barely withstand Hannibal and his forces. Brought also before the popular assembly, Laelius there delivered the same information. The senate proclaimed a single day of supplication[45] for Publius Scipio's successes; it also ordered Gaius Laelius to return to Spain as soon as possible with the ships with which he had come.[46] I have, on the basis of many sources, placed the capture of New Carthage in this year (although I am not unaware that some have recorded it as taken the following year) because it seemed to me less plausible that Scipio spent a whole year in Spain without actually doing anything.[47]

Quintus Fabius Maximus and Quintus Fulvius Flaccus became consuls on the Ides of March,[48] Fabius for the fifth time and Fulvius for the fourth and on the day on which they entered office both were assigned Italy as their province, but with their authority demarcated by region: Fabius was to operate around Tarentum, Fulvius in Lucania and Bruttium. Marcus Claudius' *imperium* was prorogued for a year. In the praetorian sortition of provinces, Gaius Hostilius Tubulus received the urban jurisdiction,

elder Scipios to 212 instead of to 211 and cannot understand why nothing more was done in 210; cf. 26.41.1 note.

[48] Cf. 26.1.1 note.

lus urbanam, L. Veturius Philo peregrinam cum Gallia, T.
Quinctius Crispinus Capuam, C. Aurunculeius Sardiniam.

9   Exercitus ita per provincias divisi: Fulvio duae legiones
quas in Sicilia M. Valerius Laevinus haberet, Q. Fabio[13]

10 quibus in Etruria C. Calpurnius praefuisset; urbanus exercitus ut in Etruriam succederet, C. Calpurnius eidem
praeesset provinciae exercituique; Capuam exercitumque

11 quem Q. Fulvius habuisset T. Quinctius obtineret; C. Hostilius ab C. Laetorio propraetore provinciam exercitumque qui tum Arimini erat acciperet. M. Marcello quibus consul rem gesserat legiones decretae. M. Valerio cum
L. Cincio—iis quoque enim prorogatum in Sicilia impe-

12 rium—Cannensis exercitus datus, eumque supplere ex
militibus qui ex legionibus Cn. Fulvi superessent iussi.

13 conquisitos eos consules in Siciliam miserunt, additaque
eadem militiae ignominia sub qua Cannenses militabant
quique ex praetoris Cn. Fulvi exercitu ob similis iram fu-

14 gae missi eo ab senatu fuerant. C. Aurunculeio eaedem in
Sardinia legiones quibus P. Manlius Vulso eam provinciam

15 obtinuerat decretae. P. Sulpicio eadem legione eademque
classe Macedoniam obtinere iusso prorogatum in annum
imperium. triginta quinqueremes ex Sicilia Tarentum ad

16 Q. Fabium consulem mitti iussae; cetera classe placere
praedatum in Africam aut ipsum M. Valerium Laevinum

---

[13] Fulvio . . . Fabio Σ: Fulvio . . . Q. Fabio *P*: ⟨Q.⟩ Fulvio . . .
Q. Fabio *Walsh*

---

[49] Cn. Fulvius Flaccus, praetor in 212, was badly defeated by
Hannibal at Herdonea but escaped with some of his cavalry
(25.21.1–10; 26.2.7–16).

[50] P. Manlius Vulso, praetor there in 210 (26.28.12).

Lucius Veturius Philo the foreigners' jurisdiction plus Gaul, Titus Quinctius Crispinus Capua, and Gaius Aurunculeius Sardinia.

Distribution of armies among provinces was as follows: Quintus Fulvius was assigned the two legions that Marcus Valerius Laevinus had charge of in Sicily, and Quintus Fabius the legions that Gaius Calpurnius had been commanding in Etruria. The city army was to move into Etruria, and Gaius Calpurnius would again have charge of that same province and its army. Titus Quinctius would take charge of Capua and the army Quintus Fulvius had commanded. Gaius Hostilius was to take over from the propraetor Gaius Laetorius command of his province and the army that was then at Ariminum. Marcus Marcellus was assigned the legions with which the consul had been operating. Marcus Valerius and Lucius Cincius (for they too had their *imperium* prorogued in Sicily) were delegated the Cannae army, and were ordered to supplement it from soldiers surviving from the legions of Gnaeus Fulvius.[49] Having sought these out, the consuls sent them off to Sicily, and they were also to serve under the same humiliating conditions as the Cannae veterans were serving and those troops from the praetor Gnaeus Fulvius' army that were sent to Sicily by the senate in its displeasure over a similar flight in battle. Gaius Aurunculeius was assigned the same legions in Sardinia with which Publius Manlius Vulso[50] had held the province. Publius Sulpicius, ordered to hold Macedonia with the same legion and fleet as before, had his *imperium* extended a year. Orders were given for thirty quinqueremes to be sent from Sicily to the consul Quintus Fabius at Tarentum; the remainder of the fleet, it was decided, would be used for raids on Africa—Marcus Vale-

traicere aut mittere seu L. Cincium seu M. Valerium Mes-
17 sallam vellet. nec de Hispania quicquam mutatum nisi
quod non in annum Scipioni Silanoque, sed donec revocati
ab senatu forent prorogatum imperium est. ita provinciae
exercituumque in eum annum partita imperia.

8. Inter maiorum rerum curas comitia maximi curionis,
cum in locum M. Aemili sacerdos crearetur, vetus excita-
verunt certamen, patriciis negantibus C. Mamili Atelli,
2 qui unus ex plebe petebat, habendam rationem esse quia
nemo ante eum nisi ex patribus id sacerdotium habuisset.
tribuni appellati ad senatum reiecerunt,[14] senatus populi
3 potestatem fecit; ita primus ex plebe creatus maximus
curio C. Mamilius Atellus.

4   Et flaminem Dialem invitum inaugurari coegit P. Licinius pontifex maximus C. Valerium Flaccum; decemvir[15]
sacris faciundis creatus in locum Q. Muci Scaevolae de-
5 mortui C. Laetorius. causam inaugurari coacti flaminis
libens reticuissem ni ex mala fama in bonam vertisset. ob
adulescentiam neglegentem luxuriosamque C. Flaccus
flamen captus a P. Licinio pontifice maximo erat, L. Flacco
6 fratri germano cognatisque aliis ob eadem vitia invisus. is,

---

[14] ⟨rem⟩ reiecerunt *Gron.*
[15] decemvir *Drak.*: decemvirum *P*

---

[51] However, Livy reports below (22.7) that in 208 both had
their commands prorogued for a year.
[52] Cf. 6.16 and note. Although until this year the post of *curio
maximus* had been held only by patricians, the election does in-
dicate that members of the *curiae* were from both orders. Atellus
was plebeian aedile in 208 and praetor in Sicily in 207 (35.1, below) and remained *curio maximus* until his death in 174.

rius Laevinus was either to sail over in person or, if he chose, send Lucius Cincius or Marcus Valerius Messalla in his stead. Nor was any change made in the case of Spain apart from Scipio and Silanus receiving prorogation of their *imperium,* not for a year but until such time as they were recalled by the senate.[51] Such was the distribution of provinces and commands for that year.

8. While attention was focused on more pressing matters, elections to the post of chief *curio,* when a priest was to be chosen to replace Marcus Aemilius, aroused an old quarrel, because the patricians claimed that the nomination of Gaius Mamilius Atellus, the sole candidate from the plebs, could not be entertained as no one outside the patrician order had held that priesthood before him. An appeal was made to the tribunes and they referred the matter to the senate; the senate granted the people authority to decide; and so Gaius Mamilius Atellus became the first from the plebeian order elected chief *curio.*[52]

The Pontifex Maximus Publius Licinius also forced Gaius Valerius Flaccus to be inaugurated as flamen of Jupiter against his will; and Quintus Mucius Scaevola was, on his death, replaced as decemvir for sacrifices by Gaius Laetorius. About the reason for a flamen being forced to accept his position I would readily have remained silent had it not been a case of a bad reputation turning into a good one. It was because of his shiftless and dissipated youth that Gaius Flaccus was chosen as flamen by the Pontifex Maximus Publius Licinius, although the young man was hated by his brother and other relatives for these

ut animum eius cura sacrorum et caerimoniarum cepit,
ita repente exuit antiquos mores ut nemo tota iuventute
haberetur prior nec probatior primoribus patrum suis
7 pariter alienisque esset. huius famae consensu elatus ad
iustam fiduciam sui, rem intermissam per multos annos ob
indignitatem flaminum priorum repetivit, in senatum ut
8 introiret. ingressum eum curiam cum P. Licinius praetor
inde eduxisset, tribunos plebis appellavit. flamen vetus-
tum ius sacerdotii repetebat: datum id cum toga praetexta
9 et sella curuli ei flamonio esse. praetor non exoletis vetus-
tate annalium exemplis stare ius sed recentissimae cuiusque consuetudinis usu volebat: nec patrum nec avorum
10 memoria Dialem quemquam id ius usurpasse. tribuni rem
inertia flaminum oblitteratam ipsis, non sacerdotio, damno
fuisse cum aequum censuissent, ne ipso quidem contra
tendente praetore, magno adsensu patrum plebisque flaminem in senatum introduxerunt, omnibus ita existiman-
tibus magis sanctitate vitae quam sacerdotii iure eam rem
flaminem obtinuisse.

11   Consules priusquam in provincias irent, duas urbanas
legiones in supplementum quantum opus erat ceteris
12 exercitibus militum scripserunt. urbanum veterem exercitum Fulvius consul C. Fulvio Flacco legato—frater hic
consulis erat—in Etruriam dedit ducendum, et legiones
13 quae in Etruria erant Romam deducendas. et Fabius con-

---

53 Cf. Val. Max. 6.9.3 (from Livy).
54 C. Fulvius Flaccus had also served well under his brother
Q. Fulvius Flaccus at Capua: cf. 26.5.8, 26.14.6–7, 26.33.5–7.

very shortcomings.[53] When the religious and ceremonial duties captured his interest, so swiftly did he slough off his old ways that none of the younger men, whether family relations or strangers, enjoyed greater esteem or approval among the leading senators. Gaining justifiable self-confidence from the general agreement over his new reputation, he reclaimed something that had over the years been suspended because of earlier flamens' disreputable conduct, namely entry into the senate. When he set foot in the senate house and the praetor Publius Licinius ushered him out, he appealed to the plebeian tribunes. He was, as a flamen, reclaiming a time-honored prerogative of his priesthood: that, together with the toga praetexta and curule chair, was granted to the office of flamen, he said! The praetor maintained that that prerogative lay not in outdated precedents from ancient history but in all the most recent practice, and no *flamen Dialis* had exercised that prerogative in either their fathers' or grandfathers' day. The tribunes ruled that since the privilege had fallen into disuse through some flamens' indolence it was correct for the loss to be theirs, not the priesthood's, and, with no opposition even from the praetor, they escorted the flamen into the senate with great approval from the senators and plebs, although everyone thought the flamen had gained his end more from the probity of his life than the prerogative of the priesthood.

Before leaving for their provinces, the consuls raised two city legions to supplement the numbers required for the other armies. The consul Fulvius assigned to Gaius Fulvius Flaccus[54]—he was the consul's brother—the responsibility of taking the old city army to Etruria and bringing back to Rome the legions that were in Etruria.

sul reliquias exercitus Fulviani conquisitas—fuere autem
ad quattuor milia trecenti quadraginta quattuor—Q.
Maximum filium ducere in Siciliam ad M. Valerium
proconsulem iussit, atque ab eo duas legiones et triginta
14 quinqueremes accipere. nihil eae deductae ex insula legiones minuerunt nec viribus nec specie eius provinciae
15 praesidium; nam cum praeter egregie suppletas duas veteres legiones transfugarum etiam Numidarum equitum
peditumque magnam vim haberet, Siculos quoque qui in
exercitu Epicydis aut Poenorum fuerant, belli peritos vi-
16 ros, milites scripsit. ea externa auxilia cum singulis Romanis legionibus adiunxisset, duorum speciem exercituum
servavit. altero L. Cincium partem insulae, qua regnum[16]
17 Hieronis fuerat, tueri iussit; altero ipse ceteram insulam
tuebatur divisam quondam Romani Punicique imperii finibus, classe quoque navium septuaginta partita ut omni
18 ambitu litorum praesidio orae maritimae essent. ipse cum
Muttinis equitatu provinciam peragrabat ut viseret agros
cultaque ab incultis notaret et perinde dominos laudaret
19 castigaretque. ita tantum ea cura frumenti provenit ut et
Romam mitteret et Catinam conveheret unde exercitui
qui ad Tarentum aestiva acturus esset posset praeberi.

---

[16] qua regnum Σ: regnum qua P

---

55 Q. Fabius Maximus, son of Q. Fabius Verrucosus, had been
praetor in 214 and consul in 213.

56 Epicydes (and Hippocrates) replaced the assassinated tyrant Hieronymus and figure prominently in Books 24 and 25: cf.
26.30.2 and note.

57 No such demarcation between the two powers is known.
Hoyos (HW, 675) comments: "'Greek and Punic' would make

The consul Fabius also instructed his son Quintus Maximus[55] to seek out the remnants of Fulvius' army—they amounted to some 4,344 men—and lead them to the proconsul Marcus Valerius in Sicily, and then to take over from him two legions and thirty quinqueremes. Removing these legions from the island in no way diminished that province's defenses in real or perceived strength; for apart from an excellent job in bringing the two old legions up to strength, Valerius also had large numbers of Numidian deserters, both infantry and cavalry, and he also recruited Sicilians, battle-hardened men who had been in Epicydes' army[56] or that of the Carthaginians. By adding those foreign auxiliaries to individual Roman legions, Valerius maintained the appearance of two armies. With one he ordered Lucius Cincius to defend the part of the island that had been Hieron's kingdom; with the other he himself undertook defense of the rest of the island, once divided by boundaries of Roman and Punic control,[57] and he also split his fleet of seventy ships so they could defend the entire coastline. He personally traversed his province with Muttines' cavalry to visit farms and take note of what was and what was not cultivated and on that basis commend or criticize landowners. Thanks to such diligence, the grain yield was great enough for him both to send some to Rome and also transport some to Catina[58] so the army that would be spending the summer around Tarentum could be provisioned from there.

more sense, for Sicily had indeed once been partially under Greek and partially under Punic rule."

[58] Modern Catania.

9. Ceterum transportati milites in Siciliam—et erant
maior pars Latini nominis sociorumque—prope magni
motus causa fuere; adeo ex parvis saepe magnarum mo-
2 menta rerum pendent. fremitus enim inter Latinos sociosque in conciliis ortus: decimum annum dilectibus stipen-
3 diis se exhaustos esse; quotannis ferme clade magna
pugnare; alios in acie occidi, alios morbo absumi. magis
perire sibi civem qui ab Romano miles lectus sit quam qui
ab Poeno captus, quippe ab hoste gratis remitti in patriam,
ab Romanis extra Italiam in exsilium verius quam in mili-
4 tiam ablegari. octavum iam ibi annum senescere Cannensem militem, moriturum ante quam Italia hostis, quippe
5 nunc cum maxime florens viribus, excedat. si veteres milites non redeant in patriam, novi legantur, brevi neminem
superfuturum. itaque quod propediem res ipsa negatura
sit, priusquam ad ultimam solitudinem atque egestatem
6 perveniant, negandum populo Romano esse. si consenti-
entes in hoc socios videant Romani, profecto de pace cum
Carthaginiensibus iungenda cogitaturos; aliter nunquam
vivo Hannibale sine bello Italiam fore. haec acta in conciliis.

7 Triginta tum coloniae populi Romani erant; ex iis duodecim, cum omnium legationes Romae essent, negaverunt
consulibus esse unde milites pecuniamque darent. eae
fuere Ardea, Nepete, Sutrium, Alba, Carseoli, Sora,
8 Suessa, Circeii, Setia, Cales, Narnia, Interamna. nova re
consules icti cum absterrere eos a tam detestabili consilio

---

59 Livy refers to casual, not official, meetings.
60 Latin colonies including originally Roman citizens. On Roman colonies, see *OCD* s.v. colonization, Roman.

9. However, the soldiers shipped to Sicily—and they were mostly of Latin or allied status—were nearly the cause of serious unrest; so true is it that great and critical events often come from the insignificant! For grumbling started among the Latins and allies in their gatherings;[59] for nine years, they said, they had been drained raising troops and supplying their pay; almost every year they faced some terrible defeat in battle; and some were being killed in battle and others taken off by disease. A compatriot conscripted by the Roman was more lost to them than one captured by the Carthaginian; for by the enemy he was sent home without ransom but by the Romans he was taken out of Italy into what was more truly exile than military service. For seven years now any soldier from Cannae had been growing old in that exile, and would die before the enemy (now at the height of his strength) left Italy. If veteran soldiers did not return home and new ones kept being conscripted, there would soon be none left! So they must refuse the Roman people what circumstances would soon refuse them anyway, and do it now before they reached utter depopulation and poverty. If the Romans saw their allies agreeing on this, they would surely consider making peace with the Carthaginians; otherwise, Italy would never be free of war while Hannibal remained alive. So went discussions at their meetings.

The Roman people then had thirty colonies;[60] and twelve of them had told the consuls—they all now had delegations in Rome—that they lacked the means to supply fighting men and cash. The twelve were Ardea, Nepete, Sutrium, Alba, Carsioli, Sora, Suessa, Circeii, Setia, Cales, Narnia, and Interamna. Taken aback by the surprising turn, the consuls tried deterring delegates from such a

vellent, castigando increpandoque plus quam leniter
9 agendo profecturos rati, eos ausos esse consulibus dicere
aiebant quod consules ut in senatu pronuntiarent in animum inducere non possent; non enim detractationem
eam munerum militiae, sed apertam defectionem a po-
10 pulo Romano esse. redirent itaque propere in colonias, et
tamquam integra re, locuti magis quam ausi tantum nefas,
cum suis consulerent. admonerent non Campanos neque
11 Tarentinos esse eos sed Romanos, inde oriundos, inde in
colonias atque in agrum bello captum stirpis augendae
causa missos. quae liberi parentibus deberent, ea illos
Romanis debere, si ulla pietas, si memoria antiquae pa-
12 triae esset. consulerent igitur de integro; nam tum quidem
quae temere agitassent ea prodendi imperii Romani, tra-
dendae Hannibali victoriae esse.
13   Cum alternis haec consules diu iactassent, nihil moti
legati neque se quod domum renuntiarent habere dixerunt neque senatum suum quid novi consuleret, ubi nec
miles qui legeretur nec pecunia quae daretur in stipen-
14 dium esset. cum obstinatos eos viderent consules, rem ad
senatum detulerunt, ubi tantus pavor animis hominum est
iniectus ut magna pars actum de imperio diceret. idem
alias colonias facturas, idem socios; consensisse omnes ad
prodendam Hannibali urbem Romanam.
  10. Consules hortari et consolari senatum, et dicere
alias colonias in fide atque officio pristino fore; eas quoque

---

61 That is, the administrative body of each colony.

terrible idea; and thinking they would have more success with censure and reproach than with gentle treatment, they told them that what they had dared to say to the consuls they, the consuls, could not conceivably articulate in the senate; for that would be not a refusal of military obligations but open defection from the Roman people. So they should return immediately to their colonies and discuss it with their people as if the subject had not been broached, since they had only discussed and not taken such a frightful step. They should remind their people that they were not Capuans or Tarentines but Romans, that it was from them that they were descended, and from them sent out into colonies and territory captured in war to increase the Roman race. What children owed to their parents was what they owed to the Romans—if they had any sense of duty or any memory of their mother city of old. So they should reconsider; for their earlier reckless deliberations meant betraying the Roman empire and handing victory to Hannibal.

Although the consuls pressed these arguments in turn for quite some time, the delegates, quite unmoved, said they had no suggestion to take home and their senate[61] had no new business to discuss when they had neither soldiers for conscription nor money to be given as pay. When the consuls saw them inflexible, they brought the matter before the senate, where such panic struck the members that most said the empire was done for. The other colonies would do the same, they said, and so would the allies—all had banded together to betray the city of Rome to Hannibal!

10. The consuls encouraged and reassured the senate, and they said the other colonies would remain just as loyal

ipsas quae officio decesserint, si legati circa eas colonias
mittantur qui castigent non qui precentur, verecundiam
2 imperii habituras esse. permissum ab senatu iis cum esset
agerent facerentque ut e re publica ducerent, pertempta-
tis prius aliarum coloniarum animis, citaverunt legatos
quaesiveruntque ab iis ecquid milites ex formula paratos
3 haberent. pro duodeviginti coloniis M. Sextilius Fregellanus respondit et milites paratos ex formula esse, et si plu-
4 ribus opus esset plures daturos, et quidquid aliud impera-
ret velletque populus Romanus enixe facturos. ad id sibi
5 neque opes deesse,[17] animum etiam superesse. consules
parum sibi videri praefati pro merito eorum sua voce
conlaudari eos nisi universi patres iis in curia gratias
6 egissent, sequi in senatum[18] iusserunt. senatus quam poterat honoratissimo decreto adlocutus eos, mandat consulibus ut ad populum quoque eos producerent et inter
multa alia praeclara quae ipsis maioribusque suis praesti-
tissent recens etiam meritum eorum in rem publicam
commemorarent.

7 Ne nunc quidem post tot saecula sileantur frauden-
turve laude sua; Signini fuere et Norbani Saticulanique et
Fregellani et Lucerini et Venusini et Brundisini et Ha-
8 driani et Firmani et Ariminenses, et ab altero mari Pon-
tiani et Paestani et Cosani, et mediterranei Beneventani
et Aesernini et Spoletini et Placentini et Cremonenses.

---

17 deesse *C*Σ: deesset *P*: deesse et *Alschefski*
18 senatum Σ: senatu eos *P*: senatum eos *A*[c]

---

62 The *formula togatorum* was a register of the manpower
available to allied states and formed the basis on which Rome
made its annual troop demands.

and reliable as before; and even those that had failed in
their duty would have respect for Roman power if envoys
were sent around those colonies to chasten them, not
plead with them. They were allowed by the senate to take
any actions or measures they thought in the state's interest,
and after first sounding the feelings of the other colonies
they summoned representatives from them and asked if
they had soldiers mobilized from the register.[62] Speaking
for the eighteen colonies, Marcus Sextilius of Fregellae
replied that there were indeed men mobilized from the
register, they would supply more if more were needed,
and they would also assiduously carry out any other instructions or wishes of the Roman people. For that they
did not lack resources, he said, and in loyalty they had
even a superabundance. The consuls began by saying that
they felt any praise the representatives received from
them would be less than they deserved without all the
senators offering them their thanks in the senate house;
and they told them to accompany them into the senate.
After addressing them with the most courteously worded
decree possible, the senate then instructed the consuls to
bring them also before the popular assembly and there
enumerate the many outstanding benefits they had conferred upon the Romans and their ancestors, noting especially their recent service to the state.

Not even today, after the passage of so many genera-
tions, should these people be passed over in silence or
deprived of their mead of praise. They were the peoples
of Signia, Norba, Saticula, Fregellae, Luceria, Venusia,
Brundisium, Hadria, Firmum, and Ariminum; on the Tyr-
rhenian Sea, Pontia, Paestum, and Cosa; and, inland,
Beneventum, Aesernia, Spoletium, Placentia, and Cre-

9   harum coloniarum subsidio tum imperium populi Romani
10   stetit, iisque gratiae in senatu et apud populum actae. duodecim aliarum coloniarum quae detractaverunt imperium
mentionem fieri patres vetuerunt, neque illos dimitti neque retineri neque appellari a consulibus; ea tacita casti-
gatio maxime ex dignitate populi Romani visa est.

11   Cetera expedientibus quae ad bellum opus erant consulibus, aurum vicensimarium quod in sanctiore aerario
12   ad ultimos casus servaretur[19] promi placuit. prompta ad
quattuor milia pondo auri. inde quingena pondo data consulibus et M. Marcello et P. Sulpicio proconsulibus et L.
Veturio praetori qui Galliam provinciam erat sortitus;
13   additumque Fabio consuli centum pondo auri praecipuum quod in arcem Tarentinam portaretur. cetero auro
usi sunt ad vestimenta praesenti pecunia locanda exercitui
qui in Hispania bellum secunda sua fama ducisque gerebat.

11. Prodigia quoque priusquam ab urbe consules pro-
2   ficiscerentur procurari placuit. in Albano monte tacta de
caelo erant signum Iovis arborque templo propinqua, et
Ostiae lucus,[20] et Capuae murus Fortunaeque aedes, et
3   Sinuessae murus portaque. haec de caelo tacta. cruentam
etiam fluxisse aquam Albanam quidam auctores erant, et
Romae intus in cella aedis Fortis Fortunae de capite sig-

[19] servaretur Σ: servabatur P
[20] lucus *Crév.*: lacus P: locus Σ

---

[63] A tax imposed on the value of a slave manumitted by the owner.   [64] Cf. 26.21.6 note.

[65] In fact, there was more than one temple, located on the Tiber's right bank: Richardson 154–55, and Oakley 4.453–54.

mona. Through the assistance provided by these colonies the power of the Roman people then stood firm, and they were thanked in the senate and popular assembly. As for the twelve other colonies that refused to heed the requisition, the senators ordered no mention to be made of them, and their representatives were not to be sent away, detained, or addressed by the consuls; such a reprimand in silence seemed most appropriate to the dignity of the Roman people.

As the consuls were making all the other necessary preparations for war, a decision was taken to withdraw gold raised by the five percent tax that was being kept in reserve in the inner treasury to meet emergencies.[63] Some four thousand pounds of gold were withdrawn. From it the consuls, the proconsuls Marcus Marcellus and Publius Sulpicius, and the praetor Lucius Veturius (who had drawn Gaul as his province) were each given five hundred pounds; and a further one hundred pounds was especially given to the consul Fabius to be transported to the citadel of Tarentum. The rest of the gold they used for contracting out, for ready money, the provisioning of clothing for the army that was waging war in Spain, winning renown for itself and its commander.

11. It was also decided that prodigies should be expiated before the consuls left the city. There had been lightning strikes on a statue of Jupiter and a tree close to the temple on the Alban Mount,[64] on a grove at Ostia, on the city wall and temple of Fortuna at Capua, and on the city wall and gate at Sinuessa. Such were the lightning strikes; and some also reported that the water of the Alban Lake had flowed with blood, and that in the sanctuary of the temple of Fors Fortuna in Rome[65] a statuette on the god-

num quod in corona erat in manum sponte sua prolapsum.
4 et Priverni satis constabat bovem locutum, volturiumque
frequenti foro in tabernam devolasse, et Sinuessae natum
5 ambiguo inter marem ac feminam sexu infantem, quos
androgynos volgus, ut pleraque faciliore ad duplicanda
verba Graeco sermone, appellat, et lacte pluvisse, et cum
6 elephanti capite puerum natum. ea prodigia hostiis maioribus procurata et supplicatio circa omnia pulvinaria,
obsecratio in unum diem indicta; et decretum ut C. Hostilius praetor ludos Apollini sicut iis annis voti factique
erant voveret faceretque.

7 Per eos dies et censoribus creandis Q. Fulvius consul
comitia habuit. creati censores ambo qui nondum consules fuerant, M. Cornelius Cethegus P. Sempronius Tudi-
8 tanus. duo censores ut agrum Campanum fruendum loca-
rent ex auctoritate patrum latum ad plebem est, plebesque
9 scivit. Senatus lectionem contentio inter censores de prin-
10 cipe legendo tenuit. Semproni lectio erat; ceterum Cornelius morem traditum a patribus sequendum aiebat, ut qui
primus censor ex iis qui viverent fuisset, eum principem
11 legerent; is T. Manlius Torquatus erat. Sempronius cui di
sortem legendi dedissent, ei ius liberum eosdem dedisse

---

66 On hermaphrodites and the Roman attitude toward them,
cf. Briscoe, *A Commentary on Livy Books 31–33*, 89.
   67 After the death of one and abdication of the other (6.18,
above).   68 M. Cornelius Cethegus, curule aedile (213) and
praetor (211); P. Sempronius Tuditanus, praetor (213). They were
later consuls together (204).   69 A prestigious office: he was
the member first called on to express an opinion concerning the
matter under discussion.   70 Presumably by sortition (cf.
Sempronius' comment on the gods immediately below).

dess's garland had spontaneously fallen from her head into her hand. At Privernum it was also confidently believed that an ox had talked and that a vulture had swooped down on a shop in the forum when it was crowded; and that at Sinuessa a child of indeterminate sex had been born, part male and part female,[66] which people generally call "androgynous" (a Greek term, as usual, a language easier for forming compound words), and that it had rained milk and a boy had been born with an elephant's head. These prodigies were expiated with full-grown victims, and supplication was proclaimed at all the couches, plus one day of public prayer; and it was further decreed that the praetor Gaius Hostilius make a vow of games for Apollo, and celebrate them as they had been vowed and celebrated in recent years.

At that time the consul Quintus Fulvius also held the assembly for electing censors.[67] The men elected censors were Marcus Cornelius Cethegus and Publius Sempronius Tuditanus,[68] neither of whom had yet been consuls. A motion was brought to the plebs, with senatorial authorization, that the two censors put the farmland of Capua up for lease, and the plebs approved it. Revision of senate membership was delayed by infighting among the censors over the selection of the *princeps senatus*.[69] It was for Sempronius to choose;[70] Cornelius, however, insisted they should follow the practice, handed down from their forefathers, of selecting as leader the man who was the oldest of all the ex-censors still alive. That man was Titus Manlius Torquatus. Sempronius, however, claimed that the man to whom the gods had granted the right of choice they had

deos; se id suo arbitrio facturum lecturumque Q. Fabium
Maximum, quem tum principem Romanae civitatis esse
12 vel Hannibale iudice victurus esset. cum diu certatum verbis esset, concedente collega lectus a Sempronio princeps
in senatu Q. Fabius Maximus consul.

Inde alius lectus senatus octo praeteritis, inter quos M.
Caecilius Metellus erat, infamis auctor deserendae Italiae
13 post Cannensem cladem. in equestribus quoque notis
eadem servata causa, sed erant perpauci quos ea infamia
14 attingeret. illis omnibus—et multi erant—adempti equi
qui Cannensium legionum equites in Sicilia erant. addide-
runt acerbitati etiam tempus, ne praeterita stipendia pro-
cederent iis quae equo publico emeruerant,[21] sed dena
15 stipendia equis privatis facerent. magnum praeterea numerum eorum conquisiverunt qui equo merere deberent,
atque ex iis qui principio eius belli septemdecim annos
nati fuerant neque militaverant omnes aerarios fecerunt.
16 locaverunt inde reficienda quae circa forum incendio con-
sumpta erant, septem tabernas, macellum, atrium regium.

12. Transactis omnibus quae Romae agenda erant, con-
2 sules ad bellum profecti. prior Fulvius praegressus Capuam; post paucos dies consecutus Fabius, qui et collegam coram obtestatus et per litteras Marcellum ut quam
acerrimo bello detinerent Hannibalem dum ipse Taren-

---

[21] emeruerant *P*: meruerant Σ

---

[71] Cf. 22.53.5; 24.18.3–4.   [72] The normal minimum term.
[73] *aerarii:* "a class of Roman citizens who had incurred the censors' condemnation for some moral or other misbehavior. They were required to pay the poll-tax (*tributum*) at a higher rate than other citizens" (*OCD* s.v.).   [74] Cf. 26.27.2–3 and notes.

also granted the right to choose freely; and he would exercise his own judgment and select Quintus Fabius Maximus, whom he could conclusively prove was then the Roman state's leading man even if Hannibal were the judge. When his colleague conceded after a long argument, the consul Quintus Fabius Maximus was chosen as senate leader by Sempronius.

The rest of the senate membership was then revised, with eight men being deselected, including Marcus Caecilius Metellus, infamous for having advocated leaving Italy after the Cannae defeat.[71] That same issue was also used in attaching censure to equestrians, but those touched by that scandal were very few. All those horsemen who had been in the legions at Cannae and were serving in Sicily—and they were many—had their horses taken from them. The censors also added consideration of time to this harsh punishment, not recognizing past service in the case of individuals who had served with a public horse but stipulating all must serve ten seasons[72] with their own horses. They also rooted out a large number who should be serving in the cavalry, and they reduced to the grade of *aerarii*[73] all who had been seventeen years old at the beginning of that war but had not served. They then contracted out projects for rebuilding what had been destroyed by fire around the forum—seven shops, the food market and the Royal Atrium.[74]

12. All their necessary business completed in Rome, the consuls left for the war. Fulvius went first, going ahead to Capua. Fabius followed a few days later, and he pleaded both with his colleague in person, and with Marcellus by letter, to hold back Hannibal with the strongest military pressure while he himself attacked Tarentum; deprived of

247

3 tum oppugnaret; ea urbe adempta hosti iam undique pulso, nec ubi consisteret nec quid fidum[22] respiceret
4 habenti, ne remorandi quidem causam in Italia fore. Regium etiam nuntium mittit ad praefectum praesidii quod
5 ab Laevino consule adversus Bruttios ibi locatum erat—octo milia hominum, pars maxima ab Agathyrna sicut ante dictum est ex Sicilia traducta, rapto vivere hominum adsuetorum; additi erant Bruttiorum indidem perfugae, et
6 audacia et audendi omnia necessitatibus pares. hanc manum ad Bruttium primum agrum depopulandum duci iussit, inde ad Cauloniam urbem oppugnandam. imperata non impigre solum sed etiam avide exsecuti, direptis fugatisque cultoribus agri, summa vi urbem oppugnabant.
7 Marcellus et consulis litteris excitus et quia ita in animum induxerat neminem ducem Romanum tam parem Hannibali quam se esse, ubi primum in agris pabuli copia fuit, ex hibernis profectus ad Canusium Hannibali occur-
8 rit. sollicitabat ad defectionem Canusinos Poenus; ceterum ut appropinquare Marcellum audivit, castra inde movit. aperta erat regio sine ullis ad insidias latebris; ita-
9 que in loca saltuosa cedere inde coepit. Marcellus vestigiis instabat, castraque castris conferebat; et opere perfecto extemplo in aciem legiones educebat. Hannibal turmatim per equites peditumque iaculatores levia certamina se-

---

[22] fidum Σ: fidem P

---

[75] Cf. 26.40.16–18.

[76] On the east coast of the toe of Italy (*Barr.* 46 D5).

[77] In Apulia, about ten miles inland from the Adriatic (*Barr.* 45 D2), earlier a refuge for the Cannae survivors (22.50.4–12).

that city, and now driven back everywhere, and having nowhere to make a stand and no secure base behind him, he would, he said, no longer even have any reason for remaining in Italy. He also sent a message to Rhegium, to the commander of the garrison that had been stationed there by the consul Laevinus against the Bruttii (eight thousand strong, this comprised, as noted above,[75] mostly men from Agathyrna shipped over from Sicily, who were accustomed to a life of larceny; and to their numbers had been added Bruttian deserters from the area who, in their straightened circumstances, were just as reckless and ready for any desperate measures). Fabius ordered this band to be taken out first to conduct raids on Bruttian territory and then to assault the city of Caulonia.[76] Their orders they carried out not only with energy but even with passion, and after plundering and chasing off the farmers they proceeded with a full-scale assault on the city.

Marcellus was prompted to action both by the consul's letter and by his conviction that no Roman general was as great a match for Hannibal as he, and as soon as he saw there was plenty of forage in the fields he left his winter quarters and encountered Hannibal near Canusium.[77] The Carthaginian was trying to induce the citizens of Canusium to defect, but on hearing of Marcellus' approach he struck camp from there. The surrounding countryside was open, with no cover for an ambush; and so he proceeded to fall back into wooded areas. Marcellus kept dogging his footsteps and pitching his camp close to his; and, that done, he would immediately deploy his legions for battle. Hannibal would skirmish with him, using only individual squadrons of his cavalry and his infantry's javelin throwers, but

rens, casum universae pugnae non necessarium ducebat.
10 tractus est tamen ad id quod vitabat certamen.

Nocte praegressum adsequitur locis planis ac patenti-
bus Marcellus; castra inde ponentem pugnando undique
in munitores operibus prohibet. ita signa conlata pugna-
tumque totis copiis, et cum iam nox instaret Marte aequo
discessum est. castra exiguo distantia spatio raptim ante
11 noctem permunita. postero die luce prima Marcellus in
aciem copias eduxit; nec Hannibal detractavit certamen,
multis verbis adhortatus milites ut memores Trasumenni
12 Cannarumque contunderent ferociam hostis. urgere atque instare eum; non iter quietos facere, non castra ponere pati, non respirare aut circumspicere; cottidie simul
orientem solem et Romanam aciem in campis videndam
esse. si uno proelio haud incruentus abeat, quietius deinde
tranquilliusque eum bellaturum.
13   His inritati adhortationibus, simulque taedio ferociae
hostium cottidie instantium lacessentiumque, acriter
14 proelium ineunt. pugnatum amplius duabus horis est.
cedere inde ab Romanis dextra ala et extraordinarii
coepere. quod ubi Marcellus vidit, duodevicensimam le-
15 gionem in primam aciem inducit. dum alii trepidi cedunt
alii segniter subeunt, turbata tota acies est, dein prorsus
16 fusa, et vincente pudorem metu terga dabant. cecidere in
pugna fugaque ad duo milia et septingenti civium soci-

---

78 Latin *extraordinarii*: a crack unit of allied infantry and cavalry selected from the allies and reserved for special tasks. They
had their own place in camp (cf. Polyb. 6.26.6–9, with Walbank's
note).

felt no need to risk total engagement. He was, however, drawn into the confrontation he had been trying to avoid.

Having advanced by night, he was overtaken by Marcellus on flat and open terrain; then, as he was establishing camp, Marcellus stopped him by attacking the men working on it from all directions. Thus there was a pitched battle and full-scale engagement, and when night started to fall they parted on equal terms. The camps, standing only a short distance from each other, were hurriedly fortified before dark. At dawn the next day, Marcellus led out his forces into the battle line; and Hannibal did not decline combat, either, giving his men fulsome encouragement and exhorting them to remember Trasimene and Cannae and crush their enemy's arrogance; he was constantly pressing and goading them, he said, never allowing them to march undisturbed or to pitch camp, never letting them catch their breath or look round—every day, with the rising of the sun, they must see a Roman army before them on the plains. If the enemy left just one battle bloodied he would be more tempered and restrained in his operations after that!

Stimulated by these exhortations, and tired of an enemy relentlessly pressing and provoking them every day, they went into battle ferociously. The fight lasted more than two hours. Then the right wing and elite allied troops[78] on the Roman side started faltering. Marcellus, seeing that, brought the eighteenth legion into the front line. With a number falling back in fear, and others slow in coming into line, the whole formation was thrown into turmoil and then completely beaten back; and, fear vanquishing shame, they began to flee. There fell in the battle and flight some twenty-seven hundred citizens and allies,

orumque, in iis quattuor Romani centuriones, duo tribuni
17 militum M. Licinius et M. Helvius. signa militaria quattuor de ala prima quae fugit, duo de legione quae ceden-
tibus sociis successerat amissa.

13. Marcellus postquam in castra reditum est contionem adeo saevam atque acerbam apud milites habuit ut
proelio per diem totum infeliciter tolerato tristior iis irati
2 ducis oratio esset. "Dis immortalibus ut in tali re laudes
gratesque" inquit "ago quod victor hostis, cum tanto
pavore incidentibus vobis in vallum portasque, non ipsa
castra est adgressus; deservissetis profecto eodem terrore
3 castra quo omisistis pugnam. qui pavor hic, qui terror,
quae repente qui et cum quibus pugnaretis oblivio animos
cepit? nempe iidem sunt hi hostes quos vincendo et victos
4 sequendo priorem aestatem absumpsistis, quibus dies
noctesque fugientibus per hos dies institistis, quos levibus
proeliis fatigastis, quos hesterno die nec iter facere nec
castra ponere passi estis.

5 "Omitto ea quibus gloriari potestis; cuius et ipsius pu-
dere ac paenitere vos oportet, referam. nempe aequis
6 manibus hesterno die diremistis pugnam. quid haec nox,
quid hic dies attulit? vestrae iis copiae imminutae sunt, an
illorum auctae? non equidem mihi cum exercitu meo lo-
qui videor, nec cum Romanis militibus; corpora tantum
7 atque arma eadem sunt. an si eosdem animos habuissetis,
terga vestra vidisset hostis, signa alicui manipulo aut co-

including four Roman centurions and two military tribunes, Marcus Licinius and Marcus Helvius. Four military standards were lost from the allied contingent first to flee, and two from the legion that had replaced the allies as they were retreating.

13. On their return to camp, Marcellus delivered an address to his men so biting and caustic that their angry commander's words were more depressing for them than the losing battle they had endured throughout the day. "To the immortal gods I can in this situation offer praise and thanks for one thing," he said, "that when you rushed panic-stricken for the rampart and gates the victorious foe did not attack the camp itself! You would certainly then have deserted the camp with the same terror with which you quit the fight! What fear was this, and what terror, that suddenly made you forget yourselves and who you were fighting? Surely these are the same enemies you spent last summer defeating and chasing from the field after defeating them, men you have pursued in recent days as they fled before you day and night, men you wore out in skirmishes and yesterday did not allow either to march or pitch camp!

"I pass over things on which you can pride yourselves, but I *will* mention something for which you should feel both shame and remorse; I mean, of course, that you broke off the fight yesterday when the battle was even. What did last night bring you, or what today? Did they bring some lessening of your strength, or some increase in theirs? Frankly, I do not think I am conversing with my own army or Roman soldiers—only your bodies and weapons are the same. Had you retained your same valor, would the enemy have seen your backs or taken standards from

horti ademisset? adhuc caesis legionibus Romanis gloria-
batur; vos illi hodierno die primum fugati exercitus dedis-

8 tis decus." clamor inde ortus ut veniam eius diei daret; ubi
vellet, deinde experiretur militum suorum animos. "Ego
vero experiar," inquit, "milites, et vos crastino die in aciem
educam ut victores potius quam victi veniam impetretis
quam petitis."

9   Cohortibus quae signa amiserant hordeum dari iussit,
centurionesque manipulorum quorum signa amissa fuerant districtis gladiis discinctos destitui;[23] et ut postero die

10 omnes pedites equites armati adessent edixit. ita contio
dimissa fatentium iure ac merito sese increpitos, neque
illo die virum quemquam in acie Romana fuisse praeter
unum ducem, cui aut morte satisfaciendum aut egregia
victoria esset.

11   Postero die armati ornatique ad edictum aderant. imperator eos conlaudat pronuntiatque a quibus orta pridie
fuga esset cohortesque quae signa amisissent se in primam

12 aciem inducturum; edicere iam sese omnibus pugnandum
ac vincendum esse, et adnitendum singulis universisque
ne prius hesternae fugae quam hodiernae victoriae fama

13 Romam perveniat. inde cibo corpora firmare iussi ut si
longior pugna esset viribus sufficerent. ubi omnia dicta
factaque sunt quibus excitarentur animi militum, in aciem
procedunt.

[23] destitui *Gron.*: destutui *Ta*: destitui iussit *P*: destituit Σ

---

[79] That is, legionaries in the past preferred death to flight.
[80] Not wheat, with which they could bake bread.

any maniple or cohort? Until now he could gloat only over cutting down some Roman legions; but today you have for the first time granted him the glory of putting an army to flight."[79] With that a cry went up begging his forgiveness for that day; he should put his soldiers' courage to the test whenever he wished. "All right, men, I *will* put it to the test," he replied, "and tomorrow I shall lead you out into battle so you can gain the pardon you seek, as victors not the vanquished."

He ordered the cohorts that had lost their standards to be kept on barley rations[80] and centurions of the maniples whose standards had been lost to stand to one side, swords drawn and belts removed; and he also instructed everybody to assemble under arms the next day, both infantry and cavalry. The meeting was then dismissed, the men admitting that the tongue-lashing they had received was well and truly deserved, that no one had that day shown himself a man in the Roman battle line apart from their commander himself, whom they must satisfy either by dying themselves or with an outstanding victory.

The next day they appeared armed and equipped as ordered. The commander complimented them and announced that he would bring into the front line the men with whom the flight had begun the previous day, and the cohorts that had lost their standards. He was now declaring, he said, that they must all fight and win, and one and all make every effort to see that news of yesterday's defeat not reach Rome before that of today's victory. They were then ordered to strengthen themselves with food in order to have sufficient stamina if the battle were prolonged. When everything was said and done for boosting of the men's morale, they proceeded to the battle line.

14. Quod ubi Hannibali nuntiatum est, "Cum eo nimirum" inquit "hoste res est qui nec bonam nec malam ferre
2 fortunam possit. seu vicit, ferociter instat victis; seu victus est, instaurat cum victoribus certamen." signa inde canere iussit, et copias educit.

Pugnatum utrimque aliquanto quam pridie acrius est, Poenis ad obtinendum hesternum decus adnitentibus,
3 Romanis ad demendam ignominiam. sinistra ala ab Romanis et cohortes quae amiserant signa in prima acie pugnabant, et legio duodevicensima ab dextro cornu in-
4 structa. L. Cornelius Lentulus et C. Claudius Nero legati cornibus praeerant; Marcellus mediam aciem hortator
5 testisque praesens firmabat. ab Hannibale Hispani primam obtinebant frontem, et id roboris in omni exercitu erat.

6 Cum anceps diu pugna esset, Hannibal elephantos in primam aciem induci iussit si quem inicere ea res tumul-
7 tum ac pavorem posset. et primo turbarunt signa ordinesque, et partim occulcatis partim dissipatis terrore qui
8 circa erant, nudaverant una parte aciem, latiusque fuga manasset ni C. Decimius Flavus tribunus militum signo arrepto primi hastati manipulum eius signi sequi se iussis-set. duxit ubi maxime tumultum conglobatae beluae facie-
9 bant, pilaque in eas conici iussit. haesere omnia tela, haud

---

81 Latin *ala* (lit., "wing"): "a unit of auxiliary troops (usually posted on a flank)" (*OLD*).

82 L. Cornelius Lentulus, praetor in 211; C. Claudius Nero, praetor in 212 (and later consul in 207, playing a major role in the battle at the River Metaurus).

83 Cf. 26.5.15, where the centurion Quintus Navius does the same.

14. When brought the news, Hannibal declared: "We are clearly up against an enemy who can tolerate neither good fortune nor bad. Winning, he puts fierce pressure on his defeated foe; losing, he renews the fight with his victors." With that he had the trumpet signal sounded and led out his troops.

On both sides the fighting was considerably fiercer than on the previous day, the Carthaginians struggling to secure yesterday's glory, the Romans to remove their disgrace. On the Roman side, the left allied contingent[81] and the cohorts that had lost their standards were fighting in the front line, and the eighteenth legion was deployed on the right wing. The legates Lucius Cornelius Lentulus and Gaius Claudius Nero[82] commanded the wings; and Marcellus was keeping the center solid by encouraging and witnessing its performance on the spot. On Hannibal's side the Spaniards formed the front line and represented the main strength in his entire army.

After a long period of indecisive fighting, Hannibal ordered elephants to be brought to the front, hoping they could create some havoc and panic. And, indeed, the beasts did at first disrupt the standards and ranks; and partly by trampling down and partly by scattering in terror anybody near them, they had created a gap in the line at one point; and the flight from there would have spread had not Gaius Decimius Flavus, a military tribune, seized the standard of the first maniple of *hastati* and ordered the maniple under that standard to follow him.[83] He led them to the point where the beasts, crowded together, were causing most trouble and gave the order for spears to be hurled at them. All the weapons stuck fast in their target,

difficili ex propinquo in tanta corpora ictu et tam[24] conferta turba; sed ut non omnes volnerati sunt, ita in quorum tergis infixa stetere pila, ut est genus anceps, in fugam versi etiam integros avertere.

10 Tum iam non unus manipulus sed pro se quisque miles, qui modo adsequi agmen fugientium elephantorum poterat, pila conicere. eo magis ruere in suos beluae, tantoque maiorem stragem edere quam inter hostes ediderant quanto acrius pavor consternatam agit quam insidentis 11 magistri imperio regitur. in perturbatam transcursu beluarum aciem signa inferunt Romani pedites, et haud magno 12 certamine dissipatos trepidantesque avertunt. tum in fugientes equitatum immittit Marcellus, nec ante finis sequendi est factus quam in castra paventes compulsi 13 sunt. nam super alia quae terrorem trepidationemque facerent elephanti forte[25] duo in ipsa porta corruerant, coactique erant milites per fossam vallumque ruere in castra. ibi maxima hostium caedes facta; caesa ad octo milia hominum, 14 quinque elephanti. nec Romanis incruenta victoria fuit; mille ferme et septingenti de duabus legionibus, et sociorum supra mille et trecentos occisi; volnerati per- 15 multi civium sociorumque. Hannibal nocte proxima castra movit. cupientem insequi Marcellum prohibuit multitudo sauciorum.

15. Speculatores qui prosequerentur agmen missi pos- 2 tero die rettulerunt Bruttios Hannibalem petere. isdem

---

24 tam Γ: tum *P*: eum Σ
25 forte Σ: que *P*: quoque *det.*

for hitting at close range such huge bodies so densely packed together was not difficult. Although not all were wounded, those with weapons stuck in their backs turned to run and in doing so—such is their undependable nature—they also stampeded uninjured animals.

It was then not just one maniple hurling javelins; so too was every single soldier who could keep pace with the herd of fleeing elephants. The beasts charged their own side with all the more force and created greater carnage than they had among their enemy—a startled elephant's panic drives it on with a fury that cannot be controlled by the driver on its back. The Roman infantry charged forward into the line broken by the animals' charge through it, and with no great effort forced back the disordered and panic-stricken Carthaginians. Marcellus then sent his cavalry against the fugitives, and the chase did not end until they were driven back into their camp in panic. For, in addition to everything else that was causing terror and alarm, two elephants happened to have collapsed right in the gateway, and the Carthaginian soldiers' dash back to their camp had to be made over their ditch and rampart. That was where the heaviest enemy casualties occurred: some eight thousand men and five elephants were killed there. Nor was it a bloodless victory for the Romans; about seventeen hundred men were killed from the two legions, and of the allies more than thirteen hundred; and a large number of citizens and allies were wounded. Hannibal struck camp the following night. Marcellus wanted to give chase but the large number of his wounded prevented him.

15. Scouts sent out to track the column brought news the next day that Hannibal was heading for Bruttium. At

ferme diebus et ad Q. Fulvium consulem Hirpini et Lucani et Volceientes traditis praesidiis Hannibalis quae in urbibus habebant dediderunt sese clementerque a consule cum verborum tantum castigatione ob errorem praeteritum accepti sunt,[26] et Bruttiis similis spes veniae facta est cum ab iis Vibius et Paccius fratres, longe nobilissimi gentis eius, eandem quae data Lucanis erat condicionem deditionis petentes venissent.

4   Q. Fabius consul oppidum in Sallentinis Manduriam vi cepit; ibi ad quattuor[27] milia hominum capta et ceterae praedae aliquantum. inde Tarentum profectus in ipsis faucibus portus posuit castra. naves quas Laevinus tutandis commeatibus habuerat partim machinationibus onerat apparatuque moenium oppugnandorum, partim tormentis et saxis omnique missilium telorum genere. instruit onerarias quoque, non eas solum quae remis agerentur, ut alii machinas scalasque ad muros ferrent, alii procul ex navibus volnerarent moenium propugnatores. hae naves ab aperto mari ut urbem adgrederentur instructae parataeque sunt; et erat liberum mare, classe Punica cum Philippus oppugnare Aetolos pararet Corcyram tramissa. in Bruttiis interim Cauloniae oppugnatores sub adventum Hannibalis ne opprimerentur, in tumulum a praesenti impetu tutum, ad cetera inopem concessere.

---

[26] accepti sunt Γ: acceptis P: accepti Σ
[27] quattuor Σ: tria P

---

[84] Manduria (still so-named) lay twenty-two miles southeast of Tarentum (*Barr.* 45 G4). The Sallentini were a people further to the southeast (45 H4 and inset).

[85] Cf. 26.20.7–10 for the fleet's arrival and departure.

about this time the Hirpini, Lucani, and Volceians all capitulated to the consul Quintus Fulvius, surrendering to him the garrisons of Hannibal that they had in their cities, and were welcomed with kindly words by the consul, who merely reprimanded them for their past mistake. The Bruttii, too, were given similar hope of pardon after the brothers Vibius and Paccius, by far the most distinguished members of their people, had come requesting the same terms of surrender as had been granted to the Lucanians.

The consul Quintus Fabius stormed the town of Manduria in the territory of the Sallentini;[84] there about four thousand men were captured, and a considerable amount of other booty. Leaving there for Tarentum, he established camp right at the harbor entrance. He loaded some ships (which Laevinus had kept for protecting supplies) partly with engines and tackle for assaulting city walls and partly with catapults, rocks, and all manner of projectiles. He also equipped freighters—and not just those propelled by oars—so that some of his men could bring engines and ladders up to the walls and others inflict wounds at long range on enemy defenders on the battlements. These ships were equipped and readied for attacking the city from the open sea; and the sea was now clear of the enemy since, when Philip was preparing to attack the Aetolians, the Punic fleet had been transferred to Corcyra.[85] Meanwhile, in Bruttium, the forces besieging Caulonia, fearing a surprise assault, withdrew to some higher ground before Hannibal's arrival and this provided protection from an immediate attack, though no further advantage.

9   Fabium Tarentum obsidentem leve dictu momentum
ad rem ingentem potiundam adiuvit. praesidium Bruttio-
10 rum datum ab Hannibale Tarentini habebant. eius praesidii praefectus deperibat amore mulierculae cuius frater in
exercitu Fabi consulis erat. is certior litteris sororis factus
de nova consuetudine advenae locupletis atque inter populares tam honorati, spem nactus per sororem quolibet
impelli amantem posse, quid speraret ad consulem detulit.
11 quae cum haud vana cogitatio visa esset, pro perfuga
iussus Tarentum transire; ac per sororem praefecto con-
ciliatus primo occulte temptando animum, dein satis explorata levitate blanditiis muliebribus perpulit eum ad
12 proditionem custodiae loci cui praepositus erat. ubi et
ratio agendae rei et tempus convenit, miles nocte per in-
tervalla stationum clam ex urbe emissus ea quae acta erant
quaeque ut agerentur convenerat ad consulem refert.
13   Fabius vigilia prima dato signo iis qui in arce erant
quique custodiam portus habebant, ipse circumito portu
14 ab regione urbis in orientem versa occultus consedit. canere inde tubae simul ab arce, simul a portu et ab navibus
quae ab aperto mari adpulsae erant, clamorque undique
cum ingenti tumultu unde minimum periculi erat de in-
15 dustria ortus. consul interim silentio continebat suos.
    Igitur Democrates qui praefectus antea classis fuerat

---

[86] Literally, "trivial to tell."
[87] The night was divided into four watches.

While Fabius was blockading Tarentum, a seemingly trivial[86] situation helped him pull off a magnificent coup. The Tarentines had a garrison that had been supplied to them by Hannibal. The commander of that garrison was deeply in love with a young woman whose brother was in the consul Fabius' army. The brother was informed in a letter from his sister of a new relationship she had now with a foreigner, one rich and very well respected among his people; and, conceiving a hope that the lover could be driven to any lengths by his sister, the man reported his hope to the consul. As this seemed no idle speculation, he was ordered to go to Tarentum posing as a deserter; and there, striking up a relationship with the commander through the sister, he first discreetly probed his feelings, and then, having evidence enough of his fickle character, he used the woman's charms to push him into betraying the post he had been assigned to guard. When a plan of action and its timing were established, a soldier was furtively dispatched at night from the city between the outposts, and he brought the consul a report on what had been done and what had been agreed to be done next.

At first watch,[87] Fabius gave the signal to those in the citadel and those standing watch over the harbor, and he himself made his way around the harbor and took up a position, out of sight, in the town's eastern sector. Trumpets then blared out simultaneously from the citadel, from the harbor, and from ships that had been brought to shore from the open sea; and shouting and, at every point where danger was actually at a minimum, an enormous racket were deliberately raised. The consul meanwhile held back his men in silence.

Now Democrates, who had earlier been the com-

forte illi loco praepositus, postquam quieta omnia circa se
vidit, alias partes eo tumultu personare ut captae urbis
16 interdum excitaretur clamor, veritus ne inter cunctati-
onem suam consul aliquam vim faceret ac signa inferret,
praesidium ad arcem unde maxime terribilis accidebat
17 sonus traducit. Fabius cum et ex temporis spatio et ex silentio ipso—quod ubi paulo ante strepebant excitantes
vocantesque ad arma, inde nulla accidebat vox—deductas
custodias sensisset, ferri scalas ad eam partem muri qua
Bruttiorum cohortem praesidium agitare proditionis con-
18 ciliator nuntiaverat iubet. ea primum captus est murus
adiuventibus recipientibusque Bruttiis, et transcensum in
urbem est; deinde[28] proxima refracta porta ut frequenti
19 agmine signa inferrentur. tum clamore sublato sub ortum
ferme lucis nullo obvio armato in forum perveniunt,
omnesque undique qui ad arcem portumque pugnabant
in se converterunt.

16. Proelium in aditu fori maiore impetu quam perse-
verantia commissum est. non animo, non armis, non arte
belli, non vigore ac viribus corporis par Romano Tarenti-
2 nus erat; igitur pilis tantum coniectis, prius paene quam
consererent manus terga dederunt, dilapsique per nota
3 urbis itinera in suas amicorumque domos. duo ex ducibus
Nico et Democrates fortiter pugnantes cecidere. Phileme-

---

[28] deinde Σ: inde P

---

[88] Cf. 26.39.6.

mander of the fleet,[88] happened then to be assigned to that
sector, and he could see that while all was quiet around
him, other areas were ringing with the noisy commotion
and shouting that sometimes attends a city's capture; and
fearing that while he hesitated the consul was taking some
action and mounting an attack, he led a force over to the
citadel from which all the most alarming noise was coming. From the time that had elapsed and the silence that
had fallen, Fabius judged that the defensive troops had
been withdrawn from that point—for where, shortly before, there had been noisy voices rousing soldiers and calling them to arms, there was now no sound coming at all
and so he had ladders advanced to the section of the wall
at which, according to the report of the negotiator of the
betrayal, the Bruttian cohort was on guard duty. It was
there, with the Bruttii helping and welcoming the Romans, that the wall was taken first, and they climbed over
into the city; after that the closest gate was also broken
down so a massed column of troops could be brought in.
Then a cry went up at about the break of day, and, meeting
no armed resistance, the Romans reached the forum, and
from all around brought upon themselves the men fighting
at the citadel or the harbor.

16. The battle at the entrance to the forum was more
violent than it was sustained. Neither in his courage,
weaponry and military expertise, nor in his vigor and
physical strength, was the Tarentine any match for the
Roman. Thus, after only throwing their javelins, they
turned in flight almost before coming to grips with their
foe, and they slipped away along city streets they knew to
their own homes or those of friends. Two of their officers,
Nico and Democrates, went down fighting bravely. Phile-

nus qui proditionis ad Hannibalem auctor fuerat cum ci-
4   tato equo ex proelio avectus esset, vagus[29] paulo post
equus errans per urbem cognitus, corpus nusquam inventum est; creditum volgo est in puteum apertum ex equo
5   praecipitasse. Carthalonem autem praefectum Punici
praesidii, cum commemoratione paterni hospitii positis
6   armis venientem ad consulem, miles obvius obtruncat. alii
alios passim sine discrimine armatos inermes caedunt,
Carthaginienses Tarentinosque pariter; Bruttii quoque
multi passim interfecti, seu per errorem seu vetere in eos
insito odio seu ad proditionis famam, ut vi potius atque
armis captum Tarentum videretur, exstinguendam.
7   Tum a caede ad diripiendam urbem discursum. triginta
milia servilium capitum dicuntur capta, argenti vis ingens
facti signatique, auri tria milia octoginta pondo, signa[30]
tabulae prope ut Syracusarum ornamenta aequaverint.
8   sed maiore animo generis eius praeda abstinuit Fabius
quam Marcellus; qui interroganti scribae[31] quid fieri signis
vellet ingentis magnitudinis—di sunt, suo quisque habitu
in modum pugnantium formati—deos iratos Tarentinis

[29] vagus P: vacuus: *ed. Rom. 1472*

[30] signa Σ: signata P: signa et *Alschefski*

[31] interroganti scribae C^cΣ: interrogatis scribae P: interrogante scriba *Drak.*

[89] For Nico and Philemenus, cf. 25.8.3–25.9.15, 26.39.15
(Nico); Democrates, previous note.

[90] According to Plutarch (*Fab.* 22.4) Fabius "overcome by his
ambition . . . ordered his men to put the Bruttians first of all to
the sword, that his possession of the city might not be known to
be due to treachery."

menus,[89] the man responsible for betraying the city to Hannibal, galloped off from the battle, and his horse was recognized a little later wandering aimlessly through the city, though his body was nowhere to be found. (It was generally thought that he had fallen headlong from his mount into an open well.) The commander of the Punic garrison, Carthalo, put down his weapons and was coming to the consul to remind him of ties of hospitality between their fathers when a soldier met him and cut him down. Men were everywhere indiscriminately slaughtering each other, armed and unarmed, Carthaginians and Tarentines alike; Bruttians, too, were killed in large numbers in all quarters,[90] perhaps by mistake, perhaps from longstanding hatred toward them, or perhaps to snuff out the rumor of betrayal and make it appear that Tarentum had instead been captured by force of arms.

Then they scattered from the carnage to sack the city. Thirty thousand slaves are said to have been taken, and huge quantities of silver plate and coin, three thousand and eighty pounds of gold, and statues and paintings almost to rival the artwork of Syracuse. But in passing up booty of that sort Fabius showed more strength of character than Marcellus. When a secretary asked what he wanted done with some colossal statues (gods represented as fighting in battle, each with his appropriate clothing), Fabius ordered that "the people of Tarentum be left their

9   relinqui iussit. murus inde qui urbem ab arce dirimebat dirutus est ac disiectus.

    Dum haec Tarenti[32] aguntur Hannibal, iis qui Cau-
10 loniam obsidebant in deditionem acceptis, audita oppugnatione Tarenti dies noctesque cursim agmine acto,
cum festinans ad opem ferendam captam urbem audisset,
"Et Romani suum Hannibalem" inquit "habent. eadem
qua ceperamus arte Tarentum amisimus."

11   Ne tamen fugientis modo convertisse agmen videretur,
quo constiterat loco quinque milia ferme ab urbe posuit
castra; ibi paucos moratus dies Metapontum sese recepit.
12 inde duos Metapontinos cum litteris principum eius civitatis ad Fabium Tarentum mittit, fidem ab consule accep-
turos impunita iis priora fore si Metapontum cum prae-
13 sidio Punico prodidissent. Fabius vera quae adferrent esse
ratus, diem qua accessurus esset Metapontum constituit,
litterasque ad principes dedit quae ad Hannibalem dela-
14 tae sunt. enimvero laetus successu fraudis si ne Fabius
quidem dolo invictus fuisset, haud procul Metaponto in-
15 sidias ponit. Fabio auspicanti priusquam egrederetur ab
Tarento, aves semel atque iterum non addixerunt. hostia
quoque caesa consulenti deos haruspex cavendum a

---

[32] Tarenti Σ: *om.* P

---

[91] That is, in allowing the city to be captured, the gods of
Tarentum must have been angry with its people. The same account is found in Plut. *Fab.* 22.5. Strabo (6.3.1) claims that most
of the dedicated objects "were either destroyed by the Carthaginians . . . or carried off as booty by the Romans when they took the
place by storm."   [92] For the same comment, cf. Plut. *Fab*.
23.1 (probably derived from Livy).

angry gods."[91] The wall that separated the city from its citadel was then pulled down and demolished.

While this was happening in Tarentum, Hannibal received news of the surrender of the troops blockading Caulonia; and after hearing of the attack on Tarentum he had driven his column along speedily day and night, but hearing then, as he hastened to bring assistance, that the city had been captured, he said: "The Romans have *their* Hannibal, too. We have lost Tarentum the same way we took it."[92]

Not to appear to have turned back his force like a man in flight, however, he pitched camp where he had halted, some five miles from the city; and after a few days there he withdrew to Metapontum. From there he sent two Metapontine citizens to Fabius in Tarentum with a letter from that city's leading men, who were to accept a guarantee from the consul that, if they betrayed Metapontum to him together with its garrison, they would receive amnesty for their earlier actions. Assuming the offer they brought to be sincere, Fabius fixed a date for coming to Metapontum and gave the men a letter to be taken to their leaders, which was then delivered to Hannibal. Hannibal, of course, pleased with the success of his ruse, since not even Fabius had proved immune to his cunning, laid an ambush for him not far from Metapontum. When Fabius took the *auspices* before leaving Tarentum, the birds time and again gave no favorable signs.[93] Furthermore, as he consulted the gods with an animal sacrifice, the priest

---

[93] That is, they refused to eat. A commander had a number of sacred chickens with him; their refusal to eat was a dire warning.

16   fraude hostili et ab insidiis praedixit. Metapontini, post-
      quam ad constitutam non venerat diem, remissi ut cunc-
      tantem hortarentur, ac repente comprehensi metu gravio-
      ris quaestionis detegunt insidias.

      17. Aestatis eius principio qua haec agebantur, P. Scipio
      in Hispania cum hiemem totam reconciliandis barbaro-
      rum animis partim donis partim remissione obsidum cap-
      tivorumque absumpsisset, Edesco ad eum clarus inter

2   duces Hispanos venit. erant coniunx liberique eius apud
      Romanos; sed praeter eam causam etiam velut fortuita
      inclinatio animorum, quae Hispaniam omnem averterat
      ad Romanum a Punico imperio, traxit eum. eadem causa

3   Indibili Mandonioque fuit, haud dubie omnis Hispaniae
      principibus, cum omni popularium manu relicto Hasdru-
      bale secedendi in imminentes castris eius tumulos, unde
      per continentia iuga tutus receptus ad Romanos esset.

4   Hasdrubal cum hostium res tantis augescere incre-
      mentis cerneret, suas imminui, ac fore ut, nisi audendo
      aliquid moveret, qua coepissent ruerent,[33] dimicare quam

5   primum statuit. Scipio avidior etiam certaminis erat, cum
      a spe quam successus rerum augebat tum quod, prius-
      quam iungerentur hostium exercitus, cum uno dimicare

6   duce exercituque quam simul cum universis malebat. ce-

---

[33] ruerent Σ: fluerent P

---

[94] That is, with torture.

[95] This is actually the summer of 208, Livy now dating all
Spanish events a year too early (cf. 7.1 note, above).

[96] For chapters 17 to 20, cf. Polyb. 10.34–39, on which Livy
clearly draws.

warned him to beware of enemy treachery and an ambush. When he failed to arrive on the agreed date, the citizens of Metapontum were sent back to coax him out of his hesitation, and, arrested on the spot and fearing a more serious investigation,[94] they disclosed the ambush.

17. At the start of the summer when this was happening in Italy,[95] Publius Scipio had spent all winter in Spain trying to enlist the barbarians' support, partly with gifts and partly by restoring hostages and prisoners of war,[96] when Edesco,[97] a man distinguished among Spanish chieftains, came to him. His wife and children were in Roman hands; but, that aside, a virtually spontaneous shift of sympathy that had turned all Spain away from Carthaginian and toward Roman power also attracted him. The same thing prompted Indibilis and Mandonius, undoubtedly the leading men in all of Spain,[98] to abandon Hasdrubal and to withdraw to the hills above his camp with all their countrymen's forces, so they would have a safe retreat to the Romans along the unbroken mountain chain.

When Hasdrubal saw that his enemy's forces were growing by such leaps and bounds while his own were diminishing, and that his numbers would continue declining unless he took some drastic action, he decided to engage as soon as possible. Scipio was even more eager for battle, since his confidence was being increased by success and also because he preferred to fight one commander and one army before the enemy armies could join up rather than

97 He is called Edecon by Polybius (10.34.2) and was chief of the Edetani tribe (TIR *J-30*, 171).

98 The two were brothers (cf. 26.49.11), called the "two greatest princes in Spain" by Polybius (10.35.6).

terum etiamsi cum pluribus pariter dimicandum foret,
arte quadam copias auxerat. nam cum videret nullum esse
navium usum, quia vacua omnis Hispaniae ora classibus
Punicis erat, subductis navibus Tarracone navales socios
7 terrestribus copiis addidit; et armorum adfatim erat ⟨et⟩[34]
captorum Carthagine et quae post captam eam fecerat
tanto opificum numero incluso.

8   Cum iis copiis Scipio veris principio ab Tarracone
egressus—iam enim et Laelius redierat ab Roma, sine quo
nihil maioris rei motum volebat—ducere ad hostem per-
9 git. per omnia pacata eunti, ut cuiusque populi fines trans-
iret prosequentibus excipientibusque sociis, Indibilis et
10 Mandonius cum suis copiis occurrerunt. Indibilis pro
utroque locutus haudquaquam ⟨ut⟩[35] barbarus stolide
incauteve, sed potius cum verecundia ⟨ac⟩[36] gravitate,
propiorque excusanti transitionem ut necessariam quam
11 glorianti eam velut primam occasionem raptam: scire
enim se transfugae nomen exsecrabile veteribus sociis,
novis suspectum esse, neque eum se reprehendere morem hominum si tam[37] anceps odium causa, non nomen
12 faciat. merita inde sua in duces Carthaginienses commemoravit, avaritiam contra eorum superbiamque et omnis
13 generis iniurias in se atque populares. itaque corpus dum-
taxat suum ad id tempus apud eos fuisse; animum iam

[34] ⟨et⟩ *Alschefski*
[35] ⟨ut⟩ *dett.*
[36] ⟨ac⟩ *dett.*
[37] tam *P*: tamen Σ

face all of them together. Even if he had to fight a number simultaneously, however, he had with a clever stroke increased his troop numbers: for when he saw his ships serving no purpose since the entire Spanish coastline was clear of Punic fleets, he had beached the ships at Tarraco and added the crews to his land forces. He also had a good stock of weapons, both those captured at New Carthage and also those that he had had manufactured after its capture by the large numbers of tradesmen he had interned.

With these troops Scipio left Tarraco at the start of spring—for Laelius, without whom he did not want to undertake any major operation, had also returned from Rome—and proceeded to lead them against the enemy. As he was passing through completely pacified lands, with allies escorting or welcoming him as he traversed the territory of each tribe, Indibilis and Mandonius met him with their troops. Indibilis spoke for the two of them, with no trace of the rough, crude language of a barbarian but rather with modesty and dignity; and he inclined more to justifying their defection to Rome as necessary than boasting about seizing the first opportunity for it; he was aware that the word "turncoat" aroused hatred among old allies and suspicion among new ones, he said, and he did not object to this tendency in men if what caused such antipathy was the motive for the desertion and not just the word itself. He then reminded them of services he had rendered Carthaginian commanders and of the Carthaginians' greed and arrogance and the injustices of all kinds inflicted on them and their people in return. Thus they had till then been just a physical presence among the Carthaginians; their heart had long been where they be-

pridem ibi esse ubi ius ac fas crederent coli. ad deos quoque confugere supplices qui nequeant hominum vim at-
14 que iniurias pati. se id Scipionem orare ut transitio sibi nec
fraudi apud eum nec honori sit. quales ex ea[38] die ex-
periundo cognorit, perinde operae eorum pretium faceret.

15 Ita prorsus respondet facturum Romanus, nec pro
transfugis habiturum qui non duxerint societatem ratam
16 ubi nec divini quicquam nec humani sanctum esset. pro-
ductae deinde in conspectum iis coniuges liberique lacri-
mantibus gaudio redduntur, atque eo die in hospitium
17 abducti; postero die foedere accepta fides dimissique ad
copias adducendas. iisdem deinde castris tendebant donec
ducibus iis ad hostem perventum est.

18. Proximus Carthaginiensium exercitus Hasdrubalis
prope urbem Baeculam erat; pro castris equitum stationes
2 habebant. in eas velites antesignanique et qui primi agminis erant advenientes ex itinere, priusquam castris locum
acciperent,[39] adeo contemptim impetum fecerunt ut facile
3 appareret quid utrique parti animorum esset. in castra
trepida fuga compulsi equites sunt, signaque Romana por-
4 tis prope ipsis inlata. atque illo quidem die inritatis tantum
5 ad certamen animis castra Romani posuerunt. nocte Hasdrubal in tumulum copias recepit plano campo in summo
patentem; fluvius ab tergo, ante circaque velut ripa prae-

---

[38] ea Σ: hac P   [39] acciperent P: caperent Σ

---

[99] South of the Guadalquivir, but exact location unknown; it
is probably Bailen in the province of Jaén: TIR *J-30*, 97. For Polybius' account of the battle of Baecula, cf. Polyb. 10.34–40, with
Walbank 2.245–55.

lieved justice and fairness were respected; people unable to endure men's violence and injustice also seek refuge as suppliants with the gods. What they were asking of Scipio was for their defection to be regarded as neither unconscionable nor creditable. Whatever qualities he personally saw in them from then on, let him gauge the value of their service from that.

That was just what he would do, replied the Roman, and he would not regard as turncoats men who did not think an alliance binding when it was not based on respect for obligations either human or divine. When their wives and children were then brought before them and restored to them, they wept tears of joy, and that day they were welcomed as guests; on the next day their allegiance was accepted, with a treaty concluded, and they were sent off to bring up their troops. After that they shared the same camp until, under their guidance, they reached the enemy.

18. The closest Carthaginian army was Hasdrubal's, close to the city of Baecula;[99] there they had cavalry outposts stationed before their camp. On these, the Roman skirmishers, advance troops, and the men at the head of the column launched an attack as they were arriving off the march and before they chose a location for camp, and they did so with such contempt that each side's morale was readily apparent. The Carthaginian cavalry was driven back into their camp in panic-stricken flight, and the Roman standards were brought forward almost to their gates. On that day, in fact, it was with their appetite for the fight merely whetted that the Romans pitched camp. During the night Hasdrubal withdrew his troops to a hill that spread out to form a broad plateau on its summit; a river lay to his rear, and before and around him a kind of steep

6   ceps oram eius omnem cingebat. suberat et altera inferior
summissa fastigio planities; eam quoque altera crepido
7   haud facilior in adscensum ambibat. in hunc inferiorem
campum postero die Hasdrubal, postquam stantem pro
castris hostium aciem vidit, equites Numidas leviumque
armorum Baliares et Afros demisit.

8   Scipio circumvectus ordines signaque ostendebat hostem, praedamnata spe aequo dimicandi campo captantem
tumulos, loci fiducia non virtutis aut armorum, stare in
conspectu. sed altiora moenia habuisse Carthaginem quae
9   transcendisset miles Romanus; nec tumulos nec arcem, ne
mare quidem armis obstitisse suis. ad id fore altitudines,
quas cepissent, hostibus ut per praecipitia et praerupta
salientes fugerent; eam quoque se illis fugam clausurum.
10 cohortesque duas alteram tenere fauces vallis per quam
deferretur amnis iubet, alteram viam insidere quae ab
urbe per tumuli obliqua in agros ferret. ipse expeditos qui
pridie stationes hostium pepulerant ad levem armaturam
11 infimo stantem supercilio ducit. per aspreta primum, nihil
aliud quam via impediti, iere; deinde ut sub ictum venerunt telorum primo omnis generis vis ingens effusa in eos
12 est. ipsi contra saxa, quae locus strata passim, omnia ferme
missilia, praebet, ingerere, non milites solum sed etiam
turba calonum immixta armatis.

---

[100] Not so Polybius, according to whom Scipio remained with
the rest of his army, "took one half of it and skirting the ridge to
the left of the enemy fell upon the Carthaginians; the other half
he gave to Laelius to attack the enemy on their right" (10.39.3).

slope hedged his entire position. Below him there was another piece of even ground with a gentle gradient, and that, too, was bordered by a second steep slope no easier to climb than the other. To this lower plain, when he saw the enemy line standing before their camp the next day, Hasdrubal sent down his Numidian cavalry and his Balearic and African light infantry.

Riding around his ranks and standards, Scipio would point out to his men an enemy now trying to cling to the hills after losing hope of fighting on level ground; only from confidence in their position, not in their courage and weapons, could they stand in sight of the Romans, he said. But New Carthage had had higher walls, which the Roman soldier had scaled; neither hills nor a citadel, and not even the sea had withstood their weapons. The high ground they had taken would serve only one purpose, allowing the enemy to flee jumping over cliffs and precipices; but even that path of flight he would close off to them. He then gave orders to two cohorts, one to hold the entrance to the valley through which the river ran, and the other to block the hillside road that led at an angle from the city into the country. Scipio himself took the light-armed troops that had driven back the enemy outposts the previous day and led them against the light infantry standing on the brow of the lower slope.[100] They first proceeded over rough terrain, hampered only by the difficulty of their path, but then, as they came within the enemy's range, a huge number of all sorts of weapons at first rained down on them. They, in retaliation, hurled stones that were scattered in profusion in the area, nearly all suitable for throwing—and not just the soldiers but even the crowd of camp followers among fighting men did that.

13   Ceterum quamquam adscensus difficilis erat et prope
obruebantur telis saxisque, adsuetudine tamen succe-
14 dendi muros et pertinacia animi subierunt primi. qui simul cepere aliquid aequi loci ubi firmo consisterent gradu,
levem et concursatorem hostem atque intervallo tutum
cum procul missilibus pugna eluditur, instabilem eundem
ad comminus conserendas manus expulerunt loco, et cum
caede magna in aciem altiori superstantem tumulo impe-
15 gere. inde Scipio, iussis adversus mediam evadere aciem
victoribus, ceteras copias cum Laelio dividit, atque eum
parte dextra tumuli circumire donec mollioris adscensus
viam inveniret iubet; ipse ab laeva circuitu haud magno in
transversos hostes incurrit.
16   Inde primo turbata acies est dum ad circumsonantem
undique clamorem flectere cornua et obvertere ordines
17 volunt. hoc tumultu et Laelius subiit; et dum pedem referunt ne ab tergo volnerarentur, laxata prima acies locus-
18 que ad evadendum et mediis datus est, qui per tam iniquum locum stantibus integris ordinibus elephantisque
19 ante signa locatis nunquam evasissent. cum ab omni parte
caedes fieret Scipio, qui laevo cornu in dextrum incucur-
20 rerat, maxime in nuda latera hostium pugnabat. et iam ne
fugae quidem patebat locus; nam et stationes utrimque
Romanae dextra laevaque insederant vias, et porta castro-

Although the climb was difficult, and they were almost overwhelmed by spears and stones, nevertheless, thanks to their experience in scaling walls and their sheer determination, the first men reached the top. As soon as they reached ground level enough for firmly planting their feet, they dislodged the enemy (here light-armed skirmishers, protected by their distance from the foe and avoiding combat while hurling weapons at long range, but also unstable in hand-to-hand fighting at close quarters), and they drove them back against the battle line standing on higher ground above them, inflicting severe losses. Then, ordering his victorious men to advance against the enemy line's center, Scipio divided the rest of the troops between himself and Laelius and ordered him to move to the right around the hill until he found a way up with a gentler gradient; he himself then advanced a short distance around to the left and attacked the enemy flank.

With that their line was at first thrown into disarray as they tried to wheel the wings around and turn the ranks to face shouting that was resounding on every side. In this chaos, Laelius also came up; and as the enemy retreated in order to avoid wounds from the rear their front broke, giving even men in the center room to climb to the top (though they could never have escaped over such uneven ground if the Carthaginian ranks had remained solid, with their elephants positioned before the standards). When there was now slaughter on every side, Scipio, who with his left wing had charged the enemy's right, began to concentrate his attack on their exposed flanks. There was then no opportunity even for flight; for Roman detachments had blocked the roads both sides, right and left; and the camp gate had been closed by the commander and his

rum ducis principumque fuga clausa erat, addita trepidatione elephantorum quos territos aeque atque hostes timebant. caesa igitur ad octo milia hominum.

19. Hasdrubal iam antequam dimicaret pecunia rapta elephantisque praemissis, quam plurimos poterat de fuga excipiens praeter Tagum flumen ad Pyrenaeum tendit.

2 Scipio castris hostium potitus cum praeter libera capita omnem praedam militibus concessisset, in recensendis captivis decem milia peditum duo milia equitum invenit. ex iis Hispanos sine pretio omnes domum dimisit, Afros

3 vendere quaestorem iussit. circumfusa inde multitudo Hispanorum et ante deditorum et pridie captorum regem

4 eum ingenti consensu appellavit. tum Scipio silentio per praeconem facto sibi maximum nomen imperatoris esse dixit quo se milites sui appellassent; regium nomen, alibi

5 magnum, Romae intolerabile esse. regalem animum in se esse, si id in hominis ingenio amplissimum ducerent, ta-

6 citi[40] iudicarent; vocis usurpatione abstinerent. sensere etiam barbari magnitudinem animi, cuius miraculo nominis alii mortales stuperent, id ex tam alto fastigio asper-

7 nantis. dona inde regulis principibusque Hispanorum divisa, et ex magna copia captorum equorum trecentos quos vellet eligere Indibilem iussit.

8 Cum Afros venderet iussu imperatoris quaestor, pue-

---

[40] taciti Σ: tacite P

---

[101] For the plans for Hasdrubal to link up with Hannibal in Italy, cf. 5.12, above. Polybius' account (10.37.1–5, 39.8) is much clearer.

officers on making their escape; and in addition the elephants had been startled and the Carthaginians were as
frightened of the panic-stricken beasts as they were of the
enemy. Thus some eight thousand men were killed.

19. Before joining battle Hasdrubal had hurriedly
seized his war chest and sent the elephants on ahead,[101]
and now he gathered up as many fugitives as he could and
made his way toward the Pyrenees along the River Tagus.
After taking possession of the enemy camp, Scipio awarded
his soldiers all the plunder apart from free persons; and in
making an inventory of the prisoners he found the number
to be ten thousand infantrymen and two thousand cavalrymen. Of these he sent all the Spaniards home without
ransom, but he instructed his quaestor to sell off the Africans. A crowd of Spaniards then swarmed around him,
men who had surrendered earlier as well as those taken
prisoner the previous day, and they of one accord hailed
him as their king. With that Scipio, calling for silence
through a herald, declared that the greatest name for him
was that with which his own soldiers had hailed him—
"general"; the title "king," revered elsewhere, was anath-
ema in Rome, he said. As for his having a regal spirit—if
that was what they considered best in a man's character—
that was for them to judge in silence, but they should avoid
using the word. Barbarians though they were, they sensed
the greatness of a soul that from such a lofty position rejected the wonderful title of which all other mortals stood
in awe. Gifts were then distributed among the Spaniards'
chieftains and princes, and Scipio told Indibilis to choose
any three hundred he liked of the captured horses.

When, following his commander's orders, the quaestor

rum adultum inter eos forma insigni cum audisset regii
9 generis esse, ad Scipionem misit. quem cum percontare-
tur Scipio quis et cuias et cur id aetatis in castris fuisset,
Numidam esse se[41] ait, Massivam populares vocare. or-
bum a patre relictum apud maternum avum Galam, regem
Numidarum, eductum; cum avunculo Masinissa, qui nuper cum equitatu subsidio Carthaginiensibus venisset, in
10 Hispaniam traiecisse. prohibitum propter aetatem a Masinissa nunquam ante proelium inisse. eo die quo pugnatum
cum Romanis esset inscio avunculo clam armis equoque
sumpto in aciem exisse; ibi prolapso equo effusum in praeceps captum ab Romanis esse.

11   Scipio cum adservari Numidam iussisset, quae pro tribunali agenda erant peragit; inde cum se in praetorium
recepisset, vocatum eum interrogat velletne ad Masinis-
12 sam reverti. cum effusis gaudio lacrimis cupere vero diceret, tum puero anulum aureum, tunicam lato clavo cum
Hispano sagulo et aurea fibula, equumque ornatum donat;
iussisque prosequi quoad vellet equitibus dimisit.

   20. De bello inde consilium habitum; et auctoribus
quibusdam ut confestim Hasdrubalem persequeretur,[42]
2 anceps id ratus ne Mago atque alter Hasdrubal cum eo

---

[41] esse se Σ (se esse A^p): esse P
[42] persequeretur Σ: consequeretur P

---

[102] Cf. 5.11 and note, above, on Gala and Masinissa.

[103] A toga praetexta, which had a broad purple stripe along its
upper edge; a flattering gift, as it was worn by boys of high status
and certain officeholders.

was selling off Africans and heard that a strikingly good-looking adolescent male among them was of royal stock, he sent him to Scipio. Scipio then questioned the boy on his identity and nationality and asked why at his age he had been in military service; and he replied that he was Numidian, that his people called him Massiva and that, left an orphan by his father, he had been brought up by his maternal grandfather, Gala, king of the Numidians; he had crossed to Spain with his uncle Masinissa, who had recently come with cavalry to assist the Carthaginians.[102] Forbidden by Masinissa because of his age, he had never before gone into battle; and on the day of the battle with the Romans he had furtively taken weapons and a horse and gone out into the fight without his uncle's knowledge; there his horse had fallen, he had been thrown headlong and then been captured by the Romans.

Ordering the Numidian kept under watch, Scipio completed the business he had in hand at his tribunal; then he withdrew to his headquarters, summoned him, and asked if he wanted to return to Masinissa. When he replied, with tears of joy in his eyes, that he truly would, Scipio then presented the boy with a gold ring, a tunic with the broad stripe,[103] together with a Spanish cloak and a golden brooch, and a horse with its full trappings; and after instructing some horsemen to escort him as far as he wished to go, he sent him off.

20. A council of war was held next; and although some advised immediate pursuit of Hasdrubal, Scipio felt this was dangerous as he feared that Mago and the other Hasdrubal might join forces with him, and so he merely sent

LIVY

iungerent copias, praesidio tantum ad insidendum Pyrenaeum misso, ipse reliquum aestatis recipiendis in fidem
Hispaniae populis absumpsit.

3   Paucis post proelium factum ad Baeculam diebus, cum
Scipio rediens iam Tarraconem saltu Castulonensi excessisset, Hasdrubal Gisgonis filius et Mago imperatores ex
ulteriore Hispania ad Hasdrubalem venere, serum post
male gestam rem auxilium, consilio in cetera exsequenda
4 belli haud parum opportuni. ibi conferentibus quid in cuiusque provinciae regione animorum Hispanis esset, unus
Hasdrubal Gisgonis ultimam Hispaniae oram quae ad
Oceanum et Gades vergit ignaram adhuc Romanorum
5 esse, eoque Carthaginiensibus satis fidam censebat; inter
Hasdrubalem alterum et Magonem constabat beneficiis
Scipionis occupatos omnium animos publice privatimque
esse, nec transitionibus finem ante fore quam omnes Hispani milites aut in ultima Hispaniae amoti aut traducti in
6 Galliam forent. itaque etiam si senatus Carthaginiensium
non censuisset eundum tamen Hasdrubali fuisse in Italiam, ubi belli caput rerumque summa esset, simul ut
Hispanos omnes procul ab nomine Scipionis ex Hispania
7 abduceret. exercitum eius cum transitionibus tum adverso
proelio imminutum Hispanis repleri militibus, et Mago-
8 nem, Hasdrubali Gisgonis filio tradito exercitu, ipsum
cum grandi pecunia ad conducenda mercede auxilia in

104 Cf. Polyb. 10.39.9 (with Walbank's note) for Scipio's failure
to give chase to Hasdrubal. For the "tactical blunder" he was
some three years later criticized in the senate by Fabius Maximus
(28.42.14–15).   105 On Castulo, cf. 26.20.6 and note.
106 Hasdrubal Barca, brother of Hannibal and Mago.
107 In 216 (23.27.9).

a contingent to blockade the pass over the Pyrenees.[104] He himself spent the rest of the summer accepting the submission of Spanish tribes.

A few days after the battle at Baecula, Scipio left the pass of Castulo[105] on his return journey to Tarraco, and the commanders Hasdrubal son of Gisgo and Mago then came to Hasdrubal from Further Spain; and while this was assistance brought too late for Hasdrubal after his defeat, it was not at all inopportune for planning the conduct of the rest of the war. As they discussed there the sympathies of Spaniards in each man's theater of operations, only Hasdrubal son of Gisgo thought that furthest Spain—the area on the Ocean around Gades—still had no experience of the Romans and therefore remained staunchly loyal to the Carthaginians; the other Hasdrubal[106] and Mago were agreed in believing that everyone, tribally and individually, had been deeply impressed by the benefits conferred by Scipio, and there would be no end to defections to the Romans until all Spanish troops were either removed to Spain's remotest areas or taken over to Gaul. So, they said, even if the Carthaginian senate had not so decided,[107] Hasdrubal would still have had to go to Italy, the heart of war and center of everything, and he would at the same time be taking all the Spaniards out of Spain, far away from Scipio's reputation. Hasdrubal's army, now reduced both by desertions and his defeat, should be supplemented with Spanish troops; Mago should transfer his army to Hasdrubal son of Gisgo and himself cross to the Balearic Islands with large sums of money to hire mer-

Baliares traicere; Hasdrubalem Gisgonis cum exercitu penitus in Lusitaniam abire, nec cum Romano manus conserere; Masinissae ex omni equitatu quod roboris esset tria milia equitum expleri, eumque vagum per citeriorem Hispaniam sociis opem ferre, hostium oppida atque agros populari. his decretis ad exsequenda quae statuerant duces digressi. haec eo anno in Hispania acta.

9   Romae fama Scipionis in dies crescere, Fabio Tarentum captum astu magis quam virtute gloriae tamen esse,
10 Fulvi senescere fama, Marcellus etiam adverso rumore esse, superquam quod primo male pugnaverat, quia vagante per Italiam Hannibale media aestate Venusiam in
11 tecta milites abduxisset. inimicus erat ei C. Publicius Bibulus tribunus plebis. is iam a prima pugna quae adversa fuerat adsiduis contionibus infamem invisumque plebei
12 Claudium fecerat; et iam de imperio abrogando eius agebat, cum tamen necessarii Claudi obtinuerunt ut relicto Venusiae legato Marcellus Romam veniret ad purganda ea quae inimici obicerent, nec de imperio eius abrogando
13 absente ipso ageretur. forte sub idem tempus et Marcellus ad deprecandam ignominiam et Q. Fulvius consul comitiorum causa Romam venit.

    21. Actum de imperio Marcelli in circo Flaminio est
2 ingenti concursu plebisque et omnium ordinum. accusa-

---

108 In fact, Mago is hiring troops in Celtiberia the next year (28.1.4).

109 Because of his capture of Carthago Nova (the date now is late 209).

110 *tecta* (lit., "roofs") means "buildings" rather than "tents" (the usual quarters for soldiers). It is also still summer, when the men should still have been on active duty.

cenary auxiliaries;[108] and Hasdrubal son of Gisgo should withdraw deep into Lusitania with his army and not engage the Romans in battle; Masinissa should have a force of three thousand cavalrymen comprising the cream of all their cavalry, and he should crisscross Hither Spain, assisting allies and plundering enemy towns and farms. Such were that year's developments in Spain.

In Rome, Scipio's reputation was growing by the day;[109] for Fabius Tarentum, though taken by treachery rather than valor, nevertheless redounded to his credit; Fulvius' reputation was on the wane; and even Marcellus was in disrepute—apart from losing his first battle, he had led his men off to quarters[110] in Venusia in midsummer while Hannibal was still at large in Italy. A personal enemy of his was Gaius Publicius Bibulus, a plebeian tribune. Ever since the first battle of his that had been unsuccessful, the man had been making Claudius unpopular and hated by the plebs by constantly discrediting him in his speeches; and now he was advocating annulment of his *imperium*.[111] Claudius' relatives, however, gained authorization for him to leave a legate in Venusia and come to Rome to clear himself of charges that his enemies were bringing against him, with no debate of the annulment of his *imperium* to be allowed while the man himself was absent. It so happened that Marcellus also came Rome to fend off the humiliation at the same time as the consul Quintus Fulvius came for the elections.

21. The debate over Marcellus' *imperium* took place in the Circus Flaminius before a huge gathering of plebeians

111 For the following episode, cf. also Plut. *Marc.* 27.

vit[43] tribunus plebis non Marcellum modo sed omnem nobilitatem: fraude eorum et cunctatione fieri ut Hannibal decimum iam annum Italiam provinciam habeat,

3 diutius ibi quam Carthagine vixerit. habere fructum imperii prorogati Marcello populum Romanum; bis caesum

4 exercitum eius aestiva Venusiae sub tectis agere. Hanc tribuni orationem ita obruit Marcellus commemoratione rerum suarum ut non rogatio solum de imperio eius abrogando antiquaretur, sed postero die consulem eum ingenti

5 consensu centuriae omnes crearent. additur collega T. Quinctius Crispinus qui tum praetor erat. postero die praetores creati P. Licinius Crassus Dives pontifex maximus, P. Licinius Varus, Sex. Iulius Caesar, Q. Claudius.

6 Comitiorum ipsorum diebus sollicita civitas de Etruriae defectione fuit. principium eius rei ab Arretinis fieri C. Calpurnius scripserat, qui eam provinciam pro praetore obtinebat. itaque confestim eo missus Marcellus con-

7 sul designatus qui rem inspiceret ac, si digna videretur, exercitu accito bellum ex Apulia in Etruriam transferret.

8 eo metu compressi Etrusci quieverunt. Tarentinorum legatis pacem petentibus cum libertate ac legibus suis responsum ab senatu est ut redirent cum Fabius consul Romam venisset.

9 Ludi et Romani et plebeii eo anno in singulos dies instaurati. aediles curules fuere L. Cornelius Caudinus et

---

[43] accusavit Σ: accusavitque P

---

[112] This is the first Julius Caesar in the historical record. On the praetors, cf. *MRR* 290–91.   [113] Modern Arezzo (*Barr.* 42 B2).   [114] The Roman Games took place from September 4 to 19, the Plebeian from November 4 to 17.

and all the classes. The tribune of the plebs accused not only Marcellus but all the nobility: it was because of their treachery and hesitation that this was now the tenth year that Hannibal had been holding Italy as his province, and he had lived longer there than in Carthage! The Roman people were reaping the benefits of Marcellus' prorogued *imperium*; his twice-beaten army was having its summer season quartered in Venusia! This address from the tribune Marcellus so effectively rebutted by listing his achievements that not only was the bill annulling his *imperium* rejected but he was elected consul the following day with overwhelming unanimity by all the centuries. As colleague he was given Titus Quinctius Crispinus, then a praetor. The next day the following praetors were elected: the Pontifex Maximus Publius Licinius Crassus Dives, Publius Licinius Varus, Sextus Iulius Caesar,[112] and Quintus Claudius.

On the very days of the election the state was anxious about a revolt in Etruria. The unrest had started among the people of Arretium[113] according to a report from Gaius Calpurnius, who was acting as propraetor in that province. The consul designate Marcellus was therefore hurriedly sent there to investigate the matter and, if the situation appeared to warrant it, to send for an army and transfer the theater of operations from Apulia to Etruria. The Etruscans were intimidated by this and restored to order. When ambassadors from the Tarentines came seeking a peace settlement that included independence and their own laws, the senate's reply was that they should return when the consul Fabius arrived in Rome.

The Roman and Plebeian games were that year both repeated for one day.[114] The curule aediles were Lucius

Ser. Sulpicius Galba, plebeii C. Servilius et Q. Caecilius
10 Metellus. Servilium negabant iure aut tribunum plebis
fuisse aut aedilem esse quod patrem eius, quem triumvi-
rum agrarium occisum a Boiis circa Mutinam esse opinio
per decem[44] annos fuerat, vivere atque in hostium potestate esse satis constabat.

22. Undecimo anno Punici belli consulatum inierunt
M. Marcellus quintum, ut numeretur consulatus quem
2 vitio creatus non gessit, et T. Quinctius Crispinus. utrisque
consulibus Italia decreta provincia est et duo consulum
prioris anni exercitus—tertius Venusiae tum erat cui
Marcellus praefuerat—ita ut ex tribus eligerent duo quos
vellent, tertius ei traderetur cui Tarentum et Sallentini
provincia evenisset.

3 Ceterae provinciae ita divisae: praetoribus P. Licinio
Varo urbana, P. Licinio Crasso pontifici maximo peregrina
et quo senatus censuisset, Sex. Iulio Caesari Sicilia, Q.
4 Claudio Flamini[45] Tarentum. prorogatum imperium in
annum est Q. Fulvio Flacco ut provinciam Capuam quae
T. Quincti praetoris fuerat cum una legione obtineret. pro-

---

44 decem ΛΣ: nexem P: novem C
45 Flamini P: Flaminio M^c Λ: om. V

---

115 A powerful Gallic tribe living between the Po and the
Apennines (Barr. 39 H4); cf. OCD s.v.

116 A member of a board of three charged with supervising
the distribution of land when a colony was founded.

117 The son of a father who had held a curule office could not
hold a plebeian (i.e., noncurule) office while the father was still
alive: cf. 30.19.9.

118 The augurs had declared his election flawed because of
thunder when he was entering office (23.31.12–13).

Cornelius Caudinus and Servius Sulpicius Galba, the plebeian Gaius Servilius and Quintus Caecilius Metellus. Servilius, people said, had had no right to have been tribune of the plebs earlier or aedile now, because, although it had for ten years been thought that his father had been killed by the Boii[115] near Mutina while serving as an agrarian triumvir,[116] it was now well established that he was alive and in the enemy's hands.[117]

22. In the eleventh year of the Punic War, Marcus Marcellus and Titus Quinctius Crispinus entered the consulship, Marcellus for the fifth time (counting the consulship that, through an electoral flaw, he did not serve).[118] Both consuls were assigned as their province Italy and the two armies of the previous year's consuls (and there was also a third army that was then at Venusia under Marcellus' command): they were to select from the three the two they wanted, and the third would be passed on to whichever would be allotted Tarentum and the Sallentini[119] as his province.

Distribution of the other provinces went as follows: of the praetors, Publius Licinius Varus received the urban jurisdiction, and Publius Licinius Crassus, the Pontifex Maximus, received that over foreigners and a further responsibility at the senate's discretion; Sicily came to Sextus Iulius Caesar and Tarentum to Quintus Claudius. Quintus Fulvius Flaccus' *imperium* was prorogued for a year for him to administer his province of Capua (formerly under the praetor Titus Quinctius) with one legion. Gaius Hos-

119 Cf. 15.4, above, and note.

rogatum et C. Hostilio Tubulo est ut pro praetore in Etru-
5 riam ad duas legiones succederet C. Calpurnio. prorogatum et L. Veturio Philoni est ut pro praetore Galliam
eandem provinciam cum iisdem duabus legionibus obti-
6 neret quibus praetor obtinuisset. quod in L. Veturio, idem
in C. Aurunculeio decretum ab senatu, latumque de pro-
rogando imperio ad populum est,[46] qui praetor Sardiniam
provinciam cum duabus legionibus obtinuerat; additae ei
ad praesidium provinciae quinquaginta longae naves quas
P. Scipio ex Hispania misisset.
7   Et P. Scipioni et M. Silano suae Hispaniae suique exercitus in annum decreti. Scipio ex octoginta navibus quas
aut secum ex Italia adductas aut captas Carthagine habe-
8 bat quinquaginta in Sardiniam tramittere iussus, quia
fama erat magnum navalem apparatum eo anno Carthagine esse, ducentis navibus omnem oram Italiae Siciliae-
9 que ac Sardiniae impleturos. Et in Sicilia ita divisa res est:
Sex. Caesari exercitus Cannensis datus est; M. Valerius
Laevinus—ei quoque enim prorogatum imperium est—
classem quae ad Siciliam erat navium septuaginta obtineret, adderet eo triginta naves quae ad Tarentum priore
anno fuerant; cum ea centum navium classe, si videretur
10 ei, praedatum in Africam traiceret. et P. Sulpicio ut eadem
classe Macedoniam Graeciamque provinciam haberet
prorogatum in annum imperium est. de duabus quae ad
11 urbem Romam fuerant legionibus nihil mutatum; supple-

[46] est *P*: eius *Walsh*

---

[120] On the much-disputed number of Scipio's ships, cf. Jal *ad loc.* (112 n. 8). [121] On the survivors of Cannae, cf. 22.59–61, 23.25.7, 24.18.9, 25.5.10.

tilius Tubulus also had his *imperium* prorogued so he could succeed Gaius Calpurnius as propraetor in Etruria at the head of two legions. Lucius Veturius Philo's *imperium* was also prorogued for him to have Gaul as his province as before, now as propraetor, and with the same two legions with which he had held it as praetor. By senatorial decree what was done for Lucius Veturius was also to apply to Gaius Aurunculeius who, as praetor, had held the province of Sardinia with two legions, and a proposal to prorogue his *imperium* was brought before the people; and for the defense of his province he was further assigned fifty warships that Publius Scipio was to send from Spain.

Both Publius Scipio and Marcus Silanus were assigned for a year the provinces they currently held in Spain, along with their armies. Scipio was ordered to send over to Sardinia fifty of the eighty ships now under his command that he had either brought with him from Italy or captured at New Carthage,[120] because it was rumored that there were intensive naval preparations in Carthage that year, and that they would blockade the whole coastline of Italy, Sicily, and Sardinia with two hundred vessels. In Sicily resources were divided as follows: Sextus Caesar was given the army from Cannae;[121] Marcus Valerius Laevinus (for he too had his *imperium* prorogued) would assume command of the fleet of seventy ships lying off Sicily and add thirty vessels that had been off Tarentum the previous year; and with this hundred-strong fleet he should, if he agreed, cross to Africa on raiding expeditions. Publius Sulpicius also had his *imperium* prorogued for a year so that he could with the same fleet administer Macedonia and Greece as his province. In the two legions stationed at the city of Rome there was no change made; and the consuls

293

mentum quo opus esset ut scriberent consulibus permissum. una et viginti legionibus eo anno defensum imperium Romanum est.

12   Et P. Licinio Varo praetori urbano negotium datum ut naves longas triginta veteres reficeret quae Ostiae erant, et viginti novas naves sociis navalibus compleret, ut quinquaginta navium classe oram maris vicinam urbi Romanae

13   tueri posset. C. Calpurnius vetitus ab Arretio movere exercitum nisi cum successor venisset. idem et Tubulo imperatum ut inde praecipue caveret ne qua nova consilia orerentur.

23. Praetores in provincias profecti; consules religio tenebat quod prodigiis aliquot nuntiatis non facile litabant. et ex Campania nuntiata erant Capuae duas aedes

2   Fortunae et Martis et sepulcra aliquot de caelo tacta, Cumis—adeo minimis etiam rebus prava religio inserit deos—mures in aede Iovis aurum rosisse, Casini examen

3   apium ingens in foro consedisse; et Ostiae murum portamque de caelo tactam, Caere volturium volasse in aedem

4   Iovis, Volsiniis sanguine lacum manasse. horum prodigiorum causa diem unum supplicatio fuit. per dies aliquot hostiae maiores sine litatione caesae, diuque non impetrata pax deum. in capita consulum re publica incolumi exitiabilis prodigiorum eventus vertit.

5   Ludi Apollinares Q. Fulvio Ap. Claudio consulibus a P.

---

[122] On Livy's apparent skepticism here and elsewhere, see Levene *Religion*, 19.   [123] Volsinii and its lake (today Lake Bolsena): *Barr.* 42 B3.   [124] See note on 26.21.3.

[125] Cf. Levene (*Religion*, 63) on Livy's use of the prodigy list as a prelude to the consuls' deaths below (chapter 27); on his use of the lists in general, see *Religion*, 19–23.

were authorized to raise supplementary forces where necessary. The defense of the Roman Empire that year rested on twenty-one legions.

The urban praetor Publius Licinius Varus was also tasked with refurbishing thirty old warships docked at Ostia and with furnishing twenty new ships with crews so he could patrol the coastline close to the city of Rome with a fleet of fifty vessels. Gaius Calpurnius was forbidden to move his army from Arretium until his successor had arrived. Tubulus, too, was ordered to take strict precautions against subversion arising there.

23. The praetors left for their provinces; but the consuls were detained by religion because after several prodigies were reported they could not easily get favorable omens. From Campania had come reports of lightning strikes on two temples in Capua, those of Fortuna and Mars, and of a number of tombs also being struck; at Cumae mice were said to have gnawed at some gold in the temple of Jupiter—into such banalities does religion insert the gods![122]—and a huge swarm of bees to have settled in the forum. At Ostia the city wall and a gate had been struck by lightning; at Caere a vulture had flown into the temple of Jupiter; and at Volsinii the lake had been suffused with blood.[123] For these prodigies there was a day's supplication.[124] For several days full-grown victims were sacrificed without favorable omens obtained, and it was some time before the favor of the gods was regained. It was on the consuls' heads that the deadly events prophesied descended, the state remaining untouched.[125]

The games of Apollo had first been celebrated in the consulship of Quintus Fulvius and Appius Claudius by the

Cornelio Sulla praetore urbano primum facti erant; inde omnes deinceps praetores urbani fecerant, sed in unum
6 annum vovebant dieque incerto[47] faciebant. eo anno pestilentia gravis incidit in[48] urbem[49] agrosque, quae tamen
7 magis in longos morbos quam in perniciabiles[50] evasit. eius pestilentiae causa et supplicatum per compita tota urbe est, et P. Licinius Varus praetor urbanus legem ferre ad populum iussus ut ii ludi in perpetuum in statam diem voverentur. ipse primus ita vovit fecitque ante diem tertium nonas Quinctiles; is dies deinde sollemnis servatus.

24. De Arretinis et fama in dies gravior et cura crescere patribus. itaque C. Hostilio scriptum est ne differret obsides ab Arretinis accipere; cui[51] traderet Romam de-
2 ducendos C. Terentius Varro cum imperio missus. qui ut venit, exemplo Hostilius legionem unam quae ante urbem castra habebat signa in urbem ferre iussit, praesidiaque locis idoneis disposuit; tum in forum[52] citatis
3 senatoribus obsides imperavit. cum senatus biduum ad considerandum peteret,[53] aut ipsos extemplo dare aut se postero die senatorum omnes liberos sumpturum edixit. inde portas custodire iussi tribuni militum praefectique

47 incerto *P*: incerta Σ   48 in *P*: per Σ

49 urbem *M*^cΣ: urbe *P*

50 perniciabiles *C*Γ: permitiabilis *P*: perniciales Σ: permitiales *Sp*, pernic(t)iales *VN*^cθ

51 cui Σ: et cui *P*

52 forum *Duker*: foro *P*

53 peteret *Duker*: tempus peteret *P*

---

126 Crossroads (*compita*) were important in Roman religion. There were later priests of the crossroads (*Compitales*) created

urban praetor Publius Cornelius Sulla; after that all urban praetors had celebrated them, but they made their vow for one year only and did not celebrate them on a fixed date. That year a serious disease fell on the city and the countryside, but one that led to lingering rather than fatal illnesses. Because of that disease, supplication was made at crossroads throughout the city,[126] and the urban praetor Publius Licinius Varus was also ordered to bring before the people a bill that those games be vowed as a permanent event on a set date. Varus himself was the first to make such a vow, and he celebrated the games on July 5th; that date was subsequently kept as the official holiday.

24. As for the people of Arretium, reports were every day becoming more serious and the concerns of the senators mounting. Gaius Hostilius therefore received written instructions not to delay taking hostages from the Arretines; and Gaius Terentius Varro, to whom Hostilius was to deliver them for removal to Rome, was sent there with *imperium*.[127] On arriving, Hostilius immediately ordered one legion that was encamped before the city to advance into it, and he deployed armed units at appropriate points; then, calling the senators into the forum, he demanded hostages. When the senate requested two days to consider the matter, he declared they must hand them over immediately or he would the next day seize all the senators' children. Then military tribunes, allied officers, and centurions were ordered to keep watch on the gates so no one

by Augustus, and there was also a festival (*Compitalia*) linked with them.

[127] Defeated at Cannae as consul, he was now a private citizen and needed to be invested with *imperium* by the senate.

4   socium et centuriones ne quis nocte urbe exiret. id segnius neglegentiusque factum; septem principes senatus priusquam custodiae in portis locarentur ante noctem cum liberis evaserunt. postero die luce prima cum senatus in forum citari coeptus esset desiderati, bonaque eorum venierunt; a ceteris senatoribus centum viginti obsides liberi ipsorum accepti traditique C. Terentio Romam deducendi.

     Is omnia suspectiora quam ante fuerant in senatu fecit.

6   itaque tamquam imminente Etrusco tumultu legionem unam, alteram ex urbanis, Arretium ducere iussus ipse C.

7   Terentius, eamque habere in praesidio urbis; C. Hostilium cum cetero exercitu placuit[54] totam provinciam peragrare et cavere ne qua occasio novare cupientibus res daretur.

8   C. Terentius ut Arretium cum legione venit, claves portarum cum magistratus poposcisset, negantibus iis comparere, fraude amotas magis quam neglegentia intercidisse ipse alias claves omnibus portis imposuit, cavitque

9   cum cura ut omnia in potestate sua essent. Hostilium intentius monuit ut in eo spem non moturos quicquam Etruscos poneret, si ne quid moveri posset praecavisset.

     25. De Tarentinis inde magna contentione in senatu actum coram Fabio, defendente ipso quos ceperat armis, aliis infensis et plerisque aequantibus eos Campanorum

---

[54] placuit Σ: placet P

could leave the city at night. That order was carried out in a rather slack and negligent manner: before nightfall seven of the leading members of the senate slipped away with their children before sentinels could be posted at the gates. At dawn the next day their absence was noted when the senators began to be summoned to the forum, and their property was sold off. From the other senators a hundred and twenty hostages, all of them senators' children, were taken and handed over to Gaius Terentius Varro to be taken to Rome.

Varro, in the senate, made everything seem more threatening than it had been earlier. Thus, as if an Etruscan uprising were imminent, Gaius Terentius was personally instructed to take a single legion (one of the two urban legions) to Arretium and keep it there to secure the city; Gaius Hostilius, it was decided, should make a sweep of the entire province with the rest of the army and ensure that no subversive elements be given any opportunity for insurrection. When Gaius Terentius reached Arretium with his legion and demanded the keys to the city gates from the magistrates, they claimed they could not be found; and so, believing they had been surreptitiously removed rather than carelessly lost, he himself had different keys made for all the gates, and he took pains to ensure everything remained under his control. Hostilius he urgently warned that hope of averting Etruscan insurrection lay in taking steps to make insurrection impossible.

25. The matter of the Tarentines then raised heated debate in the senate in Fabius' presence and, though he himself defended those he had taken by force, others were hostile, a number claiming that as their crime equaled the

2 noxae poenaeque. senatus consultum in sententiam M.'
Acili factum est ut oppidum praesidio custodiretur Taren-
tinique omnes intra moenia continerentur, res integra
postea referretur cum tranquillior status Italiae esset.

3 Et de M. Livio praefecto arcis Tarentinae haud minore
certamine actum est, aliis senatus consulto notantibus
praefectum quod eius socordia Tarentum proditum hosti

4 esset, aliis praemia decernentibus quod per quinquennium
arcem tutatus esset maximeque unius eius opera recep-

5 tum Tarentum foret, mediis ad censores non ad senatum
notionem de eo pertinere dicentibus. cuius sententiae et
Fabius fuit; adiecit tamen fateri se opera Livi Tarentum
receptum, quod amici eius volgo in senatu iactassent; neque enim recipiundum fuisse nisi amissum foret.

6 Consulum alter T. Quinctius Crispinus ad exercitum
quem Q. Fulvius Flaccus habuerat cum supplemento in

7 Lucanos est profectus. Marcellum aliae atque aliae obiec-
tae animo religiones tenebant; in quibus quod, cum bello
Gallico ad Clastidium aedem Honori et Virtuti vovisset,

8 dedicatio eius a pontificibus impediebatur quod negabant
unam cellam amplius quam uni deo recte dedicari, quia si

9 de caelo tacta aut prodigii aliquid in ea factum esset, difficilis procuratio foret, quod utri deo res divina fieret sciri
non posset; neque enim duobus nisi certis deis rite una

---

128 According to Polybius (8.27.1), he had been feasting and
drinking all day.

129 Fabius evidently had a penchant for caustic remarks. For
this one, cf. also Cic. *De or.* 2.273; Plut. *Fab.* 23.3.

130 At Clastidium (west of Placentia: *Barr.* 39 F3) Marcellus
had won the *spolia opima* in 222 (*MRR* 233). "Honos and Virtus":
"Honor and Courage."

Capuans', so should their punishment. A senatorial decree was passed on a motion of Manius Acilius that the town be garrisoned and all the Tarentines confined within its walls, with the whole matter shelved for later discussion when Italy's situation was calmer.

About Marcus Livius, commander in the citadel of Tarentum, there was a no less acrimonious argument, some wanting to censure the commander by senatorial decree for Tarentum's betrayal to the enemy through his negligence,[128] and others proposing rewards because he had defended the citadel for five years and because Tarentum had been recovered mostly though his individual effort, while those in between stated that examining Livius' record was the censors' responsibility not the senate's. Fabius also shared this opinion; he added, however, that he accepted that the recovery of Tarentum was, as Livius' friends had often declared in the senate, due to Livius; for the town would not have had to be recovered had it not been lost.[129]

One of the consuls, Titus Quinctius Crispinus, set off for Lucania with supplementary troops to join the army that had been under the command of Quintus Fulvius Flaccus. Marcellus was being detained in Rome by religious problems that time and again came to worry him, one being that although he had vowed a temple to Honos and Virtus at Clastidium during the Gallic War[130] its dedication was being blocked by the pontiffs; for, they said, one shrine could not rightly be dedicated to two gods because, if struck by lighting or if there were some supernatural occurrence within it, expiation would be difficult since it could not be known to which deity the sacrifice was to be made. (For, except for certain gods, one victim

hostia fieri. ita addita Virtutis aedes adproperato opere;
10 neque tamen ab ipso aedes eae dedicatae sunt. tum demum ad exercitum quem priore anno Venusiae reliquerat
cum supplemento proficiscitur.

11 Locros in Bruttiis Crispinus oppugnare conatus quia
magnam famam attulisse Fabio Tarentum[55] rebatur, omne
genus tormentorum machinarumque ex Sicilia arcessierat,
et naves indidem accitae erant quae vergentem ad mare
12 partem urbis oppugnarent. ea omissa oppugnatio est
quia Lacinium Hannibal admoverat copias, et collegam
13 eduxisse iam a Venusia exercitum fama erat, cui coniungi
volebat. itaque in Apuliam ex Bruttiis reditum; et inter
Venusiam Bantiamque minus trium milium passuum in-
14 tervallo consules binis castris consederant. in eandem re-
gionem et Hannibal rediit averso ab Locris bello. ibi consules ambo ingenio feroces prope cottidie in aciem exire,
haud dubia spe, si duobus exercitibus consularibus iunctis
commisisset sese hostis, debellari posse.

26. Hannibal quia cum Marcello bis priore anno con-
gressus vicerat victusque erat, ut cum eodem si dimicandum foret nec spem nec metum ex vano habebat,[56] ita
duobus consulibus haudquaquam sese parem futurum
2 censebat;[57] itaque totus in suas artes versus insidiis locum

[55] Tarentum *P*: Tarentum ⟨receptum⟩ *Walsh*
[56] habebat *Gron.*: haberet *P*: habere *Harant*
[57] censebat Σ: credebat *P*

---

[131] Near the porta Capena: cf. 29.11.13, where Marcellus' son
sees to the dedication, but only a shrine to Virtus is mentioned.
[132] A promontory south of Croton (*Barr.* 46 F3).

could not properly be sacrificed to two.) Thus, with the work hurriedly carried out, a shrine to Virtus was added, but the temples were not dedicated by Marcellus himself.[131] He then finally set off with reinforcements for the army that he had left at Venusia the previous year.

Crispinus was attempting an attack on Locri in Bruttium because he thought Tarentum had earned Fabius a great reputation, and he had sent for all manner of artillery and siege engines from Sicily; and ships were also brought from there to make an assault on the seaward part of the city. That assault was abandoned, however, because Hannibal had moved his forces to Lacinium,[132] and also because there was a report that Crispinus' colleague, Marcellus, with whom he wished to join up, had already led his army from Venusia. He therefore moved back into Apulia from Bruttium; and the consuls took up a position between Venusia and Bantia[133] in two camps not three miles apart from each other. Hannibal also returned to the same region, the war having been now diverted from Locri. There the consuls, both impetuous by nature, deployed their battle lines almost on a daily basis, fully confident that if the enemy dared to face two united consular armies the war could be ended.

26. Since Hannibal had the previous year both prevailed and been defeated in two engagements with Marcellus, he thought neither hope nor fear to be unreasonable if he were obliged to fight the same man, but he certainly believed he would be no match for both consuls together; and so, turning entirely to his old tactics, he

133 Modern Banzi, about fifteen miles southeast of Venusia (*Barr.* 45 D3).

3 quaerebat. levia tamen proelia inter bina castra vario eventu fiebant. quibus cum extrahi aestatem posse consules crederent, nihilo minus oppugnari Locros posse rati L. Cincio ut ex Sicilia Locros cum classe traiceret scribunt.
4 et ut ab terra quoque oppugnari moenia possent, ab Tarento partem exercitus qui in praesidio erat duci eo iusserunt.
5 ea ita futura per quosdam Thurinos comperta Hannibali cum essent, mittit ad insidendam ab Tarento viam. ibi sub tumulo Peteliae tria milia equitum, duo pe-
6 ditum in occulto locata; in quae inexplorato euntes Romani cum incidissent, ad duo milia armatorum caesa, mille et quingenti ferme vivi capti, alii dissipati fuga per agros saltusque Tarentum rediere.

7   Tumulus erat silvestris inter Punica et Romana castra ab neutris primo occupatus, quia Romani qualis pars eius quae vergeret ad hostium castra esset ignorabant, Hanni-
8 bal insidiis quam castris aptiorem eum crediderat. itaque nocte ad id missas aliquot Numidarum turmas medio in saltu condiderat, quorum interdiu nemo ab statione mo-
9 vebatur ne aut arma aut ipsi procul conspicerentur. fremebant volgo in castris Romanis occupandum eum tumulum esse et castello firmandum, ne si occupatus ab Hannibale
10 foret velut in cervicibus haberent hostem. movit ea res

---

134 *Barr.* 46 D5 (Lokroi Epizephyrioi).   135 L. Cincius Alimentus, propraetor in Sicily in 210, with *imperium* prorogued for 209.   136 Petelia (*Barr.* 46 F3) was roughly equidistant from Tarentum and Locri (which were more that 150 miles apart). For the town's famous siege, in which the inhabitants were obliged to live on such things as grass, roots, and tree bark, cf. 23.30.1–5.   137 The main camps, probably near Venusia in Apulia (but in Bruttium according to Val. Max. 1.6.9).

began looking for a spot for an ambush. Some skirmishes between the two camps still continued, however, with mixed results. As the consuls believed the summer could be drawn out with such encounters and that an attack could still be made on Locri,[134] they wrote to Lucius Cincius telling him to cross from Sicily to Locri with his fleet.[135] So the walls could also be assaulted from the landward side they ordered part of the army that was garrisoning Tarentum to be brought there. When Hannibal learned from some Thurians that this was going to happen, he sent men to lie in ambush on the road from Tarentum. There, at the foot of the hill of Petelia,[136] three thousand cavalry and two thousand infantry were set in hiding; and when the Romans, advancing without reconnoitering, fell among them, some two thousand soldiers were killed, about fifteen hundred were taken alive, and the rest scattered in flight and returned to Tarentum through fields and woods.

There was a tree-covered hill between the Carthaginian and Roman camps,[137] initially occupied by neither force because the Romans knew nothing of the part that was facing the enemy camp and Hannibal had considered it better suited for an ambush than a camp. For that reason he had sent some Numidian squadrons out to it during the night and hidden them in the middle of its woods, and none made any move from the position in daylight in case their weapons or they themselves might be spotted from afar. Noisy demands were now going up in the Roman camp for the hill to be seized and secured with a fort so they would not have their enemy virtually at their throats if it were occupied by Hannibal. That disturbed Marcel-

Marcellum, et collegae "Quin imus" inquit "ipsi cum equitibus paucis exploratum? subiecta res oculis certius dabit
11 consilium." adsentiente Crispino cum equitibus ducentis
viginti, ex quibus quadraginta Fregellani, ceteri Etrusci
12 erant, proficiscuntur; secuti tribuni militum M. Marcellus
consulis filius et A. Manlius, simul et duo praefecti socium
L. Arrenius et M.' Aulius.

13 Immolasse eo die quidam prodidere memoriae con-
14 sulem Marcellum, et prima hostia caesa iocur sine capite
inventum, in secunda omnia comparuisse quae adsolent,
auctum etiam visum in capite; nec id sane haruspici pla-
cuisse quod secundum trunca et turpia exta nimis laeta
apparuissent.

27. Ceterum consulem Marcellum tanta cupiditas tenebat dimicandi cum Hannibale ut nunquam satis castra
2 castris conlata diceret. tum quoque vallo egrediens signum dedit ut ad locum miles esset paratus: si collis in
quem speculatum irent placuisset, vasa conligerent et se-
querentur.

3 Exiguum campi ante castra erat. inde in collem aperta
undique et conspecta ferebat via. Numidis speculator,
nequaquam in spem tantae rei positis[58] sed si quos vagos
pabuli aut lignorum causa longius a castris progressos possent excipere, signum dat ut pariter ab suis quisque late-
4 bris exorerentur. non ante apparuere quibus obviis ab iugo

---

[58] positis *Luchs*: positus P

---

[138] The "head" is one of the lobes of the liver, and its absence
was a bad omen (cf. 30.2.13; Cic. *Div.* 1.119). Valerius Maximus
(1.6.8) and Plutarch (*Marc.* 29.4–5) also give the story.

306

lus, and he said to his colleague: "Why do we not go out ourselves to reconnoiter with a few horsemen? Seeing things up close will give us a better plan of action." Crispinus agreeing, they set off with two hundred and twenty cavalrymen, forty of whom were Fregellans and the rest Etruscans. With them went the military tribunes Marcus Marcellus, the son of the consul, and Aulus Manlius, plus two allied officers, Lucius Arrenius and Manius Aulius.

Some have recorded that the consul Marcellus held a sacrifice that day, and that after the first victim had been slaughtered the liver was found to be lacking its "head."[138] In the second everything normally there was found in place, and there was even enlargement found in the "head," but the priest was not at all pleased with entrails simply too propitious appearing after ones undersized and deformed.

27. The consul Marcellus, however, was seized by such an urge to engage Hannibal that he would say the camps were never close enough to each other. Then, too, as he emerged from the defense works, he signaled to his soldiers to be prepared in their places: if the hill they were going to reconnoiter were to their liking, they should be ready to gather up the baggage and follow him.

A small piece of flat ground lay before the camp; from it a road, open and easily visible from all sides, went up the hill. Some Numidians were posted there, not with any hope of such an opportunity arising but merely on the off-chance of intercepting some men straying too far from their camp for food or wood; but now a scout gave them the signal for all to emerge from their hiding places. Those who were to rise up from the brow of the hill to confront the Romans did not make their appearance until the

ipso consurgendum erat quam circumiere qui ab tergo
intercluderent viam; tum undique omnes exorti, et cla-
5 more sublato impetum fecere. cum in ea valle consules
essent ut neque evaderent[59] in iugum occupatum ab hoste
nec receptum ab tergo circumventi haberent, extrahi tamen diutius certamen potuisset ni coepta ab Etruscis fuga
6 pavorem ceteris iniecisset. non tamen omisere pugnam
deserti ab Etruscis Fregellani equites[60] donec integri consules hortando ipsique ex parte pugnando rem sustine-
7 bant; sed postquam volneratos ambo consules, Marcellum
etiam transfixum lancea prolabentem ex equo moribun-
dum videre, tum et ipsi—perpauci autem supererant—
cum Crispino consule duobus iaculis icto et Marcello adu-
lescente saucio et ipso effugerunt.
8 Interfectus A. Manlius tribunus militum, et ex duobus
praefectis socium M.' Aulius occisus, ‹L.›[61] Arrenius captus. et lictores consulum quinque vivi in hostium potestatem venerunt, ceteri aut interfecti aut cum consule
9 effugerunt; equites[62] tres et quadraginta aut in proelio aut
10 in fuga ceciderunt, duodeviginti vivi capti. tumultuatum
et[63] in castris fuerat ut consulibus irent subsidio, cum consulem et filium alterius consulis saucios exiguasque infeli-
cis expeditionis reliquias ad castra venientes cernunt.
11 mors Marcelli cum alioqui miserabilis fuit tum quod nec
pro aetate—iam enim maior sexaginta annis erat—neque

[59] evaderent Σ: evadere possent P
[60] equites Σ: om. P
[61] ‹L.› Fr. 1
[62] equites Σ: equitum P
[63] et Σ: om. P

others had gone around to cut off the path to their enemy's rear; then they all rose up on every side and attacked with a shout. The consuls were in a hollow such that neither climbing to the ridge occupied by the enemy nor retreating when they were cut off at the rear was possible; but the engagement could still have been drawn out had not the Etruscans struck panic into the others by starting to flee. Nevertheless, though deserted by the Etruscans, the Fregellan cavalry did not abandon the fight as long as the consuls, still unscathed, were keeping the fight going, shouting encouragement and themselves doing what they could; but when they saw both consuls wounded and Marcellus even run through by a lance and, at death's door, slipping from his horse, they, too—the mere handful that was left—fled with the consul Crispinus, who had been struck by two javelins, and the young Marcellus, also wounded himself.

The military tribune Aulus Manlius was killed in the battle, and of the two allied officers Manius Aulius was killed and Lucius Arrenius taken prisoner. Five of the two consuls' lictors also fell into enemy hands alive, and the others were either killed or made their escape with the consul; forty-three cavalrymen fell either in the engagement or flight, and eighteen were taken alive. There had also been noisy clamoring in the camps for men to go to the consuls' aid; but then they saw the consul and the other consul's son, both wounded, coming back to camp, and the meager remnants of the ill-starred venture. Distressing in any case, Marcellus' death was all the more so for his recklessly having thrown himself, his colleague, and, one might almost say, the entire republic into a desperate

pro veteris prudentia ducis tam improvide se collegamque
et prope totam rem publicam in praeceps dederat.

12   Multos circa unam rem ambitus fecerim si quae de
13 Marcelli morte variant auctores omnia exsequi velim. ut
omittam alios, Coelius triplicem gestae rei †ordinem†[64]
edit, unam traditam fama, alteram scriptam in laudatione[65]
filii qui rei gestae interfuerit, tertiam quam ipse pro inqui-
14 sita ac sibi comperta adfert. ceterum ita fama variat ut
tamen plerique loci speculandi causa castris egressum,
omnes insidiis circumventum tradant.

28. Hannibal magnum terrorem hostibus morte consulis unius, volnere alterius iniectum esse ratus, ne cui
deesset occasioni, castra in tumulum in quo pugnatum
2 erat extemplo transfert. ibi inventum Marcelli corpus se-
pelit. Crispinus, et morte collegae et suo volnere territus,
silentio insequentis noctis profectus, quos proximos nanc-
tus est montes in iis loco alto et tuto undique castra posuit.

3   Ibi duo duces sagaciter moti sunt alter ad inferendam,
4 alter ad cavendam fraudem. anulis[66] Marcelli simul cum
corpore Hannibal potitus erat. eius signi errore ne qui
dolus necteretur a Poeno metuens, Crispinus circa civi-

---

[64] ordinem *P*: seriem *Perizonius*: ordine m<emoriam> *Casti-glioni*   [65] scriptam in laudatione *N*ᶜ: scriptam laudationem *P*:
scripta laudatione Σ: scriptam laudatione<m> *Walsh*
[66] anulis *P*: anulo Σ

---

[139] The text is unsound here: see textual note. On Coelius
Antipater, cf. Introduction to vol. V.
[140] Polybius (10.32.7–12) is merciless in his criticism of Marcellus, who "brought this misfortune on himself by behaving not
so much like a general as like a simpleton."

situation, something befitting neither his age—for he was by then more than sixty—nor the caution of a veteran commander.

I would be making many detours around a single event if I chose to give in detail all the variant accounts of Marcellus' death. To pass over others, Coelius gives three different sequences of action:[139] first the traditional version; then that in the text of the eulogy given by the son who participated in the action; and a third that Coelius presents as researched and established by himself. However, while versions vary, most report that Marcellus left camp to reconnoiter, and all that he was caught in an ambush.[140]

28. Thinking his enemy greatly demoralized by one consul's death and the other's wounding, and not to miss any opportunity, Hannibal immediately moved camp to the hill on which the engagement had been fought. There he found and buried Marcellus' body.[141] Crispinus, daunted both by his colleague's death and his own wound, left in the silence of the following night and pitched his camp on the first mountains he reached, in a spot elevated and protected on all sides.

There the two commanders showed ingenuity, one in setting a trap, the other in avoiding one. Together with Marcellus' body, Hannibal had also come into possession of his signet ring.[142] Fearing some duplicity on the Carthaginian's part through a mistake being made over that ring, Crispinus had sent messengers around nearby com-

[141] There are various accounts of this: Val. Max. (5.1.ext.6); Plut. *Marc.* 30.1–3 (citing Valerius Maximus, Cornelius Nepos, Livy, and Augustus as authorities).

[142] The plural is unusual and *anulo* may be right.

tates proximas miserat nuntios occisum collegam esse,
anulisque eius hostem potitum; ne quibus litteris cre-
5 derent nomine Marcelli compositis. paulo ante hic nuntius
consulis Salapiam venerat cum litterae ab Hannibale alla-
tae sunt Marcelli nomine compositae se nocte quae diem
illum secutura esset Salapiam venturum; parati milites
essent qui in praesidio erant, si quo opera eorum opus
6 esset. sensere Salapitani fraudem; et ab ira non defectionis
modo sed etiam equitum interfectorum rati occasionem
7 supplicii peti, remisso retro nuntio—perfuga autem Romanus erat—ut sine arbitro milites quae vellent agerent,
oppidanos per muros urbisque opportuna loca in stationi-
8 bus disponunt, custodias vigiliasque in eam noctem intentius instruunt, circa portam qua venturum hostem re-
bantur quod roboris in praesidio erat opponunt.
9   Hannibal quarta vigilia ferme ad urbem accessit. primi
agminis erant perfugae Romanorum, et arma Romana
habebant. ii, ubi ad portam est ventum, Latine omnes lo-
quentes excitant vigiles aperirique[67] portam iubent: con-
10 sulem adesse. vigiles velut ad vocem eorum excitati tumul-
tuari, trepidare, moliri portam. cataracta deiecta[68] erat;
eam partim vectibus levant partim funibus subducunt in
11 tantum altitudinis ut subire recti possent. vixdum satis
patebat iter cum perfugae certatim ruunt per portam; et
cum sescenti ferme intrassent, remisso fune quo suspensa

[67] aperirique $M^cC^c\Gamma$: aperique *P*   [68] clausa *P*: *del. Walsh*

[143] That is, a letter with a seal from Marcellus' ring.
[144] Cf. 1.1 (and note) and 1.5, above.
[145] Cf. 26.38.11–14.

munities informing them that his colleague had been killed and the enemy had his signet ring in his possession; they should not trust any letter written in Marcellus' name.[143] This message from the consul had reached Salapia[144] slightly before a letter was brought there from Hannibal, written in Marcellus' name and stating that he would be coming to Salapia the night of that very day, and the soldiers in the garrison should be at the ready in case he needed their services. The people of Salapia saw through the trick; and they thought that, from anger not only over their abandoning his cause but also over the killing of his cavalrymen,[145] Hannibal was looking for a way to punish them. Accordingly, sending back the messenger (he was actually a Roman deserter) so their soldiers could, unobserved, do what they wanted done, they placed townspeople along the walls and at strategic points, put sentries and patrols on special alert for the night, and posted the strongest troops in the garrison around the gate by which they thought the enemy would come.

Hannibal approached the city at about the fourth watch. At the head of his column were some Roman deserters, and they were bearing Roman arms. When they reached the gate, these men, all speaking Latin, called out to the watchmen and ordered the gates to be opened—the consul was coming. As if awakened by the shouting, the watchmen bustled, scurried about, and strained to open the gate. The portcullis had been lowered; some used crowbars and others ropes to raise it to a height that would allow men pass under it standing up. No sooner was there enough room to pass than the deserters came racing through the gateway; and, when about six hundred had entered, the rope by which it was held was released and

12 erat cataracta magno sonitu cecidit. Salapitani alii per-
fugas neglegenter ex itinere suspensa umeris, ut inter
pacatos, gerentes arma invadunt, alii e turribus portae
13 murisque saxis sudibus pilis absterrent hostem. ita inde
Hannibal suamet ipse fraude captus abiit, profectusque ad
Locrorum solvendam obsidionem, quam ⟨urbem L.⟩[69]
Cincius summa vi operibus tormentorumque omni genere
ex Sicilia advecto oppugnabat.

14   Magoni iam haud ferme fidenti retenturum defensu-
rumque se urbem, prima spes morte nuntiata Marcelli
15 adfulsit. secutus inde nuntius Hannibalem Numidarum
equitatu praemisso ipsum quantum adcelerare posset cum
16 peditum agmine sequi. itaque ubi primum Numidas edito
e speculis signo adventare sensit, et ipse patefacta repente
porta ferox in hostes erumpit. et primo magis quia improviso id fecerat quam quod par viribus esset anceps certa-
17 men erat; deinde ut supervenere Numidae tantus pavor
Romanis est iniectus ut passim ad mare ac naves fugerent,
relictis operibus machinisque quibus muros quatiebant.
ita adventu Hannibalis soluta Locrorum obsidio est.

29. Crispinus postquam in Bruttios profectum Hannibalem sensit, exercitum cui collega praefuerat M. Marcel-
2 lum tribunum militum Venusiam abducere iussit. ipse
cum legionibus suis Capuam profectus vix lecticae agita-
tionem prae gravitate volnerum patiens, Romam litteras

[69] quam ⟨urbem L.⟩ . . . oppugnabat *Riemann*: quam Cinus
. . . oppugnas *P*: quam Cincius . . . oppugnabat Σ: quam ⟨instrux-
erat L.⟩ Cincius . . . oppugnans *Walsh*

[146] Son of the dead consul (26.12 and 27.7, above).

the portcullis dropped with a loud crash. A number of Salapians then attacked the deserters who, anticipating a peaceable reception, had their weapons nonchalantly slung from their shoulders after their march; others, on the gate towers and walls, kept their enemy at bay with stones, stakes, and javelins. And so, hoist by his own petard, Hannibal left the area and headed off to raise the siege of Locri, a city that Lucius Cincius was attacking with the utmost vigor, employing siege works and all kinds of artillery brought over from Sicily.

By now Mago had little confidence that he would be able to hold and defend the city, and his first glimmer of hope came with the news of Marcellus' death. There followed a report that Hannibal had sent ahead his Numidian cavalry and was himself making all possible haste following with his infantry column. Thus, as soon as he learned from a signal sent from watchtowers that the Numidians were approaching, Mago himself suddenly flung open the gate and made a fierce sortie against the enemy. At first the battle hung in the balance, more because Mago had taken the Romans by surprise than because he matched them in strength; then when the Numidians arrived, such panic struck the Romans that they bolted in disorder to the sea and their ships, abandoning siege works and the machines with which they had been pounding the walls. Thus, with Hannibal's arrival, the siege of Locri was raised.

29. On discovering that Hannibal had left for Bruttium, Crispinus ordered the military tribune Marcus Marcellus[146] to lead off to Venusia the army that his colleague had commanded. He himself set off for Capua with his own legions, barely able to tolerate the jolting of his litter because of the severity of his wounds, and he wrote a let-

de morte collegae scripsit quantoque ipse in discrimine
3 esset: se comitiorum causa non posse Romam venire, quia
nec viae laborem passurus videretur et de Tarento sollici-
tus esset ne ex Bruttiis Hannibal eo converteret agmen;
legatos opus esse ad se mitti viros prudentes cum quibus
quae vellet de re publica loqueretur.

4   Hae litterae recitatae magnum et luctum morte alterius consulis et metum de altero fecerunt. itaque et Q.
Fabium filium ad exercitum Venusiam miserunt, et ad
consulem tres legati missi, Sex. Iulius Caesar, L. Licinius
Pollio, L. Cincius Alimentus cum paucis ante diebus ex
5 Sicilia redisset. hi nuntiare consuli iussi ut si ad comitia
ipse venire Romam non posset, dictatorem in agro Ro-
6 mano diceret comitiorum causa; si consul Tarentum profectus esset, Q. Claudium praetorem placere in eam re-
gionem inde abducere legiones in qua plurimas sociorum
urbes tueri posset.

7   Eadem aestate M. Valerius cum classe centum navium
ex Sicilia in Africam tramisit, et ad Clupeam urbem escen-
sione facta agrum late, nullo ferme obvio armato, vastavit.
inde ad naves raptim praedatores recepti, quia repente
8 fama accidit classem Punicam adventare. octoginta erant
et tres naves; cum his haud procul Clupea prospere pugnat

---

[147] These are elections for the consuls of 207.
[148] *Barr.* 32 H3: Clupea (var. Clipea).

ter to Rome about his colleague's death and the great danger he faced himself. He could not come to Rome for the elections, he said, because he thought he would be unable to stand the rigors of the journey, and he was also concerned about Tarentum in case Hannibal directed his army there from Bruttium; so legates should be sent to him, discerning individuals with whom he could discuss his wishes vis-à-vis state policy.

This letter, when it was read out, aroused deep sorrow over the death of the one consul and grave fear for the other. The senators therefore sent Quintus Fabius the younger to the army in Venusia, and three legates were also sent to the consul: Sextus Iulius Caesar, Lucius Licinius Pollio, and Lucius Cincius Alimentus (who had returned from Sicily a few days earlier). These had instructions to inform the consul that, if unable to come to Rome for the elections himself, he should appoint a dictator within Roman territory to supervise them;[147] and if the consul had left for Tarentum, it was the will of the senate that the praetor Quintus Claudius lead his legions into the area where he could protect the greatest number of their allied cities.

That same summer Marcus Valerius crossed from Sicily to Africa with a fleet of a hundred ships, and landing at the city of Clupea[148] he inflicted widespread devastation on the countryside, meeting virtually no armed resistance. The marauding troops were then swiftly brought back to the ships because word suddenly came that a Punic fleet was approaching. There were eighty-three ships; and against them the Roman admiral fought a successful engagement not far off Clupea. After eighteen ships were

317

Romanus. duodeviginti navibus captis, fugatis aliis cum magna terrestri navalique praeda Lilybaeum rediit.

9 Eadem aestate et Philippus implorantibus Achaeis auxilium tulit, quos et Machanidas tyrannus Lacedaemoniorum finitimo bello urebat, et Aetoli navibus per fretum quod Naupactum et Patras interfluit—Rhion incolae vo-
10 cant—exercitu traiecto depopulati erant. Attalum quoque regem Asiae, quia Aetoli summum gentis suae magistratum ad eum proximo[70] concilio detulerant, fama erat in Europam traiecturum.

30. Ob haec Philippo in Graeciam descendenti ad Lamiam urbem Aetoli duce Pyrrhia, qui praetor in eum an-
2 num cum absente Attalo creatus erat, occurrerunt; habebant et ab Attalo auxilia secum et mille ferme ex Romana classe a P. Sulpicio missos. adversus hunc ducem atque has copias Philippus bis prospero eventu pugnavit; mille ad-
3 modum hostium utraque pugna occidit. inde cum Aetoli metu compulsi Lamiae urbis moenibus tenerent sese, Philippus ad Phalara exercitum reduxit. in Maliaco sinu is locus est, quondam frequenter habitatus propter egregium portum tutasque circa stationes et aliam opportunitatem maritimam terrestremque.

[70] proximo Σ: proximo anno P: proximo annuo Weiss.

---

[149] Cf. 5.9 and note, above.
[150] Tyrant at this time (following the death of Lycurgus), he possessed "large and strong forces" (Plut. Phil. 10.1), but in 206 he died at Mantinea at the hands of Philopoemen (Plut. Phil. 10.7; Polyb. 11.11.1–11.18.5).
[151] Attalus I (269–197) was ruler of Pergamum, which in 129 became the Roman province of Asia ("Asia" here is thus anach-

captured and the rest put to flight, Valerius then returned to Lilybaeum[149] with ample spoils from his land and sea operations.

That same summer Philip also brought help to the Achaeans in response to their appeals; the Spartan tyrant Machanidas[150] was causing them great distress with a border war, and the Aetolians had also been conducting raids with an army ferried across the strait between Naupactus and Patrae (locally called "Rhion"). There was also a report that Attalus king of Asia was going to cross to Europe because the Aetolians had conferred on him their people's highest office at their most recent council meeting.[151]

30. Philip therefore came down into Greece and was met at the city of Lamia by the Aetolians with their leader Pyrrias, who had been elected praetor[152] for that year together with Attalus, who was absent at this time; they had with them auxiliary forces from Attalus and also about a thousand men from the Roman fleet, who had been sent to them by Publius Sulpicius. Against this general and these forces Philip fought two successful battles, and in each he killed about a thousand of his enemy. As the Aetolians, daunted by this, kept within the walls of the city of Lamia after that, Philip led his army back to Phalara.[153] This is a place on the Malian Gulf, once thickly populated because of its fine harbor, safe anchorages close by, and other maritime and land advantages.

ronistic). He was the first to adopt the royal title. The office here conferred on him was purely honorary.

[152] That is, *strategos*.

[153] *Barr.* 55 D3 (tentatively).

4   Eo legati ab rege Aegypti Ptolomaeo Rhodiisque et Atheniensibus et Chiis venerunt ad dirimendum inter Philippum atque Aetolos bellum. adhibitus ab Aetolis et
5   ex finitimis pacificator Amynander rex Athamanum. omnium autem non tanta pro Aetolis cura erat, ferociore quam pro ingeniis Graecorum gente,[71] quam ne Philippus regnumque eius rebus Graeciae, grave libertati futurum,
6   immisceretur. de pace dilata consultatio est in concilium Achaeorum, concilioque ei et locus et dies certa indicta; interim triginta dierum induttiae impetratae.
7   Profectus inde rex per Thessaliam Boeotiamque Chalcidem Euboeae venit ut Attalum, quem classe Euboeam petiturum audierat, portibus et litorum adpulsu arceret.
8   inde, praesidio relicto adversus Attalum si forte interim traiecisset, profectus ipse cum paucis equitum levisque
9   armaturae Argos venit. ibi curatione Heraeorum Nemeorumque suffragiis populi ad eum delata quia se Macedonum reges ex ea civitate oriundos referunt, Heraeis peractis ab ipso ludicro extemplo Aegium profectus est ad indictum multo ante sociorum concilium.
10   Ibi de Aetolico finiendo bello actum ne causa aut Ro-

---

[71] ferociore . . . gente *Walsh*: ferocioris . . . gentis *P*: ferociori . . . genti M^c: ferociori . . . gente *Gron.*

---

[154] Athamania was an area in the southeast of Epirus (*Barr.* 55 A2), from which it became independent about 230 (*OCD* s.v. Athamenes). Aetolia lay south of it.

[155] The Achaean Confederacy, originally a federation of Achaean cities, later expanded to absorb the whole of the Peloponnese. Its biennial meetings (spring and autumn) were held at Aegium (Aigion: *Barr.* 55 4C).

Ambassadors came there from Ptolemy, king of Egypt, and from the Rhodians, Athenians, and Chians to settle the conflict between Philip and the Aeolians. Also invited to the negotiations, as a peace broker, was Amynander king of the Athamanians, one of their neighbors.[154] Everybody's concern, however, was less for the Aetolians (a people more aggressive than is usual for Greeks) than for keeping Philip and his kingdom out of the affairs of Greece, to whose freedom they would pose a serious threat. Discussion of peace was postponed until the council meeting of the Achaeans,[155] and both venue and date for that meeting were established; and a thirty-day truce was obtained for the meantime.

Leaving there, the king came to Chalcis in Euboea by way of Thessaly and Boeotia; his aim was to keep Attalus out of its harbors or from landing on its coastline, having heard that he would be heading for Euboea with a fleet. Leaving a force in Chalcis to face Attalus in case he made the crossing in the meantime, he himself then set off with a few cavalrymen and light infantry and came to Argos. There, by vote of the people, he was granted superintendence of the Festival of Hera and the Nemean Games, since the kings of Macedon claim descent from that city-state,[156] and when the Festival of Hera was concluded he went straight from the event itself to Aegium for the council meeting of his allies scheduled much earlier.

There was discussion there of ending the Aetolian war

[156] Through the mythical Caranus: Plut. *Alex.* 2.2; Justin 7.1.7; Livy 32.22.11 (with Briscoe's note). The Festival of Hera took place in Argos, the Nemean Games at Nemea about eight miles away (in the second and fourth year of each Olympiad).

11 manis aut Attalo intrandi Graeciam esset. sed ea omnia,
vixdum indutiarum tempore circumacto, Aetoli turbavere,
postquam et Attalum Aeginam venisse et Romanam clas-
12 sem stare ad Naupactum audivere. vocati enim in concilium Achaeorum, in quo et eae legationes erant quae ad
Phalara egerant de pace, primum questi sunt quaedam
parva contra fidem conventionis tempore indutiarum
13 facta; postremo negarunt dirimi bellum posse nisi Messe-
niis Achaei Pylum redderent, Romanis restitueretur Atin-
tania, Scerdilaedo et Pleurato Ardiaei.
14 Enimvero indignum ratus Philippus victos victori sibi
ultro condiciones ferre, ne antea quidem se aut de pace
audisse aut indutias pepigisse dixit spem ullam habentem
quieturos Aetolos, sed uti omnes socios testes haberet se
15 pacis, illos belli causam quaesisse. ita infecta pace concilium dimisit, quattuor milibus armatorum relictis ad
praesidium Achaeorum et quinque longis navibus accep-
16 tis, quas si adiecisset missae nuper ad se classi Carthaginiensium et ex Bithynia ab rege Prusia venientibus navibus,
statuerat navali proelio lacessere Romanos iam diu in re-
17 gione ea potentes maris. ipse ab eo concilio Argos regressus; iam enim Nemeorum appetebat tempus, quae cele-
brari volebat praesentia sua.

31. Occupato rege apparatu ludorum et per dies festos

---

157 An area about twenty miles east of Dyrrhachium (*Barr.* 49
C2).

158 Cf. 26.24.9.

159 Prusias I Cholus ("The Lame") (ca. 230–182) was the ally
and brother-in-law of Philip.

so neither the Romans nor Attalus would have reason to enter Greece. But, with the truce barely expired, all such plans were upset by the Aetolians after they heard that Attalus had reached Aegina and that a Roman fleet was also anchored off Naupactus. For when invited to the Achaeans' council, which was also attended by the deputations that had participated in the peace discussions at Phalara, the Aetolians began with complaints about some minor infractions of the agreement during the truce; but finally they declared that the war could not be terminated unless the Achaeans gave Pylus back to the Messenians, and unless Antintania[157] were restored to the Romans and the Ardiaei to Scerdilaedus and Pleuratus.[158]

Philip thought it quite outrageous that the conquered party should be offering terms to him, the conqueror; even earlier, he said, when he had listened to peace proposals and concluded a truce, it was not with any hope that the Aetolians would remain calm, but so that all his allies could witness that he had sought grounds for peace and they grounds for war. He thus adjourned the council without achieving peace, leaving four thousand troops behind to protect the Achaeans and accepting their offer of five warships: he had decided that, if he added these to the Carthaginian fleet recently sent to him and the ships coming from Bithynia from King Prusias,[159] he would, in a naval battle, challenge the long-standing Roman supremacy at sea in that region. Philip himself withdrew to Argos after that meeting; for now the time of the Nemean games was at hand, and he wanted them honored by his presence.

31. While the king was preoccupied with planning the games and enjoying during the festival season more relax-

licentius quam inter belli tempora remittente animum, P.
Sulpicius ab Naupacto profectus classem adpulit inter
Sicyonem et Corinthum agrumque nobilissimae fertilitatis
2 effuse vastavit. fama eius rei Philippum ab ludis excivit;
raptimque cum equitatu profectus, iussis subsequi pediti-
bus, palatos passim per agros gravesque praeda, ut qui
nihil tale metuerent, adortus Romanos compulit in[72]
3 naves. classis Romana haudquaquam laeta praeda Naupactum rediit.[73]

Philippo ludorum quoque qui reliqui erant celebrita-
tem quantaecumque, de Romanis tamen, victoriae partae
4 fama auxerat, laetitiaque ingenti celebrati festi dies, eo
magis etiam quod populariter dempto capitis insigni pur-
puraque atque alio regio habitu, aequaverat ceteris se in
5 speciem, quo nihil gratius est civitatibus liberis. praebuis-
setque haud dubiam eo facto spem libertatis nisi omnia
intoleranda libidine foeda ac deformia effecisset. vagaba-
tur enim cum uno aut altero comite per maritas domos
6 dies noctesque; et summittendo se in privatum fastigium
quo minus conspectus eo solutior erat, et libertatem cum
aliis vanam ostendisset totam in suam licentiam verterat.
7 neque enim omnia emebat aut eblandiebatur sed vim
etiam flagitiis adhibebat, periculosumque et viris et parentibus erat moram incommoda severitate libidini regiae

[72] in P: ad Σ
[73] rediit P: redit Σ

ation than he could in time of war, Publius Sulpicius set sail from Naupactus, put in with his fleet between Sicyon and Corinth, and there inflicted widespread damage on farmlands renowned for their fertility. Word of that called Philip away from the games; and he swiftly set off with his cavalry, ordering his infantry to follow; and, attacking the Romans, who were wandering in disorder through the fields—heavily laden with plunder and in no fear of such an attack—he drove them back into their ships. The Roman fleet returned to Naupactus, not at all pleased with its plunder.

For Philip the news of his victory had also increased the crowds for the remainder of the games—slight though it was, it *was* over the Romans!—and the days of the festival were celebrated with effusive joy, all the more so after a popularity-seeking gesture of setting aside his diadem, his purple robe, and the rest of his royal apparel, and seemingly bringing himself down to everybody else's level (for nothing gives free societies more pleasure than this). And by such a gesture he might have offered some genuine hope of freedom had he not made everything filthy and degrading by his unconscionable debauchery. For he would prowl around homes of married people day and night with one or two companions; and the less noticed he was in bringing himself down to the level of a private person the less restrained he was; and freedom, only a fleeting glimpse of which he had given others, he had in his own case turned completely into profligacy. For he did not gain all his ends by money or seduction but would even add violence to his scandalous behavior, and it was dangerous for husbands and parents alike to have obstructed the king's sexual appetite with an inconvenient

8 fecisse. uni etiam principi Achaeorum Arato adempta uxor
nomine Polycratia, ac spe regiarum nuptiarum in Macedoniam asportata fuerat.

9 Per haec flagitia sollemni Nemeorum peracto pau-
cisque additis diebus, Dymas est profectus ad praesidium
Aetolorum, quod ab Eleis accitum acceptumque in urbem
10 erat, eiciendum. Cycliadas—penes eum summa imperii
erat—Achaeique ad Dymas regi occurrere, et Eleorum
accensi odio quod a ceteris Achaeis dissentirent, et infensi
Aetolis quos Romanum quoque adversus se movisse bel-
11 lum credebant. profecti ab Dymis coniuncto exercitu
transeunt Larisum amnem, qui Eleum agrum ab Dymaeo
dirimit.

32. Primum diem quo fines hostium ingressi sunt populando absumpserunt; postero die acie instructa ad urbem accesserunt, praemissis equitibus qui obequitando
portis promptum ad excursiones genus lacesserent Aeto-
2 lorum. ignorabant Sulpicium cum quindecim navibus ab
Naupacto Cyllenen traiecisse, et expositis in terram quattuor milibus armatorum silentio noctis ne conspici agmen
3 posset intrasse Elim. itaque improvisa res ingentem iniecit
terrorem postquam inter Aetolos Eleosque Romana signa
4 atque arma cognovere. et primo recipere suos voluerat
rex; deinde contracto iam inter Aetolos et Tralles—Illyrio-

---

160 She became the mother of Philip's son Perseus, who later
disputed the throne with his brother Demetrius (39.53.3). Cf.
Briscoe, *A Commentary on Livy Books* 38–40, 399–400.

161 Philip heads for Dymae (*Barr.* 58 B1) en route for Elis (58
A2), where the Aetolian garrison is installed.

162 He was *strategos* for 209.

163 Cyllene (Kyllene) and Elis: *Barr.* 58 A2.

moral firmness. Even one of the most important Achaeans, Aratus, saw his wife—her name was Polycratia[160]—taken from him and whisked off to Macedonia with the hope of a royal marriage.

The Nemean festival and a few extra days having been spent in such debauchery, he set off for Dymae in order to drive out its Aetolian garrison, which had been invited, and then admitted, into their city by the Eleans.[161] Cycliadas (supreme command lay with him)[162] and the Achaeans met the king at Dymae; they were inflamed with hatred for the Eleans for distancing themselves from the other Achaeans, and they were also furious with the Aetolians who, they believed, had also incited the Romans to war against them. Setting off from Dymae with their armies united, they crossed the River Larisus, which divides Elean territory from that of Dymae.

32. The first day that they entered their enemy's territory they spent on looting; on the next day they approached the city with their battle line formed up, having first sent cavalry ahead to provoke the Aetolians—a race ever ready to make sorties—by riding up to their gates. They were unaware that Sulpicius had crossed from Naupactus to Cyllene with fifteen ships and that, after setting four thousand soldiers ashore, he had entered Elis[163] in the dead of night so his column could not be spotted. Thus, the shock at recognizing Roman standards and armor among the Aetolians and Eleans struck sheer terror into them. The king first wanted to withdraw his troops; but then there was a clash between the Aetolians and the

rum id est genus—certamine, cum urgeri videret suos, et
5   ipse rex cum equitatu in cohortem Romanam incurrit. ibi
equus pilo traiectus cum prolapsus super caput regem
effudisset, atrox pugna utrimque accensa est, et ab Roma-
6   nis impetu in regem facto et protegentibus regiis; insignis
et ipsius pugna fuit cum pedes inter equites coactus esset
proelium inire. dein cum iam impar certamen esset, cade-
rentque circum eum multi et volnerarentur, raptus ab suis
7   atque alteri equo iniectus fugit. eo die castra quinque
milia passuum ab urbe Eleorum posuit; postero die
ad propinquum Eleorum castellum—Pyrgum vocant—
copias omnes eduxit, quo agrestium multitudinem cum
8   pecoribus metu populationum compulsam audierat. eam
inconditam inermemque multitudinem primo statim terrore adveniens cepit, compensaveratque ea praeda quod
ignominiae ad Elim acceptum fuerat.
9   Dividenti praedam captivosque—fuere autem quattuor milia hominum, pecorumque[74] omnis generis ad viginti milia—nuntius ex Macedonia venit Aeropum quen-
dam corrupto arcis praesidiique praefecto Lychnidum
cepisse, tenere et Dassaretiorum quosdam vicos et Dardanos etiam concire. omisso igitur Achaico atque Aetolico
10 bello, relictis tamen duobus milibus et quingentis omnis
generis armatorum cum Menippo et Polyphanta ducibus
11 ad praesidium sociorum, profectus ab Dymis per Achaiam

---

[74] pecorumque Σ: pecoris P

---

[164] Little is known of them; they are also called Illyrian by
Stephanus of Byzantium, but Thracian by Strabo and Hesychius
(cf. Briscoe on 31.35.1).

[165] Lychnidus: *Barr.* 49 C2; Dassaretis: C3; Dardania: C1.

Tralles, an Illyrian tribe,[164] and when he saw his men hard pressed he himself charged at a Roman cohort with his cavalry. There his horse was run through by a javelin, unseating the king and flinging him over its head onto the ground, and a struggle flared up, furious on both sides, with the king under attack from the Romans and the king's men protecting him. The fight the man himself put up was remarkable despite his being forced to enter battle on foot amid his cavalry. Then, when the struggle was already one-sided, and many were falling or being wounded around him, he was seized by his men and put on another horse, on which he fled the field. That day he pitched camp five miles from the city of Elis; on the next day he led out all his troops against a nearby stronghold of the Eleans (they call it Pyrgus), to which he had heard a crowd of peasants had been driven with their animals from fear of marauding. That disorganized and unarmed crowd he captured through the immediate panic caused by his arrival, and he had with that plunder compensated for the humiliation inflicted at Elis.

As he was dividing up the plunder and prisoners—there were four thousand men, and some twenty thousand farm animals of all kinds—a message arrived from Macedonia that a certain Aeropus had captured Lychnidus through bribing the officer in command of its citadel and garrison, and that the man was also holding some villages of the Dessaretii and even inciting the Dardanians to revolt.[165] He therefore abandoned the Achaean and Aetolian war but left in place twenty-five hundred fighting men of all categories under Menippus and Polyphas for his allies' protection; then, setting off from Dymae, he

Boeotiamque et Euboeam decimis castris Demetriadem
in Thessaliam pervenit.

33. Ibi alii maiorem adferentes tumultum nuntii occur-
runt, Dardanos in Macedoniam effusos Orestidem iam
tenere ac descendisse in Argestaeum campum, famamque

2 inter barbaros celebrem esse Philippum occisum. expedi-
tione ea, qua cum populatoribus agri ad Sicyonem
pugnavit, in arborem inlatus impetu equi ad eminentem

3 ramum cornu alterum galeae praefregit; id inventum ab
Aetolo quodam perlatumque in Aetoliam ad Scerdilae-
dum, cui notum erat insigne galeae, famam interfecti regis

4 volgavit. post profectionem ex Achaia regis Sulpicius Aegi-
5 nam classe profectus cum Attalo sese coniunxit. Achaei
cum Aetolis Eleisque haud procul Messene prosperam
pugnam fecerunt. Attalus rex et P. Sulpicius Aeginae hi-
bernarunt.

6 Exitu huius anni T. Quinctius consul, dictatore comitiorum ludorumque faciendorum causa dicto T. Manlio
Torquato, ex volnere moritur; alii Tarenti alii in Campania

7 mortuum tradunt. ita[75] quod nullo ante bello acciderat,
duo consules sine memorando proelio interfecti velut or-
bam rem publicam reliquerant. dictator Manlius ma-
gistrum equitum C. Servilium—tum aedilis curulis erat—

8 dixit. senatus quo die primum est habitus ludos magnos
facere dictatorem iussit quos M. Aemilius praetor urbanus
C. Flaminio Cn. Servilio consulibus fecerat et in quin-

[75] ita *Weiss.*: id *P*

---

[166] Orestis and the Argestaean plain (Argestaeus Campus):
Barr. 49 D3.   [167] 31.1–2, above.   [168] The winter of 209–8.

came through Achaea, Boeotia, and Euboea, and after a ten-day march reached Demetrias in Thessaly.

33. There other messengers met him with news of more serious trouble: the Dardanians, who had been streaming into Macedonia, were now occupying Orestis and had come down into the Argestaean plain,[166] and among the barbarians it was rumored that Philip had been killed. Now during the operation on which he fought raiders near Sicyon,[167] he had crashed into a tree when his horse bolted and on a projecting tree branch had broken off one of the horns on his helmet; this had been found by some Aetolian and taken to Scerdilaedus in Aetolia, who was familiar with the helmet's distinctive feature, and that spread the rumor that the king had been killed. After the king's departure from Achaea, Sulpicius set off with his fleet for Aegina and joined up with Attalus. The Achaeans fought a successful battle against the Aetolians and Eleans not far from Messene. King Attalus and Publius Sulpicius wintered on Aegina.[168]

At the close of this year the consul Titus Quinctius appointed Titus Manlius Torquatus dictator for conducting the elections and the games, but then he died from his wound; some place his death in Tarentum, others in Campania. Thus—something unparalleled in any war to that date—two consuls, killed without fighting a battle of any consequence, had left the state parentless, as it were. The dictator Manlius appointed Gaius Servilius (he was then curule aedile) as his master of horse. On the first day of its session, the senate instructed the dictator to stage the same great games that the urban praetor Marcus Aemilius had staged in the consulship of Gaius Flaminius and Gnaeus Servilius, and which Aemilius had also vowed

331

quennium voverat; tum dictator et fecit ludos et in insequens lustrum vovit.

9   Ceterum cum duo consulares exercitus tam prope hostem sine ducibus essent, omnibus aliis omissis una prae-
cipua cura patres populumque incessit consules primo
quoque tempore creandi, et ut eos crearent potissimum

10   quorum virtus satis tuta a fraude Punica esset; cum toto
eo bello damnosa praepropera ac fervida ingenia imperatorum fuisse,[76] tum eo ipso anno consules nimia cupiditate
conserendi cum hoste manum in necopinatam fraudem

11   lapsos esse. ceterum deos immortales miseritos nominis
Romani pepercisse innoxiis exercitibus, temeritatem consulum ipsorum capitibus damnasse.

       34. Cum circumspicerent patres quosnam consules fa-

2   cerent, longe ante alios eminebat C. Claudius Nero. ei
collega quaerebatur; et virum quidem eum egregium
ducebant, sed promptiorem acrioremque quam tempora

3   belli postularent aut hostis Hannibal; temperandum acre
ingenium eius moderato et prudenti viro adiuncto collega
censebant.

       M. Livius erat, multis ante annis ex consulatu populi

4   iudicio damnatus; quam ignominiam adeo aegre tulerat ut
rus migrarit et per multos annos et urbe et omni coetu

---

[76] fuisse Σ: fuissent *PTa*?

---

[169] In 217, in relation to the vow of a Sacred Spring (cf.
22.10.7–9).

[170] *Punica fraus*, a favorite Livian expression, used five times
by him (all, not surprisingly, in this decade) and in classical Latin
found elsewhere only in Florus (who is much indebted to Livy)
and, much later, in Orosius.   [171] Cf. 14.4 and note, above.

would be celebrated in five years.[169] The dictator then staged the games and also vowed they would be celebrated again in the following *lustrum*.

However, since two consular armies were so close to the enemy without leaders, everything else was shelved and there was only one pressing concern for the senators and people: electing consuls as soon as possible, and especially electing men with a valor resistant to Punic duplicity.[170] Throughout that war, they reasoned, their commanders' impulsive and hotheaded character had proved disastrous, and that very year in particular the consuls had, from being too eager to engage the enemy, fallen into a trap that they had not foreseen. However, the immortal gods had taken pity on the Roman people, they said, and had spared the guiltless armies and made the consuls themselves pay for their recklessness with their own lives.

34. As the senators were casting about for men to make consuls, one stood head and shoulders above the rest: Gaius Claudius Nero.[171] What he needed was a colleague; and while they thought him an excellent candidate they also thought him too impetuous and volatile for the present military situation or for an enemy like Hannibal; his impulsive nature needed to be tempered through pairing with a cool-headed, prudent colleague.

A possibility was Marcus Livius who, after his consulship many years earlier, had been convicted of a crime by the popular assembly,[172] a disgrace he had so taken to heart that he moved to the country and for many years

---

[172] M. Livius Salinator (33). Consul in 219, he had been convicted of peculation at the end of his term (Frontin. *Str.* 4.1.45; cf. also Livy 22.35.3).

5 caruerit[77] hominum. octavo ferme post damnationem
anno M. Claudius Marcellus et M. Valerius Laevinus consules reduxerant eum in urbem; sed erat veste obsoleta
capilloque et barba promissa, prae se ferens in voltu habi-

6 tuque insignem memoriam ignominiae acceptae. L. Veturius et P. Licinius censores eum tonderi et squalorem
deponere, et in senatum venire fungique aliis publicis

7 muneribus coegerunt. sed tum quoque aut verbo adsen-
tiebatur aut pedibus in sententiam ibat donec cognati
hominis eum causa M. Livi Macati, cum fama eius agere-

8 tur, stantem coegit in senatu sententiam dicere. tunc ex
tanto intervallo auditus convertit ora hominum in se, cau-
samque sermonibus praebuit: indigno iniuriam a populo
factam, magnoque id damno fuisse quod tam gravi bello

9 nec opera nec consilio talis viri usa res publica esset. C.
Neroni neque Q. Fabium neque M. Valerium Laevinum
dari collegam posse, quia duos patricios creari non liceret;

10 eandem causam in T. Manlio esse, praeterquam quod re-
cusasset delatum consulatum recusaturusque esset. egregium par consulum fore si M. Livium C. Claudio collegam
adiunxissent.

11 Nec populus mentionem eius rei ortam a patribus est
12 aspernatus. unus eam rem in civitate is cui deferebatur

---

[77] caruerit *Ta*Σ: careret *P*

---

[173] Literally, "go over with his feet to the opinion," referring
to showing support for a motion at division by walking over to the
appropriate side.

[174] Cf. 25.3–5, above.

[175] This resulted from the Licinio-Sextian rogations and, later,
the Lex Genucia (on which see Oakley 1.645–85).

avoided the city and all public gatherings. Some seven years after the conviction the consuls Marcus Claudius Marcellus and Marcus Valerius Laevinus had brought him back into the city; but he wore old clothes, had long hair and a long beard, and in his demeanor and expression showed he well remembered his humiliation. The censors Lucius Veturius and Publius Licinius pressed him to have his hair and beard cut, to put aside his rags, and to attend senate meetings and carry out other duties of public life. Even then, however, he would utter only one word in support of a motion or silently vote for it,[173] until, that is, the case of his relative Marcus Livius Macatus, when the man's reputation was at stake,[174] forced him to stand and give his opinion before the senate. Being heard then after so long an interval, he had everybody's eyes riveted on him and became a topic of conversation. The slight he had received from the people was undeserved, said the senators, and in so serious a war the state had suffered serious loss in not availing itself of the help or advice of a man of such qualities. Gaius Nero could be given neither Quintus Fabius nor Marcus Valerius Laevinus as his colleague because electing two patrician candidates was not allowed;[175] and the same argument applied in the case of Titus Manlius (who, in any case, had refused the consulship when offered it and would refuse it again). They would have an excellent pair of consuls if they paired Marcus Livius as colleague with Gaius Claudius!

Nor did the people object to this notion raised by the senators. The only man in the community opposed to the idea was the one on whom the office was being conferred,

honos abnuebat, levitatem civitatis accusans: sordidati rei non miseritos candidam togam invito offerre, eodem ho-
13 nores poenasque congeri. si bonum virum ducerent, quid ita pro malo ac noxio damnassent? si noxium compe-rissent, quid ita male credito priore consulatu alterum
14 crederent? haec taliaque arguentem et querentem casti-gabant patres, et M. Furium memorantes revocatum de exsilio patriam pulsam sede sua restituisse. ut parentium saevitiam, sic patriae patiendo ac ferendo leniendam esse.
15 adnisi omnes cum ⟨C.⟩[78] Claudio M. Livium consulem fecerunt.

35. Post diem tertium eius diei praetorum comitia habita. praetores creati L. Porcius Licinus C. Mamilius C. et A. Hostilii Catones. comitiis perfectis ludisque factis
2 dictator et magister equitum magistratu abierunt. C. Te-rentius Varro in Etruriam pro praetore missus ut ex ea provincia C. Hostilius Tarentum ad eum exercitum iret quem T. Quinctius consul habuerat. et L. Manlius trans
3 mare legatus iret viseretque quae res ibi gererentur; si-mul, quod Olympiae ludicrum ea aestate futurum erat quod maximo coetu Graeciae celebraretur, ut, si tuto per
4 hostem posset, adiret id concilium ut, qui Siculi bello ibi

---

[78] ⟨C.⟩ ed. Rom.

---

[176] Not the usual white toga, but the toga of the candidate for office specially whitened (*candidatus*) with chalk.   [177] M. Fu-rius Camillus, almost a legendary figure. Reputedly exiled (the charges vary), he was recalled to save his country from the Gauls, who had invaded and sacked Rome. Cf. Cornell 316–19.
[178] C. Hostilius Tubulus, *praetor urbanus* in 209 and then *propraetor* in Etruria this year (208; cf. 6.12 and 22.5, above).

who accused his fellow citizens of fickleness: after showing
no pity for him as a defendant in rags, they were now offering him a white toga[176] that he did not want—offices
and punishments heaped on the same person! If they
thought him a good man, why had they condemned him
as a criminal and lawbreaker? If they had found him guilty,
why, after so wrongly entrusting him with the first consulship, should they entrust him with a second? When he
adduced these and other such arguments and complaints,
the senators proceeded to reprimand him, reminding him
that it was after being recalled from exile that Marcus
Furius Camillus had restored his fatherland to her proper
place from which she had been removed.[177] Like parents'
harshness, they said, the harshness of a country must be
soothed with patience and acceptance. With a united effort
they made Marcus Livius consul alongside Gaius Claudius.

35. Two days later the praetorian elections were held.
The praetors elected were Lucius Porcius Licinus, Gaius
Mamilius, Gaius Hostilius Cato and Aulus Hostilius Cato.
When the elections were over and the games held, the
dictator and master of horse resigned their magistracy.
Gaius Terentius Varro was sent into Etruria as propraetor
so Gaius Hostilius[178] could leave that province for Tarentum to the army that the consul Titus Quinctius had commanded. Lucius Manlius[179] was also to proceed overseas
as a legate and keep an eye on developments there; at the
same time, since the Olympic Games were to be held that
summer and would be celebrated with large crowds of
spectators from Greece, he was to attend this meeting (if
he could safely get through the enemy) so that any Sicilian

179 L. Manlius Acidinus, urban praetor in 210 (4.4, above).

profugi aut Tarentini cives relegati ab Hannibale essent,
domos redirent scirentque sua omnia[79] quae ante bellum
habuissent reddere populum Romanum.

5   Quia periculosissimus annus imminere videbatur neque consules in re publica erant, in consules designatos
omnes versi quam primum eos sortiri provincias et prae-
sciscere quam quisque eorum provinciam, quem hostem
6 haberet, volebant. de reconciliatione etiam gratiae eorum
in senatu actum est, principio facto a Q. Fabio Maximo;
7 inimicitiae autem nobiles inter eos erant, et acerbiores eas
indignioresque Livio sua calamitas fecerat quod spretum
8 se in ea fortuna credebat. itaque is magis implacabilis erat,
et nihil opus esse reconciliatione aiebat: acrius et intentius
omnia gesturos timentes ne crescendi ex se inimico colle-
9 gae potestas fieret. vicit tamen auctoritas senatus ut positis
simultatibus communi animo consilioque administrarent
rem publicam.

10   Provinciae iis non permixtae regionibus sicut superio-
ribus annis, sed diversae extremis Italiae finibus, alteri
adversus Hannibalem Bruttii Lucani, alteri Gallia adversus Hasdrubalem, quem iam Alpibus adpropinquare fama
11 erat, decreta. exercitum e duobus qui in Gallia quique in
Etruria esset, addito urbano, eligeret quem mallet qui
12 Galliam esset sortitus. cui Bruttii provincia evenisset,
novis legionibus urbanis scriptis utrius mallet consulum
13 prioris anni exercitum sumeret; relictum a consule exerci-

[79] omnia Σ: omnia iis P

war refugees present, or any Tarentine citizens driven out by Hannibal, might return home and know that all property that they had possessed before the war was being restored to them by the Roman people.

Because the oncoming year seemed fraught with danger and there were no consuls in office in the state, everyone turned to the consuls designate, wanting them to hold their provincial sortition as soon as possible and have advance notice of which province each would have and the enemy he would face. There was also discussion in the senate, started by Quintus Fabius Maximus, of reconciling the two; the animosity between them was well known, and had been made even more bitter and difficult for Livius by his personal misfortune because he believed he had been shabbily treated in his time of adversity. Thus he was the more implacable of them, and he kept saying there was no need of reconciliation—each would show more careful attention to everything from fear of a spiteful colleague profiting at his expense. Senatorial authority prevailed, however, making them discharge their public duties with harmony and cooperation.

Their provinces were not geographically connected as in previous years, but set apart at both ends of Italy, with one assigned the Bruttii and Lucanians to face Hannibal, and the other Gaul to face Hasdrubal who, it was said, was already approaching the Alps. The consul drawing Gaul was instructed to choose for himself one of the two armies located respectively in Gaul and in Etruria, with the army of the city also added. The one to whom Bruttium fell as his province would enroll new city legions and take over one of the two armies—the choice was his—of the previous year's consuls; the proconsul Quintus Fulvius would

tum Q. Fulvius proconsul acciperet, eique in annum im-
14 perium esset. et C. Hostilio, cui pro Etruria Tarentum
mutaverant provinciam, pro Tarento Capuam mutave-
runt; legio una data est cui Fulvius proximo anno praefuerat.

36. De Hasdrubalis adventu in Italiam cura in dies
crescebat. Massiliensium primum legati nuntiaverant eum
2 in Galliam transgressum erectosque adventu eius, quia
magnum pondus auri attulisse diceretur ad mercede auxi-
3 lia conducenda, Gallorum animos. missi deinde cum iis
legati ab Roma Sex. Antistius et M. Raecius ad rem inspiciendam rettulerant misisse se cum Massiliensibus ducibus qui per hospites eorum principes Gallorum omnia
4 explorata referrent: pro comperto habere Hasdrubalem
ingenti iam coacto exercitu proximo vere Alpes traiecturum, nec tum eum quicquam aliud morari nisi quod clausae hieme Alpes essent.

5 In locum M. Marcelli P. Aelius Paetus augur creatus
inauguratusque, et Cn. Cornelius Dolabella rex sacrorum
inauguratus est in locum M. Marci qui biennio ante mor-
6 tuus erat. hoc eodem anno et lustrum conditum est a censoribus P. Sempronio Tuditano et M. Cornelio Cethego.
7 censa civium capita centum triginta septem[80] milia centum octo, minor aliquanto numerus quam qui ante bellum
8 fuerat. eo anno primum ex quo Hannibal in Italiam venisset comitium tectum esse memoriae proditum est: et lu-

---

[80] CXXXVII *P*: CLXXVII *Walsh, cl. 29.37.6 et Per. 20*

---

[180] That is, with the guides.
[181] Cf. 6.16 and note, above.

take the army left by the consul, and he would have *imperium* for a year. In the case of Gaius Hostilius, for whom the senators had already substituted Tarentum for Etruria as his province, they now substituted Capua for Tarentum; and he was assigned the one legion that Fulvius had commanded the previous year.

36. Concern over Hasdrubal's arrival in Italy was growing by the day. First, Massiliot ambassadors had reported that he had crossed into Gaul and that there was excitement over his coming among the Gauls because he was said to have brought a large amount of gold to hire mercenaries. Then Sextius Antistius and Marcus Raecius, sent with them as legates from Rome to investigate the matter, had informed the senate that they had sent men with Massiliot guides to make a full report based on intelligence gathered from Gallic chieftains through their ties of hospitality;[180] and they were certain that Hasdrubal would cross the Alps the following spring with a huge army he had already assembled, and all that was holding him back at that time was that the Alps were impassable in winter.

Publius Aelius Paetus was elected and installed as augur to replace Marcus Marcellus, and Gnaeus Cornelius Dolabella was installed as *rex sacrorum* to replace Marcus Marcius, who had died two years earlier.[181] This same year the census purification was also performed by the censors Publius Sempronius Tuditanus and Marcus Cornelius Cethegus. The number of citizens in the census came to 137,108, a considerably smaller figure than before the war. It is on record that for the first time since Hannibal had entered Italy the Comitium was that year provided with

dos Romanos semel instauratos ab aedilibus curulibus Q.
9 Metello et C. Servilio, et plebeiis ludis biduum instauratum a C. Mamilio et M. Caecilio Metello aedilibus plebis.
et tria signa ad Cereris eidem dederunt. et Iovis epulum
fuit ludorum causa.

10 Consulatum inde ineunt C. Claudius Nero et M. Livius
iterum; qui, quia iam designati provincias sortiti erant,
praetores sortiri iusserunt. C. Hostilio iurisdictio urbana
11 evenit; addita et peregrina ut tres in provincias exire possent. A. Hostilio Sardinia, C. Mamilio Sicilia, L. Porcio
12 Gallia evenit. summa legionum trium et viginti ita per
provincias divisa: binae consulum essent, quattuor Hispania haberet, binas tres praetores in Sicilia et Sardinia et
13 Gallia, duas C. Terentius in Etruria, duas Q. Fulvius in
Bruttiis, duas Q. Claudius circa Tarentum et Sallentinos,
unam C. Hostilius Tubulus Capuae; duae urbanae ut scri-
14 berentur. primis quattuor legionibus populus tribunos
creavit; in ceteras consules miserunt.

37. Priusquam consules proficiscerentur, novendiale
2 sacrum fuit quia Veiis de caelo lapidaverat. sub unius prodigii, ut fit, mentionem alia quoque nuntiata: Minturnis
aedem Iovis et lucum Maricae, item Atellae murum et

---

182 Shade for the *comitium* (the earliest place of public assembly in Rome and always the venue for the *comitia curiata*) was
provided by awnings (on which cf. Plin. *HN* 19.23).

183 That is, the consular legions.

184 The ceremony was the normal expiation process for stone
showers. This section on prodigies is unusually long and, according to Levene (*Religion*, 65–66), "matches the treatment of the
crisis with which it is associated" (that is, the action of Hasdrubal
up to the battle of the Metaurus).

185 The shrine and grove of the nymph Marica lay on the coast

shade;[182] that the Roman Games were repeated for one day by the curule aediles Quintus Metellus and Gaius Servilius; and also that the Plebeian Games were repeated for two days by the plebeian aediles Gaius Mamilius and Marcus Caecilius. These same aediles also offered three statues at the temple of Ceres; and there was a feast of Jupiter in honor of the games.

Gaius Claudius Nero and Marcus Livius then entered their consulship, Livius for the second time. As they had already drawn their provinces as consuls designate, they ordered the praetors to draw theirs. The urban jurisdiction fell to Gaius Hostilius; he was further assigned the foreigners' jurisdiction so the three other praetors could leave the city for their provinces. Sardinia fell to Aulus Hostilius, Sicily to Gaius Mamilius, and Gaul to Lucius Porcius. A total of twenty-three legions was apportioned among the provinces as follows: there would be two each for the consuls; Spain would have four; the three praetors would have two each, in Sicily, Sardinia, and Gaul respectively; Gaius Terentius would have two in Etruria; Quintus Fulvius two in Bruttium; Quintus Claudius two near Tarentum, plus the Sallentini; and Gaius Hostilius Tubulus one in Capua; and two city legions were to be raised. The people elected the tribunes for the first four legions;[183] the consuls sent them to the others.

37. Before the consuls could set out there was a nine-day ceremony because a shower of stones had fallen at Veii.[184] After the mention of one prodigy others were also reported, as usual. The temple of Jupiter and Grove of Marica at Minturnae,[185] as well as the city wall and a gate

just south of Minturnae (*Barr.* 44 E3; Nisbet-Rudd on Hor. *Carm.* 3.17.9–12 p. 216).

3   portam de caelo tacta; Minturnenses, terribilius quod esset, adiciebant sanguinis rivum in porta fluxisse; et Capuae
4   lupus nocte portam ingressus vigilem laniaverat. haec procurata hostiis maioribus prodigia, et supplicatio diem unum fuit ex decreto pontificum. inde iterum novendiale instauratum quod in Armilustro lapidibus visum pluere.
5   liberatas religione mentes turbavit rursus nuntiatum Frusinone natum infantem esse quadrimo parem, nec magnitudine tam mirandum quam quod is quoque, ut Sinuessae
6   biennio ante, incertus mas an femina esset natus erat. id vero haruspices ex Etruria acciti foedum ac turpe prodigium dicere: extorre[81] agro Romano, procul terrae contactu alto mergendum. vivum in arcam condidere, provectumque in mare proiecerunt.
7   Decrevere item pontifices ut virgines ter novenae per urbem euntes carmen canerent. id cum in Iovis Statoris aede discerent conditum ab Livio poeta carmen, tacta de
8   caelo aedes in Aventino Iunonis reginae; prodigiumque id ad matronas pertinere haruspices cum respondissent do-

---

[81] extorre *P*: extorrem ΛΣ

---

[186] About ten miles south of Capua (*Barr.* 44 F4).

[187] On supplication, cf. 26.21.3 note.

[188] An area on the Aventine, where a ceremony of arms purification took place each October 19.

[189] Sixty miles southeast of Rome on the Via Latina (*Barr.* 44 D2).

[190] Cf. 31.12.6–8 for the same fate of a hermaphrodite baby.

[191] Richardson 225: Iuppiter Stator, Aedes (1).

[192] Livius Andronicus (ca. 280–200), generally regarded as Rome's earliest poet. Brought to Rome as a captive from Taren-

at Atella, were said to have been struck by lightning;[186] the people of Minturnae, to make their report more terrifying, added that a stream of blood had flowed in the temple doorway; at Capua, too, a wolf had come through a gate at night and badly mauled a guard. These prodigies were expiated with full-grown victims, and by decree of the pontiffs there was one day of supplication.[187] The nine-day ceremony was then repeated because a shower of stones had been seen in the Armilustrum.[188] But minds freed from religious concerns were once again troubled by a report of a child at Frusino[189] being born equal in size to a four-year-old, and it was not so much its size that excited wonder as that it was unclear at its birth whether it was male or female (as at Sinuessa two years before). Sooth-sayers brought in from Etruria called it a foul and loath-some prodigy and said it must be taken from Roman ter-ritory, kept from all contact with the ground, and drowned in the sea. They placed it alive in a coffin, took it out to sea, and threw it in.[190]

The pontiffs also decreed that three groups of nine young girls should sing a hymn in a procession through the city. When the girls were in the temple of Jupiter Stator[191] learning the hymn, a composition by the poet Livius,[192] the temple of Queen Juno on the Aventine[193] was struck by lightning; and the soothsayers interpreted that as a prodigy affecting married women[194] and said the goddess

tum in 272, he adapted Greek comedies and tragedies and trans-lated Homer's *Odyssey* into Latin. Only meager fragments of his works remain.

193 Cf. Richardson 215–16: Iuno Regina, Aedes (2).

194 Juno being a goddess of women and marriage.

9 noque divam placandam esse, aedilium curulium edicto in
Capitolium convocatae, quibus in urbe Romana intraque
decimum lapidem ab urbe domicilia essent, ipsae inter se
quinque et viginti delegerunt ad quas ex dotibus stipem

10 conferrent; inde donum pelvis aurea facta lataque in
Aventinum, pureque et caste a matronis sacrificatum.

11   Confestim ad aliud sacrificium eidem divae ab decemviris edicta dies, cuius ordo talis fuit. ab aede Apollinis
boves feminae albae duae porta Carmentali in urbem duc-

12 tae; post eas duo signa cupressea Iunonis reginae porta-

13 bantur. tum septem et viginti virgines longam indutae
vestem carmen in Iunonem reginam canentes ibant, illa
tempestate forsitan laudabile rudibus ingeniis, nunc ab-
horrens et inconditum si referatur. virginum ordinem
sequebantur decemviri coronati laurea praetextatique. a

14 porta Iugario vico in forum venere; in foro pompa constitit, et per manus reste data virgines sonum vocis pulsu

15 pedum modulantes incesserunt. inde vico Tusco Vela-
broque per bovarium forum in clivum Publicium atque
aedem Iunonis reginae perrectum. ibi duae hostiae ab
decemviris immolatae, et simulacra cupressea in aedem
inlata.

---

[195] Gate in the Servian wall through which passed the Vicus
Iugarius (see below): Richardson 301 and fig. 58.16.

[196] Street above the Forum Romanum, running along the
Capitoline hill: Richardson 424 and fig. 19.

[197] The main street between the Forum Romanum and the
Velabrum (which was between the Forum Romanum and the
Forum Boarium): Richardson 429.

[198] The main road on the Aventine, built in 241 or 238 (cf.
Book 26 note 61) and named after its builders, the aediles L. and

needed to be appeased with a gift. Married women with homes in the city of Rome or within ten miles of the city were therefore summoned to the Capitol by edict of the curule aediles, and they selected twenty-five of their number to whom they would bring a small contribution from their dowries; from that a golden bowl was made as the gift and taken to the Aventine where, with ritual purification and cleansing, the sacrifice was offered by the married women.

A date for a second sacrifice to the same goddess was immediately proclaimed by the *decemvirs* and its program was as follows: from the temple of Apollo two white cows were led into town by way of the Porta Carmentalis;[195] behind them were carried two statues of Queen Juno made from cypress wood. Then came twenty-seven young girls dressed in long robes, singing a hymn to Queen Juno that at the time might to their rude intellects have seemed to have some merit but which, recited now, would be thought tasteless and uncouth. The train of girls was followed by the *decemvirs* wearing laurel garlands and the *toga praetexta*. From the gate they came along the Vicus Iugarius[196] into the forum; in the forum the procession halted, and the girls, passing a cord through their hands, moved forward beating their feet in time with their singing. From there, by way of the Vicus Tuscus[197] and the Velabrum, they came through the Forum Boarium to the Clivus Publicius[198] and the temple of Queen Juno. There the two victims were sacrificed by the *decemvirs* and the cypress-wood statues carried into the temple.

M. Publicius Malleolus: Richardson 90 and fig. 14 (p. 47). It descended (*clivus* means "slope") to the Forum Boarium.

38. Dis rite placatis dilectum consules habebant acrius intentiusque quam prioribus annis quisquam meminerat

2 habitum. nam et belli terror duplicatus novi hostis in Italiam adventu, et minus iuventutis erat unde scriberent

3 milites. itaque colonos etiam maritimos, qui sacrosanctam vacationem dicebantur habere, dare milites cogebant. quibus recusantibus edixere in diem certam ut quo quisque

4 iure vacationem haberet ad senatum deferret. ea die ad senatum hi populi venerunt, Ostiensis Alsiensis Antias Anxurnas Minturnensis Sinuessanus, et ab supero mari

5 Senensis. cum vacationes suas quisque populus recitaret, nullius cum in Italia hostis esset praeter Antiatem Ostiensemque vacatio observata est; et earum coloniarum iuniores iure iurando adacti supra dies triginta non pernoctaturos se extra moenia coloniae suae donec hostis in Italia esset.

6 Cum omnes censerent primo quoque tempore consulibus eundum ad bellum—nam et Hasdrubali occurrendum esse descendenti ab Alpibus, ne Gallos Cisalpinos neve Etruriam erectam in spem rerum novarum sollicitaret, et Hannibalem suo proprio occupandum bello,

7 ne emergere ex Bruttiis atque obviam ire fratri posset—Livius cunctabatur, parum fidens suarum provinciarum

8 exercitibus: collegam ex duobus consularibus egregiis exercitibus et tertio cui Q. Claudius Tarenti praeesset

---

199 The maritime colonies, inhabited by Roman citizens, were exempt from military service because their duty to protect the coast was thought an equivalent.

200 Literally, "from the upper sea."

201 Sena Gallica (mod. Senigallia), some eighteen miles northwest of Ancona (*Barr.* 42 E1).

38. The gods ritually appeased, the consuls held a troop levy with greater vigor and intensity than anyone had remembered in earlier years. For the dread occasioned by the war had been doubled by the new enemy arriving in Italy, and there were fewer young men for enrolling soldiers. They therefore started forcing even colonists on the coast, men said to have an inviolable exemption,[199] to provide soldiers. When they refused, the consuls publicly announced a date on which each was to bring its grounds for exemption before the senate. On that day peoples of the following settlements came to the senate: Ostia, Alsium, Antium, Anxur, Minturnae, Sinuessa, and, from the Adriatic coast,[200] Sena.[201] When they all read out their agreements for exemption, in no case apart from Antium and Ostia[202] was the agreement considered valid while the enemy remained in Italy; and even from those two colonies men of fighting age were bound by oath not to spend more than thirty nights outside the walls of their colony as long as the enemy remained in Italy.

Everyone thought the consuls should go into battle as soon as possible: Hasdrubal must be confronted during his descent from the Alps to prevent him fomenting unrest among the Cisalpine Gauls or in Etruria, which was already looking for a chance to rebel; and Hannibal had to be kept occupied with his own campaign so he could not leave Bruttium and meet up with his brother. Livius, however, was hesitant, having little confidence in the armies assigned to his provinces (his colleague could choose from two fine consular armies and a third under the command

[202] The two towns mostly responsible for coastal security.

electionem habere. intuleratque mentionem de volonibus
9　revocandis ad signa. senatus liberam potestatem consulibus fecit et supplendi unde vellent et eligendi de omnibus
exercitibus quos vellent permutandique ⟨et⟩[82] ex provinciis quos e re publica censerent esse traducendi.

10　　Ea omnia cum summa concordia consulum acta. volones in undevicensimam et vicensimam legiones scripti.
11　magni roboris auxilia ex Hispania quoque a P. Scipione M.
Livio missa quidam ad id bellum auctores sunt, octo milia
Hispanorum Gallorumque, ad duo milia de legione militum, equitum mille octingentos mixtos Numidas Hispa-
12　nosque; M. Lucretium has copias navibus advexisse. et
sagittariorum funditorumque ad tria milia ex Sicilia C.
Mamilium misisse.

　　39. Auxerunt Romae tumultum litterae ex Gallia alla-
2　tae ab L. Porcio praetore: Hasdrubalem movisse ex hibernis et iam Alpes transire; octo milia Ligurum conscripta
armataque coniunctura se transgresso in Italiam esse, nisi
mitteretur in Ligures qui eos bello occuparet; se cum inva-
3　lido exercitu quoad tutum putaret progressurum. hae litterae consules raptim confecto dilectu maturius quam
constituerant exire in provincias coegerunt, ea mente ut
uterque hostem in sua provincia contineret, neque con-
4　iungi aut conferri[83] in unum vires pateretur. plurimum in

---

82 ⟨et⟩ *Ald.*　　　83 conferri Σ: conferre *P*

---

203 Latin *volones*, lit. "volunteers," but during the Punic War
the word was used of the slaves, purchased from their owners
after Cannae, who volunteered to serve in the army.

204 Elected praetor for this year, 207 (35.1, above), and given
Sicily as his province (36.11, above).

of Quintus Claudius at Tarentum). He had also raised the suggestion of recalling slave volunteers[203] to service. The senate gave the consuls carte blanche to draw supplementary troops from wherever they wished and also to select any troops they liked from all the armies, as well as to exchange and transfer from their provinces any men they thought would be of service to the state.

All these measures were put into effect by the consuls in perfect harmony. Slave volunteers were drafted into the nineteenth and twentieth legions. Some authorities state that for this campaign Marcus Livius was also sent powerful auxiliary forces from Spain by Publius Scipio: eight thousand Spaniards and Gauls, about two thousand legionaries, and eighteen hundred cavalrymen, a mixture of Numidians and Spaniards. Marcus Lucretius, they add, brought these troops by sea, and Gaius Mamilius[204] also sent some three thousand archers and slingers from Sicily.

39. Alarm in Rome was heightened by a dispatch brought from the praetor Lucius Porcius in Gaul: Hasdrubal had moved from his winter quarters and was already on his way over the Alps, and eight thousand Ligurians, already mobilized and armed, would join him once he crossed into Italy, unless someone were sent into Liguria to keep them preoccupied with a war; with his own army, weak though it was, he would advance as far as he thought safe. This dispatch forced the consuls to complete their troop levy and leave for their provinces earlier than planned, their idea now being for each to hold the enemy back in his province and not permit them to meet up or join forces. In this they had great help from

eam rem adiuvit opinio Hannibalis quod, etsi ea aestate transiturum in Italiam fratrem crediderat, recordando quae ipse in transitu nunc Rhodani nunc Alpium cum hominibus locisque pugnando per quinque menses exhau-
5 sisset, haudquaquam tam facilem maturumque transitum exspectabat. ea tardius movendi ex hibernis causa fuit.

6   Ceterum Hasdrubali et sua et aliorum spe omnia cele-riora atque expeditiora fuere. non enim receperunt modo Arverni eum deincepsque aliae Gallicae atque Alpinae
7 gentes, sed etiam secutae sunt ad bellum; et cum per munita pleraque transitu fratris quae antea invia fuerant ducebat, tum etiam duodecim annorum adsuetudine per-viis Alpibus factis inter mitiora iam transibant hominum
8 ingenia. invisitati namque antea alienigenis nec videre ipsi advenam in sua terra adsueti, omni generi humano inso-ciabiles erant; et primo ignari quo Poenus pergeret, suas rupes suaque castella et pecorum hominumque praedam
9 peti crediderant. fama deinde Punici belli quo duodeci-mum annum Italia urebatur satis edocuerat viam tantum Alpes esse; duas praevalidas urbes, magno inter se maris terrarumque spatio discretas, de imperio et opibus cer-tare.

10   Hae causae aperuerant Alpes Hasdrubali. ceterum
11 quod celeritate itineris profectum erat, id mora ad Pla-centiam, dum frustra obsidet magis quam oppugnat, cor-

---

205 The inhabitants of what is now the Auvergne, which would mean that Hasdrubal came through central France before the Alpine crossing. This seems unlikely, and the text or Livy's geography may be suspect. Cf. Hoyos *HW*, 680.

Hannibal's assumptions, since he had believed his brother would cross into Italy that summer; but reflecting on his own exhausting experiences—first the Rhone crossing, then the Alps and five months of battling men and the terrain—he had not been expecting Hasdrubal's journey to be anything like as easy and swift as it actually was. That was why he was rather slow in moving from winter quarters.

In fact, for Hasdrubal everything went more quickly and easily than either he or others had expected. For the Averni,[205] and then other Gallic and Alpine tribes, not only welcomed his coming but even went to war alongside him. He was also leading his army along a path which, though impassable earlier, had now become a largely open thoroughfare from his brother's crossing; and they were passing through peoples whose character had already been softened through the Alps being regularly crossed for twelve years. For, earlier, receiving no visits from outsiders and being unused to setting eyes on a stranger in their land, they were xenophobic toward the entire human race; and having no idea at first of where the Carthaginian was headed they had believed his objective to be their own rocky homes and strongholds and plunder in the form of animals and men. Then news of the Punic war, with which Italy had now been ablaze for eleven years, had shown them that the Alps were merely a passageway, that this was two mighty cities, separated by a large expanse of sea and land, fighting for power and dominion.

Such were the things that had opened up the Alps for Hasdrubal. The progress he had made by the speed of his march, however, he squandered by delaying at Placentia, which he besieged unsuccessfully rather than attacked.

353

12 rupit. crediderat campestris oppidi facilem expugnationem esse, et nobilitas coloniae induxerat eum, magnum se excidio eius urbis terrorem ceteris ratum iniecturum.

13 non ipse se solum ea oppugnatione impediit, sed Hannibalem, post famam transitus eius tanto spe sua celeriorem,

14 iam moventem ex hibernis continuerat, quippe reputantem non solum quam lenta urbium oppugnatio esset, sed etiam quam ipse frustra eandem illam coloniam ab Trebia victor regressus temptasset.

40. Consules diversis itineribus profecti ab urbe velut in duo pariter bella distenderant curas hominum, simul recordantium quas primus adventus Hannibalis intulisset

2 Italiae clades, simul cum illa angeret cura, quos tam propitios urbi atque imperio fore deos ut eodem tempore utrobique res publica prospere gereretur. adhuc adversa

3 secundis pensando rem ad id tempus extractam esse. cum in Italia ad Trasumennum et Cannas praecipitasset Romana res, prospera bella in Hispania prolapsam eam

4 erexisse. postea cum in Hispania alia super aliam clades duobus egregiis ducibus amissis duos exercitus ex parte delesset, multa secunda in Italia Siciliaque gesta quassa-

5 tam rem publicam excepisse, et ipsum intervallum loci, quod in ultimis terrarum oris alterum bellum gereretur,

6 spatium dedisse ad respirandum. nunc duo bella in Italiam accepta, duo celeberrimi nominis duces circumstare urbem Romanam, et unum in locum totam periculi molem, omne onus incubuisse. qui eorum prior vicisset intra pau-

---

206 Livy has earlier mentioned only an unsuccessful attack on a storage depot near Placentia (21.57.7–8) and an inconclusive battle outside the town the following spring (21.59.1–9).

207 Since they seemed to be setting off for separate wars.

He had thought a town on a plain would be easily taken, and the colony's renown had induced him to make the attempt, since he thought that by destroying that city he would strike terror in everyone else. Not only did he slow his own progress by that siege but he had also held back Hannibal, now moving from winter quarters after hearing that his brother's crossing had gone much faster than expected; for Hannibal was thinking not only about how slow the investment of cities could be but also about his own failed attempt on that same colony[206] when he was returning victorious from the Trebia.

40. In setting off from the city in opposite directions, as though for two wars at the same time, the consuls had only divided people's worries;[207] they remembered the disasters that Hannibal's first arrival had brought on Italy, and they were at the same time plagued by anxiety over what gods would be so kind to their city and empire as to grant the republic success on two fronts at the same time. Thus far they had drawn things out by compensating for reverses with successes. When Roman fortunes had taken a fall at Trasimene and Cannae, victorious wars in Spain had raised them again. Later, when defeat after defeat in Spain had partly destroyed two armies, with the loss of two fine commanders, numerous successes in Italy and Sicily had sustained the shaken republic; and the very geographic separation—because one of the wars was being fought at the world's end—had also allowed some breathing space. Now two wars had been brought into Italy; two commanders of great fame stood around the city of Rome, and it was on one area that the whole brunt and burden of this perilous war had come down. The first of those commanders to win a victory would join forces with the other

355

7 cos dies castra cum altero iuncturum. terrebat et proximus
annus lugubris duorum consulum funeribus.

His anxii curis homines digredientes in provincias con-
8 sules prosecuti sunt. memoriae proditum est plenum adhuc irae in cives M. Livium ad bellum proficiscentem
monenti Q. Fabio ne priusquam genus hostium cognosset
temere manum consereret, respondisse ubi primum ho-
9 stium agmen conspexisset pugnaturum. cum quaereretur
quae causa festinandi esset, "aut ex hoste egregiam gloriam" inquit "aut ex civibus victis gaudium meritum certe,
etsi non honestum, capiam."

10 Priusquam Claudius consul in provinciam perveniret,[84] per extremum finem agri Larinatis[85] ducentem in
Sallentinos exercitum Hannibalem expeditis cohortibus
adortus C. Hostilius Tubulus incomposito agmini terribi-
11 lem tumultum intulit; ad quattuor milia hominum occidit,
novem signa militaria cepit. moverat ex hibernis ad famam
hostis Q. Claudius, qui per urbes agri Sallentini castra
12 disposita habebat. itaque ne cum duobus exercitibus simul
confligeret, Hannibal nocte castra ex agro Tarentino movit
13 atque in Bruttios concessit. Claudius in Sallentinos agmen
convertit; Hostilius Capuam petens obvius ad Venusiam

[84] perveniret Σ: veniret P
[85] Larinatis P^c Σ: Laritanis P: Tarentini *Madvig*

[208] The text is defective. The manuscripts (see textual note)
read *Laritanis* or *Larinatis* (of Larinum), but Larinum is some
two hundred miles northwest of the Sallentini as the crow flies
(cf. *Barr.* 45 A1: Larinum; H4: Sallentini). Madvig's suggested
emendation "Tarentine" makes sense but is paleographically difficult.

in a matter of days. They were frightened, too, by the previous year, darkened by the deaths of the two consuls.

Tormented by such worries, the people saw off the consuls as they left for their provinces. It is recorded that as Marcus Livius left for the campaign, still full of anger with his fellow citizens, Quintus Fabius had warned him against recklessly engaging before he knew the kind of enemy he faced, but Livius had answered that he would fight as soon as he saw the enemy column. Asked why there was such haste, Livius replied: "Either I shall gain a great reputation from my enemy, or else I shall have from my fellow citizens' defeat some well deserved, even if not honorable, pleasure."

Before the consul Claudius reached his province, Hannibal was leading his army along the fringes of †Larinine†[208] territory into that of the Sallentini when Gaius Hostilius Tubulus[209] attacked him with some light-armed cohorts, causing terrible panic; he killed about four thousand men and captured nine military standards. Quintus Claudius,[210] who had his troops billeted throughout the cities in Sallentine territory, had moved out of winter quarters on hearing of the enemy's movements; and so, to avoid clashing with two armies at the same time, Hannibal struck camp at night from the area of Tarentum and withdrew into Bruttium. Claudius directed his army toward the Sallentini; Hostilius, who was making for Capua, met

---

[209] Now propraetor at Tarentum (35.2, above).
[210] Now praetor at Tarentum (21.5 and 36.13, above).

14 fit[86] consuli Claudio. ibi ex utroque exercitu electa peditum quadraginta milia, duo milia et quingenti equites quibus consul adversus Hannibalem rem gereret; reliquas
copias Hostilius Capuam ducere iussus ut Q. Fulvio
proconsuli traderet.

41. Hannibal undique contracto exercitu, quem in hibernis aut in praesidiis agri Bruttii habuerat, in Lucanos
ad Grumentum venit spe recipiendi oppida quae per
2 metum ad Romanos defecissent. eodem a Venusia consul
Romanus exploratis itineribus contendit, et mille ferme
3 et quingentos passus castra locat ab hoste.[87] Grumenti
moenibus prope iniunctum videbatur Poenorum vallum;
4 quingenti passus intererant. castra Punica ac Romana in-
teriacebat campus; colles imminebant nudi sinistro lateri
Carthaginiensium, dextro Romanorum, neutris suspecti
quod nihil silvae neque ad insidias latebrarum habebant.
5 In medio campo ab stationibus procursantes certamina
haud satis digna dictu serebant. id modo Romanum quae-
rere apparebat, ne abire hostem pateretur; Hannibal inde
6 evadere cupiens totis viribus in aciem descendebat. tum
consul ingenio hostis usus, quo minus in tam apertis collibus timeri insidiae poterant, quinque cohortes additis
quinque manipulis nocte iugum superare et in aversis col-
7 libus considere iubet; tempus exsurgendi ex insidiis et
adgrediendi hostem Ti. Claudium Asellum tribunum militum et P. Claudium praefectum socium edocet quos cum

---

[86] fit Σ: fuit P
[87] locat ab hoste P: ab hoste locat Σ

---

[211] An ancient (ca. 600) settlement, allied to Rome since the
fourth century: *Barr.* 45 C4; *OCD* s.v.

the consul at Venusia. There forty thousand infantry and twenty-five hundred cavalry were chosen from each army for the consul's operation against Hannibal; and Hostilius was instructed to lead the remaining troops to Capua to be transferred to the proconsul Quintus Fulvius.

41. Bringing together the army that he had been keeping in winter quarters or garrisons in Bruttian territory, Hannibal came to Grumentum[211] in Lucania in the hope of recovering towns that had from fear defected to the Romans. The Roman consul, after reconnoitering the roads, also marched there from Venusia and encamped about one and a half miles from the enemy. The rampart of the Carthaginian camp seemed almost to abut the walls of Grumentum; there was half a mile between them. Between the Punic and Roman encampments was level ground; treeless hills rose up to the Carthaginians' left and to the Romans' right, and neither side harbored suspicions about the other because they had no woods or hiding place for an ambush.

On the level ground between them there were some forays from both armies' advance posts precipitating skirmishes barely worth a mention. The Roman's only aim seemed to be not to let his enemy leave; Hannibal, eager to get away from there, would take the field in full force. Then the consul adopted his enemy's tactics: since there could be little fear of ambush on such open hills, he ordered five cohorts to cross the mountain ridge at night with an additional five maniples and take up a position on the far side of the hills. The time for these to emerge from their hiding place and attack the enemy he gave to Tiberius Claudius Asellus, a military tribune, and to Publius Claudius, a prefect of the allies, both of whom he was

8 iis mittebat. ipse luce prima copias omnes peditum equitumque in aciem eduxit. paulo post et ab Hannibale signum pugnae propositum est, clamorque in castris ad arma
discurrentium est sublatus; inde eques pedesque certatim
portis ruere ac palati per campum properare ad hostes.
9 quos ubi effusos consul videt, tribuno militum tertiae legionis C. Aurunculeio imperat ut equites legionis quanto
10 maximo impetu possit in hostem emittat: ita pecorum
modo incompositos toto passim se campo effudisse[88] ut
sterni obterique priusquam instruantur possint.

42. Nondum Hannibal e castris exierat cum pugnantium
2 clamorem audivit; itaque excitus tumultu raptim ad hostem copias agit. iam primos occupaverat equestris terror;
peditum etiam prima legio et dextra ala proelium inibat.
incompositi hostes, ut quemque aut pediti aut equiti casus
3 obtulit, ita conserunt manus. crescit pugna subsidiis et
procurrentium ad certamen numero augetur; pugnantes-
que, quod nisi in vetere exercitu et duci veteri haud facile
4 est, inter tumultum ac terrorem instruxisset Hannibal, ni
cohortium ac manipulorum decurrentium per colles clamor ab tergo auditus metum ne intercluderentur a castris
5 iniecisset. inde pavor incussus et fuga passim fieri coepta
est; minorque caedes fuit quia propinquitas castrorum
breviorem fugam perculsis fecit. equites enim tergo in-
6 haerebant; in transversa latera invaserant cohortes secun-

[88] effudisse Σ: fudisse P

sending with them. At dawn, Nero himself led all the troops, infantry and cavalry, into the battle line. Shortly afterward the signal for battle was also put up by Hannibal, and in the camp the shouting of men rushing to arms arose. Cavalry and infantry then raced from their gates and made a disordered rush at the enemy all over the plain. Seeing their disarray, the consul ordered a military tribune of the third legion, Gaius Aurunculeius, to unleash the legion's cavalry on the enemy with all possible force; in such disorder had they poured out like animals all over the plain that they could be charged down and crushed before they formed up, he said.

42. Hannibal had not even left camp when he heard the shouting of the combatants; and so, roused to action by the commotion, he hurriedly led his troops against his enemy. The closest of them had already been struck with panic by the cavalry, and the first legion and left allied contingent of their infantry were entering the battle. In disarray, the enemy engaged with whatever chance put in their way, be it foot soldier or cavalryman. The battle grew with reinforcements, and spread further as greater numbers rushed into the fray; and amid the uproar and panic all round, Hannibal might still have formed up his fighters—something not easy for any but a seasoned force and a seasoned commander—had not shouting they heard from cohorts and maniples running down the hills behind them struck fear into them of being cut off from their camp. With that they were panic-stricken and a rout began everywhere; but the slaughter was less because the closeness of their camp made the flight of the demoralized Carthaginians shorter. For the cavalry were hard on their heels; and their flanks had been attacked side-on by co-

7   dis collibus via nuda ac facili decurrentes. tamen supra octo milia hominum occisa, supra septingentos capti. signa militaria novem adempta; elephanti etiam, quorum nullus usus in repentina ac tumultuaria pugna fuerat, quattuor

8   occisi duo capti. circa quingentos Romanorum sociorumque victores ceciderunt.

    Postero die Poenus quievit; Romanus in aciem copiis eductis, postquam neminem signa contra efferre vidit, spolia legi caesorum hostium et suorum corpora conlata

9   in unum sepeliri iussit. inde insequentibus continuis diebus aliquot ita institit portis ut prope inferre signa videretur, donec Hannibal tertia vigilia crebris ignibus taber-

10   naculisque, quae pars castrorum ad hostes vergebat, et Numidis paucis qui in vallo portisque se ostenderent re-

11   lictis, profectus Apuliam petere intendit. ubi inluxit, successit vallo Romana acies; et Numidae ex composito paulisper in portis se valloque ostentavere, frustratique aliquamdiu hostes citatis equis agmen suorum adsequun-

12   tur. consul ubi silentium in castris et ne paucos quidem qui prima luce obambulaverant parte ulla cernebat, duobus equitibus speculatum in castra praemissis, postquam satis tuta omnia esse exploratum est, inferri signa iussit;

13   tantumque ibi moratus dum milites ad praedam discurrunt, receptui deinde cecinit multoque ante noctem copias reduxit.

14   Postero die prima luce profectus, magnis itineribus

---

[212] A well-documented stratagem: Frontin. *Str.* 1.1.7, 1.1.9, 1.5.22, 2.5.17, 2.12.4, 3.11.5.

horts running downward on a clear and easy path. Even so, more than eight thousand men were killed and more than seven hundred captured. Nine military standards were taken; of the elephants, which had served no purpose in such a swift and disordered battle, four were killed and two captured. About five hundred of the victorious Romans and their allies were lost.

The next day the Carthaginian remained inactive; the Roman led his troops into the battle line but on seeing no one carry out the standards to face him he ordered the spoils from the enemy dead to be gathered up and his own men's bodies brought together in one spot and buried. Then, for several days in a row, he threatened the enemy gates so closely as to seem to be almost mounting an assault, until eventually, at the third watch, Hannibal left numerous fires and tents behind in the part of his camp that faced his enemy,[212] plus a few Numidians (who were to make themselves visible on the rampart and at the gates) and set off at the third watch, heading for Apulia. At dawn, the Roman force approached the rampart, and the Numidians, following the prearranged plan, briefly let themselves be seen at the gateways and rampart and then, after duping their enemy for a while, galloped off to join their comrades on the march. When the consul observed there was silence in the camp and that not even the few men who had been walking about at dawn were anywhere to be found, he sent two cavalrymen forward into the camp to investigate, and on learning that all was secure he ordered the advance into it; and, remaining there only long enough for the men to run off for their spoils, he sounded the retreat and led back the troops well before nightfall.

Setting out at dawn the next day, he followed his enemy

famam et vestigia agminis sequens haud procul Venusia
15 hostem adsequitur. ibi quoque tumultuaria pugna fuit;
supra duo milia Poenorum caesa. inde nocturnis monta-
nisque itineribus Poenus ne locum pugnandi daret Me-
16 tapontum petiit. Hanno inde—is enim praesidio eius loci
praefuerat—in Bruttios cum paucis ad exercitum novum
comparandum missus: Hannibal, copiis eius ad suas additis, Venusiam retro quibus venerat itineribus repetit, at-
17 que inde Canusium procedit. nunquam Nero vestigiis
hostis abstiterat, et Q. Fulvium, cum Metapontum ipse
proficisceretur, in Lucanos ne regio ea sine praesidio esset
arcessierat.

43. Inter haec ab Hasdrubale, postquam ab Placentiae
obsidione abscessit,[89] quattuor Galli equites duo Numidae
2 cum litteris missi ad Hannibalem, cum per medios hostes
totam ferme longitudinem Italiae emensi essent dum
Metapontum cedentem Hannibalem sequuntur, incertis
itineribus Tarentum delati a vagis per agros pabulatoribus
3 Romanis ad Q. Claudium propraetorem deducuntur. eum
primo incertis implicantes responsis, ut metus tormentorum admotus fateri vera coegit, edocuerunt litteras se ab
4 Hasdrubale ad Hannibalem ferre. cum iis litteris sicut
erant signatis L. Verginio tribuno militum ducendi ad
Claudium consulem traduntur; duae simul turmae Samni-
tium praesidii causa emissae.

[89] a Placentiae obsidione abscessit *P*: ad Placentiam obsidionem accessit Σ

---

213 *Barr.* 45 E4.
214 *Barr.* 45 D2.

with forced marches, guided by reports and the tracks of their column, and overtook him not far from Venusia. There, too, there was a scrappy engagement, and more than two thousand Carthaginians were killed. The Carthaginian then headed for Metapontum,[213] marching at night and on mountain roads so as to allow no room for battle. From there Hanno—for he had been put in command of that area—was sent into Bruttium with a handful of men to raise a new army; and after adding Hanno's troops to his own Hannibal returned to Venusia by the roads on which he had come, and from there went ahead to Canusium.[214] At no time had Nero stopped tracking his enemy, and when he was himself setting out for Metapontum he had summoned Quintus Fulvius to Lucania so the region would not be undefended.

43. Meanwhile, after he abandoned the siege of Placentia, four Gallic horsemen and two Numidians had been sent off by Hasdrubal with a letter for Hannibal. They traveled almost the length of Italy through the midst of their enemies, but while following Hannibal as he was withdrawing to Metapontum they came upon roads unknown to them, ended up in Tarentum and were brought to the propraetor Quintus Claudius by some Roman foragers who were wandering through the countryside. At first they tried to mislead him with evasive responses, but when the threat of torture forced the truth out of them they told him they were bearing a letter to Hannibal from Hasdrubal. Together with this letter, which was still sealed, they were handed over to the military tribune Lucius Verginius to be taken to the consul Claudius Nero; two squadrons of Samnites were also sent with them as an escort.

5 Qui ubi ad consulem pervenerunt litteraeque lectae
6 per interpretem sunt et ex captivis percontatio facta, tum
   Claudius non id tempus esse rei publicae ratus quo consi-
7 liis ordinariis, provinciae suae quisque finibus, per exercitus suos cum hoste destinato ab senatu bellum gereret—
   audendum ac novandum aliquid improvisum, inopinatum,
   quod coeptum non minorem apud cives quam hostes ter-
8 rorem faceret, perpetratum in magnam laetitiam ex magno
   metu verteret—litteris Hasdrubalis Romam ad senatum
   missis simul et ipse patres conscriptos quid pararet edocet.
9 monet ut cum in Vmbria se occursurum Hasdrubal fratri
   scribat, legionem a Capua Romam arcessant, dilectum
   Romae habeant, exercitum urbanum ad Narniam hosti
   opponant.
10 Haec senatui scripta. praemissi item per agrum Lari-
   natem Marrucinum Frentanum Praetutianum, qua exercitum ducturus erat, ut omnes ex agris urbibusque commeatus paratos militi ad vescendum in viam deferrent,
   equos iumentaque alia producerent ut vehiculorum fessis
11 copia esset. ipse de toto exercitu civium sociorumque
   quod roboris erat delegit, sex milia peditum mille equites.
   pronuntiat occupare se in Lucanis proximam urbem
   Punicumque in ea praesidium velle; ut ad iter parati om-
12 nes essent. profectus nocte flexit in Picenum. et consul
   quidem quantis maximis itineribus poterat ad collegam
   ducebat, relicto Q. Catio legato qui castris praeesset.

---

215 Modern Narni, on the via Flaminia north of Rome (*Barr.*
42 D3), an effective point at which to block Hasdrubal's advance.
   216 That is, areas along the Adriatic. Larinum: *Barr.* 44 G2;
the Frentani, Marrucini, and Praetuttii: 42 G4 and F3.
   217 South of Ancona (*Barr.* 42 F2–3).

When they reached the consul, the letter was read by means of an interpreter and the prisoners interrogated, and Claudius thereupon decided that the crisis facing the state did not require conventional plans, with each consul functioning within the confines of his province and engaging with his own troops an enemy assigned by the senate—there must be some bold new stroke, startling and unexpected, something that would terrify citizens as much as the enemy, but which, successfully concluded, would turn great fear into great joy; and so he sent Hasdrubal's letter to the senate in Rome and at the same time explained to the conscript fathers what his plan was. His advice was that, since Hasdrubal was writing to his brother that he would meet him in Umbria, they should recall a legion to Rome from Capua, hold a troop levy in Rome, and station the city army at Narnia[215] to face the enemy.

Such was his letter to the senate. People were also sent ahead through the territory of Larinum, the Marrucini, Frentani, and Praetutii, through which he would be leading his army,[216] to instruct everyone to carry to the roadside from farms and cities provisions for his men that were ready to eat, and to bring out horses and other pack animals so there would be plenty of transport for men suffering fatigue. He personally selected from his entire army the strongest citizen and allied troops—six thousand infantry and a thousand cavalry. He gave notice that he intended seizing the closest city in Lucania and the Carthaginian garrison in it; and everyone was to be ready for the march. Setting off at night, he veered toward Picenum.[217] In fact, the consul was, with the longest possible forced marches, leading the men to join his colleague, with his legate Quintus Catius now left in charge of the camp.

44. Romae haud minus terroris ac tumultus erat quam fuerat biennio[90] ante, cum castra Punica obiecta Romanis moenibus portisque fuerant. neque satis constabat animis tam audax iter consulis laudarent vituperarentne; apparebat, quo nihil iniquius est, ex eventu famam habiturum.
2 castra prope Hannibalem hostem relicta sine duce, cum exercitu cui detractum foret omne quod roboris quod floris fuerit. et consulem in Lucanos ostendisse iter cum
3 Picenum et Galliam peteret, castra relinquentem nulla alia re tutiora quam errore hostis, qui ducem inde atque
4 exercitus partem abisse[91] ignoraret. quid futurum si id palam fiat, et aut insequi Neronem cum sex milibus armatorum profectum Hannibal toto exercitu velit aut castra invadere praedae relicta sine viribus, sine imperio, sine auspicio?
5 Veteres eius belli clades, duo consules proximo anno interfecti terrebant: et ea omnia accidisse cum unus imperator, unus exercitus hostium in Italia esset. nunc duo bella Punica facta, duos ingentes exercitus, duos prope Hanni-
6 bales in Italia esse; quippe et Hasdrubalem patre eodem Hamilcare genitum, aeque impigrum ducem, per tot annos in Hispania Romano exercitatum bello, gemina victoria insignem duobus exercitibus cum clarissimis ducibus
7 deletis. nam itineris quidem celeritate ex Hispania, et concitatis ad arma Gallicis gentibus, multo magis quam

90 biennio *P*: quadriennio *Glar., fort. recte*
91 abisse Σ: abesset *P*

218 Cf. 26.9.6–26.11.13. However, this present alarm is to be dated to 207, so either Livy is mistaken or Jal (*ad loc.*) is correct in accepting Glareanus' emendation to "four."

44. In Rome there was no less alarm and panic than two years earlier when a Carthaginian camp had been pitched before its walls.[218] People could not decide in their minds whether to praise or condemn the consul's daring march; what was clear, and most unfair, was that opinion of it would rest on the outcome. A camp had been left without a leader close to an enemy like Hannibal—and left with an army depleted of all its strength, all its elite troops! And the consul had made a show of heading into Lucania while really making for Picenum and Gaul, and was leaving behind a camp whose security depended on nothing more than their enemy's misperception, on their being unaware that the commander and part of the army had gone. What would happen if that became known and Hannibal, with his entire army, chose either to chase Nero who had left with six thousand troops or else attack a camp now left wide open to looting, without strength, without supreme command, and without *auspices*?

That war's past defeats and two consuls having been killed the previous year terrified people; and all of that had occurred when there was only one enemy commander and one enemy army in Italy. Now it had become *two* Punic wars, two mighty armies, and almost two Hannibals in Italy! For Hasdrubal, too, was born of Hamilcar and was just as dynamic a leader;[219] he had had so many years' of training in war against the Romans in Spain, and he had made a name for himself with his twin victories, wiping out two armies with their famous commanders. In the speed of his journey from Spain, too, and in inciting Gallic tribes

219 That is, as his brother Hannibal.

8 Hannibalem ipsum gloriari posse; quippe in iis locis hunc
coegisse exercitum quibus ille maiorem partem militum
fame ac frigore, quae miserrima mortis genera sint, ami-
9 sisset. adiciebant etiam periti rerum Hispaniae haud cum
ignoto eum duce C. Nerone congressurum, sed quem in
saltu impedito deprensus forte haud secus quam puerum
conscribendis fallacibus condicionibus pacis frustratus
10 elusisset. omnia maiora etiam vero praesidia hostium,
minora sua, metu interprete semper in deteriora inclinato,
ducebant.

45. Nero postquam iam tantum intervalli ab hoste fecerat ut detegi consilium satis tutum esset, paucis milites
2 adloquitur. negat ullius consilium imperatoris in speciem
3 audacius, re ipsa tutius fuisse quam suum. ad certam eos
se victoriam ducere, quippe ad quod bellum collega non
antequam ad satietatem ipsius peditum atque equitum
datae ab senatu copiae fuissent maiores instructioresque
quam si adversus ipsum Hannibalem iret profectus sit, eo
ipsos[92] quantumcumque virium momentum addiderint
4 rem omnem inclinaturos. auditum modo in acie—nam ne
ante audiatur daturum operam—alterum consulem et alterum exercitum advenisse haud dubiam victoriam factu-
5 rum. famam bellum conficere, et parva momenta in spem
metumque impellere animos. gloriae quidem ex re bene
gesta partae fructum prope omnem ipsos laturos; semper
quod postremum adiectum sit id rem totam videri traxisse.

[92] eo ipsos *P*: eos ipsos Λ: eo ipsi si *Madvig*

[220] 26.17.4–16.

to war, he had far more reason for boasting than Hannibal himself—for Hasdrubal had assembled this army in that same region where Hannibal had lost most of his soldiers to hunger and freezing temperatures, the most wretched of deaths! Those acquainted with the Spanish situation would also add that in engaging with Gaius Nero Hasdrubal would be facing a commander not unfamiliar to him: when he chanced to be caught in a difficult pass, he had, with a charade of framing peace terms,[220] duped and hoodwinked him just like a little boy. They also kept assuming all the enemy's strength to be greater than it really was, and their own smaller, fear always leaning toward a more pessimistic analysis.

45. When Nero had covered enough distance from the enemy for his plan to be revealed quite safely, he briefly addressed his men. He said no commander had ever had a plan that looked more foolhardy but was really more sound than his. It was to certain victory that he was leading them, for his colleague had not left for the campaign before receiving from the senate more than enough infantry and cavalry to meet his needs, forces stronger and better equipped than if he were going to face Hannibal himself, and they themselves would completely tip the scale with whatever strength they added! Once it was merely heard on the battlefield—for he would ensure that it was not heard earlier—that a second consul and a second army had arrived, this would put their victory beyond doubt. Hearsay decides the outcome of a battle, and insignificant factors push the mind toward hope or fear. And as for the glory, they themselves would from success reap nearly all of it—what came at the end was always considered to have been the decisive factor. They could see for themselves by

371

6   cernere ipsos quo concursu, qua admiratione, quo favore
hominum iter suum celebretur.

7   Et hercule per instructa omnia ordinibus virorum mu-
lierumque undique ex agris effusorum inter vota ac preces
et laudes ibant. illos praesidia rei publicae, vindices urbis
Romanae imperiique appellabant: in illorum armis dex-
trisque suam liberorumque suorum salutem ac libertatem

8   repositam esse. deos omnes deasque precabantur ut illis
faustum iter, felix pugna, matura ex hostibus victoria esset,
damnarenturque ipsi votorum quae pro iis suscepissent ut,

9   quemadmodum nunc solliciti prosequerentur eos, ita pau-
10   cos post dies laeti ovantibus victoria obviam irent. invitare
inde pro se quisque et offerre et fatigare precibus ut quae
ipsis iumentisque usui essent ab se potissimum sumerent.

11   benigne omnia cumulata dare; modestia certare milites ne
quid ultra usum necessarium sumerent. nihil morari nec
ab signis[93] absistere[94] cibum capientes, diem ac noctem
ire; vix quod satis ad naturale desiderium corporum esset

12   quieti dare. et ad collegam praemissi erant qui nuntiarent
adventum percontarenturque clam an palam, interdiu an
noctu venire sese vellet, iisdem an aliis considere castris.
nocte clam ingredi melius visum est.

    46. Tessera per castra ab Livio consule data erat ut
tribunus tribunum, centurio centurionem, eques equi-

---

[93] signis Σ: signis nec P   [94] absistere *Fr.* 2: subsistere P

---

[221] Literally, "to be condemned for their vows." When making
a vow, the petitioner promised the gods a gift if the petition were
granted. If it were granted, the petitioner was "condemned" to
make good on the promise.

[222] A small wooden tablet (*tessera*) bearing the orders of the
day was circulated among the maniples of the legion.

what crowds of people they were celebrated as they passed by, and with what admiration and support.

And certainly they were marching along amid vows, prayers, and words of praise from rows of men and women who had poured in from all over the countryside. Defenders of the state, they kept calling them, champions of the city of Rome and her empire; in their weapons and sword arms lay their and their children's safety and freedom. They prayed to all the gods and goddesses to grant those men a prosperous journey, a successful battle and swift victory over the enemy; and prayed, too, that they themselves would be obliged to repay the vows they had made on their behalf[221] and that, just as they now anxiously sent those men on their way, so would they in a few days go happily to meet them as they rejoiced in their victory. Then they all issued invitations, proffered gifts, and persistently entreated the men to take whatever might be of use to them or to their beasts of burden, and take it from them in particular. They showered everything on them without stint; and the soldiers competed in showing restraint, not taking anything beyond their needs. There was no dawdling, no breaking formation when they took food, and they marched day and night; and barely did they give themselves enough rest to meet the body's natural requirements. Men had also been sent ahead to Nero's colleague to announce the army's coming and ask whether he wanted them arriving secretly or openly, by day or at night, and whether they would be housed in the same camp or another. Entering secretly during the night was thought preferable.

46. The tablet[222] had been circulated through the camp by the consul Livius: a tribune was to house a tribune, a centurion to house a centurion, a cavalryman a cavalry-

2 tem, pedes peditem acciperet: neque enim dilatari castra opus esse, ne hostis adventum alterius consulis sentiret. et coartatio plurium in angusto tendentium facilior futura erat quod Claudianus exercitus nihil ferme praeter arma secum in expeditionem tulerat; ceterum in ipso itinere

3 auctum voluntariis agmen erat offerentibus ultro sese, et veteribus militibus perfunctis iam militia et iuvenibus quos certatim nomina dantes, si quorum corporis species roburque virium aptum militiae videbatur, conscripserat.

4 ad Senam castra alterius consulis erant, et quingentos ferme inde passus Hasdrubal aberat. itaque cum iam ap-propinquaret tectus montibus substitit Nero ne ante noc-tem castra ingrederetur. silentio ingressi ab sui quisque

5 ordinis hominibus in tentoria abducti cum summa om-nium laetitia hospitaliter excipiuntur.

Postero die consilium habitum cui et L. Porcius Lici-

6 nus praetor adfuit. castra iuncta consulum castris habebat; et ante adventum eorum per loca alta ducendo exercitum, cum modo insideret angustos saltus ut transitum claude-ret, modo ab latere aut ab tergo carperet agmen, ludifica-

7 tus hostem omnibus artibus belli fuerat. is tum in consilio aderat. multorum eo inclinant sententiae ut, dum fessum via ac vigiliis reficeret militem Nero, simul et ad noscen-dum hostem paucos sibi sumeret dies, tempus pugnandi[95]

---

[95] pugnandi Σ: pugnae P

---

[223] On Sena, cf. 38.4 and note, above. There is however a problem with Livy's location of the camp here because it lay too far south if Hasdrubal considered joining Hannibal in Umbria: see Hoyos *ad loc.* (*HW*, 681).

[224] Given the number of prisoners taken by the Carthaginians (49.7, below), he must have been defeated more often than not.

man, and a foot soldier a foot soldier. For, Livius decided, the camp should not be enlarged in case the enemy surmised that the other consul had arrived. And restricting men to a small space for their quarters would actually prove quite easy since Claudius' troops had brought with them for the operation almost nothing but their weapons. However, the column had on the march itself been enlarged by volunteers, as well as by older soldiers whose service was over offering to join, and also by younger men racing to enlist whom Claudius had enrolled if their physique and bodily strength seemed fit for service. The other consul's camp was at Sena,[223] and Hasdrubal was about half a mile away from there. Therefore, as he drew near, Nero halted where he had some cover from mountains so as not to enter the camp before nightfall. The men then filed in silently and were each taken to their tents by soldiers of their own rank and, amid general rejoicing, were offered hospitality.

The next day there was a council of war that was also attended by the praetor Lucius Porcius Licinus. He had his camp adjoining the consuls'; and before their arrival· he had been leading his force over the high country, at one time seizing narrow passes to obstruct their passage, at another harrying the enemy column with strikes at its flanks or rear, using all the arts of war in playing tricks on them.[224] He was now attending the war council. The opinions of many there inclined toward delaying engagement with the enemy to give Nero time to refresh his men, now exhausted from the journey and lack of sleep, and also to allow him a few days to familiarize himself with his enemy.

8   differretur. Nero non suadere modo sed summa ope orare
institit ne consilium suum quod tutum celeritas fecisset
9   temerarium morando facerent; errore qui non diuturnus
futurus esset velut torpentem Hannibalem nec castra sua
sine duce relicta adgredi nec ad sequendum se iter inten-
disse. antequam se moveat, deleri exercitum Hasdrubalis
10 posse, redirique in Apuliam. qui prolatando spatium hosti
det, eum et illa castra prodere Hannibali et aperire in
Galliam iter ut per otium ubi velit Hasdrubali coniunga-
11 tur. extemplo signum dandum et exeundum in aciem,
abutendumque errore hostium absentium praesentium-
que dum neque illi sciant cum paucioribus nec hi cum
12 pluribus et validioribus rem esse. consilio dimisso signum
pugnae proponitur confestimque in aciem procedunt.

     47. Iam hostes ante castra instructi stabant. moram
pugnae attulit quod Hasdrubal, provectus ante signa cum
paucis equitibus, scuta vetera hostium notavit quae ante
non viderat et strigosiores equos; multitudo quoque maior
2   solita visa est. suspicatus enim id quod erat, receptui propere cecinit, ac misit ad flumen unde aquabantur, ubi et
excipi aliqui possent et notari oculis si qui forte adustioris
3   coloris ut ex recenti via essent; simul circumvehi procul

Nero, however, proceeded not just to urge them but to beg them abjectly not to make his plan, which speed had made sound, a risky one by delaying. It was because of a bluff, one that would not last long, he said, that Hannibal was virtually frittering away time: he was not attacking his camp, which had been left without a commander, nor had he taken to the road to pursue him. Before he made any move, Hasdrubal's army could be destroyed and they could return to Apulia. Anyone giving the enemy time by delaying was both betraying that camp to Hannibal and also opening up a path into Gaul for him to join up with Hasdrubal at his leisure wherever he wished. They must immediately give the signal and go out into battle; they must fully capitalize on the bluff pulled on the absent enemy and the one present, while the former was still unaware that he faced fewer troops than he imagined and the latter that he faced more and stronger ones. When the council adjourned, the signal for battle was put up and they immediately went forward to battle stations.

47. The enemy was already standing in formation before their camp. There was a delay in engagement because, as Hasdrubal rode forward before his standards with a few cavalrymen, he noticed among the enemy some battle-worn shields that he had not observed earlier and horses that were rather emaciated; and their numbers also seemed unusually large. Suspecting what was actually the case, he quickly sounded the retreat, and he sent men to the river from which the Romans drew water so some prisoners could be seized there and inspected for any signs of a darker tan such as there would be after a recent journey; at the same time he ordered men to ride around

castra iubet specularique num auctum aliqua parte sit vallum, et ut attendant semel bisne signum canat in castris.

4   Ea cum ordine relata omnia essent, castra nihil aucta
errorem faciebant. bina erant sicut ante adventum consulis alterius fuerant, una M. Livi, altera L. Porci; neutris
quicquam quo latius tenderetur ad munimenta adiectum.

5 illud veterem ducem adsuetumque Romano hosti movit,
quod semel in praetoris castris signum, bis in consularibus
referebant cecinisse; duos profecto consules esse, et quonam modo alter ab Hannibale abscessisset cura angebat.

6 minime id quod erat suspicari poterat, tantae rei frustra-
tione Hannibalem elusum ut ubi dux, ubi exercitus esset

7 cum quo castra conlata habuerit ignoraret: profecto haud
mediocri clade absterritum insequi non ausum. magno
opere vereri ne perditis rebus serum ipse auxilium venisset, Romanisque eadem iam fortuna in Italia quae in His-

8 pania esset. interdum litteras suas ad eum non pervenisse
credere, interceptisque iis consulem ad sese opprimen-
dum accelerasse.

His anxius curis exstinctis ignibus, vigilia prima dato
9 signo ut taciti vasa conligerent, signa ferri iussit. in trepidatione et nocturno tumultu duces parum intente adser-

the Roman encampment at some remove and examine whether the rampart had been extended at any point, and also take note of whether in the camp there was one bugle call or two.

When this was all duly reported to Hasdrubal, the fact that there had been no camp enlargement fooled him. There were two camps (as there had been before the other consul's arrival), one belonging to Marcus Livius and the other to Lucius Porcius; in neither had there been any extension of fortifications to accommodate more tents. What concerned this veteran commander, one also used to facing a Roman enemy, was the news his men brought him that there had been one bugle call sounded in the praetor's camp, but two in the consul's; *both* consuls must be there, and the question of how one had slipped away from Hannibal kept tormenting him. The last thing he could suspect was what was actually the case, that Hannibal had been duped so thoroughly that he had no idea where the commander or the army that he had had encamped beside him could possibly be. It must be that his brother had not dared give chase because he had suffered a serious defeat; he greatly feared things must have gone badly wrong, that he himself had come too late to help, and that the Romans were now enjoying the same success in Italy as they were in Spain. Occasionally the thought crossed his mind that his letter had not reached Hannibal, that the consul had intercepted it, and that he had now come with all speed to crush him.

Vexed by such worries, Hasdrubal had the fires extinguished at the first watch, gave the signal for the men to quietly gather their equipment, and then ordered them to move out. In all the consternation and confusion of the

vati alter in destinatis iam ante animo latebris subsedit,
alter per vada nota Metaurum flumen tranavit. ita deser-
tum ab ducibus agmen primo per agros palatur, fessique
aliquot somno ac vigiliis sternunt corpora passim atque
10 infrequentia relinquunt signa. Hasdrubal dum lux viam
ostenderet ripa fluminis signa ferri iubet; et per tortuosi
amnis sinus flexusque cum errore ⟨iter re⟩volvens[96] haud
multum processisset, ubi prima lux transitum opportunum
11 ostendisset transiturus erat.[97] sed cum, quantum a mari
abscedebat, tanto altioribus coercentibus amnem ripis
non inveniret vada, diem terendo spatium dedit ad insequendum sese hosti.

48. Nero primum cum omni equitatu advenit; Porcius
2 deinde adsecutus cum levi armatura. qui cum fessum
agmen carperent ab omni parte incursarentque, et iam
omisso itinere quod fugae simile erat, castra metari Poe-
3 nus in tumulo super fluminis ripam vellet, advenit Livius
peditum omnibus copiis non itineris modo sed ad conse-
4 rendum extemplo proelium instructis armatisque. sed ubi
omnes copias coniunxerunt derectaque acies est, Claudius
dextro in cornu, Livius ab sinistro pugnam instruit; media
5 acies praetori tuenda data. Hasdrubal omissa munitione
castrorum postquam pugnandum vidit, in prima acie ante

---

[96] errore ⟨iter re⟩volvens *Riemann*: errorem volvens *P*: errore
volvens *CΓΣ*: orbem volvens *Weiss.*: errore ⟨re⟩volvens *Walsh*
[97] erat *Σ*: *om. P*

---

[225] If the camp is located near Sena, the man would have to
trek more than ten miles to reach the river (*Barr.* 42 E1). Cf. also
46.4 note, above.

night little attention was paid to the two guides, one of whom settled into a hiding place of which he had earlier made a mental note, while the other swam across the River Metaurus where he knew it was shallow.[225] Thus deserted by its guides, the column at first drifted aimlessly through the countryside and some, exhausted and weary from lack of sleep, threw themselves down here and there, leaving only a few around the standards. Hasdrubal ordered an advance along the riverbank until daylight could show them the way; but doubling back after losing his direction along the twisting and turning banks of the winding river, he made little headway. He was intending to cross as soon as dawn revealed a suitable fording point, but unable to find shallow spots, since the further he drew back from the sea the higher became the banks confining the river, he frittered away the day and gave his enemy the time to catch up.

48. Nero arrived first, together with all his cavalry; then Porcius followed with the light infantry. As they were harassing and charging the weary column from every direction, and the Carthaginian, now abandoning a march that resembled a flight, was wanting to lay out a camp on a knoll overlooking the riverbank, Livius arrived with all his infantry deployed and armed, not just in marching order but drawn up for immediate engagement. When the Romans brought all their troops together and the battle line was deployed, Claudius took the right wing and Livius the left; the praetor was assigned command of the center. Hasdrubal, who stopped fortifying a camp when he saw that he had to fight, positioned his elephants in the front line

signa elephantos conlocat.[98] circa eos laevo in cornu adversus Claudium Gallos opponit, haud tantum iis fidens
6 quantum ab hoste timeri eos credebat; ipse dextrum cornu
adversus M. Livium sibi atque Hispanis—et ibi maxime in
7 vetere milite spem habebat—sumpsit; Ligures in medio
post elephantos positi. sed longior quam latior acies erat;
8 Gallos prominens collis tegebat. ea frons quam Hispani
tenebant cum sinistro Romanorum cornu concurrit. dextra omnis[99] acies extra proelium eminens cessabat; collis
oppositus arcebat ne aut a fronte aut ab latere adgrederentur.
9 Inter Livium Hasdrubalemque ingens contractum cer-
10 tamen erat, atroxque caedes utrimque edebatur. ibi duces
ambo, ibi pars maior peditum equitumque Romanorum,
ibi Hispani, vetus miles peritusque Romanae pugnae, et
Ligures, durum in armis genus. eodem versi elephanti, qui
primo impetu turbaverant antesignanos, et iam signa mo-
11 verant loco; deinde crescente certamine et clamore impo-
tentius iam regi et inter duas acies versari velut incerti
quorum essent, haud dissimiliter navibus sine guberna-
culo vagis.

[98] conlocat *P*: locat Σ
[99] omnis *P*: ⟨R⟩om⟨a⟩nis *Walsh*

---

[226] Polybius, whose account of the battle survives (11.1.2–
11.2.1) gives the number of elephants as ten (App. *Hann.* 52 has
fifteen). For a detailed examination of Livy's account compared
with other sources (especially Appian and Dio-Zonaras), see Jal,
Introduction, 25–31.

[227] The Latin here (*longior*) would normally refer to length,
but it is generally accepted as referring to depth because Polybius

before the standards.[226] Close to them on the left wing and facing Claudius he set the Gauls, not so much from confidence in them as because he believed they were feared by the enemy. The right wing, facing Marcus Livius, he took for himself and the Spaniards—it was in these veteran troops that he placed his greatest hope. The Ligurians were stationed in the middle behind the elephants. But the formation had depth[227] rather than breadth, and the Gauls received cover from a hill before them. The part of the front line that the Spaniards held clashed with the Romans' left wing. The entire Roman right, standing beyond the fighting, remained out of it; the hill before them prevented any frontal or flank attack.

Between Livius and Hasdrubal there had been a huge confrontation, and terrible carnage was being wreaked on both sides. There stood the two commanders, there most of the Roman infantry and cavalry, and there the Spaniards, veteran troops familiar with Roman fighting, and the Ligurians, a race tough in battle. To this same spot the elephants had been driven, and with their first charge they had caused havoc in the front lines and already made the standards give ground; then, as the conflict and battle cries intensified, controlling them became more difficult and they strayed back and forth between both lines as though uncertain to which side they belonged, not unlike rudderless ships.

(11.1.3) refers to Hasdrubal "increasing the depth of his line, making the front of his whole army very narrow." That Livy has again misread Polybius is possible, but it must have been the shortness of Hasdrubal's line that enabled Claudius to outflank it (§14, below).

12 Claudius "quid ergo praecipiti cursu tam longum iter emensi sumus?" clamitans militibus, cum in adversum col-
13 lem frustra signa erigere conatus esset, postquam ea regione penetrari ad hostem non videbat posse, cohortes aliquot subductas e dextro cornu, ubi stationem magis
14 segnem quam pugnam futuram cernebat, post aciem circumducit, et non hostibus modo sed etiam suis inopinantibus in sinistrum[100] hostium latus incurrit; tantaque celeritas fuit ut cum ostendissent se ab latere mox in terga iam
15 pugnarent. ita ex omnibus partibus, a fronte ab latere ab tergo, trucidantur Hispani Liguresque, et ad Gallos iam
16 caedes pervenerat. ibi minimum certaminis fuit; nam et pars magna ab signis aberant, nocte dilapsi stratique somno passim per agros, et qui aderant itinere ac vigiliis fessi, intolerantissima laboris corpora, vix arma umeris
17 gerebant;[101] et iam diei medium erat, sitisque et calor hiantes caedendos capiendosque adfatim praebebat.

49. Elephanti plures ab ipsis rectoribus quam ab hoste interfecti. fabrile scalprum cum malleo habebant; id, ubi saevire beluae ac ruere in suos coeperant, magister inter aures positum ipsa in compage qua[102] iungitur capiti cervix
2 quanto maximo poterat ictu adigebat. ea celerrima via mortis in tantae molis belua inventa erat ubi regendi spem vicissent; primusque id Hasdrubal instituerat, dux cum
3 saepe alias memorabilis tum illa praecipue pugna. ille

---

[100] sinistrum *P*: dextrum *Glar.*: sinistrum ⟨evectus in dextrum⟩ *Conway*   [101] gerebant Σ: gestabant *P*
[102] ipsa in compage qua Σ: ipso in articulo quo *P*

---

[228] Throughout Livy, and Roman literature generally, the Gauls are represented as lacking stamina in battle.

"So why did we bother covering so much ground so quickly?" Claudius kept shouting to his men, after vainly trying to march his troops up a hill facing him; but when he saw it impossible to penetrate to the enemy there, he withdrew a number of cohorts from the right wing (where he could see they would be standing inactive rather than fighting), led them around behind the battle line, and launched an attack on the enemy left that took not only the enemy but even his own side by surprise; and such was its speed that just after appearing on the flank the cohorts were soon attacking the rear. Thus on every side—front, flank and rear—Spaniards and Ligurians were being massacred; and by now the slaughter had also reached the Gauls. There the fighting was lightest: for most had left their positions, slipping away in the night and lying asleep throughout the countryside, and those still around, exhausted from the journey and sleep deprivation, were physically incapable of exerting themselves[228] and barely able to shoulder their weapons; and now it was already midday, and thirst and heat left them gasping and ready to be cut down or captured in droves.

49. As for the elephants, more were killed by their drivers than by the enemy. These had a workman's chisel plus a mallet; and when the animals began rampaging and charging their own side the keeper would place the chisel between their ears, just where the neck joins the head, and drive it home with all his might. That had been found to be the swiftest way of killing a beast of such a size once the animals left no hope of being controlled; and the first to have introduced the practice was Hasdrubal, a leader memorable for many things and especially for that battle.

pugnantes hortando pariterque obeundo pericula susti-
nuit, ille fessos abnuentesque taedio et labore nunc pre-
cando, nunc castigando accendit, ille fugientes revocavit

4 omissamque pugnam aliquot locis restituit. postremo,
cum haud dubie fortuna hostium esset, ne superstes tanto
exercitui suum nomen secuto esset, concitato equo se in
cohortem Romanam immisit; ibi, ut patre Hamilcare et
Hannibale fratre dignum erat, pugnans cecidit.

5   Nunquam eo bello una acie tantum hostium interfectum est, redditaque aequa Cannensi clades vel ducis

6 vel exercitus interitu videbatur. quinquaginta septem[103]
milia hostium occisa, capta quinque milia et quadringenti,
magna praeda alia cum omnis generis tum auri etiam

7 argentique; civium etiam Romanorum qui capti apud hostes erant supra quattuor milia capitum recepta. id solacii
fuit pro amissis eo proelio militibus, nam haudquaquam
incruenta victoria fuit; octo ferme milia Romanorum sociorumque occisa.

8   Adeoque etiam victores sanguinis caedisque ceperat
satias ut postero die, cum esset nuntiatum Livio consuli
Gallos Cisalpinos Liguresque qui aut proelio non ad-
fuissent aut inter caedem effugissent uno agmine abire
sine certo duce sine signis sine ordine ullo aut imperio,

9 posse si una equitum ala mittatur omnes deleri, "quin
supersint" inquit "aliqui nuntii et hostium cladis et nostrae
virtutis."

103 septem Σ: sex P

---

229 Polybius' postmortem assessment of Hasdrubal (11.2.3–
10) is much longer than Livy's.

It was he who by his encouragement kept men fighting and faced the dangers with them, he who by alternating entreaties and reproaches energized them when they were weary and giving up the fight from fatigue and exhaustion; and it was he who called back fleeing men and rekindled a battle where it had in some places been abandoned. In the end, when fortune clearly favored his enemies, he galloped straight into a Roman cohort, not to outlive such a great an army that had followed his famous name. There he went down fighting—a death worthy of his father Hamilcar and his brother Hannibal.[229]

Never during that war were so many of the enemy killed in one battle, and with the loss, whether of the commander or of the army, repayment for Cannae seemed to have been made with an equally crushing defeat. Fifty-seven thousand of the enemy were killed and fifty-four hundred taken prisoner, and there were large quantities of booty of all kinds, including gold and silver. More than four thousand Roman citizens who had been prisoners in enemy hands were also recovered. That was some consolation for losing the soldiers in that battle, for it was by no means a bloodless victory: Roman and allied losses were about eight thousand.

How far the victors also felt they had seen enough of bloodshed and killing became clear the following day after a report was brought to the consul Livius of some Cisalpine Gauls and Ligurians, who had either had no part in the battle or had escaped during the massacre; they were retreating in a single column, with no recognized leader and no standards, and without formation or chain of command, and they could all be wiped out if a cavalry squadron were let loose on them. "No," said Livius, "let some survive to tell of the enemy's defeat and our courage."

50. Nero ea nocte quae secuta est pugnam profectus[104] citatiore quam inde venerat agmine die sexto ad stativa sua

2 atque ad hostem pervenit. iter eius frequentia minore— nemo enim[105] praecesserat nuntius—laetitia vero tanta vix ut compotes mentium prae gaudio essent celebratum est.

3 nam Romae neuter animi habitus satis dici enarrarique potest, nec quo incerta exspectatione eventus civitas fue-

4 rit[106] nec quo victoriae famam acceperit.[107] nunquam per omnes dies, ex quo Claudium consulem profectum fama attulit, ab orto sole ad occidentem aut senator quisquam a curia atque a magistratibus abscessit aut populus e foro.

5 matronae quia nihil in ipsis opis erat in preces obtestationesque versae per omnia delubra vagae suppliciis votisque fatigavere[108] deos.

6 Tam sollicitae ac suspensae civitati fama incerta primo accidit duos Narnienses equites in castra quae in faucibus Vmbriae opposita erant venisse ex proelio nuntiantes cae-

7 sos hostes. et primo magis auribus quam animis id acceptum erat ut maius laetiusque quam quod mente capere aut satis credere possent; et ipsa celeritas fidem impediebat

8 quod biduo ante pugnatum dicebatur. litterae deinde ab L. Manlio Acidino missae ex castris adferuntur de Narnien-

9 sium equitum adventu. hae litterae per forum ad tribunal praetoris latae senatum curia exciverunt; tantoque certamine ac tumultu populi ad fores curiae concursum est ut

[104] pugnam ⟨profectus⟩ *Sartorius*: pugnam *P*: properans *Walsh*

[105] nemo enim Σ: quia nemo *P*

[106] fuerit Σ: fuerat *P*

[107] acceperit Σ: accepit *P*

[108] fatigavere Σ: fatigare *P*

50. Nero left on the night that followed the battle, and moving the column along at greater speed than on his outward journey he reached his base camp and the enemy in five days. Along his route crowds were smaller—for no messenger had preceded him—but with such elation did they welcome his coming that they were almost beside themselves with joy. As for Rome, no words can be found to recount or describe either of its emotional states—neither that in which the citizens were anxiously awaiting the outcome nor that with which they received the news of victory. Throughout the days following the news that the consul Claudius had left, not once between sunrise and sunset did any senator leave the senate house and magistrates or the people leave the forum. Married women, unable to provide any material assistance themselves, turned to prayer and appeals to heaven as they roamed through all the shrines and urgently petitioned the gods with entreaties and vows.

While the city was gripped by such anxiety and tension, a vague rumor arose that two riders from Narnia had reached the camp that had been set up to barricade the entrance to Umbria, and that they brought news of an enemy massacre. At first this entered ears without registering in their minds; it was news too great and too joyful to be mentally absorbed or believed, and the very speed of its arrival also made acceptance difficult since the battle was said to have occurred only two days earlier. Then a dispatch, sent from his camp, was brought from Lucius Manlius Acidinus about the arrival of the two Narnian riders. This dispatch, borne through the forum to the praetor's tribunal, brought the senators out of the senate house; and with such fighting and scrambling did people

389

adire nuntius non posset, sed traheretur a percontantibus
vociferantibusque ut in rostris prius quam in senatu litte-
10 rae recitarentur. tandem summoti et coerciti a magistratibus; dispensarique laetitia inter impotentes eius animos
11 potuit. in senatu primum, deinde in contione litterae recitatae sunt; et pro cuiusque ingenio aliis iam certum
gaudium, aliis nulla ante futura fides erat quam legatos
consulumve litteras audissent.

51. Ipsos deinde appropinquare legatos allatum est.
tunc enimvero omnis aetas currere obvii, primus quisque
oculis auribusque haurire tantum gaudium cupientes;
ad Mulvium usque pontem continens agmen pervenit.
2 legati—erant L. Veturius Philo P. Licinius Varus Q. Cae-
3 cilius Metellus—circumfusi omnis generis hominum frequentia in forum pervenerunt, cum alii ipsos alii comites
4 eorum quae acta essent percontarentur; et ut quisque
audierat exercitum hostium imperatoremque occisum,
legiones Romanas incolumes, salvos consules esse, extemplo aliis porro impertiebant gaudium suum.
5 Cum aegre in curiam perventum esset, multo aegrius
summota turba ne patribus misceretur, litterae in senatu
6 recitatae sunt; inde traducti in contionem legati. L. Vetu-

---

230 The bridge carrying the Via Flaminia across the Tiber,
later made famous by Constantine's defeat of Maxentius in AD
312. This is its earliest mention: cf. *OCD* s.v. *pons Mulvius.*

converge on the doors of the senate house that the messenger could not get near, but was instead pulled away by people who kept questioning him and noisily demanding to have the letter read out on the Rostra before it was in the senate. Finally these people were pushed aside and restrained by the magistrates; and the happy news could then be spread among minds incapable of taking it in. The letter was read out, first in the senate and then in the popular assembly; and reactions varied with each person's temperament, some feeling unreserved joy, others suspending belief until they heard the envoys or a letter from the consuls.

51. Next came news that the consular legates were themselves approaching. Then for sure people of all ages ran to meet them, all wishing to be first to take in such joy with eyes and ears; and one long line stretched all the way to the Mulvian Bridge.[230] The envoys—they were Lucius Veturius Philo, Publius Licinius Varus, and Quintus Caecilius Metellus—reached the forum surrounded by crowds of people of every class, some asking the envoys themselves and others their attendants to recount what had happened; and as each heard that the enemy army and its leader had been destroyed and that the Roman legions were unharmed and the consuls safe, they would immediately go on to share their joy with others.

When, with difficulty, the envoys had reached the senate house and, with much greater difficulty, the crowd had been pushed aside so as not to intermingle with senators, the letter was read out in the senate; and then the envoys were conducted to the popular assembly. After reading out the letter, Lucius Veturius himself gave a detailed ac-

rius litteris recitatis ipse planius omnia quae acta erant
exposuit cum ingenti adsensu, postremo etiam clamore
universae contionis, cum vix gaudium animis caperent.
7 discursum inde ab aliis circa templa deum ut grates
agerent, ab aliis domos ut coniugibus liberisque tam lae-
tum nuntium impertirent.

8 Senatus quod M. Livius et C. Claudius consules incolumi exercitu ducem hostium legionesque occidissent
supplicationem in triduum decrevit. eam supplicationem
C. Hostilius praetor pro contione edixit, celebrataque a
9 viris feminisque est. omnia templa per totum triduum
aequalem turbam habuere, cum matronae amplissima
veste cum liberis, perinde ac si debellatum foret, omni
10 solutae metu dis immortalibus grates agerent. statum quoque civitatis ea victoria movit, ut iam inde haud secus
quam in pace res inter se contrahere vendendo, emendo,
mutuum dando argentum creditumque solvendo au-
derent.

11 C. Claudius consul cum in castra redisset caput Hasdrubalis, quod servatum cum cura attulerat, proici ante
hostium stationes, captivosque Afros vinctos ut erant ostendi, duos etiam ex iis solutos ire ad Hannibalem et ex-
12 promere quae acta essent iussit. Hannibal tanto simul
publico familiarique ictus luctu, adgnoscere se fortunam
13 Carthaginis fertur dixisse; castrisque inde motis, ut omnia

---

231 Into Hannibal's camp, according to Frontinus (*Str.* 2.9.2).

count of events, which was received with great approval from the entire gathering, and finally even with noisy applause since people could barely contain their delight. They then dispersed, some making the rounds of the temples of the gods to offer thanks, and others returning home to share such happy news with their wives and children.

To mark Marcus Livius' and Gaius Claudius' destruction of the enemy commander and his legions while preserving intact their own army, the senate decreed three days' supplication. That supplication the praetor Gaius Hostilius announced at an assembly, and the ceremonies were attended by both men and women. All the temples saw the same large crowds throughout the three-day period, as women and their children, dressed in their finest clothes and, now free from all fear, offered thanks to the immortal gods just as if the war were over. The state's financial situation was also affected by that victory; from then on people ventured to transact business no differently than in peacetime: selling, buying, putting out loans, and discharging debt.

On returning to his camp, the consul Gaius Claudius ordered Hasdrubal's head—which he had carefully kept and brought with him—to be tossed before the enemy outposts;[231] and he also had his African prisoners put on display just as they were, in their chains, but two he also released, ordering them to go to Hannibal and tell him what had happened. Shaken by such a blow to his people as well as his family, Hannibal is said to have stated that he now saw the destiny of Carthage. He struck camp,

auxilia quae diffusa latius tueri non poterat in extremum
Italiae angulum Bruttios contraheret, et Metapontinos
civitatem universam excitos sedibus suis et Lucanorum
qui suae dicionis erant in Bruttium agrum traduxit.

intending to gather together in Bruttium, in the furthest corner of Italy, all his supporting troops, whom he could not protect if they were widely dispersed; and he removed from their homes the entire population of Metapontum and all Lucanians that were under his control, sending them into Bruttian territory.

LIBRI XXVII PERIOCHA

Cn. Fulvius proconsul cum exercitu ab Hannibale ad Herdoneam caesus est. meliore eventu ab Claudio Marcello cos. adversus eundem ad Numistronem pugnatum est. inde Hannibal nocte recessit. Marcellus insecutus est et subinde cedentem pressit, donec confligeret. priore pugna Hannibal superior, sequenti Marcellus. Fabius Maximus pater consul Tarentinos per proditionem recepit. Claudius Marcellus T. Quinctius Crispinus consules speculandi causa progressi e castris insidiis ab Hannibale circumventi sunt. Marcellus occisus, Crispinus fugit. lustrum a censoribus conditum est. censa sunt civium capita $\overline{\text{CXXXVII}}$ CVIII; ex quo numero apparuit quantum hominum tot proeliorum adversa fortuna populo R. abstulisset. in Hispania ad Baeculam Scipio cum Hasdrubale et Hamilcare conflixit et vicit. inter alia captum regalem puerum eximiae formae ad avunculum Masinissam cum donis dimisit. Hasdrubal, qui cum exercitu novo Alpes transcenderat ut se Hannibali iungeret, cum milibus hominum LVI caesus

---

[232] Only here among our sources.

SUMMARY OF BOOK XXVII

The proconsul Gnaeus Fulvius was destroyed by Hannibal, along with his army, near Herdonea. A battle with a more successful outcome was fought against that same leader near Numistro by the consul Claudius Marcellus. Hannibal left there by night. Marcellus pursued him and put pressure on him as he retreated, until he engaged him in the field. In the first battle Hannibal emerged the winner, and in the second Marcellus. The consul Fabius Maximus (the father), as consul, recovered Tarentum through betrayal. The consuls Claudius Marcellus and Titus Quinctius Crispinus went forward from the camp to reconnoiter and were caught in an ambush by Hannibal. Marcellus was killed and Crispinus escaped. The *lustrum* was closed by the censors, and the census revealed 137,108 citizens, from which figure it became clear how many men the misfortunes of the Roman people had taken from them in so many wars. At Baecula in Spain Scipio fought with Hasdrubal and Hamilcar[232] and was victorious. Among the other spoils a boy of royal birth and exquisite looks had been captured, and he was sent away to his maternal uncle Masinissa by Scipio with gifts. Hasdrubal, who had crossed the Alps with a new army to unite with Hannibal, was killed with fifty-six thousand men, and

est, capta V̄CCCC M. Livi cos. ductu, sed non minore opera Claudi Neronis cos., qui, cum Hannibali oppositus esset, relictis castris ita ut hostem falleret, cum electa manu profectus Hasdrubalem circumvenerat. res praeterea feliciter a P. Scipione in Hispania et a P. Sulpicio praetore adversus Philippum et Achaeos gestas continet.

fifty-four hundred were captured; this occurred under the command of the consul Marcus Livius, but no less significant was the part played by the consul Claudius Nero, who, after being assigned to confront Hannibal, left his camp in such a way as to dupe his enemy and, having set out with a handpicked force, got the better of Hasdrubal. In addition, the book contains the successful operations conducted in Spain by Publius Scipio, and by the praetor Publius Sulpicius against Philip and the Achaeans.

INDEX

Citations are by Livy's book and chapter numbers.

INDEX

INDEX